The Land Office Business

THE
LAND OFFICE
BUSINESS

*The Settlement and Administration of American
Public Lands, 1789-1837*

MALCOLM J. ROHRBOUGH

New York · Oxford University Press · 1968

To My Father and Mother

CONTENTS

MAPS

INTRODUCTION

This is a book about the public domain.

It is not a history of legislation. Other historians have studied in detail the passage of laws relative to the public lands. Payson Jackson Treat's *The National Land System, 1785–1820* is a detailed analysis of the origins of the land system and the twenty-year credit period in the sale of the public domain. The other two principal works, Roy M. Robbins's *Our Landed Heritage: The Public Domain, 1776–1936* and Benjamin H. Hibbard's *A History of the Public Land Policies,* are both larger and more comprehensive studies. Hibbard's is a detailed factual account of the alienation of the public lands, supported by quantities of statistics and written from the perspective of an agricultural economist. Robbins's is more interpretative and derives much of his framework from the theories of Frederick Jackson Turner in stressing the rise of sectionalism, the growth of democracy, and the eternal conflict between settler and speculator. These three accounts were written almost entirely from the published sources, principally the accounts of debates in Congress, and the large number of published government documents dealing with the public lands. What emerged as significant were the statements made by important national figures about the public lands, the opinions of editors, and the number of acres alienated under various Congressional laws. The most recent important works on the public domain are state and regional studies. The leading works of this genre are Paul Wallace Gates's *The Wisconsin Pine Lands of Cornell University* and *Fifty Million Acres: Conflicts over Kansas Land Policy,* and two studies by Allan G. Bogue, *Money at Interest: The Farm Mortgage on the Middle Border* and *From Prairie to Corn Belt: Farming on the Illinois and Iowa Prairies in the Nineteenth Century.* The bulk of the contributions by other recent historians is in the form of articles. The most significant of these have been collected in *The Public Lands*, edited by Vernon Carstensen, whose introduction to the volume is a perceptive account of the confusion, uncertainty, and combination of innocence and venality that accompanied the distribution of the public lands.

The signature of the President on an act of Congress was only the first step in a long cycle of events conveying the lands from the nation to its citizens. In order to administer the transfer of land under the regulations established, Congress early recognized the need for bureaucratic machinery. At first a few clerks sufficed, but as the land business grew—and it did grow enormously in the first part of the nineteenth century—so did the administrative apparatus that supervised this business. The story of the alienation of the public domain is not told in the accounts of Congressional debates and legislation, however interesting and illuminating these may be. Instead, men took the lands in endless daily transactions at the land offices all over the West. The United States surrendered its lands in many ways and at many points in the administrative system. Louis Pelzer once wrote, "And who will say that the operations of the land office at Marietta or at Zanesville are less worthy of the work of the historians than are events like the taking of Fort Ticonderoga or the battle of Bunker Hill?" [1] The story of the land offices in the West is a difficult one, for little survives of the actual face-to-face negotiations that accompanied the confrontation between the citizens and the administrative officer of the government. The story that emerges, however, tells us much about the development of the nation and its expansion in the early nineteenth century.

This study is, of necessity, incomplete. Congress filled the *Statutes at Large* with legislation concerning the public lands. To study all of it would be a staggering task. Here much is treated briefly; some not at all. The actual administration and operation of numerous Congressional laws dealing with the public lands would provide the subject matter for numerous monographs. The New Madrid claims, the administration of the many laws for the adjudication of private claims, and the pre-emption acts—to mention only a few—deserve fuller treatment than they receive here. Perhaps this study may arouse interest in the

1. Louis Pelzer, "The Public Domain as a Field for Historical Study," *Iowa Journal of History and Politics*, 12 (1914): 575.

question of how the well-studied and documented land "policy" of this nation actually functioned.

In a larger sense the real subject of this book is the land itself. It fascinated men. For generations the ancestors of the early settlers had sought it without success in the closed society and economic structure of Europe. The promise of land drew them to the New World. From the very first establishment of permanent English colonies on this continent, men actively sought land. The drive for it lay behind much of the movement of the colonial period. No sooner had men settled on their land and tasted the independence of ownership, or at least possession, than some men began to seek more fertile, cheaper lands. This search drew them constantly to the West. Initially they moved up the rivers of Virginia and to the fertile interior valleys of New England. When lands in Pennsylvania became dear, men moved to western Maryland; and when supply and demand made lands expensive there (as growing numbers of people did almost everywhere), they went down the Great Valley of the Appalachians to the back country of Virginia and the Carolinas. Later this same urge sent their sons across the mountains to the interior of the continent. Wesley Frank Craven noted that land was the common denominator of all the colonies: "Surely, if there was one thing which bound the colonists together in a common experience, it was the necessity they found, most of them at least, to dig their livelihood out of the soil." [2] For the sake of the land, men defied the Indians who had used it for so long; they challenged the authority of men, like Judge Richard Henderson, who would have restricted their rights to it; and they had few qualms about flouting established authority by settling illegally on the public lands and remaining there.

Land was not simply the object of the small cultivator. Because it was limited in quantity while the numbers of people always increased, it rose in value. Its value could also be affected by improvements, new crops, and proximity to transportation routes, to mention only a few of the ways. Speculation in land was a powerful force in colonial America and subsequently in the Republic of the Constitution. As early as the first settlements by land-stock companies, lands in the New World attracted the entrepreneurial talents and surplus capital

2. Wesley Frank Craven, *Diversity and Unity—Two Themes in American History* (Princeton, 1964), 6.

of men of affairs. Land speculation was part of the American scene from the first settlements. Its colonial practitioners were legion. Land speculators have been among our leading national heroes: figures such as George Washington, who once held extensive tracts of land in the West; Robert Morris, the financier of the American Revolution; Benjamin Franklin, in spite of his strictures on prudence and frugality; Albert Gallatin, who kept lands in Ohio until well after his resignation from the Treasury Department, where he controlled the administration of the public lands; and, of course, Andrew Jackson, a man of frontier habits and orientation, who never rid himself of the frontier habit of dabbling in the public lands. From the days when men first stripped the Indian of his land with beads and rum, to the intricate combinations of talent, capital, and technique that controlled the public land sales in the mid-1830's, land was a principal outlet for the capital and the talents of the entrepreneur.

This story opens on a relatively motionless nation. "Even after two centuries of struggle the land was still untamed; forests covered every portion, except here and there a strip of cultivated soil; the minerals lay undisturbed in their rocky beds, and more than two thirds of the people clung to the seaboard within fifty miles of tide-water, where alone the wants of civilized life could be supplied," Henry Adams wrote in his description of the nation in 1800. "The centre of population rested within eighteen miles of Baltimore, north and east of Washington," he continued, "except in political arrangement, the interior was little more civilized than in 1750, and was not much easier to penetrate than when La Salle and Hennepin found their way to the Mississippi more than a century before." [3] The same might be said of the United States at the outbreak of the War of 1812. Within the quarter-century after peace, a great change took place. The migration that engulfed the eastern half of the continent was one of the greatest in the history of the world. The ensuing flood of humanity brought new states into the Union, redrew the economic and political map of the nation, and led to unparalleled sales of the public domain.

Land was the nation's most sought-after commodity in the first half-century of the republic, and the effort of men to acquire it was one of the dominant forces of the period. The fabled tracts of rich land, fertile

3. Henry Adams, *History of the United States of America* (9 vols., New York, 1891–98), 1: 1.

beyond all imagination, became the markers of the two centuries of advance from the Tidewater to the Mississippi. The gardens of Eden of this two hundred years were the Shenandoah Valley of Virginia, the Connecticut River Valley, the bluegrass region of Kentucky, the valleys of the Muskingum and the Wabash, Harrison's Purchase in Indiana, the Creek Purchase in Alabama, the Boon's Lick country in Missouri, the Sangamon River Valley, and the Choctaw Cession of 1830 in central Mississippi. All drew men with the promise of cheap, fertile land; all marked the way to the West. This book is the account of how these men took the land, and of how in the face of the great pressure generated by the movement of people, the government and its administrators attempted to control the distribution of the public domain.

July 1968
Swampscott, Mass.   M. J. R.

THE LAND OFFICE BUSINESS

The Early
Administrative Experience,
1785–1800

1

With the close of the Revolutionary War the attention of the new American nation turned to the West. It lay beyond the formidable Appalachians, a vast unknown, with a few blank spaces filled in. By 1781 there were only sparse settlements across the mountains, and these existed at the pleasure of the numerous and powerful Indian tribes that still effectively controlled the region from the Appalachians to the Mississippi. Settlements in western Virginia and across the mountains in the Kentucky country were an exception. This extension of the Old Dominion had achieved a permanence during the war. Substantial islands of population also existed in eastern Tennessee and at the broad bend of the Tennessee River. Farther west the ancient French settlements at Vincennes, Kaskaskia, and Cahokia and the thriving town of St. Louis across the Mississippi gave indication of inroads on the wilderness, but hardly of American influence. To the northwest of the Ohio River only a few squatter cabins broke the stillness of a forest solitude that existed much as it had before the first English settlements on the continent more than a century and a half earlier.

From the earliest settlements, occupants had been drawn to the West by the desire for cheap, fertile lands. Indeed the search for and the acquisition of new lands was a dominant theme of the colonial period. The movement for better lands began when the first settlers on the James sought lands up the river. In New England, town fathers viewed the fertile lands in the interior valleys and felt the call to establish a congregation in the wilderness. Eventually the desire for land broke down the cohesiveness of settlement everywhere. The advance to the interior of the continent increased considerably in the second quarter of the eighteenth century with the movement of the

Germans and the Scotch-Irish down the Great Valley, the narrow corridor of fertile land lying between the Blue Ridge and the Appalachian mountains and extending from Pennsylvania to Georgia. By the French and Indian wars the back country to the eastern edge of the Alleghenies was largely filled. With the English military victory and the assurance of the primacy of English institutions, an outburst of expansion to the interior appeared imminent; but it was arrested by a decision of the British government. Policy makers in Whitehall resented the desultory, rambling, disorganized absorption of the western lands. It flouted royal authority and upset the Indians—and the royal treasury had no funds to finance an Indian war. So the British government sought to control the occupation of the interior by bringing to it the same order and regularity that characterized the operation of the Empire, at least in the minds of those responsible for policy. The Proclamation Line down the backbone of the mountain ranges established an easily defined and recognizable boundary beyond which settlement was forbidden. Indian tribes enforced the line of demarcation far more successfully than the British Empire; in the Kentucky and Tennessee areas it was honored only in the breach. To the northwest, Indian strength and the smaller pressure of population combined to prevent the crossing of the Ohio in any substantial numbers. The search for new lands continued unabated during the War for Independence; and with the success of the American cause, the authority of the Empire vanished. The rules governing the occupation of the interior of the continent and the power behind them disappeared. A new set of forces was in control. What the new rules would be for the settlement of the trans-Appalachian region remained to be determined.

Several needs forced the government of the Confederation to consider immediately a policy for the new public domain. The movement of settlers onto the vacant lands—long a problem for landlords in colonial America—increased with the end of the war. The staggering national debt demanded the exploitation of all revenue resources, and the ceded public lands promised to be one of the nation's richest. Congress also needed to placate the Indian tribes of the West, so recently allied with the British. Veterans who had been guaranteed land bounties demanded that machinery be created to give them their promised reward. And everywhere the rush to the West threatened to make any policy obsolete before it was instituted. When he returned from a western trip to view his lands, George Washington wrote of this phenomenon, "The spirit for emigration is great, people have got impatient, and tho' you cannot stop the road, it is yet in your power to mark the way; a little while and you will not be able to do either."[1]

In order to weigh the merits of various plans for the distribution of the public domain, the Confederation Congress established a committee on the matter in 1784. Its chairman was Thomas Jefferson of Virginia. This group of men from all parts of the nation sifted through a century and a half of colonial precedents for the distribution of land.

In the seventeenth century the real estate of an unknown continent had often been granted in large chunks to a few individual proprietors. Although interested in the landed estates that signified the wealth of that day, these men soon recognized that the sale of their grants —or of part of them, in most cases—offered enormous opportunities for profit. This discovery led to the sale of lands and quickly to speculation in real estate; for lands could be bought, held, and sold, and the varying value gave opportunities for great profit. From the sale of shares in the Virginia Company to the outbreak of the American Revolution, the buying and selling of land occupied a prominent position in colonial America. In the middle and southern colonies, proprietors sold extensive tracts of their lands through private sales at a fixed price in land offices established for that purpose. By the middle of the eighteenth century even the New England colonies (heretofore an exception to the rule) witnessed sales of lands, both in small tracts to individuals for cultivation and in large blocks to speculators.[2]

Since profits were of great importance, the proprietors sought an administrative system that would establish the sale of land under regulations easily understood by all prospective purchasers. For the convenience of a large number of buyers, the proprietors or their representatives established land offices, both for sale and to control squat-

---

1. George Washington to Richard Henry Lee, President of Congress, Dec. 14, 1784, John C. Fitzpatrick, ed., *The Writings of George Washington* (39 vols., Washington, 1931–44), 28: 12.
2. Amelia Clewley Ford, *Colonial Precedents of Our National Land System as it Existed in 1800* (Bulletin of the University of Wisconsin, no. 352, Madison, 1910), 83–84; Marshall D. Harris, *Origin of the Land Tenure System in the United States* (Ames, 1953), 237–54.

ting or trespassing on the proprietary lands. The presence of a symbol of authority, it was hoped, would retard this colonial disease. Gradually these offices spread to the interior in order to extend the authority of the proprietors and to offer a larger number the opportunity to purchase. The office of surveyor general was also developed, first in Maryland and gradually throughout the middle and southern colonies. By the outbreak of the Revolution the land office, the surveyor general, and boards of commissions on land decisions were familiar institutions in colonial America.[3]

The financial possibilities of the American wilderness also became apparent to the administrators in Whitehall. After 1772 the Lords of Trade developed their own system for the disposal of American lands by means of sale in large and small lots at a fixed price. The outbreak of the American Revolution aborted English plans to sell American lands and, in turn, made the several states masters of their respective domains or rather free to disagree about their mutual boundaries without outside interference. Since the western lands of the various states were handsome sources of revenue in a time of meager resources, the states continued to sell them during the war. Virginia and North Carolina were especially active in the sale of lands, with an extensive system of land offices, attractive terms, and fertile tracts. The states had no common system or even a consistent one, but varied their techniques in order to attract the maximum amount of business at the lowest administrative cost. This administrative machinery also served to distribute the bounty lands given soldiers by their various states for services during the Revolutionary War.[4]

Because the new independent states were uncertain what form of government they wished to adopt, they were reluctant to part with their claims to the interior—claims that dated back to their colonial charters. This reluctance increased because of the disproportionate quantities of real estate claimed by some of the states. Indeed, Maryland refused to join the Confederation government until the landed states (particularly Virginia) ceded their claims. Long negotiations

3. Milton Conover, *The General Land Office, Its History, Activities and Organization* (Service Monograph of the United States Government, no. 13, Baltimore, 1923), 2–5.
4. Ford, *Colonial Precedents of Our National Land System,* 86–89; Henry Tatter, "State and Federal Land Policy during the Confederation Period," *Agricultural History,* 9 (1935): 176–86.

followed. Finally some eight months before the surrender of Lord Cornwallis at Yorktown, New York redrew her western boundary to exclude her claims; and Maryland's reluctance to join the Confederation weakened. Ultimately all states with claims to the western country ceded their rights, some unconditionally, others with reservations. In this fashion the new nation found herself with a vast public domain in the interior of the continent.[5]

In its reports the Congressional committee established to formulate a policy for orderly disposal of the new public domain favored the New England system of survey before settlement over the southern tradition of indiscriminate occupation and identification of a tract by means of natural boundaries. In making provision for the administration of the public domain, however, Jefferson drew primarily on the Virginia experience. Indeed, in some places he repeated word for word portions of the state's 1779 law. His plan, entitled "Report of a Committee to Establish a Land Office," recommended precisely located, square surveyed tracts administered by several "registers," who would be appointed by Congress for each public land state. The register would inspect the surveying certificates, record land grants, and report the quantity and location of grants annually to the Secretary of Congress. Land was granted by the general government to the grantee and his heirs forever, and the receipts of the sales should be applied to the sinking fund. The surveying system of New England was thus joined to the administrative apparatus of the South.[6]

Congress adjourned for the summer without taking action on the plan, and Thomas Jefferson went to France as ambassador. When the report finally came before Congress in the spring of 1785, it was referred to a committee of one member from each state. The new committee retained the rectangular townships, reduced their size from seven to six square miles, and provided that land would be sold at auction and in tracts of township size. The full Congress then debated the committee's recommendations at length. Of the ensuing discussion

5. On the creation of the national domain and the various reservations, see Merrill Jensen, "The Cession of the Old Northwest," *Journal of American History*, 23 (1936): 27–48; Merrill Jensen, "The Creation of the National Domain," *ibid.*, 26 (1939): 323–42.
6. Julian P. Boyd, ed., *The Papers of Thomas Jefferson* (17 vols. to date, Princeton, 1950—), 7: 140–48n; Ford, *Colonial Precedents of Our National Land System*, 91.

to frame "an ordinance for the disposal of the Western territory," William Grayson wrote to Timothy Pickering, "I think there has been as much said and wrote about it as would fill forty Volumes. . . ."[7] One result of the discussion was an amendment to permit the sale of smaller tracts. The ordinance became law on May 20, 1785.[8]

The Ordinance of 1785 was in part an exposition and analysis of the persistent problems of the past; and, as it turned out, those same problems would cause much trouble in the future. The law provided for the identification, care, and husbanding of the great natural resources of the Republic. The government would note mines, salt springs, salt licks, and mill seats in order to preserve them. The ordinance also retained for the government parts of the gold, silver, lead, and copper deposits, reserved four federal lots (numbers 8, 11, 26, and 29) in every township, and designated section 16 for the "maintenance of public schools within the said township." With the exception of the school reservations, efforts to preserve the resources of the public domain proved futile; Congress eventually gave up and opened these to unlimited exploitation. The ordinance correctly identified the objects of national interest and tried to secure them. The concepts were clear. The execution was faulty, and the results were disappointing.[9]

The administrative arrangements introduced under the ordinance were more successful. They combined the concern of Congress for revenue with the colonial heritage of a century and a half. The rectangular survey, with its precise system for surveying and describing the land, remained central to the preparation of the lands for sale. A "geographer" appointed by the President would lay down "directions" for surveys, set up "regulations" for the "conduct" of surveyors, and make reports to Congress. The surveyors, one from each state, were to divide the land into townships six miles square and subsequently by

7.　Edmund Cody Burnett, ed., *Letters of Members of the Continental Congress* (8 vols., Washington, 1921–36), 8: 106.

8.　On the creation of the Ordinance of 1785, see Payson Jackson Treat, "Origin of the National Land System under the Confederation," American Historical Association, *Annual Report for 1905*, 1: 231–39; Harris, *Origin of the Land Tenure System in the United States*, 389–91; Clarence E. Carter, ed., *Territorial Papers of the United States* (26 vols. to date, Washington, 1934—), 2: 12n. This last work is cited hereafter as *Territorial Papers*.

9.　Vernon Carstensen, ed., *The Public Lands, Studies in the History of the Public Domain* (Madison, 1963), xv–xx.

subdivision into sections of 640 acres; each was to be numbered in an orderly fashion and plainly marked on the ground. As soon as seven ranges of townships had been surveyed, the geographer would transmit one plat—a scaled diagram of the tract—to the Board of the Treasury. Herein lay the seeds of a bookkeeping and recording enterprise that would later assume enormous proportions. First priority in the seven ranges went for military bounties promised to veterans of the Revolutionary War. The remaining lands were to be allotted to the several states in proportion to their quotas at the time of the most recent requisition. Each state's allotment was to be administered by the commissioner of the loan office for that state, "who after giving notice of not less than two nor more than six months by causing advertisements to be posted up at the court houses or other noted places in every county and to be inserted in one newspaper published in the states of their residence respectively . . ." should sell the townships at public auction. It was hoped that the competition would increase the revenue.

In order to give opportunity for the purchaser of modest means, commissioners auctioned whole townships alternately with townships divided into lots. The minimum price was one dollar per acre, paid in specie or in land office certificates reduced to specie value. The prospective purchaser also paid the cost of survey, estimated at $36 for the township. The buyer had to make payment at the time of sale or forfeit the lands for immediate resale. Upon payment the commissioner issued a deed for a specified tract of land, not a warrant permitting future location on some tract of land (a system common in the middle and southern states in the colonial period). The commissioners recorded their transactions in a regular manner and transmitted quarterly accounts to the Board of the Treasury. The ordinance limited the time for state sale and directed the return to Congress of any lands unsold eighteen months after receipt of the plat. In spite of the authority of the Board of the Treasury, the composition of the surveying force and control over the public sales remained in the hands of the states themselves.[10]

10. The full text of the ordinance is printed in Carter, ed., *Territorial Papers,* 2: 12–18, with numerous useful notes. Congress also moved to make the western country more attractive to prospective settlers (and, hopefully, purchasers) by establishing a form of government that would provide both order and assurance of later acceptance into the Union on the basis of equality. The full text of the Or-

Congress hastened to prepare the public lands for sale. Its immediate concern was the proper survey of the first seven ranges west of the base line. The Board of the Treasury immediately recalled the Geographer of the United States, Thomas Hutchins, who was then engaged in running the boundary line between Virginia and Pennsylvania. Hutchins hastened to Pittsburgh, where he met the assembled surveyors from the various states. The survey of the first seven ranges began, hampered by problems of internal dissensions and by threats of Indian unrest. After setting the enterprise under way, Hutchins immediately returned east in order to attend to more state boundary lines. The surveys in the western country moved along by fits and starts. The surveyors completed four ranges by February 1787, and Hutchins immediately submitted the plats to Congress.[11]

Congress was impatient. The debts of the nation pressed heavily upon few outward assets. One of these assets was certainly the public lands, but the surveys insisted upon by a majority of its members proved long and costly. Simultaneously with the arrival at Congress of the plats of the first four ranges came recommendations from the Board of the Treasury for the immediate sale of the western lands. The board felt "that considering the Surveyors have already been employed two years, it is not probable that in the course of another, they will have completely Surveyed the first seven Ranges." Acting under this impression, the board asked for alteration in the Ordinance of 1785 in order to place the first four ranges of land on sale at once. The terms were also somewhat at variance with those laid down two years earlier. After notice of four months Congress should place the lands on sale "in the place where Congress shall sit," which was New York. The sales should continue until all lands were disposed of, with the minimum price of one dollar per acre. At the time of sale the purchaser must pay one-third of the purchase money "in any of the Public Securities of the United States to the Treasurer of the said States"; the remainder was to be paid within three months.[12] Congress

dinance of 1787, dated July 13, 1787, is in *ibid.*, 39–50, with explanatory notes on its passage and interpretation.
11. William D. Pattison, "The Survey of the Seven Ranges," *Ohio Historical Quarterly*, 68 (1959): 115–40; Joseph Ernst, "With Compass and Chain: Federal Land Surveyors in the Old Northwest, 1785–1816" (Unpublished doctoral dissertation, Columbia University, 1958), Ch. 2.
12. "Report of Board of Treasury on Western Land Sales," April 4, 1787, Carter, ed., *Territorial Papers*, 2: 24–25.

agreed. In the autumn of 1787 the Confederation Government auctioned 72,934 acres of land for the sum of $117,108.22. No entire townships were sold. The receipts were smaller than Congress had hoped.[13]

The real estate northwest of the Ohio River remained attractive to speculators, however; and through their influence in Congress and the failure of established practices to produce sufficient revenue through small sales, entrepreneurs succeeded in introducing the policy of sale by large tracts. If the public domain were to serve as a basis of revenue, it was persuasively argued, sales of large tracts to groups of capitalists would realize such revenue and would at the same time transfer the administrative expense from the Confederation government to the new owners. Acting on this assumption, and urged on by members with a direct interest in the proceedings, Congress now sold one million acres to the Ohio Company of Associates in the same week that it passed the Northwest Ordinance. Since the Treasury received depreciated certificates of indebtedness at par, the Ohio Associates paid less than ten cents per acre—a transaction that testified both to the willingness of Congress to rid itself of the expense and difficulty of administering a large section of the public domain and to the need for immediate revenue of some kind, or at least for a decrease in the large debt outstanding. The whole affair was also a tribute to the lobbying skill of the Reverend Manassah Cutler and to the duplicity of William Duer, secretary of the Board of the Treasury.

Congress subsequently passed a resolution in the fall of 1787 that authorized the Board of the Treasury to enter into negotiations with others for the purchase of "not less than one million of acres in one body" on the same terms offered Cutler and Sargent of the Ohio Company.[14] Cutler and Sargent also signed a contract on behalf of the Scioto Company for a large tract, and John Cleves Symmes concluded an arrangement with the Treasury Board for one million acres.[15]

13. *American State Papers: Documents, Legislative and Executive of the Congress of the United States* (38 vols. in 10 classes, Washington, 1832–61), *Public Lands*, 3: 459.
14. Carter, ed., *Territorial Papers*, 2: 78.
15. The standard accounts of the various purchases and their principals, are Archer B. Hulbert, *The Records of the Ohio Company* (2 vols., Marietta, 1917), especially the introduction to Vol. 1; Beverly W. Bond, Jr., ed., *The Correspon-*

By the beginning of 1789, then, the first arrangements for the disposal of the public domain stood discredited and unused. The rectangular system of surveys was a disappointment because of its slowness and expense. When Congress bypassed the Ordinance of 1785 and determined to sell four surveyed ranges immediately, the sales were so indifferent as to raise doubts about the value of the public lands in reducing the national debt. Congress now made the procedures used in the sale of the first four ranges standard for future sales. It empowered the Board of the Treasury to sell other parts of the seven ranges as they were surveyed under the same conditions as prevailed in the autumn of 1787. Sales could be held in Philadelphia as well as New York, and the members of the board might "adjourn the same from time to time, to any part or parts of the United States which they may judge most proper for the purpose." [16] The dislocation of the land system was completed with the death of Geographer Thomas Hutchins in 1789. Both surveys and sales lapsed and awaited the action of the new government to revive them.

In the spring of 1789 a new government took office under the new Constitution. The task of making a suitable policy for the distribution of the public domain in the West now merged with the greater problem of creating an administrative mechanism for the national government. The latter was a momentous task and was made more difficult and precarious by the narrow margin of approval for the new form of government and by the heavy obligations it assumed. So the public lands and their administration had to find a place in a new system. The largest and most important branch of the new government, the Treasury, was closely connected with the pressing issue of the period: the nation's debt. Its ambitious chief was Alexander Hamilton. The Congressional organic act establishing the Treasury Department provided, among other duties, that the department should execute such measures for the sale of public lands as should be given it by law. In August 1790, Congress gave the department responsibility for the survey of the seven ranges. Once again the public domain would function as

dence of *John Cleves Symmes* (New York, 1926); Archer B. Hulbert, "The Methods and Operations of the Scioto Group of Speculators," *Journal of American History*, 1 (1915): 502–15; 2 (1915): 56–73.
16.   Carter, ed., *Territorial Papers*, 2: 122–24.

an aspect of the nation's revenue.[17] The sale and administration of the public domain had to be integrated with the nation's financial program. Congress appealed to the new Secretary of the Treasury for suitable recommendations.

Alexander Hamilton had a plan for the financial and political development of the new nation, which involved securing the allegiance of the mercantile classes of the eastern cities to the support of the new government. He moved to make the public lands a part of his system. While the Secretary recognized that the principal aims of a land policy should be advantageous sales for the government and the accommodation of western settlers, he did not doubt that "the former, as an operation of finance, claims primary attention. . . ." While any plan should endeavor to give "satisfaction" to the "inhabitants of the Western country," the most important consideration was the accommodation of wealthy purchasers, men and organizations who would purchase large quantities of the public lands. He distinguished three classes of prospective buyers—"moneyed individuals and companies, who will buy to sell again; associations of persons, who intend to make settlements themselves; single persons, or families now resident in the Western country, or who may emigrate thither hereafter"—and noted that the government should provide administrative arrangements to meet the needs of each group. For the large companies and capitalists who would buy large tracts, Congress should establish a "General Land Office . . . at the seat of Government." For smaller purchasers, lands might be acquired at "subordinate" offices, one in the Northwest, another in the Southwest. Three "commissioners," either appointed or *ex officio,* should be placed in charge of the whole operation, and under them, "three commissioners" in each subordinate office. Hamilton also recommended the appointment of a surveyor general with authority to choose deputies.[18]

Hamilton's suggestions not only showed his conviction that the lands should be considered first and foremost as a part of the nation's

17. 1 Stat. 65–67 (Sept. 2, 1789); 1 Stat. 187 (June 7, 1790); Leonard D. White, *The Federalists: A Study in Administrative History* (New York, 1948), 116–22.
18. *American State Papers, Public Lands,* 1: 8–9. The concern for the Southwest arose from the recent establishment of the Territory South of the Ohio. 1 Stat. 123 (May 26, 1790).

revenue, but also demonstrated that certain basic issues supposedly
solved by the Ordinance of 1785 were still open to question. He recommended the system of prior surveys be modified in favor of indiscriminate locations. Lands might be sold in various regular tracts, but
"any quantities may, nevertheless, be sold by special contract, com-
prehended either within natural boundaries or lines, or both." The
government would run external lines of survey upon the sale of tracts,
but no systematic system of prior survey was to be established. Obviously Hamilton was concerned more with the prospect of pleasing his
customers and less with the long-range difficulties of managing the
public domain. His terms of thirty cents per acre with no credit for
tracts less than ten miles square once again affirmed his determination
to please the large capitalist.[19]

Members of Congress debated these proposals upon several occasions. The House finally passed a bill that reduced the price to
"twenty-five cents 'hard money' per acre," and established "a General
Land Office . . . at the seat of Government" and "two subordinate
Land offices in the Western territory—one to the south, and the other
to the northwest of the Ohio." The Senate did not consider the measure, and the problem of what to do with the public lands temporarily
disappeared from sight.[20]

The issue of the public domain was very much alive in the western
country and was the principal concern of the citizens of the new
Northwest Territory, to the north and west of the Ohio. Since the
close of the Revolutionary War, in spite of the constant danger from
Indians, settlers moved across the Ohio, coming down the river from
Pittsburgh and crossing from Kentucky, where conditions for the
acquisition of land were increasingly stringent. Those who came settled without regard to ownership. Squatting on lands was as old as
settlement in the New World, and illegal settlements had plagued the
proprietors of colonial America. Some occupants eventually hoped to
purchase, but they were probably a minority. Most of the settlers de-

19.   Payson Jackson Treat, The National Land System, 1785–1820 (New York,
1910), 70–74; Benjamin H. Hibbard, A History of the Public Land Policies (New
York, 1924), 59–60.
20.   Annals of the Congress of the United States (42 vols., Washington, 1834–
56), 1 Cong., 3 Sess., 2: 1829–32, 1840–42, 1864, 1873–74. On the Annals as a
source, see White, The Federalists, 18n.

pended on numbers, distance, and lack of force to keep them in possession of their plots and improvements indefinitely. Although few men defended the principle of illegal intrusion, colonial governments and large proprietors were incapable of enforcing their will in vast reaches of wilderness.[21]

No sooner was the armed conflict of the Revolutionary War ended than the movement of settlers onto the public lands noticeably increased. The problem was particularly severe north of the Ohio River, where squatters began building cabins and making clearings as early as 1779. With the close of the war the Congress tried to prevent and anticipate settlements by issuing a proclamation that prohibited settlements on Indian lands without the express permission of Congress. The Congress of the Confederation had no more success in preventing these intrusions than had the Penns, George Washington, or the British Crown. Settlers continued to move across the Ohio, establishing their tiny improvements in the vast wilderness. When George Washington toured his western lands in the summer of 1784, he reported of the intruders that "in defiance of the proclamation of Congress, they roam over the Country on the Indian side of the Ohio, mark out Lands, Survey, and even settle them."[22] Reminded of the problem again by interested and influential observers such as Washington, the Confederation Congress moved once more to assert its authority. By a proclamation passed in 1785, it forbade illegal intrusions on the public lands and ordered trespassers to depart forthwith. No change resulted.

This time Congress determined to act, in part to uphold its own self-respect, in part because of the increased friction with Indians caused by white trespassers on Indian lands. With the signing of the Treaty of Fort McIntosh in early 1785, the government bound itself to remove trespassers from Indian lands. In the summer of 1785 a detachment of troops crossed the Ohio and erected Fort Harmar at the mouth of the Muskingum, for the double purpose of protecting the surveyors from the Indians and of dispersing the squatters on the public lands. Neither this symbol of national authority nor the physical

21. Ford, *Colonial Precedents of Our National Land System*, 112–18.
22. Washington to Jacob Read, Nov. 3, 1784, Fitzpatrick, ed., *The Writings of George Washington*, 27: 486.

presence of military force inhibited the immigrants. They continued to
come.[23]

The Commissioner for Indian Affairs now instructed Colonel Joseph
Harmar to drive off the intruders. As soon as the winter weather mod-
erated, Harmar complied. He dispatched Ensign John Armstrong from
his command with a party of twenty men "to dispossess sundry persons, who had presumed to settle on the lands of the United States on
the western side of the Ohio River." [24] Armstrong encountered scattered resistance and numerous pleas for mercy. He also found the illegal settlements much more extensive than anyone had imagined. Although Armstrong drove the squatters "off as far as seventy miles
from this post," Harmar warned that "the number lower down the
river is immense, and, unless Congress enters into immediate measures, it will be impossible to prevent lands being settled." [25] The
colonel later sent a second expedition with the same object. In spite of
the army's determined efforts, the settlers continued to return. "The
men generally absconded, and the women and children were taken
across the river to the next settlement," Albert Gallatin later wrote,
"but it was necessary to repeat the operation, and I know persons
whose cabins were burnt and settlements destroyed three times." [26]

The settlers were more circumspect in their dealings with the Indian tribes. Impetus from their British advisers and the fear of engrossing settlements spurred Indian depredations along the Ohio frontier. The American military disasters of Harmar in 1790 and St. Clair
the following year made the situation even more difficult. The tribes
of the Ohio Valley now attacked along the entire frontier. Several settlements on the upper reaches of the Muskingum dispersed and returned to the safety of the forts on the Ohio. Indian raids that wiped
out at least one settlement deflected new immigrants to the relative
safety of Kentucky.[27] The period of uncertainty that followed was re-

23. On the problem of squatters, see John D. Barnhart, *Valley of Democracy*
(Bloomington, 1953), 128–31; Randolph C. Downes, *Frontier Ohio, 1788–1803*
(Columbus, 1935), 73–77.
24. Harmar to the President of the Congress, May 1, 1785, William Henry Smith,
ed., *The St. Clair Papers* (2 vols., Cincinnati, 1882), 2: 3.
25. Harmar to the Secretary at War, June 1, 1785, *ibid.*, 6.
26. Albert Gallatin to Thomas Jefferson, April 16, 1804, Henry Adams, ed., *The
Writings of Albert Gallatin* (3 vols., Philadelphia, 1879), 1: 188; this work cited
hereafter as *Gallatin Writings*.
27. Downes, *Frontier Ohio*, 69–71; Beverly W. Bond, Jr., *The Foundations of*

lieved by General Anthony Wayne's victory at Fallen Timbers in 1794. If he did not annihilate the hostile tribes, Wayne at least convinced them that they could expect no further aid from the British. At almost the same time the British gave up their posts in the Old Northwest under the terms of Jay's treaty.

Not only did Wayne's victory mean peace to the Ohio frontier, it led to a great cession of land from the Indians at the Treaty of Green-ville and also established a definite boundary line between white and Indian lands. White settlement in this part of the Old Northwest entered a new phase. The southern two-thirds of the present state of Ohio was opened to settlement, and settlers rushed to it as if these were the last public lands on the continent. They confidently expected that the government would devise a system for the sale of the public lands and would place them on the market. "But all Kentucky and the back parts of Virginia and Pennsylvania are running mad with expec-tations of the land office opening in this country—hundreds are run-ning into the wilderness west of the Great Miami, locating and mak-ing elections of land," wrote John Cleves Symmes. He added, "They almost laugh me full in the face when I ask them one dollar per acre for first-rate land, and tell me they will soon have as good for thirty cents." [28] Governor Arthur St. Clair of the Northwest Territory also noted the dramatic movement of population and warned the govern-ment to think once more about the problem of the public lands. "What the Intentions of the Government, are with regard to the Sale of the Lands in this Country I am entirely ignorant," he wrote, "but it is my duty to inform you Sir, that in my opinion, if they are not dis-posed of soon, such numbers of People will take possession of them, as may not easily be removed. . . ." [29]

Wayne's victory, the subsequent rush to the Ohio country, and the warnings of St. Clair caused Congress to turn once more to the cre-ation of a system for the disposal of the public lands. The small pur-chaser had a greater voice in the debates that developed over the

Ohio, Carl F. Wittke, ed., *The History of the State of Ohio,* Vol. 1 (Columbus, 1941), 275–311.

28. Symmes to Jonathan Dayton, Aug. 6, 1795, Bond, ed., *The Symmes Corre-spondence,* 174–75. Accounts of the dramatic spread of settlement into the Ohio country after the Indian war are Bond, *The Foundations of Ohio,* 349–95; Downes, *Frontier Ohio,* 71–73.

29. St. Clair to Sec. State, Jan. 1796, Carter, ed., *Territorial Papers,* 2: 548.

terms of sales and the administration of the public domain. Albert
Gallatin of Pennsylvania was among those who spoke of the importance of land to the nation and its citizens. "If the cause of the happi-
ness of this country was examined into . . . it would be found to
arise as much from the great plenty of land in proportion to the inhabitants, which their citizens enjoyed, as from the wisdom of their political institutions," he told his Congressional colleagues. Representative
William Findley, also from western Pennsylvania, told his fellow legislators that "they ought not only to keep a wholesale but a retail
store." [30] In a measure at least, the West achieved its wish. The law
of 1796 "for the Sale of the Lands of the United States, in the territory
northwest of the river Ohio, and above the mouth of Kentucky river,"
provided for the sale of half the townships in sections of 640 acres
each. At the price of two dollars per acre, the outlay was substantial
for the small purchaser, even with modified credit under which the
purchaser paid an immediate deposit of one-twentieth of the purchase
price, one-half within thirty days, and the remainder within one year.
Cash purchasers received a discount of 10 per cent of the purchase
price. The law also confirmed the system of rectangular survey pro-
mulgated under the Ordinance of 1785 but since fallen into disuse.
Congress now indicated that survey would always precede settlement,
and that the information compiled by the surveyors might assist in
selling the lands.[31]

Congress also made arrangements for an administrative system to
supervise the sale of the public lands. The President would appoint a
surveyor general to direct the surveying operations. The law also provided facilities for the sale of western lands at the nation's capital,
under the direction of the Secretary of the Treasury, in tracts of one-
quarter township. For the convenience of settlers on the frontier,
smaller tracts of 640 acres would be sold at auction, under the direction of the governor or the secretary of the territory and the surveyor
general in several different towns in the territory. The law directed
that the lands below the Miami should be sold at Cincinnati; those
between the Scioto and the Ohio Company's purchase, at Pittsburgh;
and tracts between the Connecticut Reserve and the seven ranges, at

30.   *Annals of Congress*, 4 Cong., 1 Sess., 5: 411, 339.
31.   1 Stat. 464–69 (May 18, 1796); Hibbard, *A History of the Public Land
Policies*, 67–68; Treat, *The National Land System*, 79–86.

Pittsburgh. The Secretary of the Treasury should give proper notice of the sales in the newspapers in each state. The Secretary of the Treasury remained the final source of record, and his office recorded or received records of the dates of sales, price, money deposited, location of land, dates of the certificates granted, and other pertinent data. The law also gave the President power to appoint a man to act for the Secretary of the Treasury in receiving monies paid in for public lands at the western sales.[32]

The task of administering this law fell to the new Secretary of the Treasury, Oliver Wolcott. Wolcott was one of the first important figures in government to achieve a career in administration. After serving as Auditor and Comptroller of the Treasury, he became Secretary in 1795 on the resignation of Hamilton.[33] Wolcott began his work by notifying John Neville of Pittsburgh of his selection as receiver of public monies and explained the duties of the post. The Secretary also advertised the forthcoming sale of lands in the appropriate newspapers, fixing the date for October 24, 1796. The Land Law of 1796 also made the Secretary of the Treasury responsible for keeping orderly accounts of the sales of the public lands. In order to establish orderly record-keeping procedures, Wolcott drew up six forms to be used in the land business. These he sent to his new receiver, Neville, with detailed instructions for their use. Wolcott also issued special instructions to the superintendents of the sales at Pittsburgh.[34]

Governor Arthur St. Clair was unhappy about his new duty. The trip from Cincinnati to Pittsburgh was a formidable undertaking, and he found it necessary to go by way of Detroit and Presque Isle on other business. On the way he suffered a severe attack of gout that increased his ill humor. Nonetheless he arrived on time. The results hardly justified his effort. Bidding on public lands at the public sale was spasmodic, and even the private sales were small.[35]

32. 1 Stat. 464–69 (May 18, 1796).
33. White, *The Federalists*, 123–25. The most complete account of Wolcott's long career in public service is George Gibbs, ed., *Memoirs of the Administrations of Washington and John Adams, Edited from the Papers of Oliver Wolcott, Secretary of the Treasury* (2 vols., New York, 1846).
34. Wolcott to Neville, National Archives, General Land Office, Letters Sent, Miscellaneous, 1: July 15, 1796; Wolcott to Winthrop Sargent, *ibid.*, July 15, 1796; Wolcott to Neville, *ibid.*, Oct. 5, 1796; Wolcott to Superintendents, *ibid.*, Oct. 5, 1796. This depository is abbreviated hereafter as NA: GLO.
35. St. Clair to Wolcott, Aug. 30, 1796; St. Clair to Sargent, Dec. 1, 1796, Smith, ed., *The St. Clair Papers*, 2: 406, 413–17.

Procedures also had to be established for handling lands granted by previous governments, and Governor St. Clair took an active role here also. The basis of this recognition of rights lay in the Virginia Act of Cession of 1783, in which the Virginia government specified "that the French and Canadian inhabitants, and other settlers of the Kaskaskies, Saint Vincents, and the neighboring villages, who have professed themselves citizens of Virginia, shall have their possessions and titles confirmed to them, and be protected in the enjoyment of their rights and liberties." The Ordinance of 1787 confirmed this right, and Congress later expanded the general declaration by providing additional reservations for the citizens of the Illinois country.[36] For his several terms as governor, Arthur St. Clair, in conjunction with his secretary, Winthrop Sargent, labored to adjudicate the claims in the Illinois country.[37] Their ceaseless work in searching records, taking testimony, and judging these cases had minimal practical results, but it laid the groundwork for the innumerable commissions on private claims that would labor at various tasks for three-quarters of the nineteenth century in the interests of amalgamating foreign grants into the American land system.

In spite of scant sales, the administrative system established under the Land Law of 1796 continued to prepare lands for sale. After a lengthy search President George Washington appointed Rufus Putnam as surveyor general.[38] Putnam immediately sought instructions from the Secretary of the Treasury. Wolcott eventually rounded up funds for the work and sent the money with detailed instructions. A system of administration gradually evolved. Putnam selected his deputies, let the contracts, ushered his men into the field with the coming of spring, welcomed them in the autumn, checked their field notes, paid

36. Francis Newton Thorpe, comp., *The Federal and State Constitutions, Colonial Charters, and other Organic Laws of the States, Territories, and Colonies Now or Heretofore Forming the United States of America* (7 vols., Washington, 1906), 2: 956; 1 Stat. 221–22 (March 3, 1791).
37. See St. Clair to Sec. War, May 1, 1790, Smith, ed., *The St. Clair Papers*, 2: 137; St. Clair to Sec. State (without date), 1796, *ibid.*, 398–400; *American State Papers, Public Lands*, 1: 9–16; Clarence Walworth Alvord, *The Illinois Country, 1673–1818*, Clarence Walworth Alvord, ed., *The Centennial History of Illinois*, Vol. 1 (Chicago, 1922), 203–07.
38. Washington to Timothy Pickering, July 25, 1796, Fitzpatrick, ed., *The Writings of George Washington*, 35: 153; Washington to John Marshall, July 15, 1796, *ibid.*, 140. On Putnam, note Rowena Buell, comp., *The Memoirs of Rufus Putnam and Certain Official Papers and Correspondence* (Boston, 1903).

them off, copied the notes, drafted the plats, accounted for the expenditures of public funds, and transmitted the surveys and accounts to the Secretary. In spite of disagreements with the Secretary over various matters, harassment by Indians, inaccuracies, and a particularly severe winter in 1797–98, Putnam made substantial progress in surveying the Ohio country in the four years after his appointment. During 1797 the surveyor general directed the running of the Greenville Treaty line and laid off the military tract. Regular surveys of the public lands began in 1798. With appropriations of slightly less than $50,000 for the three years 1797–1800, Putnam surveyed enough land to permit sales of Ohio public lands after the passage of the Land Law of 1800.[39]

Rufus Putnam's appointment showed the strong connection between the administrators of the public lands and the land business. Before taking office Putnam had served for many years as the chief representative of the Ohio Company of Associates in the Northwest Territory. The President and the Secretary of the Treasury sought prominent citizens of the territory for posts in administering the public domain, because a known occupant enhanced the office and reflected favorably on the national government; but these men were almost invariably concerned with speculation in lands. Men appointed from the East to administer the public domain acquired the habit of investment in the public lands soon after crossing the mountains. The Northwest Territory provided many examples of this phenomenon. The secretary of the territory, Winthrop Sargent, was one of the leaders in the organization of the Ohio Company. The territorial judges were likewise interested in land speculation. John Cleves Symmes was chief of a great land enterprise and a territorial judge. Rufus Putnam was the Ohio Company's representative, was nominated a territorial judge in 1790, and moved to the even more sensitive post of surveyor general in 1796. Judge George Turner, the third territorial judge, was also involved in land speculation. Most of the surveyors were speculators. Of this group Thomas Worthington, Israel Ludlow, and Putnam were notable examples.[40] The close connection between administrators and

39. William D. Pattison, *Beginnings of the American Rectangular Survey System, 1784–1800* (Chicago, 1957), 200–204; Ernst, "With Compass and Chain: Federal Land Surveyors in the Old Northwest, 1785–1816," Ch. 5.

40. Alfred Byron Sears, *Thomas Worthington, Father of Ohio Statehood* (Columbus, 1958); Bond, ed., *The Symmes Correspondence*, 40n; Bond, *The Founda-*

the land business would continue into the nineteenth century and would often serve to cast doubt on the integrity and impartiality of the administration of the public lands.

Sales under the Land Law of 1796 were small. During the first year, sales at Pittsburgh reached nearly 49,000 acres for the total sum of $112,135.45—a disappointing figure in light of the great expectations. Secretary Wolcott wrote, "The whole of the sections were repeatedly exposed to sale, at Pittsburgh, but without success, further than has been mentioned; the actual sales were confined to sections near the river Ohio." [41] The Land Law of 1796 was apparently unsatisfactory to both purchasers and government. The minimum price of two dollars per acre and the minimum tract of 640 acres meant that the buyer must be prepared to pay $1,280 within a year, a very unlikely contingency for the average settler. It was clear that the terms of the act placed the government at a disadvantage in competing with the smaller tracts, lower prices, and ample credit offered by the large speculative land companies and still available in some states. At the very moment the government asked two dollars per acre, John Cleves Symmes sold good land in the Ohio Valley for half that price, with credit and large discounts on substantial purchases.[42] Thus, the law failed to attract purchasers and so failed to raise the revenue that numerous members of Congress expected. Various committees and individual Congressmen tinkered with the law in the years after its passage, suggesting various devices such as credit, smaller tracts, and lower prices, but always without result.[43]

In 1800 Congress was moved to change the land system, following the passage in the previous year of the Northwest Territory into the second stage of government, which meant that under the conditions of the Ordinance of 1787, the legislature could send a nonvoting delegate to Congress. The man chosen was William Henry Harrison. A son-in-law of Judge John Cleves Symmes, Harrison had resigned a captaincy

tion of Ohio, 401. Governor Arthur St. Clair recognized this conflict of interest and wrote of it at length. St. Clair to Sec. State, Dec. 15, 1794; July 15, 1799, Carter, ed., Territorial Papers, 2: 499–500; 3: 57–59.
41. Wolcott to Rep. John Nicholas (Va.), Jan. 24, 1797, American State Papers, Public Lands, 1: 74.
42. Symmes to Dayton, Aug. 6, 1795, Bond, ed., The Symmes Correspondence, 174–75.
43. American State Papers, Public Lands (Duff-Green), 1: 65; ibid., Public Lands, 1: 82.

in the army to become territorial secretary in 1798. To the nation's capital he carried the desires of his constituents for changes in the land system: smaller tracts, lower prices, credit, more convenient land offices, and pre-emption. In spite of his talents, he probably would not alone have created a new land law had not Congress been ready for a change in the system. His was the duty of channeling rather than creating Congressional interest in the public lands.

Guided by Harrison and advised by Gallatin, Congress passed a land law that met many of the desires of the western country. To begin with, the act of May 10, 1800, established four land districts, each with an office, located at Cincinnati, Chillicothe, Marietta, and Steubenville, all in the Northwest Territory. Lands continued to be sold at public auctions of three weeks' duration, after proper proclamations and advertisements of the time and place of the sale and the tracts to be auctioned. The minimum price remained two dollars per acre, but the government extended credit to the purchaser. The law provided that "one fourth part of the purchase money shall be paid within forty days after the day of sale as aforesaid: another fourth part shall be paid within two Years; another fourth part within three Years; and another fourth part within four Years, after the day of sale." The government charged interest at 6 per cent on the unpaid balance and offered a discount of 8 per cent when any of the last three payments was received before the date due, "reckoning this discount always upon the sum which would have been demandable by the United States on the day appointed for such payment." The difficulties of computation that flowed from this provision plagued land officers for twenty years. Lands not paid for within five years (within one year after the date of the last payment) would be forfeited, advertised, and sold at auction. The law also directed the sale of lands in sections and half-sections, thus reducing to 320 acres the minimum tract purchasable.[44]

The Land Law of 1800 called for the appointment of two officers to conduct business in each of the district land offices, the register of the land office and the receiver of public monies. They were presidential appointments with the advice and consent of the Senate. The register entered applications for land, kept in his office the plats of the district, and attended to the affairs of the office connected with land. For his

44. 2 Stat. 73–78 (May 10, 1800); Treat, *The National Land System,* 94–99.

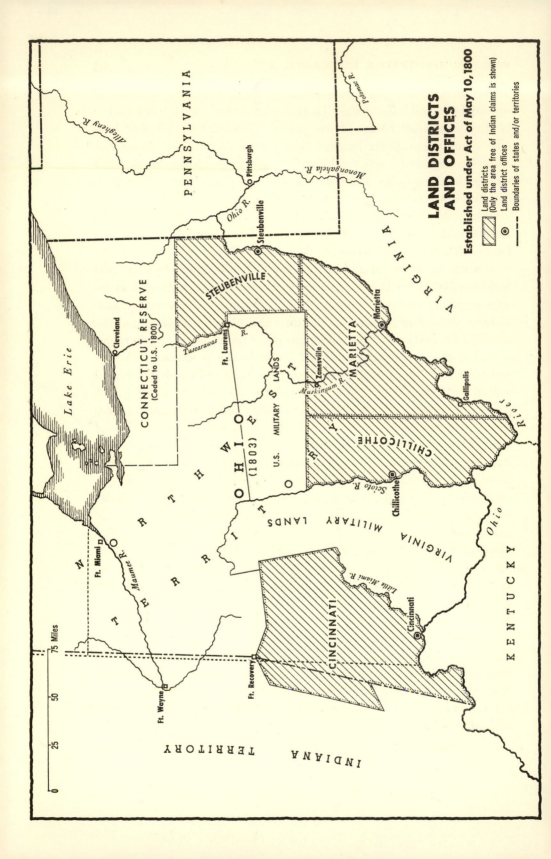

LAND DISTRICTS
AND OFFICES

Established under Act of May 10, 1800

Land districts
(Only the area free of Indian claims is shown)
Land district offices
Boundaries of states and/or territories

labor he received various small fees and a commission of one-half of 1 per cent on his sales. Near by was the office of the receiver of public monies. The receiver accepted the funds paid to the government by purchasers, issued proper receipts in duplicate, and superintended the financial aspects of the land business. He also safeguarded the funds of the government and periodically remitted them to the Treasury. His remuneration was a commission of 1 per cent on receipts "as a compensation for clerk-hire, receiving, safe keeping and transmitting it to the Treasury of the United States." Both officers posted bonds to assure their financial responsibility.[45]

Within two weeks of the passage of the law President John Adams appointed the necessary officers, and they received the approval of the Senate. The Secretary of the Treasury opened a correspondence with them and directed the surveyor general to do the same. The new land system appeared ready for operation.

The land system that had been created was the product of nearly two centuries of concern with the public lands and their administration in the New World. From the very first permanent English settlements, the overriding concern of the settlers with land made this subject a vital one to all elements of the population. This interest in the land and expansion inland in search of it varied in intensity from time to time, when an event or a particularly attractive discovery would bring it bubbling to the surface once more, but it was always present. There was nothing predetermined about the land system that emerged in 1800. In the previous two hundred years, and indeed in the first twelve years of the Republic under the Constitution, numerous other plans of policy and administration had been suggested. The experience of the new government under the Constitution in handling the issue of the public lands showed that in many respects little had changed. The same themes had always appeared, and the 1790's saw them once more: the eternal movement west, the constant search for new lands, squatting and illegal settlement, and demands for a good title. With these difficulties went certain common administrative elements, whose early examples could be found deep in colonial times: the surveyor general, land offices, land commissioners. The system of administration developed by 1800 had much to recommend it in terms of experience; whether it would prove adequate for the new situations of the future remained to be determined.

45. 2 Stat. 73–78 (May 10, 1800).

Albert Gallatin
and the Expansion of
the Land System,
1801–1812

2

The implementation of the Land Law of 1800 fell to new management. Growing ideological and political rivalry in the 1790's culminated in the election of 1800 and the triumph of the Republican cause. On March 4, 1801, Thomas Jefferson and his party assumed direction of the nation's affairs and control over the administrative machinery of the government. The new President invited the group of advisers who would form his cabinet to the new capital in Washington, a primitive little town, its unfinished streets a quagmire from the spring rains, isolated from the social and cultural life that consoled the men of government service and their wives in New York and Philadelphia. It was a fitting setting for a government that its supporters termed simple, stark, and thrifty.

Of particular concern was the Treasury Department, the most powerful force in the government and the former headquarters of the archfoe Hamilton. The new Secretary of the Treasury was Albert Gallatin. A Swiss from Geneva, Gallatin had come to America in 1780. Up to a point his was a typical immigrant's experience. He pursued a variety of trades (including that of tutor in French at Harvard College and speculator in Virginia land warrants) in several parts of the nation (on the seaboard from Maine to Richmond, and in the interior on Virginia's western frontier) before settling in western Pennsylvania. There he farmed on a small scale, speculated in lands, and became involved in politics. Of the three he was most successful in politics, becoming a delegate to the Pennsylvania Constitutional Convention and later a member of the Assembly. With the appearance of national partisan politics, Gallatin gravitated to the new opposition party of Thomas Jefferson and James Madison. Pennsylvania made him a

United States Senator in February 1793, but the Federalists in the Senate expelled him fourteen months later on the grounds of uncertain citizenship. In 1795 he returned to the national political scene as a Congressman from western Pennsylvania, where Republican strength protected him from further Federalist attacks. It was a period of great excitement over speculation in lands. As a land speculator, Gallatin readily understood the attractions of the public domain as a field for investment, and the great profits that might be realized from it. He also knew of the driving desire of the settler for a tract of his own land. As a Congressman, Gallatin manifested great interest in the public lands, and in debate he constantly supported the sale of small tracts to individual settlers.[1]

Unlike his predecessor Hamilton, Gallatin inherited an established administrative system. Part of this structure concerned the administration of the public lands. In the previous twelve years Congress had passed many laws concerned with the public domain, dealing with such diverse elements as the terms of sale, private land claims, donations, surveys, and the establishment of district land offices. Hamilton and Wolcott had supervised the creation of machinery for carrying these laws into operation. In the spring of 1801, Gallatin moved to use the administration of the Treasury Department for his own ends. His policy stressed retrenchment, minimum involvement by the Treasury Department in the life of the nation, and a reduction of the national debt. In achieving these goals, he intended to act in a way compatible with Republican principles.[2]

During Gallatin's twelve years of superintending the public lands, there was a tremendous growth in the land business, with innumerable new laws and an attendant increase in responsibility and in the time necessary to administer the public domain. It was a period of expansion to the West. Settlement in the Old Northwest filled up the Greenville Cession and then expanded north from the Ohio into the river valleys of Indiana and Illinois. Within the decade Congress created new territories in Indiana (1800) and Illinois (1809). In the

1.   Raymond Walters, Jr., *Albert Gallatin: Jeffersonian Financier and Diplomat* (New York, 1957), 14–16, 17–23, 26–64, 87–101, 119–32; Alexander Balinky, *Albert Gallatin: Fiscal Theories and Policies* (New Brunswick, 1958), 3–16; Henry M. Dater, "Albert Gallatin-Land Speculator," *Journal of American History*, 26 (1939): 21–38.
2.   Balinky, *Albert Gallatin: Fiscal Theories and Policies*, 49–51, 232–33.

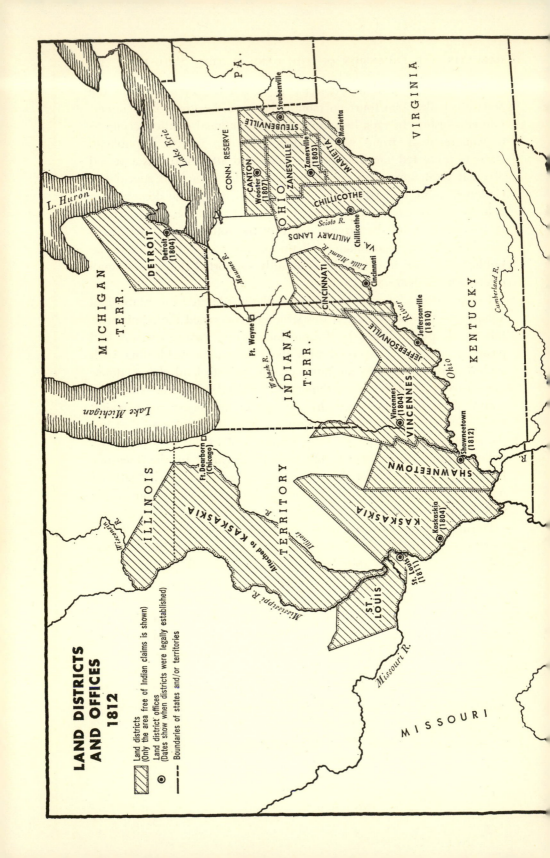

LAND DISTRICTS AND OFFICES 1812

Land districts
(Only the area free of Indian claims is shown)

Land district offices
(Dates show when districts were legally established)

Boundaries of states and/or territories

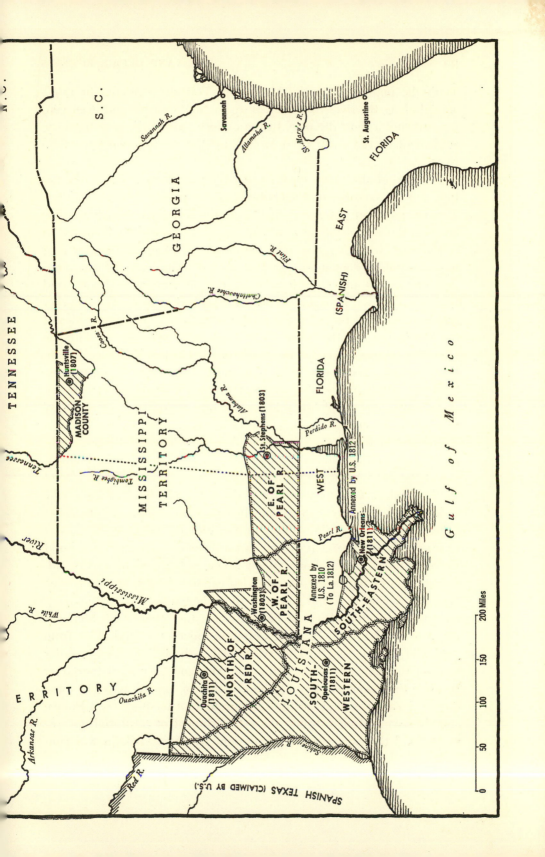

south the population in the Mississippi Territory (created in 1798) spread along the river from Vicksburg to New Orleans and even ventured inland a short distance. In the eastern part of the new territory, settlement moved north from Mobile up the rivers toward the interior.

This period also saw a great increase in the physical size of the nation and the consequent enlargement of the public domain. In 1803, Thomas Jefferson purchased the Louisiana Territory, which roughly doubled the size of the new nation. The Secretary of the Treasury, in consultation with Congress, now undertook to integrate this new area into the public domain—a complex and delicate task. It was a region of French- and Spanish-speaking people, strange traditions, and foreign land laws. Extensive grants of land had been made by earlier governments. Old French and Spanish settlements lined both sides of the Mississippi from the town of St. Louis to its intersection with the Ohio. Population moved up the rivers of the Orleans Territory (established in 1803), particularly the Red and the Ouachita. Here, too, the Secretary had to make haste in order to keep his land system abreast of an expanding population and, at the same time, to meet a variety of local conditions.

The first step was the creation of land districts and the establishment of district land offices. An act of Congress defined the boundaries of the district, but the President had the authority to fix the site of the land office. Gallatin established district land offices at Zanesville (1803) and Wooster (1803) in the State of Ohio; at Vincennes (1804) and Jeffersonville (1807) in the Indiana Territory; Kaskaskia (1804) and Shawneetown (1812) in the Illinois Territory; and also at Detroit (1804) and St. Louis (1809). The system for the orderly administration of the public domain also expanded into the South. The Secretary set up two land offices in the Mississippi Territory in 1803: one at Washington (West of Pearl River); the other at St. Stephens (East of Pearl River). In 1811, Congress moved the land office from Nashville (Tennessee) to Huntsville (Mississippi Territory) in order to meet the demands of the settlers in Madison County at the Great Bend of the Tennessee River. The creation of land districts in these dozen years followed closely on the purchase of territory from France and the several Indian tribes, the establishment of territorial governments, and the expansion of population. By 1812, Gallatin was conducting the nation's land business through eighteen district land offices, fourteen of them established under his direction.[3]

After an act of Congress established a land district and the President named the site of the land office, the district land officers were appointed. When Gallatin took over the Treasury Department, the authority of the district land officers was undefined, as was nearly everything else about the land system established under the law of 1800. Initially the offices of register and receiver were viewed as part-time appointments, something on the order of a county commissioner of roads or the postmaster in a small frontier community. Several land office appointees received assurances that they could continue to work as deputy surveyors.[4] At first the post of land officer carried no significant emolument, which confirmed an incumbent's feeling that there was little to do. Congress had established no salary, and the sole stipend was a small percentage of the sales and other modest fees for services. Registers, receivers, commissioners, and other administrators of the public lands also had to supply their own offices, furniture, and fuel. When the volume of duties became apparent, land officers complained, and Gallatin persuaded Congress to authorize a salary of $500 per annum and a commission on sales.[5]

The offices of the register and receiver turned out to be of the greatest importance. The duties were detailed and complex. The register had charge of the plats and had to identify each tract upon sale and to mark it taken. He was a direct link between the purchaser and the government. The receiver had charge of the funds received in payment for the public lands. In a credit system with its interest charges and discounts, the calculation of the accounts alone was a burdensome and exacting chore. The decision of the Secretary of the Treasury that the receiver must accept any partial payment for lands, however small, greatly complicated the calculation of interest and discount, as well as increased the number of payments that had to be calculated.[6] The calculations had to be perfect. In one unfortunate in-

3. Treat, *The National Land System*, 162–78, esp. map on p. 174.
4. Rufus Putnam to Worthington, June 12, 1800, Worthington Papers, Ohio State Library, Columbus; Gallatin to John Badollet, April 7, 1804, Gallatin Papers (microfilm), Princeton University Library.
5. 2 Stat. 282 (March 26, 1804). The land office at Marietta was an exception; the salary there was limited to $200 a year.
6. Gallatin to receivers, NA: GLO, Ltrs. Sent, Misc., 1: April 4, 1805.

stance the receiver at Steubenville misunderstood the instructions from the Treasury Department and erroneously calculated the accounts for a public sale of one hundred thousand acres of land. By the time Gallatin made the unfortunate officer aware of his error, the purchasers had long since dispersed over a land district of thousands of square miles. The receiver recalculated the accounts and spent several months searching out the buyers in order to explain his error and collect additional sums.[7]

The responsibilities connected with handling public funds were also great. Payment for public lands might be offered in the form of specie, bank notes, or certificates of credit. The receiver had to recognize counterfeit notes, to reject bank notes that would not be accepted at par at the bank of deposit (a condition requiring that he know the fifty or so banks whose notes he might currently receive), and to reject spurious certificates. In the event of a mistake he had to pay the government out of his own pocket. The receiver was also responsible for the safe deposit of the public funds. Bills he might remit through the mails, after cutting them "in two equal parts in order that each half may be forwarded by a different mail." The bulk of specie posed a special problem. In 1805, Gallatin asked James Findlay, the Cincinnati receiver, to transport his balance of $150,000 to Pittsburgh. The sum was entirely in specie, weighed four tons and required four wagons and several guards. In spite of the spring rains, the receipts reached Pittsburgh safely, but not without great anxiety and expense.[8]

It was a rare land officer who was not involved in the buying and selling of land for his own personal gain. There was no rule against it. The danger of conflict in office was clear, but in a period when governors, territorial judges, and other state and territorial officials engaged in the land business, this relaxed attitude carried over into the administration of the public domain. When a purchaser's receipt for a choice tract did not reach the land office in time, and his land was forfeited, Jared Mansfield, Putnam's successor as surveyor general, immediately gobbled up the tract, much to Gallatin's distress.[9] Clerks in the district land offices speculated in certificates of indebtedness—stocks that

7. Gallatin to Rep. Andrew Gregg (Penna.), NA: Legislative Division, Reports of the Committee on Public Lands, 1: Jan. 31, 1806.
8. Gallatin to James Findlay, NA: GLO, Ltrs. Sent, Misc., 1: Nov. 6, 1802; March 8, 1805.
9. Gallatin to Jefferson, Jan. 6, 1807, Adams, ed., *Gallatin Writings*, 1: 326–27.

circulated at less than face value but, under a law of 1797, might be received in payment for the public lands at par. The difference between the market value and the face value represented profit. Clerks often used the same stock certificates over and over.[10] Nathaniel Ewing, receiver at Vincennes, and Governor William Henry Harrison of the Indiana Territory joined a company engaged in the purchase and sale of public lands. Although Gallatin could find no evidence that either man had improperly used his authority as a superintendent of the sale, he nonetheless thought it "extremely improper" that the two administrators should be joined with a company whose object was the purchase of lands at the lowest possible price. With the President's support, the Secretary issued a circular to forbid superintendents of sales to join organizations whose purpose was "by lessening competition, to prevent the highest price being obtained for the lands." [11]

Gallatin's task of supervising his land administrators was unending and complicated. To investigate the numerous complaints, he employed Senators, Representatives, important local citizens, territorial officers, and even other land officers. Congress early recognized the possibility of speculation, fraud, and misappropriation of funds by requiring land offices to post bond and, in 1804, by providing for an annual inspection of all federal land offices. These inspections took place first in 1805 and annually thereafter. Gallatin issued specific instructions to the inspectors, stressing the examination of the register's ledger and journal, its comparison with the receipts in the hands of the receiver, and a general suggestion to note whether the books of the office "have the appearance of fairness and regularity." [12] Yet the Secretary, the land officers, and the inspectors were often political allies. Land officers were powerful men. Their great distance from Washington and their removal from Gallatin's close observation and advice increased their independence. The inspectors, of whom much was expected, were almost always appointed from the towns where the land officers resided, perhaps in the interests of economy. (Inspectors received six dollars a day and another six dollars for each twenty miles

10. *American State Papers, Finance*, 2: 163; Gallatin to Zaccheus Biggs, NA: GLO, Ltrs. Sent, Misc., 1: Jan. 9, 1806.
11. Gallatin to Jefferson, April 27, 1808, Carter, ed., *Territorial Papers*, 7: 562–63; Circular to land officers, NA: GLO, Ltrs. Sent, Misc., 1: April 30, 1808.
12. Gallatin to examiners, *ibid.*, May 2, 1806.

of travel to and from the land office.) The examiners were often friends, neighbors, business partners, and political allies of the land officers. Nonetheless, their reports disclosed maladministration, extended absences, and occasional examples of financial mismanagement.[13] Gallatin worried constantly about the reputation of his land officers. To Jefferson he confided, "My best endeavors, knowing the abuses committed in almost every State [land system], have been exerted, and, I think, with success, in preserving the purity of our land offices. . . ." [14] The purity was occasionally smudged, but the standards of land officers were higher under Gallatin than at any other time during the first half-century of the land business.

The principal object of Gallatin's administrative apparatus was the sale of public lands. Congress had passed laws dictating the terms, tract size, and rules for sale; the sales had to take place in accordance with Congressional guidelines. Much remained to be done. The preparation for a public sale began with the surveys. Throughout Gallatin's administration Congress frequently changed the rules and regulations governing the sale of public land and its survey. Under the Land Law of 1800, which directed the survey of alternate townships into sections, Rufus Putnam was obliged to resurvey all his work of the past three years. The efficiency and promptness of the surveys suffered from lack of clerical assistance and the failure of deputies to maintain their schedules. The removal of Rufus Putnam for political reasons also disturbed the continuity of the surveys. Jefferson's choice for the post of surveyor general was Jared Mansfield, a noted mathematician and acting professor of mathematics at West Point.[15] In his letter of instructions to Mansfield, Secretary Gallatin referred to the limited area of land cleared of Indian title and noted that "almost the whole of the public lands has already been surveyed. . . ." [16] But the new surveyor general did not lack for challenges. William Henry Harrison, Governor of the Indiana Territory, made a series of extensive purchases from the Indians. By 1810 a big wedge of lower Indiana and the southern third of the Illinois Territory had been freed of Indian title. Mansfield's authority expanded accordingly. In 1804,

13.   E.g. Gallatin to Zaccheus Biggs, NA: GLO, Ltrs. Sent, Misc., 2: May 10, 1811; Gallatin to Thomas Gibson, *ibid.*, July 24, 1811.
14.   Gallatin to Jefferson, Jan. 6, 1807, Adams, ed., *Gallatin Writings*, 1: 326–27.
15.   On Mansfield, see *Dictionary of American Biography*, 12: 256–57.
16.   Gallatin to Mansfield, NA: GLO, Ltrs. Sent, SG, 1: Sept. 19, 1803.

Congress gave him jurisdiction over all public lands north of the Ohio and east of the Mississippi to which Indian titles had been extinguished. Two years later, Congress broadened his jurisdiction to include the Territory of Louisiana (later the State of Missouri) and empowered him to appoint a principal deputy for that region.

The surveys moved steadily forward for the half-dozen years after Mansfield's appointment, but after 1810 rising Indian unrest once more slowed the surveys of new lands. Mansfield deplored the delay but found ample work in the surveying of private claims and their integration into the general plats. By the time the outbreak of war in 1812 brought a complete halt to all surveying under Mansfield's jurisdiction, the surveyor general had supervised the survey of the public lands in the lower third of Indiana and Illinois, in addition to those areas in Ohio free of Indian claims.[17]

In 1803 Congress extended the surveying system by establishing a new surveying district for the area south of the State of Tennessee. President Thomas Jefferson wrote of his appointee, Isaac Briggs, "in point of science, in astronomy, geometry and mathematics he stands in a line with Mr. Ellicott, and *second to no man* in the United States." [18] The appointment of Briggs was not a satisfactory one. The new surveyor was a mathematician and a perfectionist. He delayed surveys on the grounds that sufficient accuracy could not be achieved for the fee of four dollars a mile. Early in 1804, Briggs went to Washington for conferences with the President and Congress over private land claims in Mississippi. He was gone almost a year, and the surveys of the district languished. Upon his return he found a remonstrance from Gallatin. "It is a matter of regret that the surveying should have

17. Ernst, "With Compass and Chain: Federal Land Surveyors in the Old Northwest, 1785–1816," Ch. 6; Charles J. Bayard, "The Development of the Public Land Policy, 1783–1820, With Special Reference to Indiana" (Unpublished doctoral dissertation, Indiana University, 1956), Chs. 7 and 8.

18. Jefferson to William C. C. Claiborne, May 24, 1803, quoted in Ella Kent Barnard, "Isaac Briggs, A. M., F. A. P. S.," *Maryland Historical Magazine,* 7 (1912): 411. Jared Mansfield was the sole surveyor general in the United States, and the law creating the separate district stated only that "a surveyor of the lands of the United States, south of the state of Tennessee, shall be appointed. . . ." 2 Stat. 233 (March 3, 1803). In practice, however, the new district was an independent administrative unit whose head reported directly to the Secretary of the Treasury and later to the Commissioner of the General Land Office. Before the end of the decade, the surveyor South of Tennessee was often referred to as a surveyor general, and the heads of other surveying districts established after 1812 automatically assumed the title.

been so long delayed; and there is now a representation to Congress from the Mississippi Legislature, complaining of it," the Secretary wrote.[19]

Briggs finally acted. He gave his full attention to the surveys of his district, and by the fall of 1806 he could express confidence that "*the whole of the Surveying,* in the Mississippi Territory both East and West of Pearl River, will be completed by the 1st of next year, and the returns in this office within one month thereafter." [20] At the same time Congress enlarged his responsibility by giving him authority over the survey of the Territory of Orleans. An act of Congress authorized Briggs to appoint a principal deputy for each of two surveying districts in this territory. Gallatin urged especially a rapid survey of the western district to facilitate an early public sale. The Secretary continued: "I will add, that that object is considered as intimately connected with the welfare, & even safety of that newly acquired territory.—For it is the only portion where any great increase of American population can take place, and I need not comment on the importance of that object." Gallatin made it unmistakably clear that "scientific correctness" was of far less importance than "dispatch, which is indispensably necessary." [21] The part of the territory east of the Mississippi with all the parishes lying on the west bank of the river and bordering the river formed the eastern district, with its land office at New Orleans. Most of the land here was covered by private claims and occupied by French residents. The western district was composed of the settlements on the Red and the Ouachita rivers, with the parishes of Attacapas and Opelousas, and the land office was at Opelousas.[22]

Briggs for the first time began to encounter the serious problems that would plague administrators of the public lands in his part of the country far into the future. The dominant feature of the early surveys in the Southwest was the large number of private claims, which by their "complex nature and scattered position . . ." meant that "almost every Township in the Territory is partly done before one tenth part

19.   Gallatin to Briggs, NA: GLO, Ltrs. Sent, SG, 1: Feb. 20, 1805.
20.   Briggs to Gallatin, *ibid.*, Ltrs. Recd., SG, Miss., 52: Sept. 20, 1806. Most of the Mississippi Territory was still occupied by several Indian tribes.
21.   Gallatin to Briggs, *ibid.*, Ltrs. Sent, Misc., SG, 1: May 8, 1806. The principal deputies received a salary of $500 per annum, plus 25 cents for each mile of survey executed by their deputies, and 25 cents for each certified copy of a plat of survey. 2 Stat. 391–95 (April 21, 1806).
22.   See Gallatin to John W. Gurley, NA: GLO, Ltrs. Sent, Misc., 1: March 30, 1805.

of them can be completed for this office." [23] Briggs never even made a good start. In late 1806 he made a hurried journey to Washington. He never returned. The surveyor's office was thrown into confusion by his precipitate departure. Open accounts and half-completed surveys lay unattended, and the progress of the surveys in the Southwest languished amidst the irate cries of interested citizens, legislatures, unpaid deputies, and land commissioners.[24]

More than a year later, Seth Pease arrived to assume the duties of Surveyor General South of Tennessee. Pease was a New Englander, an astronomer, and a surveyor and had assisted in laying out Connecticut's Western Reserve in Ohio. To him Secretary Gallatin made known once more the importance of the work: "I will only repeat, what I had often urged to your Predecessor that the speedy completion of the surveys of the private claims & public lands in the Mississippi Territory is an object of great national importance, which has been delayed much beyond our rational expectations." [25] The new surveyor general was a diligent and practical man. Under his supervision the surveys of the Mississippi Territory made good progress.

Pease resigned in 1810. His successor was Thomas Freeman, surveyor and explorer of the Red River. A native of Ireland, he had come to the United States in 1784 and had entered the public service as a surveyor in 1793. Washington had appointed him to survey the boundary line between the United States and Spanish West Florida. Under President Thomas Jefferson he had directed an expedition up the Red River, and he had been since 1808 the register of the land office at Madison County (Huntsville).[26] Freeman's assumption of duties coincided with the rise of Indian unrest. Outlying areas became unsafe for smaller parties, and the surveyors retreated to the settlements. For the next five years Freeman attempted to survey the many private claims that covered the settled part of the Mississippi and Orleans territories.[27] Freeman's tenure of office (he served

23. Briggs to Gallatin, NA: GLO, Ltrs. Recd., SG, Miss., 52: Sept. 20, 1806.
24. A detailed account of early Mississippi Territory surveys is James Helms, Jr., "Land Tenure in Territorial Mississippi, 1798–1809" (Unpublished master's thesis, University of Virginia, 1954), Ch. 3.
25. Gallatin to Pease, NA: GLO, Ltrs. Sent, SG, 1: March 21, 1807.
26. On Freeman, see Dunbar Rowland, ed., *Encyclopedia of Mississippi History* (2 vols., Madison, 1907), 1: 728, 749–50.
27. The universal importance of these claims is thoroughly discussed in Robert Vaughn Haynes, "A Political History of the Mississippi Territory" (Unpublished doctoral dissertation, Rice University, 1958), *passim*.

until his death in 1821) gave stability to a district whose surveys had
suffered from frequent changes of personnel.

Gallatin intended that the land business should be conducted in accordance with strict Republican principles of administration—that is
to say, with a minimum of staff and the smallest expense possible. The
result was a bottleneck at crucial spots in the land system. In 1801
Rufus Putnam noted that deputy surveyors had returned more than
thirteen thousand miles of field notes to his office, but so limited was
his clerical staff that only a fraction of these notes had been transcribed into plats and transmitted to the Treasury Department and
the district land offices. The Secretary of the Treasury also refused to
reimburse expenses for office rent, fuel, and furniture—small matters,
but serious enough to officers who lived and worked in distant wilderness posts, where the cost of such items was high. Thomas Rodney, a
land commissioner, wrote from the Mississippi Territory, "I love fru-
gallity and economy in the Management of public Money, but I view
Parsimony & extravagance as extremes that are Equally productive of
Evil." [28] Gallatin's concern at the cost of administration increased
after 1808 when the expanding European war threatened to derange
his carefully created financial equilibrium. [29]

If Gallatin were to increase the nation's revenue by the sales of public lands, he first had to clear up the numerous private claims. His
Federalist predecessors had struggled with this problem, but the purchase of Louisiana immeasurably increased the numbers and area of
these foreign titles. The United States Government recognized these
claims, and Congress moved to provide for their examination and confirmation. The Republicans did not choose territorial governors as the
instrument of their policy but instead created a new administrative
mechanism, the board of commissioners, first provided for under the
act of March 3, 1803. These boards consisted of three men who were
appointed or of two special appointees acting with the register of the
local land office. Although their objects varied with specific situations,
their general mission, in the words of the Secretary of the Treasury,
was "to guard against unfounded or fraudulent claims, to confirm all
bona fide claims derived from a legitimate authority, even when the

28. Putnam to Gallatin, NA: GLO, Ltrs. Recd., SG, Ohio, 64: Aug. 10, 1801;
Thomas Rodney to Caesar Rodney, Oct. 31, 1804, Simon Gratz, ed., "Thomas
Rodney," *Pennsylvania Magazine of History and Biography*, 44 (1920): 68.
29. Balinky, *Albert Gallatin: Fiscal Theories and Policies*, 128–63.

title had not been completed, and to secure in their possessions all the actual settlers who were found on the land when the United States took actual possession . . . though they had only a right of occupancy."[30] These boards formed an intermediate administrative and judicial body between the claimant and final Congressional approval. Their activities were of the greatest importance.

The pattern of operations almost never varied. The commissioners established a headquarters, often in the largest town or at the site of the district land office, advertised their presence, and asked those with claims to come forward. For the next several months (even years in some cases) they recorded evidence and interrogated claimants and their witnesses. Congressional acts that authorized the creation of boards generally provided a clerk for recording evidence. Farsighted commissioners selected a local figure of stature, who they hoped would be both of perfect integrity and familiar with the language and the problems of the claims and claimants. His presence served to reassure the citizens that their interests would be protected.

The Territory of Mississippi (created in 1798) offers an example of the successful disposition of private land claims. At the time Gallatin became concerned with this area, the major portion of it belonged to the Indians. Only two narrow strips along the Mississippi and the Tombigbee rivers had been ceded to the white man, and "some say that there are Claims to Every foot of Land. . . ."[31] In response to Jefferson's plea for prompt settlement of the numerous claims in the territory, Congress created two land districts, one east and the other west of the Pearl River. For each land district the President appointed a register and two land commissioners, who served as boards to adjudicate private land claims and to disentangle them from the Yazoo claims. By comparison with experiences elsewhere, the two boards made rapid progress. They completed their reports in 1805; and acting on their recommendations, Congress confirmed grants of more than 450,000 acres originally made by Spain and Great Britain.[32]

30. 2 Stat. 230–32 (March 3, 1803); Adams, ed., *Gallatin Writings*, 3: 220.
31. Thomas Rodney to his son, Caesar A. Rodney, Gratz, ed., "Thomas Rodney," 43: 212.
32. Helms, "Land Tenure in Territorial Mississippi, 1798–1809," Ch. 4. The contentious Yazoo claims have been described as "a wild tangle of doubtful, overlapping, and contradictory claims without parallel in the entire history of the public domain." Ralph S. Cotterill, "The National Land System in the South, 1803–1812," *Journal of American History*, 16 (1930): 496.

Problems in the Territory of Orleans (admitted to the Union in 1812 as the State of Louisiana) were not so easily solved. The primitive state of the surveys and records, the confusion attending the transfer of national ownership, and the opportunities to acquire landed wealth by fraud were immediately recognized. In 1803, William C. C. Claiborne, then Governor of the Mississippi Territory and later Governor of the Territory of Orleans, wrote to the Secretary of State, "I have reason to believe that much of the vacant Land in Louisiana, will be covered by fraudulent grants, previous to the delivery of the province to the United States." [33] In 1805, Congress provided two boards of commissioners to inspect records, take evidence, interrogate witnesses, and judge the validity of the claims. These two administrative bodies found their way blocked by missing records, nonexistent surveys, primitive communications, language difficulties, and local hostility. An estimated ten thousand claims covered large quantities of the most fertile and best-located land. The two boards eventually rejected about one-quarter of these claims for lack of proof or suspicion of fraud. Their investigations took years. Not until 1820 were the Louisiana claims sufficiently settled to permit a sale of public land.[34]

Claims were fewer but problems were no less complex in the Territory of Louisiana (later the State of Missouri). In addition to a board of commissioners, Congress also provided for a recorder of land titles to register the many claims. To this post Jefferson appointed the able Frederick Bates, later Governor of Missouri.[35] In spite of Bates's presence, the career of the board was stormy. In 1806 one of the commissioners resigned, and the recording secretary absconded with the only copy of the records. Two other members of the board later betrayed their trust by making secret agreements with the large land holders. Gallatin chose new commissioners, and the hearings began again. The new board worked for six years and in 1812 eventually issued certifi-

33.   Claiborne to Madison, Sept. 7, 1803, Carter, ed., *Territorial Papers*, 9: 26.
34.   Harry L. Coles, Jr., "Applicability of the Public Land System to Louisiana," *Journal of American History*, 43 (1956): 51–54; Harry L. Coles, Jr., "The Confirmation of Foreign Land Titles in Louisiana," *Louisiana Historical Quarterly*, 38 (1955): 1–22; Francis P. Burns, "The Spanish Land Laws of Louisiana," *ibid.*, 11 (1928): 557–81. Coles estimates that as many as ten thousand claims were presented for confirmation in Louisiana.
35.   2 Stat. 326 (March 2, 1805); Thomas M. Marshall, ed., *The Life and Papers of Frederick Bates* (2 vols., St. Louis, 1926), 1: 6–18.

cates of confirmation to fewer than half of the three thousand claims considered. The board discovered more than seven hundred cases of perjury. Of one witness, Joseph Page, the commission wrote: "This man is a Frenchman, and has been a great swearer; we have, perhaps, two hundred of his depositions, generally given in favor of the large land-jobbers. . . ."[36] Although a land office opened in St. Louis in 1811, the first sales of public lands did not take place until 1818.[37]

Commissioners in the Old Northwest found many of the same problems. "From the character of the witnesses, and the complexion of the evidence advanced in support of a very great number of those claims," wrote the commissioners from Kaskaskia, "we are obliged to proceed on our examination of them with much slowness and caution, the public interest imperiously requires that we should do so. . . ."[38] Gallatin fully concurred about the danger of fraud and wrote to the commissioners, "I embrace this opportunity to state, that, information has been received from several quarters of gross attempts being made to impose unfounded & fraudulent claims on the Commissioners, & that full reliance is placed on your resisting & exposing every such fraud."[39] The issue of private land claims became closely intertwined with politics. Everywhere the land commissioners worked in the midst of bribery and corruption. Fortunately the high integrity and dedication of the commissioners and their great devotion to duty enabled them to deliver objective opinions on the most controversial subject of the Old Northwest.[40]

The boards of commissioners often encountered open hostility from the French and the Spanish who confronted an alien language and legal tradition, in their struggle to establish their land claims. Suspicion and resentment were easily aroused. The *Missouri Gazette*

36. Report of the Board of Commissioners, Feb. 24, 1810, *American State Papers, Public Lands*, 2: 125.

37. Louis Pelzer, "The Spanish Grants of Upper Louisiana," *Iowa Journal of History and Politics*, 11 (1913): 3–37; Lemont K. Richardson, "Private Land Claims in Missouri," *Missouri Historical Review*, 50 (1955–56): 132–44, 271–86, 387–99; Allen Henry Rose, "The Extension of the United States Land System to Missouri, 1804–1817" (Unpublished master's thesis, Washington University, St. Louis, 1941).

38. E. Bacchus and Michael Jones to H. R., NA: Legislative Division, Rpts. of the House Committee on Public Lands, 1: Feb. 24, 1806.

39. Gallatin to commissioners, NA: GLO, Ltrs. Sent, Misc., 1: Feb. 6, 1807.

40. On the private claims in the Old Northwest, see Francis A. Philbrick, ed., *The Laws of Indiana Territory, 1801–1809* (Illinois Historical Collections, Vol. 21, Springfield, 1930), lxxxvii–xcv; Treat, *The National Land System*, 198–229.

fanned them by printing inflammatory letters to the editor: "Have you forgotten that you were born free, and that you enjoyed that freedom until the latter part of 1805, when three land commissioners with their agents, constables, &c. &c. &c. established their inquisition in your capital, & tyrannized over you with the most insolent and vindictive spirit, until they dragooned you to the most abject submission, and forced you to give up your property into their hands. . . ." [41] The authority of the boards of commissioners was indeed broad. "The Commissioners are the sole judge of what should be considered by them as proper evidence," wrote Gallatin on one occasion. The finality of the judgment over claims varied, according to the wording of the law that created the board. In some instances the board of commissioners handed down absolute decisions on the validity of claims, sent the confirmed claims to the surveyor general, with instructions to survey and record them on the general plat, and forwarded a copy of its report to Congress for information. But the decision was final. "The Register and Receiver when acting as Commissioners were a court without appeal for the purpose for which they were initiated," in the words of the Secretary.[42] In other cases the board would submit recommendations to Congress, which had reserved the power of final decision. These recommendations carried great weight because of the commissioners' familiarity with the claims and local conditions; and Congress rarely disregarded them.

By 1810, Gallatin had established eight boards of commissioners—one each in the territories of Michigan, Indiana, Illinois, and Louisiana, and two each in the Mississippi and Orleans territories.[43] By that time the commissioners in Mississippi had completed their work, and sales had begun, while the boards in Michigan, Indiana, and Illinois had presented their reports to Congress. The boards of commissioners in the Orleans and Louisiana territories had neither presented their findings nor indicated when they might be available.[44]

41. St. Louis *Missouri Gazette,* Feb. 1, 1810. The *Gazette* represented the large landed interests in the Louisiana Territory.
42. Gallatin to Parke Walton, Receiver, Washington, NA: GLO, Ltrs. Sent, Misc., 1: Aug. 9, 1810.
43. Adams, ed., *Gallatin Writings,* 3: 219.
44. Gallatin to Jeremiah Morrow, Chairman of the Senate Committee on Public Lands, NA: GLO, Ltrs. Sent, Misc., 1: Jan. 26, 1810.

The settlement of private claims and the survey of the public domain were only preparatory steps to the sale of public lands. Sales took place under conditions outlined in the Land Law of 1800, which fixed the date of the first sale under the new system in April and May 1801, almost the same date on which Gallatin took over the Treasury. One of the first public auctions took place at Chillicothe. Here the interests of the United States Government were in the hands of the district land officers, particularly Thomas Worthington, the register. His was an uneasy responsibility. Crowds appeared in the little town a full two weeks before the opening of the sale. Settlers came in large numbers, hoping to acquire land at the minimum price. They were quickly joined by the prominent citizens of the territory, who expected to pick up valuable tracts at the minimum price and hold them as speculations. The proper forms failed to arrive, but Worthington worried more about the absence of the Governor and the secretary of the territory, for the law specified that one or the other of these officers should attend as a superintendent of the sale. Both forms and officials were still missing on the day the sale was scheduled to begin. The register's discomfort was not lessened by the restlessness of the large waiting crowd. "In this case I felt much undetermined as to my duty, not less than two hundred people were in the town from different parts of the Country Waiting for the Commencement of the Sale. . . ." he wrote. "The surveyor Gen. being here, I called on him for his Opinion and on three Gentlemen of the Bar all of whom agreed that it was my duty to Commence the Sale." The register did so. "I still felt a Considerable degree of reluctance at doing so but finally believing that the law enjoined it on me as a duty, between the hours of 3 & 4 OClock in the Afternoon the Sale was Commenced, having first prevailed on the Surveyor General to Assist in adapting regulations & Manageing the same." [45] On the register's signal, the crier stepped forward, announced the location of the first tract, and prepared to receive bids.

The next weeks saw the first enactment of a drama that would be repeated with many variations throughout the century. Men drifted in and out of the sale room in small groups, constantly seeking information about choice tracts. The land was so vast that no one knew much about it, except the surveyors and those who had access to surveyors'

45. Worthington to Gallatin, May 11, 1801, Carter, ed., *Territorial Papers*, 3: 133.

plats. A general atmosphere of strained good will prevailed, in which the only outward object of all citizens was to take as much land with as little return to the government as possible. In the sale room the crier called the numbers of the tracts, and the crowd waited expectantly. Everywhere individuals silently measured the value of the land against the possibility of creating a bidding competition. Silence might give them the tract later at the minimum price. Anxious settlers bid for their land in low, quiet voices and, when speculators bid against them, angrily made known their rights. When men bid for tracts in error or bid against one another for tracts they did not want, the universal advice was forfeit, wait for the resale next day, and then take them at the minimum.[46]

The land office business in the Northwest Territory had begun. The office at Chillicothe sold 99,058 acres of land for more than $220,000 in the three weeks of the public sale. At the end of eight weeks Worthington had sold more than $360,000, and a week later, $400,000. Figures through November 1, 1801, showed the four district land offices with sales of 398,646 acres for $834,887.11. These figures contrasted sharply with the sales under the Land Law of 1796, and the sum was a welcome addition to government income. On the basis of these early figures Gallatin estimated that for the next eight years the annual income from the sales of public lands would be about $400,000.[47]

Gallatin soon had expectations of an even greater income. In 1803, Congress extended the land system to the public domain south of the State of Tennessee.[48] To the Secretary fell the task of placing on the market the lands of the Mississippi, Orleans, and Louisiana territories, where the completion of the private claims and surveys lagged. The commissioners in the Mississippi Territory made substantial progress, but the confirmed private land claims remained unsurveyed and so unincorporated into the general plat. The Secretary grew more and more impatient for a sale, particularly as the international situation

46. See testimony on the charges of Elias Langham against Worthington, Worthington Papers, #3827, Ohio Historical Society Library, Columbus.
47. Sears, *Thomas Worthington*, 40; *American State Papers, Finance*, 1: 703, 715.
48. 2 Stat. 229–35 (March 3, 1803). For an analysis of the act, see Helms, "Land Tenure in Territorial Mississippi, 1798–1809," Ch. 2.

threatened to reduce the income from imposts: a substantial rise in income from the sale of public lands would be most welcome. Eventually, in spite of the unsurveyed claims, he determined to place selected tracts of Mississippi land on the market in 1809. When the President questioned the decision to sell lands prior to the completion of a general plat, Gallatin explained that "the importance of carrying the land system into operation there, for the purpose both of quieting the people & of encouraging population, had induced me to adopt that mode, rather than to delay the sales several months longer in order to wait for the Surveyor's returns." [49] Under the direction of the Secretary, sales of public lands in the Mississippi Territory began in August 1809.

Gallatin also sought to introduce some uniformity into the sales at the district land offices. The crier should call aloud each quarter-section successively in each township, he wrote, and, "if no person bids for each quarter section during half a minute to pass on to the next; by which process, each Township on which there is no bid, occupies only one hour & a quarter." The crier should wait five minutes between townships. When the bids were made, "a limited time say five minutes, is allowed for the sale. . . ." If this schedule were maintained, "a good sober Crier," "a correct Clerk," and the two land officers could auction 160,000 acres in ten days. Above all, the Secretary concluded, "The Superintendents must fix on their plan before the commencement of their sales, in all its details, so as to proceed regularly & without interruption." [50] The Secretary also established rules for the sale of relinquished lands, but active competition was rare on such occasions, and the House Committee on Public Lands once observed, "Few men are willing to incur the resentment of their neighbors by bidding for their property, at public vendue, even when other neighbors are the creditors; and when the public is concerned, scarcely a man will be found hardy enough to do it." [51]

49. Gallatin to Thomas H. Williams, Register, Washington, NA: GLO, Ltrs. Sent, Misc., 1: Oct. 20, 1808; Gallatin to Jefferson, Oct. 21, 1808, Carter, ed., *Territorial Papers*, 5: 657.
50. Gallatin to John Badollet, Register, Vincennes, NA: GLO, Ltrs. Sent, Misc., 1: March 9, 1807.
51. NA: Legislative Division, Rpts. of House Committee on Public Lands, 1: March 1, 1806.

The land system inaugurated under the Land Law of 1800 consisted of public auction, open competition for choice tracts which the highest bidder would win, and the highest possible profit would go to the government. In practice this system did not work. Both squatters and small purchasers, as well as speculators, combined to prevent competitive bidding. Jared Mansfield thought it a manifestation of the unfortunate character of the frontier population. "The composition of the people in these parts, except the industrious yeoman & mechanics, as much as indicate corruption," he complained to Gallatin. "They are fortune hunters from the Eastern States. Landed speculation, Surveying Jobbing, Pettyfogging, Fakery, Electioneering for public places, & everything except labour & industry are the means in operation. Hence the feuds & disorders in Louisiana and Indiana Territory & in this State, & the most unprincipled abuse of one another, & public officers who dare discountenance fraud, abuse, & the measures of the speculators." The country would be better off without public land sales, "than that speculation should trample underfoot all justice & should convert to its purposes with those very laws which were intended to counteract it." At Vincennes, Steubenville, and Chillicothe speculators sold off their tracts for cash before the government sale had ended, and the United States received only a quarter of the final sale price. "They are completely successful, by their numbers, vigilance, intrigues, knowledge of the Land Laws, & occasions they afford for practicing such arts," concluded the surveyor general.[52]

Gallatin protected the government's revenue from lands by limiting the power of state taxation. Under his recommendation the United States Government gave to each state salt spring reservations of six square miles and one-tenth of the net income of the lands sold for turnpike and canal construction. When they entered the Union, the public land states agreed, in exchange for these gifts, to levy no taxes on lands sold by the federal government for five years from the date of sale.[53] The Secretary was also one of a series of administrators who attempted to preserve the salt and lead deposits of the nation from exploitation, but he was not successful. The salt deposits of Illinois

52. Mansfield to Gallatin, Nov. 27, 1807, Gallatin Papers (microfilm), Princeton University Library; same to same, Sept. 8, 1806, Carter, ed., *Territorial Papers*, 7: 388.
53. *American State Papers, Misc.*, 1: 327–28; 2 Stat. 175 (April 30, 1802).

and the lead in Missouri were eventually taken over by the energetic pioneer, with little or no return to the government.[54]

The actual sales of the public lands were only the beginning of Gallatin's responsibilities. After the sales were over, the work of the Treasury Department began. The department was responsible for the records that resulted from the sale and administration of the public domain. These records were numerous, and they grew as the surveys and sales of the public lands increased. The receivers of public money transmitted monthly transcripts of sales and payments with the original receipts and assignments to the clerks of the Treasury Department, who checked and adjusted the accounts. The next step was an examination by the Auditor, with an eventual review by the Comptroller of the Treasury. The scrutiny was thorough, detailed, and often extremely slow. Gallatin thought, "The system, as it relates to the accountability of the receivers, is better checked than that of any other branch of the public revenue; but the various and contingent provisions respecting the credits, interest, discount, forfeitures, and other conditions of sale, render it rather complex, and for that reason liable to delays in the final settlement of the accounts of the receivers." [55]

Each register transmitted monthly to the department an account of money received as recorded by him from the receipts presented, and lists of all tracts of land applied for and entered by individuals, with a special notation on all tracts reverted through failure of payment. Special Treasury Department clerks took charge of the registers' monthly returns as they came in the mail, and of the receivers' accounts as they emerged from the comptroller's office. Four such clerks were assigned to the land business, and they examined and posted all transactions and records in the accounts of individual purchasers—a lengthy process where a separate account had to be opened and maintained for each purchaser under the credit system, and the principal and interest of each payment had to be calculated and entered on his

54. Donald J. Abramoske, "The Federal Lead Leasing System in Missouri," *Missouri Historical Review*, 54 (1959): 27–38.
55. Adams, ed., *Gallatin Writings*, 3: 224. On the department's system of accounting, see Leonard D. White, *The Jeffersonians: A Study in Administrative History, 1801–1829* (New York, 1951), 163–65. The auditor's correspondence with the land officers was extensive but devoted entirely to questions of bookkeeping and land patents. See NA: GLO, Ltrs. Sent, Misc., Vols. 3 and 4, *passim*.

account sheet. The records of the office became unmanageably large. On January 1, 1811, there were 173 ledgers containing the records of the sales made at eleven district land offices.[56]

The land business was large and complicated. The expense of administration was substantial. Up to December 31, 1812, the total cost of administering the public domain, including surveys, judging private land claims, the sales at public auction, and miscellaneous items, came to $945,325.71.[57] The quantity of public lands sold varied from year to year and had begun to rise once more on the eve of the War of 1812. The sales and receipts for the decade are reflected in this table: [58]

	ACRES	
1800	67,751	$ 135,501.86
1801	497,939	1,031,893.26
1802	271,080	532,160.74
1803	174,156	349,292.18
1804	398,156	817,270.50
1805	581,972	1,186,562.09
1806	506,019	1,053,792.34
1807	320,946	659,709.17
1808	209,167	490,080.35
1809	275,004	605,970.20
1810	285,796	607,867.77
1811	575,067	1,216,447.28

Albert Gallatin found the administration of the public domain a great worry and a growing drain on his time. Basic policy and administration were all very well and entirely appropriate for the Secretary of the Treasury, but Gallatin was importuned for advice on the most minute questions. He found himself occupied constantly with queries on fees, errors in purchase, lost certificates, jurisdiction, transportation of funds, interest, personalities, surveys, private claims, and numerous others. A correspondence that was burdensome from the beginning became impossible with fourteen new land offices and the increasing demands of private land claims. He wrote, "It cannot be expected that

56. *House Committee Reports,* 11 Cong., 3 Sess., Jan. 3, 1811.
57. *American State Papers, Public Lands,* 2: 739.
58. *Senate Public Document,* 27 Cong., 3 Sess., #246: 6. Leonard White notes that "the sale of public land, a modest enterprise until about 1810, became a more extensive and complicated operation." *The Jeffersonians,* 138.

I should give opinions in every case of that description which may occur; other official duties altogether forbid it." And again he remonstrated, "It is impossible that I should have time to examine and correctly to decide every doubtful case which may occur in the execution of the land law." [59] But "decide" and "give opinions" the Secretary did for a dozen years. As the land business grew, so did his, and so did that of the department.

So great was the press in 1811 that the Secretary requested additional funds for another clerk to aid in the adjustment of the receivers' accounts. Instead, the Senate Committee on the Public Lands sensibly recommended the establishment of a special bureau within the Treasury Department to handle the land business. The chairman of the committee was Thomas Worthington, former register of the land office at Chillicothe and now a Senator from Ohio. Under the guiding hand of this former land officer, the Senate quickly passed a bill to establish a "General Land Office" within the Treasury Department. The House was equally amenable, and President Madison signed the bill on April 25, 1812. With the creation of a separate bureau of the Treasury to handle the land business, the direct administration of the public domain by the Secretary of the Treasury came to an end. While future Secretaries would have a strong voice in making policy concerning the administration of the public domain, they were relieved of the pressing correspondence and details that burdened Gallatin.[60]

The Jeffersonians were always intensely interested in the public lands. Throughout his presidency Thomas Jefferson occupied himself with the public domain, with its administration, and with the decisions surrounding the new territory in the Louisiana Purchase. Gallatin strongly influenced the whole land business. His advice and interpretation, his integrity and standards of office holding, his careful accountability and minute direction of the operations of the district land offices and the submission of accounts, his concern and interest in the small settler and purchaser, all showed his personal attention. And yet he had a larger goal. Both he and the President wished to make the new territory an integral part of the Union through a prompt solu-

59. Gallatin to Jesse Spencer, Register, Chillicothe, NA: GLO, Ltrs. Sent, Misc., 1: June 16, 1803; Gallatin to Thomas Worthington, Register, Chillicothe, *ibid.*, Sept. 15, 1801.

60. *House Committee Reports*, 11 Cong., 3 Sess., Jan. 3, 1811; 2 Stat. 716–18 (April 25, 1812); Carter, ed., *Territorial Papers*, 8: 203n.

tion of the land problem (so vital to the inhabitants there, as land was vital to men everywhere in the West) and to reduce the expenses of government and to raise the revenue from the public lands, especially after the embargo of 1808, which threatened Gallatin's economic system. The two were not notably successful in achieving these goals, although they made a significant contribution by establishing the requisite administrative machinery. With the assistance of Congress, the Secretary and the President expanded the land system to meet the needs of an expanding people and an expanding public domain.

The Organization of
the General Land Office,
1812–1814

3

In the years after 1808 a series of unforseen events shattered Albert Gallatin's carefully constructed and heretofore successful financial system. His goal of liquidating the public debt suffered a grievous blow with the imposition of the embargo; and although he turned to the public domain as an additional source of revenue and rushed lands in the Mississippi Territory onto the market in 1809, the income from the land business fell far short of compensating for the loss of impost duties.

The Treasury's difficulties were accompanied by the rise of discord within the Republican party. Through the growing crisis moved the scholarly James Madison, fourth President of the Republic, eternally hopeful that the affairs of the nation abroad and of the party at home and the state of the Treasury might be repaired by caution and compromise. The confusion and anxiety that stirred the capital and the highest councils of government reached a climax in the spring of 1812 when some members of the Republican party led the nation into a war against Great Britain. Phrases about maritime grievances and national honor rolled across the pages of the President's official message, but in the background loomed the vast and tempting domain of Canada. The President sent his statement of principles to Congress on June 1, 1812.[1] While the House and the Senate debated the most important national issue since the ratification of the Constitution, the capital and the nation watched and waited. In the midst of this tense atmosphere Edward Tiffin of Ohio, the first Commissioner of the General Land Office, arrived in Washington.

Tiffin had come to administer the new bureau of the Treasury cre-

1. Walters, *Albert Gallatin*, 223–50; Balinky, *Albert Gallatin: Fiscal Theories and Policies*, 128–63.

ated by the act of April 25, 1812, which had also provided for a commissioner to work under the direction of the Secretary "to superintend, execute and perform, all such acts and things, touching or respecting the public lands of the United States, and other lands patented or granted by the United States. . . ." These tasks were formerly divided among the Secretary of State, the Secretary of War, the Secretary, the Auditor, and the Comptroller of the Treasury. The new commissioner had a seal of office and the franking privilege. He also had charge of "all records, books and papers . . . touching or concerning the public lands of the United States. . . ." The new law directed him to provide information for the President or either house of Congress when so requested, and it made his office the source of land patents, to be signed by the President and countersigned by the commissioner. The General Land Office also became an intermediate bureau of audit between the district land offices and the comptroller of the Treasury. To staff his new organization, the commissioner was allowed up to $7,000 a year in clerk hire. The law enjoined all persons employed under it from engaging, directly or indirectly, in the purchase of public lands.[2]

The new commissioner was an example of the professional man on the frontier. A native of England, Tiffin came to the United States in 1784 and settled in Charles Town, Virginia, with his father and mother. He attended the Philadelphia Medical College and, upon completing the required course of study, returned to Charles Town, married Mary Worthington, the daughter of a large Virginia landowner, and established a profitable medical practice. In 1798, Tiffin followed his brother-in-law, Thomas Worthington, to the town of Chillicothe, in the Northwest Territory. He and Worthington became leaders of the Republican party and led the opposition to Governor Arthur St. Clair. With the triumph of Republicanism in 1801, the removal of St. Clair, and the admission of Ohio to the Union in 1803, Tiffin was elected the state's first governor almost without opposition. He was re-elected in 1805, but he resigned two years later to become a candidate for the United States Senate; and the legislature gave him a two-to-one majority over his Federalist opponent. Within a year of moving to Washington, however, Tiffin's wife died, and he resigned soon thereafter and returned to his Chillicothe farm. Here he dabbled

2. 2 Stat. 716–18 (April 25, 1812).

in state and local politics while devoting himself principally to farming and a growing medical practice.[3]

Edward Tiffin owed to Thomas Worthington his second transition from rural Ohio to official Washington. Another leader of the Ohio Republicans, Worthington was a member of the territorial legislature from 1799 to 1803, for three years first register of the Chillicothe land office, and the first United States Senator from Ohio. He retired to permit Tiffin's election in 1807, but returned to the Senate again in 1810. Throughout he maintained a special interest in the public domain, and Albert Gallatin thought Worthington the only man in the Senate who understood the vital subject of land.[4] Thomas Worthington was instrumental in passing the bill for the creation of the General Land Office, and he recommended Edward Tiffin as the first commissioner. Tiffin was happily remarried, restless, and fearful of the strain imposed on his health by a growing medical practice. He accepted the appointment and arrived in Washington with his family on the evening of June 3, 1812. A new era in land management had begun—at the moment when the very existence of the Republic seemed imperiled. The new commissioner would learn, however, that the public lands remained uppermost in the minds of the citizens of the western country—a concern that was only occasionally interrupted by the war with Great Britain.[5]

Tiffin's appointment was a logical one. As a "western man" he knew the importance of the public domain to that section of the country and he could be expected to mollify those Congressmen from the West who would complain about the numerous decisions that had to be made by the new agency. He was also a Republican with a distinguished political career. The critical importance of land in the West was well known in Washington, and it was hoped that under a man of Tiffin's stature the new bureau would protect the interests of the government while remaining sympathetic to the desires of the frontier.

3.   William T. Utter, *The Frontier State, 1803–1825*, Carl F. Wittke, ed., *The History of the State of Ohio*, Vol. 2 (Columbus, 1942), 32–62; William Edward Gilmore, *Life of Edward Tiffin* (Chillicothe, 1897); C. G. Comegys, *Reminiscences of the Life and Public Services of Edward Tiffin, Ohio's First Governor* (Chillicothe, 1869).
4.   Gallatin to Jefferson, Nov. 25, 1806, Adams, ed., *Gallatin Writings*, 1: 323.
5.   Tiffin to Worthington, Oct. 31, 1811; March 15, 1812, Worthington Papers, Ohio Historical Society Library, Columbus; same to same, April 16, 1812, Worthington Papers, Ohio State Library, Columbus.

Tiffin had one other noteworthy characteristic to bring to the post: he apparently was not a speculator in lands, something of a rarity among prominent citizens on the frontier at this time.

The commissioner quickly turned to the business of organizing the new bureau. Tiffin had already indicated that he counted on the Secretary of the Treasury for guidance. "I hope that Mr. Gallatin will aid me with his Council," he confided in accepting the appointment. "Indeed Sir was it not that Mr. Gallatin is at the head of the Treasury Department—I think I could not have consented to go on." [6] Gallatin knew Tiffin and valued him highly, but the Secretary was preoccupied with the financial crisis caused by the war. Members of the Cabinet debated how to raise the needed funds to finance a war in accordance with strict Republican principles. Gallatin also knew that the War and Navy departments—long simple sinecures for successful Republican politicians—were in the hands of incompetents, and he was already making plans to assume some of the duties of these departments.[7] After a warm handshake and a few words with the new commissioner, the Secretary excused himself, and returned to his office. In the ten months during which Gallatin continued to head the Treasury Department, he had little time for the management of the public lands or for the new Commissioner of the General Land Office.

Tiffin was immediately struck with the chaos created in official Washington by the precipitate declaration of war against Great Britain. Of it he wrote, "all is confusion here, & many appear disposed to take advantage of the credulity of the people by circulating the most shameful lies of every one engaged for the public. I am also astonished to see Men who I had supposed men of Sense, acting without system, discretion or prudence." [8] The commissioner pushed ahead with his job. From the War Department he collected the clerks concerned with the military land bounties of the Revolutionary War, and from the Department of State, those men responsible for land patents. To these groups he added the record keepers from the Treasury Department. Dislocation resulted, but Tiffin organized well, and under his close direction the clerks soon developed procedures for

6.   Tiffin to Worthington, May 15, 1812, Worthington Papers, Ohio Historical Society Library.
7.   Walters, *Albert Gallatin*, 251–54.
8.   Tiffin to Worthington, Aug. 30, 1812, Worthington Papers, Ohio Historical Society Library.

meeting the heavy business. "We have been pretty industrious in the land office," he wrote Gallatin with a sense of satisfaction, "and I hope the business will soon be brought up." [9]

In spite of Washington's preoccupation with the war, Tiffin determined to carry on the land business in its usual form. Congress had made provision for eighteen district land offices and two surveyors general, and the Secretary of the Treasury had activated these administrative units. Even as the mobilization of numerous militia companies carried off surveyors and land officers, the commissioner prepared to continue the customary functions of sale, survey, and audit. His plans for the normal transaction of business suffered a severe blow with the resignation, in the autumn of 1812, of Jared Mansfield as surveyor general northwest of the Ohio. By his long service and his scientific knowledge Mansfield had transformed the surveying of the Old Northwest into a well-ordered and scientifically oriented operation. He was responsible, among other things, for the introduction of principal meridians and base lines, basic reference points for the next century of the rectangular survey.[10] Mansfield had finally obtained the post that he had so long sought—the professorship of natural philosophy at West Point. His mathematical skills had indeed greatly benefitted the surveying system of the Old Northwest by placing it on a regular scientific basis, yet his departure seemed critical particularly because President Madison chose Josiah Meigs as his successor. An unsuccessful applicant for the West Point post, Meigs was an old friend of the Republican political philosophy and a man with influential relatives. He needed a political appointment at this time, but he knew nothing about practical surveying or its administration.[11]

Because of Mansfield's sudden departure and Meigs's difficulties in moving from Georgia to Cincinnati, the office of Surveyor General of the United States (as it was officially known) stood vacant for almost five months. During this period the death of the chief clerk increased the difficulties. Returns of the deputy surveyors lay unattended and unchecked, and the deputies were unpaid, checked and certified returns were unplatted, and accounts remained open. The entire survey-

9. Tiffin to Gallatin, *ibid.*, Aug. 6, 1812.
10. Treat, *The National Land System*, 187–90.
11. Madison to Jefferson, Oct. 14, 1812, Gaillard Hunt, ed., *The Writings of James Madison* (9 vols., New York, 1900–10), 8: 219; Tiffin to Meigs, NA: GLO, Ltrs. Sent, SG, 1: Nov. 24, 1812.

ing business suffered. On his arrival in late March 1813, Meigs requested that Mansfield be granted a leave of absence in order to instruct him in his new post. The new surveyor general termed Mansfield's presence "indispensable, that his System, which was believed, by all who understood it, to be very judicious, may not be deranged by his successor." [12] Meigs's admission that he did not understand the "System" influenced the commissioner and the Secretary of War to approve a leave of four weeks for Mansfield, but the war intervened, and the West Point professor could not leave his post.[13] Mansfield was generous with his advice through the mail, but in general Meigs learned from the clerks of the office.

The operations of his office for the next two years demonstrated his inexperience. Throughout the entire period Meigs never submitted a return to the General Land Office that met Tiffin's most generous standards. The surveys for the Shawneetown district, for example, were "incorrectly done, and not either agreable to law, or in that correct manner which the principal Surveyor South of Tennessee has made his—and from which we cannot possibly make a connected plat of the country, I am constrained to request that they may be corrected . . . ," wrote Tiffin. Nor did the new surveyor general's financial accounts meet approval: they were carelessly calculated and late in submission.[14]

Added to the administrative difficulties of Josiah Meigs were the problems raised by the Indian menace in the Northwest. The surrender of General William Hull at Detroit and the massacre of the Fort Dearborn garrison exposed the frontier of the Old Northwest to hostile Indians. Raiding parties harassed the Illinois and Indiana territories. Most of the American settlements retired to the line of the Wabash and Maumee rivers. In the spring of 1813, American forces took the offensive in an attempt to retake Detroit and damage Britain's prestige among her Indian allies. Throughout the winter, correspondence and orders passed between the West and Washington; and

12. Meigs to Tiffin, *ibid.*, Ltrs. Recd., SG, NW, 4: April 8, 1813. Also see same to same, *ibid.*, March 22, 1813.
13. Tiffin to Sec. War, *ibid.*, Ltrs. Sent, Misc., 5: April 12, 1813; Tiffin to Mansfield, *ibid.*, April 17, Oct. 7, 1813.
14. Tiffin to Meigs, *ibid.*, SG, 1: Sept. 29, 28, 1813; Robert King to Tiffin, *ibid.*, Sept. 28, 1813.

with the warmer weather, a large force under the command of Major General William Henry Harrison moved north. Harrison won no dramatic victory, but he broke the British and Indian seige of Fort Meigs (named for the surveyor general's nephew, Return Jonathan Meigs, Jr., the wartime Governor of the State of Ohio) at the mouth of the Maumee. Captain Oliver Hazard Perry's autumn victory on Lake Erie finally forced the British to evacuate Detroit and Fort Malden, and many of the large Indian tribes went along with the British in their retreat. But the frontier of the Old Northwest was still far from secure.

The achievements of the surveys and the surveyors in the Old Northwest varied with the success of American arms. The changes were often sudden. "From the present flattering prospects relative to the War in our Frontier, some of the Surveyors have thought it probable that they may resume their labour within a few months," Meigs wrote in June 1813. Such optimism vanished almost immediately. The appearance of General Henry Proctor's force of British regulars and Indian allies in the spring of 1813 drove the frontier back toward the Ohio. Even the intrepid Meigs, scarred veteran of many political battles, became uneasy. All talk of surveying was forgotten. "We had a momentary calm, but, this day we are advised of a returning storm," he wrote to Tiffin and added, "I hope you will not think me *timid* if I ask you direction for my Conduct, supposing this town to become the *frontier*." [15] At the very moment when disaster threatened, Fort Meigs withstood Proctor's seige, and the Indians of Ohio failed to join his cause. The tide of war surged north once more. Meigs became more optimistic, but the possibility of resuming surveying operations on a regular basis seemed as remote as ever. Small isolated raiding parties continued to harass individual settlers and surveying parties. In the spring of 1814 the surveyor general determined to try once more, and he soon found surveyors willing to risk their lives for government funds. Still the danger was too great. Indians wounded several surveyors and drove the rest back to the safety of the settlements. The year 1814 was so discouraging that neither Meigs nor Tiffin made any estimates of funds to carry forward the surveys, and Congress

15.   Meigs to Tiffin, *ibid.*, Ltrs. Recd., SG, NW, 4: June 16, 1813; same to same, *ibid.*, Mo., 60; July 26, 1813.

made no appropriations for them. Indeed for the entire period of the war no further surveys of the public lands were made in the Old Northwest.[16]

In the Southwest the result was much the same. The surveyor general, Thomas Freeman, was a man of technical skill and administrative competence. His domain was vast, and his problems were of great difficulty and complexity. During the War of 1812 anarchy spread in the Southwest. Spanish Florida lacked an effective government. Raiders of various nationalities crossed back and forth over the boundary line, looting whenever they could, and escaped slaves added to the confusion. Surveying such an area was dangerous work. The same condition prevailed in the southern Mississippi Territory and in the new State of Louisiana. To the problems of high water, difficult terrain, and complex private claims (of which he constantly complained), Freeman added the pirates of the Southwest, for a variety of freebooters, pirates, and bandits prospered on the anarchy.[17] These "overgrown, piratical Banditti," as he called them, were securely fortified on an offshore island, which was safe from a preoccupied United States Navy, and from which they ventured forth to harass merchant ships and surveying parties. Freeman described one band of more than five hundred men that counted among its equipment half a dozen armed vessels.

Indians added to the danger. The great Creek uprising of 1813 culminated in the massacre of the garrison and numerous civilians at Fort Mims, an act that spread terror over the South. Everywhere in southern Tennessee and the Mississippi Territory isolated settlers and their families retreated to the safety of towns and forts. In the northern part of the territory at the Great Bend of the Tennessee, "the greatest alarm prevails through this country from an apprehension of an attack from the Creek Indians. . . . Hundreds of families have removed from the frontier . . . a great many of which have gone to Tennessee & others to Virginia, at this time there is not more than two or three families between this place & the Tennessee river, which con-

16.   Meigs to Tiffin, *ibid.*, NW, 4: March 19, 1814; Tiffin to Meigs, *ibid.*, Ltrs. Sent, Misc., 5: May 28, 1814. Accounts of the impact of the war on the frontier of the Old Northwest are Utter, *The Frontier State*, 88–119; Logan Esarey, *History of Indiana, from its Exploration to 1922* (3 vols., Dayton, 1923), 1: 238–39; Alvord, *The Illinois Country*, 440–47.
17.   Freeman to Tiffin, NA: GLO, Ltrs. Recd., SG, Miss., 53: March 17, 1814.

tained at least two Hundred not more than a week ago," wrote a land officer from Huntsville. "The people have not the least confidence in themselves, their being no Army in the Country, which would make but a feeble resistance against two thousand *infuriated Hell Hounds,*" he added.[18] Surveyors who ventured out worked on private claims and returned to the safety of settlements in the evening. The survey of new Indian cessions ceased.

In spite of the derangement of the surveys in the Old Northwest and the Southwest, and in spite of the government's retrenchment in Washington, the war with England did not dull interest in the public domain. Tiffin's tasks were essentially those of his predecessors and successors. Although the actual demand for the sale of the public lands varied with the military situation in different parts of the nation, the commissioner dealt with the same problems of survey, private claims, sale, trespass, and pre-emption. In Mississippi and Alabama the threat of the Creek uprising drastically curtailed the sale of new lands. Lands sold and receipts for the years immediately prior to and including the war for Mississippi and Alabama were: [19]

	ACRES	
1809	87,636	$194,872
1810	77,036	158,126
1811	81,913	164,822
1812	144,873	299,904
1813	30,261	60,659
1814	41,272	82,545

Even as the war whoops of the Indians sent the citizens of the southern frontier back to the safety of civilization, the boards of commissioners continued to settle private land claims, schemes of fraud multiplied, complaints about the laxity and slowness of the land commissioners increased, and the administration of the public domain in this area continued much as it had. Men who found their avenues of investment temporarily closed at home shifted their interest elsewhere, and the fertile Florida lands suddenly became a principal topic of conversation.[20]

18.   John Read to Tiffin, *ibid.,* Reg. & Rec., Huntsville, 4: Sept. 27, 1813.
19.   *American State Papers, Public Lands,* 3: 420.
20.   On the continued fascination of the land business for citizens in the South in time of war, see Judge Harry Toulmin to Tiffin, NA: GLO, Ltrs. Recd., Misc., T: June 7, 1814.

Hull's fiasco at Detroit and the attacks along the frontier following his surrender checked only temporarily the expansion of population into the territory northwest of the Ohio River and the lands across the Mississippi in the Missouri Territory (the name was changed from Louisiana Territory in 1812 to prevent confusion with the new State of Louisiana). In Ohio the war was a period of great prosperity for agriculture, and "applications for new lands are numerous." [21]

Prospects were equally bright in the Indiana Territory. John Badollet, register of the Vincennes land office, looked out on a quiet countryside, "the Indians harmless & we in a state of tranquility." But Badollet's contentment over the influx of settlers could not hide his chagrin at the military development of the war. "Would it not be an excellent measure," he mused, "instead of cannon, which may be swamped, to send to Canada cargoes of fourth of July toasts, the British I am confident could not stand the shock, in their dismay, they would scamper away helter-skelter and head over heels toward Quebec and if advantage was ably & spiritedly followed up by reinforcements of the same kind, Canada would ere long be ours." He took confidence from the many new settlers and the increased applications for lands even in the remote areas, and he concluded that "the apprehension of indian hostilities has but a limited influence on the minds of emigrants and is not likely to impede the proposed Sales." [22] The sales of public lands in Indiana during the war proved the continued attraction of the public domain.

When in 1813 Congress granted pre-emption rights to early settlers in Illinois, pioneers flocked to the Illinois land offices to affirm their legality. Threats of Indians did not take their minds off land, which was far more significant to them in the long run. By the later months of 1814 the pre-emption business in Illinois approached a peak. "The Business in our offices since we commenced has become so arduous & multiplied that we could do little more than make the Entries of Lands applied for and Journalize the Accompts," wrote the land officers at Kaskaskia. They continued, "Perhaps in a week we shall have Applications to the Amount of 100,000 acres." Adding to the rush of new business was the return of the early pre-emptioners, "who are also crowding on us with the balance of the first Instalments." [23]

21. William Reynolds, Canton, to Tiffin, *ibid.*, Misc., R: June 3, 1814.
22. Badollet to Tiffin, *ibid.*, Vincennes, 20: June 1, Nov. 18, 1814.
23. Michael Jones and Shadrach Bond to Tiffin, NA: GLO, Ltrs. Recd., Reg. & Rec., Kaskaskia, 13: Oct. 28, 1814.

So great was the interest in the public lands in Illinois that the government organized a new land office in April 1814 at Shawneetown; it was constructed on a flood plain of "boards, nails and other necessary materials for a proper building" floated down the Ohio. The expectation of sales was in the air as early as the spring of 1814. "The expectation of the Public of that part of the Western Territory has been excited, and they are anxious, if not, rather, clamorous, to see the Public Promise performed," the surveyor general wrote. "At the present time money is plenty among them—and the Sales would be, in my opinion, rapid and extensive." Meigs's judgment was confirmed by the substantial sales of public lands in the territory in 1814.[24]

The figures for the sales of public lands in the Old Northwest before and during the War of 1812 give graphic testimony to the desire of the frontier to continue the land office business as usual:[25]

	Ohio	Indiana	Illinois
	ACRES	ACRES	ACRES
1811	380,418	53,301	
1812	273,777	45,028	
1813	410,271	59,719	
1814	817,714	166,312	158,461

Trespassing on the public domain increased during the war, as men defied the Indians and the constituted authority of their own government in order to obtain land. By so doing, they formed a barrier between the settled areas and the violence of war. Such "buffers" had formed a protective shield on innumerable occasions since the establishment of the English colonies. Various colonial governments in periods of crisis had offered free land to men who would settle in exposed places. The prosperous citizens of the General Court in Massachusetts and the House of Burgesses in Virginia thought such bounty cheaper than the cost of mercenary troops and perhaps even more effective. The Government of the United States was less generous, but the citizens of the settled areas were as appreciative of the services rendered by the buffers as their ancestors had been. When Edward Tiffin objected to the disorderly and illegal usurpation of the public domain, he received an explanatory letter from Alexander McNair, the

24. Meigs to Tiffin, *ibid.*, SG, NW, 4: April 9, 1814.
25. *American State Papers, Public Lands,* 1: 420; *Senate Public Documents,* 27 Cong., 3 Sess., #246: 5.

register at St. Louis. McNair spoke strongly against the use of force to remove the trespassers. "At this time it is my opinion, justified by the statements of many, that five militia men of this Territory would not march against the intruders on public lands," McNair wrote. He concluded, "Much feeling has been excited on this subject, as those who may be found on public lands are the persons who have borne the storm of the Indian War, being on the frontier. . . ." [26] The same sentiments were probably true in the frontier of the Old Northwest and in the Southwest. The buffers would not be disturbed in time of war.

Superintending the surveys, supervision of commissions on private claims, and the sales of the public lands were the field duties of the commissioner of the General Land Office. He also had certain equally time-consuming tasks within his own organization. The act of establishment made the General Land Office responsible "to audit and settle all accounts relative to the public lands." The accounts "relative to the public lands" were of several different kinds. Establishing the fiscal solvency of the receivers and the registers of the district land offices and the surveyors general was one of the important but elusive duties. Land officers and surveyors general posted bond. Under this system, sureties certified their financial responsibility for any deficits left by the officer. Commissioner Tiffin struggled to keep these bonds up to date (signers were always dying, moving to distant places, disappearing from sight, and going bankrupt themselves). But financial responsibility was absolutely necessary to the accounting system of the Treasury Department. Tiffin liked sureties "wealthy and respectable" and vouched for by Congressmen. [27]

The commissioner also inspected the salary accounts of the land officers and surveyors general. Registers and receivers invariably complained about low salaries. Those who resided in cities with high costs were particularly outspoken about the inadequacy of the government's stipend. Of the eighteen offices, several had scanty sales, and five— Detroit, Ouachita, Opelousas, St. Louis, and New Orleans—had no public sales at all. "In the most expensive part of the world $500 will be found very inadequate to the support of a family," wrote the receiver

26. McNair to Tiffin, NA: GLO, Ltrs. Recd., Reg. & Rec., St. Louis, 34: Jan. 27, 1814.
27. Tiffin to Rep. James Robertson (La.), ibid., Ltrs. Sent, Misc., 5: May 24, 1813; Tiffin to William Garrard, ibid., June 14, 1813; Tiffin to Richard Rush, Comptroller of the Treasury, ibid., Aug. 17, 1813.

at New Orleans, "$1500 a year would be no more than adequate." Under cover fees augmented the small income—an illegal device, as the commissioner constantly reminded land officers. Other supplements to the government's salary were various "contingent expenses" allowed in pursuance of duties. "Contingent expenses" involved money paid for supplies or services allegedly necessary for the transaction of the land business. From the Secretary of the Treasury the commissioner inherited the responsibility of passing judgment on these expenses. Under his general policy he disallowed all charges for office rent and chests used for storing the public funds. Charges for expenses at public sales of land, criers, additional clerks, and so forth, he readjusted to a reasonable amount in accordance with earlier departmental figures. He honored no charge without proper receipts. Tiffin's views reflected those of the leaders in government and the nation at large: this was a part of that long period in the early history of the Republic when it was assumed that a public servant should not be well paid.[28]

The auditing of accounts within the Treasury Department was a careful and necessary process. The Auditor of the Treasury made an initial examination of accounts and passed them on to the Comptroller of the Treasury with the evidence, vouchers, and his recommendation. The decision of the comptroller was final. The accounts for the administrators of the public domain forced an exception to this rule. After the commissioner viewed and passed decision on them, he sent them directly to the comptroller, thus bypassing the auditor. This privilege had the advantage of saving time in a process that took far too long. And it did not affect the finality of the comptroller's decision.[29]

Tiffin realized that in order to run the land office in a regular manner, he must standardize as many aspects of the land business as possible. To this end his office "has constantly adhered to one grand principle of diffusing through all subordinate offices the same systematic means of conducting them." He also drafted a uniform letter of instructions for the annual inspection of land offices. The time and date

28.   Lloyd Posey to Tiffin, *ibid.*, Ltrs. Recd., Reg. & Rec., New Orleans, 22: May 25, 1813; Circular to Registers and Receivers, *ibid.*, Ltrs. Sent, Misc., 5: April 1, 1813. On parsimony in the public service, see White, *The Jeffersonians*, 399–404.

29.   White, *The Federalists*, 341–47; White, *The Jeffersonians*, 163–67; Willard E. Hotchkiss, *The Judicial Work of the Comptroller of the Treasury* (Ithaca, 1911), 16 n.

and format for the submission of accounts took on a uniformity designed to aid the land officer in preparing the accounts, the commissioner in answering questions about accounts, and the clerks in checking the accounts.[30]

In a manner characteristic of the land business, practice varied markedly from theory. Monthly and quarterly accounts were frequently late. Excuses were legion. The mails were poor and further deranged by the war. Indeed, during the war, and at almost every other time during the first half-century of the Republic, administrators of the growing public domain complained continually to the Postmaster General about the irregular and untrustworthy condition of the mails. And, the war caused other upsets. The British capture of Detroit meant the loss of the land records deposited in that office; the threat to the Ohio Valley caused a brief period of consternation in the land offices there; and the British expedition against Louisiana in late 1814 disrupted the orderly transaction of business in that region. Numerous land officers were high officials in the state militia and were concerned far more with military matters in this period than with the submission of accounts; yet they refused to resign their land offices, and in this decision they were generally protected by important political figures. The frontier was often unhealthy, land officers suffered the usual sicknesses, and the reports to the commissioner of deaths in the families of land officers indicated that the threat was real enough. Hazards were increased by the fact that Treasury Department regulations demanded that the land officers remain at their posts at all times. There were, of course, a few absentee land officers, men who lived at great distances and conducted the business of the office through their clerks.[31]

When the accounts had at last been received, the General Land Office began one of its most important functions: the careful scrutiny and checking of every financial transaction undertaken in the district land offices. The task was time-consuming and frustrating. With the credit system providing for endless partial payments, and the complex

30. Tiffin to Reg. & Rec., West of Pearl River, NA: GLO, Ltrs. Sent, Misc., 5: Aug. 4, 1813; the form letter from Tiffin to inspectors is at the beginning of *ibid.*, 5: n. d.
31. James Abbott to Tiffin, *ibid.*, Ltrs. Recd., Reg. & Rec., Detroit, 25: July 31, Sept. 9, 1814; Meigs to Tiffin, *ibid.*, SG, Mo., 60: July 26, 1813; John Sloane to Tiffin, *ibid.*, Reg. & Rec., Canton, 35: Oct. 5, 1813.

calculations of principal and interest according to the time lapsed in making payment, the accounts should have been kept by a competent bookkeeper. Registers and receivers of district land offices, however, did not receive appointments because of their clerical talents. They were not only important men politically, but they were sufficiently involved in other affairs to make their attendance to the land office business occasionally little more than a token. The commissioner admonished such officers to mend their ways and to perform their duties conscientiously.[32]

Once approved by the clerks of the General Land Office, and after the tracts sold had been compared with the plats in the General Land Office and suitably marked thereon, all accounts went to the comptroller. Here the same examination took place. It is not surprising that, with the growth of government administration and the necessity of achieving absolute accuracy and of funneling all accounts through the watchdog comptroller, it took increasingly longer for an account to receive final clearance. The accounts of the General Land Office particularly suffered from this delay. Comptroller Joseph Anderson wrote, "The accounts of the General Land Office are greatly in arrears; some of them remain unsettled from seven to ten years. These accounts are intricate, and generally very large; from ten to fifteen days is required for the best accounting clerk to examine one of them." [33] Interested individuals, from spiteful or sincere motives, occasionally accused land officers of being in arrears to the government. Some officers did default, but such was the delay in accounting that the true state of their balances was often unknown for years after they had actually left the land business.

Commissioner Tiffin had a modest staff at his disposal. In 1813 the entire appropriation for the General Land Office was $13,500, of which Tiffin's salary alone was $3,000. Seven clerks received a total of $7,000, and the final $3,500 was for contingent expenses—ledgers, ink, pens, fuel, paper, parchment for patents, and so forth. In 1814 the Secretary of the Treasury increased the number of clerks to nine and the total salary to $9,000. The duties of the various clerks indicated Tiffin's organization of the office. John Gardiner, the chief clerk

32. Tiffin to James Findlay, *ibid.*, Ltrs. Sent, Misc., 6: Aug. 17, 1814; Tiffin to Peter Wilson, *ibid.*, 5: Sept. 20, 1813.
33. *American State Papers, Finance*, 3: 127.

($1,350), attended to the business of visitors to the office, supervised correspondence, and prepared the reports and statements required by Congress. The draftsman ($1,100) compiled maps from the plats submitted by the surveyors general, marked the sales of the public lands on the office maps, and prepared copies of maps for Congress and the heads of the departments when so requested. Four accountant clerks ($1,000 each) examined the quarterly and monthly accounts of the receivers. The remaining three clerks ($800 to $900) posted into ledgers the accounts of registers and receivers. The clerks of the General Land Office worked from nine in the morning until three in the afternoon. All clerks, including the chief clerk and the draftsman, prepared patents in their free time. This task was a heavy one, for which the office had no regular staff. The tardy issue of patents drew fire from Congressmen who had complaining constituents, but Congress rarely relieved the situation by providing an additional clerk.[34] Not surprisingly, the land business was run by the General Land Office much as it had been by the Treasury Department in previous years. The only change was the increased volume of work.

In addition to its duties as accountant, the General Land Office also served as record keeper for the nation's land business. This function, too, had become more complex. By 1814 the accumulated monthly returns of the registers and receivers of the district land offices filled 292 ledgers, and the number increased with each passing month. Other volumes held copies of the quarterly accounts of receivers and the records of statements and estimates required by Congress and other "public functionaries." Complete records were also retained on the issue of patents on cash purchases, Revolutionary War bounty lands, pre-emption claims, donation claims, and private land claims. The office also preserved copies of outgoing and incoming correspondence. Thus, as the office contained complete records of the land business in the nation's first quarter-century, it was a central repository of information by which final answers to questions of claim and payment might be determined.[35]

The scope of the General Land Office and the duties and authority

34. Tiffin to Joseph Nourse, Register of the Treasury, NA: GLO, Ltrs. Sent, Misc., 5: Nov. 24, 1812; John Gardiner, chief clerk, to Sec. Treas., *ibid.*, 6: Nov. 16, 1814.
35. Gardiner to Sec. Treas., *ibid.*, Nov. 16, 1814.

of its commissioner in these first years of operation were undefined. Tiffin himself was undoubtedly an important figure in Washington, but his prominence was probably due more to his earlier political achievements than to his post as commissioner. The commissioner found that he and his organization were the object of a wide range of inquiries. He answered innumerable Congressional requests of a public nature. He also handled the personal business of Congressmen when so requested, and constantly defended his organization against the charges of delay and incompetence that purchasers made through their Congressmen. He corresponded extensively with his land districts and surveyors general and offered advice on matters of interpretation and decisions on local problems for which there were no general regulations. Tiffin never strayed from the guidelines of the Secretary of the Treasury; and where doubt existed, he consulted with the Secretary. Tiffin viewed the commissioner and the district land offices as "ministerial" men who administered rather than made policy.[36] Yet he frequently advised Congress on matters concerning land policy. Because of his extensive correspondence with men in the field, he could provide information on local conditions over a wide range of the frontier. This was a source to which Congressional committees rarely had access. The commissioner showed no reluctance in making his views known, and he generally backed up his opinions by reference to correspondence with his district land officers.[37] Outside of advice, the commissioner took no decisive action of his own. He became even less inclined to act with the departure of Albert Gallatin and the accession to power in the Treasury Department of new men with whom Tiffin was unacquainted.

Yet simply by his presence and the pressure of the duties of the overextended Treasury Department on its Secretary, the commissioner absorbed power over the land business. Gallatin's successors struggled to keep the nation afloat in a time of war with inadequate Republican principles of finance; they had little time for the fine points of the public lands, since they virtually ignored them as a possible source revenue. Nor had they Gallatin's abiding interest in the public do-

36. Tiffin to John Read, Register, Huntsville, NA: GLO, Ltrs. Sent, Misc., 5: June 10, 1814; Tiffin to John Badollet, *ibid.*, May 18, 1814.
37. Tiffin to Speaker, HR, *ibid.*, 5: April 2, 1814; Tiffin to Rep. James Kilbourne (Ohio), *ibid.*, March 9, 1814.

main, which came from a residence of two decades on the frontier of western Pennsylvania. Tiffin's influence seemed to depend upon the interest of the Secretary. Where the latter chose to take an aggressive interest in the land business, the commissioner operated almost entirely under his authority. Where the Secretary remained relatively indifferent, the commissioner perforce found himself with considerable influence in framing land policy, and perhaps equally important, he controlled its administration, a matter of the greatest concern on the frontier. Thus, by indirection and indifference Tiffin began to make his presence and that of his organization felt in the land business.

The tranquility of social Washington which hid the agony of a frustrating war was shattered by the British decision to make the nation's capital a military objective. In late August 1814 a British force of some four thousand veterans of the European wars landed in Maryland and began to march on the capital. The administrative staff of the government gave way to panic when the English troops routed a large force of American defenders. The fall of the city appeared imminent. Tiffin was prepared for such an eventuality. The packing of the records of the General Land Office had begun several days before the news of the British advance. Even as the defeated American military force straggled through the city on the way to the safety of Virginia, Tiffin found wagons, and the loading of the land office records commenced immediately. His clerks, directed by John Gardiner, worked from evening twilight until well past midnight. Under Gardiner's care all the records of the land business were moved to the interior of Virginia. The commissioner himself took a small force of clerks, crossed the Potomac River, and set up a temporary office. The next night he watched the flames of the burning government buildings light the sky. Josiah Meigs was philosophical about the whole affair: "The capture of *the City* is an interesting event—but I had expected it very confidently—the times are such as will eminently try men's souls." Tiffin had little time for reflection on the event. From his office in Virginia the commissioner continued to supervise the land business of the nation.[38] Thanks to Tiffin's foresight, "all the Maps of this Office, & all the books & papers necessary to the settlement of accounts, were saved from destruction," Gardiner reported to George W. Campbell, Gallatin's successor as Secretary of the Treasury. The Brit-

38.   Meigs to Tiffin, *ibid.*, Ltrs. Recd., SG, NW, 4: Sept. 10, 1814.

ish soon left, and Tiffin reoccupied his former quarters within a week of his departure.[39]

Tiffin's experience in dealing with numerous Congressional requests showed him that in spite of the great interest in the subject, even Congressmen knew little about the various aspects of the public lands and their administration. To remedy this defect, he issued the first report on the public lands and the part played by the General Land Office in their administration. He justified this "comprehensive view" by the "considerable accession of new members of the national legislature," and hoped that this information would make apparent "such legislative provisions as are required. . . ." The three-thousand-word document noted the progress of surveys in the South, discussed the settlement of private claims, and outlined the general operations of the district land offices by state and territory. Tiffin closed with a plea for additional clerks to speed the settlement of accounts. The report of the Commissioner of the General Land Office soon became an annual affair, as did the plea for more clerical assistance.[40]

Tiffin himself did not direct the postwar affairs of the General Land Office. He found himself increasingly indifferent to the duties of his post and alienated by Washington and its social functions. Still, a government post would be a useful supplement to his income and continue his influence, particularly if the office were concerned with the public lands. On March 28, 1814, after fewer than two years as commissioner, Tiffin asked to exchange posts with Josiah Meigs, the Surveyor General Northwest of the Ohio. At the same time he requested permission to transfer the office of surveyor general from Cincinnati to Chillicothe, the site of his farm and friends. President James Madison acquiesced in both requests. Tiffin resigned on October 10, 1814, and left Washington the next day with his family, as quietly as he had come.[41]

In spite of his unassuming nature and his unobtrusive work in a period better remembered for other things, Edward Tiffin represented a bench mark in the administration of the public lands. He had organized a new bureau, made it function in spite of a war, and estab-

39. Gardiner to Rep. Joseph Pearson (N.C.), *ibid.*, Nov. 1, 1814; Gardiner to Sec. Treas., *ibid.*, Oct. 26, 1814.
40. *American State Papers, Public Lands*, 2: 873–75.
41. Carter, ed., *Territorial Papers*, 8: 313n; Tiffin to Madison, NA: GLO, Ltrs. Sent, Misc., 6: Oct. 10, 1814.

lished practices and precedents for the future. He had continued
Albert Gallatin's efforts to give some order and regularity to the land
business. It was a significant achievement. The real test of his work
lay ahead, in the great westward migration and the land office business of the post war years.

The Land System and the Administration of the Military Bounty Lands, 1814–1818

4

Josiah Meigs first walked into the chambers of the General Land Office on November 27, 1814. The new commissioner introduced himself to John Gardiner, the chief clerk, and the two retired to the commissioner's office, where Gardiner explained something of the duties of the office and the problems of the land business. Soon they emerged, and the chief clerk took the new commissioner on a tour of the office, pausing to introduce Meigs to the various clerks and to explain their duties.

The early career of Josiah Meigs was noteworthy for its variety. The son of a Middletown, Connecticut, hatter, young Josiah matriculated at Yale and graduated with the class of 1778. Apparently untroubled by the American Revolution, he taught in an academy, tutored at Yale, and eventually went into law. After his admission to the bar Meigs pursued careers as an editor, a local politician, and a lecturer at Yale University. In 1789 he felt the financial pressure of a growing family and moved to Bermuda, attracted by the promise of legal business from American merchants engaged in the West Indian trade. Here he systematically alienated men of influence. Meigs was an outspoken and truculent republican. His undisguised contempt for Englishmen and English institutions led to a decline in his prosperous legal business and forced his return to the mainland in 1794. He immediately became professor of mathematics and natural philosophy at Yale. His strong republican principles and his zealous support of Thomas Jefferson soon brought him into conflict with President Timothy Dwight and led to his departure in 1800 for the new University of Georgia. Meigs was the first professor appointed to the institution, and he subsequently served as its president. He performed a notable service for the fledgling school which existed only on paper. Scouring the state for students, he held classes under trees and in taverns, according to the season of the year. Spurred by his relentless pressure, the state legislature finally voted sufficient funds for a classroom building. The dedication of this unattractive building in 1806 marked the establishment of the university—a monument to the zeal and unending labor of one man. But once more Meigs made enemies. His open contempt for Georgians, his demands for greater financial support from the legislature, his frequent political pronouncements, all gradually turned the influential citizens of the state against him. Many disputes with the board of trustees over policy and funds led him to resign the presidency in 1810. Next year the board dismissed him from his professorship. At the age of fifty-four Meigs found himself isolated on the Georgia frontier, responsible for a family of nine children, and without a job.[1]

Upon his dismissal from the University of Georgia, Josiah Meigs wrote to President James Madison seeking the professorship of natural philosophy at West Point. Madison had already promised the appointment to Jared Mansfield, so he offered the vacant post of surveyor general to Meigs, who quickly accepted. Although Josiah Meigs was interested in natural science and well versed in astronomy, he knew nothing of surveying. Fortunately for him, Indian unrest hampered the surveys in the Northwest, and his deficiences were not too visible. Only Edward Tiffin in the General Land Office was really aware of his surveyor general's inability to produce proper plats and correct accounts. Meigs learned much in two years, profiting from an extensive correspondence with Jared Mansfield and the commissioner and from the constant tutelage of his clerks. In spite of his pleasure at serving his nation and his political principles, he wanted to return to his native East; and when Tiffin offered to exchange posts, the surveyor general readily agreed. Josiah Meigs and his family arrived in Washington on November 26, 1814, "after a journey of 28 days and six hundred miles at least . . . over mountains and bad roads."[2] The new commissioner found official Washington functioning once more: the debris of war had been cleared away; temporary quarters were established.

1.   William M. Meigs, *Life of Josiah Meigs* (Philadelphia, 1887); *Dictionary of American Biography*, 12: 506–07.
2.   Quoted in Meigs, *Life of Josiah Meigs*, 63.

There had been other, intangible changes since the arrival of the first commissioner some two years before. The General Land Office had been organized in a period of optimism, at the beginning of a great war that would prove American independence and add to her continental empire. Then Albert Gallatin, a man of proven integrity and ability, ran the Treasury Department. If Tiffin found that the attention of the Treasury Department was focused elsewhere, nonetheless it was a spirited time to be engaged in the business of government. Within two years these conditions had changed. Gallatin had resigned in 1814 and gone to Europe. As a replacement for him, President James Madison had chosen the ineffectual George Washington Campbell of Tennessee, a consistent supporter of the Administration in the Senate but a man without new ideas or programs. Under his guidance the financing of the war became progressively more difficult. Adherence to the simple and straight-laced Republican principles of finance could not raise the necessary funds. Public confidence in the government began to wane; and by the time Meigs arrived on the scene, the prestige of the national government was at a low ebb. British forces had burned the Capitol and the White House, almost without resistance. Another enemy force had attacked in the South. The Treasury was empty. Campbell had resigned after only seven months in office, and Madison had named a new Secretary of the Treasury. He was Alexander James Dallas, a prominent Philadelphia lawyer, a loyal supporter of the administration throughout the war, a friend of Gallatin's, and the man whose constant negotiations with New York and Philadelphia capitalists throughout 1814 had enabled the shaky government to remain afloat financially. It remained to be seen whether he could restore the nation's finances in an official capacity.[3]

When Josiah Meigs became Commissioner of the General Land Office, he inherited an administrative empire that stretched from Detroit to New Orleans, from Steubenville to St. Louis. This system everywhere reflected the diligence, imagination, and labor of his predecessors. Albert Gallatin had established district land offices, appointed land officers, instructed them in their duties, saw them properly bonded, solved their problems, answered their letters, and counseled them on keeping accounts. He had also supervised the surveys

3. Raymond Walters, Jr., *Alexander James Dallas: Lawyer—Politician—Financier* (Philadelphia, 1943), 175–200.

of the public domain, established commissions on private land claims, and had general charge of the accounting and patenting procedures in Washington. Edward Tiffin had tried to achieve a systematic approach to the land business, a uniformity that would efficiently serve what promised to be one of the government's busiest enterprises. The system that Gallatin and Tiffin had established remained in large part stable through the first half-century of the Republic.

The disposition of the public lands was administered by three units: the surveyors general, the district land offices, and the General Land Office in Washington. Each unit had its distinct functions.

The two surveyors general prepared the lands for sale by marking them through the system of rectangular survey. The whole process began with an estimate of expenses from a surveyor general to the Commissioner of the General Land Office. Such an estimate would detail the surveying plans for the coming year, the number of miles, the location of the proposed surveys, and the total cost. The Commissioner of the General Land Office would add his suggestions and recommendation, perhaps engage in additional correspondence with the surveyor general, and then send the recommendation to the Secretary of the Treasury. Once approved by the Secretary, the Treasury Department sent the request on to Congress as part of the funds necessary to operate the federal government during the coming year. Within the annual appropriations act specific sums would be designated for the survey of the public lands. With the money appropriated, each surveyor general contracted with his deputies for the tracts to be surveyed at the price specified by the government. As soon as weather permitted, the deputies went into the field. Through the hot summer months they stretched chains over the ground, sent letters for additional funds, pacified or dimissed recalcitrant members of their units, and made field notes of what they had covered. They might also make notes of the most likely lands for purchase and speculation, to be used at public sale by themselves or perhaps sold to an investor. With the coming of winter the deputies returned from the field, presented their notes, and waited while the clerks of the surveyor general checked them. This done, they were paid and returned home to await the call to the field next spring. Meanwhile the clerks and draftsmen in the office of the surveyor general began transforming the field notes into plats, which were diagrams drawn to scale and showing the boundaries and subdivisions of a tract of land, together with other data that might be useful for identification. Through the long winter months they worked away at the task, hampered by lack of sufficient assistance and always reminded by the General Land Office of the need for haste. When the plats were finally completed, two sets were committed to the mail, one directed to the appropriate district land office, the other to the General Land Office.

Lands described in these plat books could now be sold. The cycle of sale began with a proclamation by the President of the United States, which was countersigned by the Commissioner of the General Land Office. The notice specified the tracts for sale, the dates of the sale, and the place where the sale would be held. Under the direction of the commissioner, newspapers in the appropriate districts published the proclamation. The district land officers also gave the widest possible circulation to the coming event. Even before the day of the sale, men came in groups and singly to the town where the district land office was located. Hotels and rooming houses, if any, were quickly filled, and in pleasant weather men spent much of their time outside at night. Individuals came with different expectations and varying information. Some sought only to purchase the tract on which their improvements lay. Others had greater ambitions. They had viewed the land themselves and might have purchased information from deputy surveyors or employed someone to ride over the land and search for choice tracts; they intended to purchase for purposes of speculation.

When the day of the sale came, the register emerged from his office, flanked by his clerks and a crier. They moved through the crowd to a raised platform, where the crier took his position, declared the sale open, and then cried off the first section of the first township. A pause followed, while he waited the requisite thirty seconds for a bid. The sale had begun. For the next three weeks the scene would be enacted over and over, without losing any of its drama. The process by which the public lands were brought to market through survey and public sale were known to every citizen in the western country; and a public land sale ranked with birth, marriage, and death among the most significant events in the life of any frontiersman. Here, in a few seconds, decisions were made that had a lifelong impact on the men who were present. It was invariably a moving and sobering experience, drawing forth loud outbursts which were followed by long silences. Occasionally violence erupted, but generally unofficial rules of competition had been agreed upon well before the formal opening of the sale. There were scenes of great cupidity and great generosity, with the latter all too rare.

A successful bidder went immediately to the register and received a notation of his tract. Then he moved directly to the receiver, who might be either near by or still resting in the relative quiet and safety of his own office. The purchaser paid the receiver one-twentieth of the purchase price and received duplicate receipts. He then returned to the register and presented one of the receipts. The other he retained. The register noted the tract sold on his list and marked an "A.P." on the plat in the appropriate tract—that is to say, "applied for." Perhaps the successful purchaser went home; perhaps he stayed until the end of the sale, content to avoid the work of his farm and to bask in the success of his venture. In a sense his future was secure. As a debtor to the government, he must return within ninety days and complete payment of one-quarter of the purchase price; but the government was traditionally an understanding creditor. All sales were subject to the administrative mechanism established by the United States Government. Henceforth, regardless of mistakes in location, errors in judgment, and other unfortunate accidents, all decisions were final and could be reversed only by the Secretary of the Treasury or, more probably, by an act of Congress.

Sale of the public lands was not confined to small tracts, and they were not necessarily the most common purchase. Many bidders at a public sale were interested in large blocks of land. Speculators pooled their capital and made plans well before the public auction, and then bought tracts up to ten thousand acres. They almost never paid more than the minimum price. Relatively modest entrepreneurs sought out particularly choice tracts for town-site speculation.

When a public sale had ended, the district land officers began to sort out the many details of individual transactions. Each register and each receiver had to put his books in order, the sales had to be checked against one another, with an exact accounting of the funds received, and the accounts and records had to be forwarded to the General Land Office on a regular basis. This was only the beginning. Periodically each purchaser returned to make additional payments. These might be substantial or minute. The receiver was obliged to take them all. Interest and principal had to be carefully calculated, and all according to the time elapsed. Each financial transaction went to Washington in the receiver's quarterly accounts. In order to assist them, the clerks of the receiver had the instructions and numerous examples sent from Washington, but in the wilderness, surrounded by heat and mosquitoes, with bad light and poor quillpens, the clerks never found the figures so clear as those that emanated from the antiseptic rooms of the General Land Office.

Accounting duties seemed endless. Eventually the purchaser made his final payment. The receiver or one of his clerks made the appropriate calculations, doublechecked to make sure, and issued a "final certificate." The appearance of a final certificate in the accounts rendered to the General Land Office was the signal for a careful examination of the entire account from initial to final payment. A clerk in the General Land Office checked the quantity and price of land, the date purchased, discounts allowed and interest charged, and the effect of new laws on the transaction. All too frequently errors were found that necessitated additional payments or a refund. When the entire transaction was at last found correct in all respects, the certificate went to the bottom of a large pile of tracts awaiting patents. In time the patent was prepared and sent to the White House for the President's signature. With the signatures of the President and the Commissioner of the General Land Office, title to the land passed to the purchaser, and the land became private property. Citizens of the Republic, from the authors of the Ordinance of 1785 to the most obscure settlers in the western country, believed devoutly in Blackstone's observation that a "set of words upon parchment [will] convey dominion on land."

Clerks then packed the patents in boxes for shipment to the district land offices. When he received the patent, the register sent word to the purchaser and waited for his appearance. Notified by a neighbor, a letter, the weekly newspaper, or in some other way, the purchaser eventually appeared. The final transaction between the two men was symbolic of the national ideal that land should be made available to all the nation's citizens. It also symbolized the operation of a system uniform in its demands and working for the benefit of the government and the citizen. In exchange for regular financial payments, the government awarded a perfect title to the land. Josiah Meigs commented that "so wise, beautiful and perfect a system was never before adopted by any government or nation on earth." [4]

How "wise, beautiful and perfect" the land system was depended in large part on how it was administered and how it met new problems. Now that the war was at last over and the tempo of movement to the West was quickening, the attention of the General Land Office and its commissioner was diverted to the question of the military bounty lands. The use of land to reward military service had a long history in the English colonies, where land was far more plentiful than money. Indeed, at the opening of the War of 1812, the governments of Virginia and the United States were still engaged in straightening out problems of Revolutionary War land bounties.[5]

In 1811, as a war with England became more likely, the Congress tried to increase the size of the Army and Navy and used military bounty lands very much as had other legislative bodies for the past century and a half. Under the law that emerged, the President would supervise the survey of six millions of acres of the public lands for military bounties: tracts of two million acres each in the Michigan, Illinois, and Louisiana territories. Congress directed that the selected lands should be "fit for cultivation, not otherwise appropriated, and to which the Indian title is extinguished. . . ." [6]

As Tiffin had paid little attention to the question of the military bounty lands, Commissioner Meigs inherited the full force of the problem. Already in late 1814 protests could be heard that the bounty lands were not ready. Soldiers and speculators alike recognized the value of the bounty, and they were eager to have it prepared for distribution as rapidly as possible. First Meigs needed funds. Appropriations for the survey of the public domain had touched $100,000 in 1811 but fell during the war years: $48,620 in 1812; $61,262 in 1813; and $60,000 in 1814. If the government intended to provide for sales in Missouri and Mississippi, "and to survey the Six millions of acres for military service . . . an appropriation may be necessary equal to

4. *Niles' Weekly Register,* 16: 363 (July 24, 1819).
5. Rudolf Freund, "Military Bounty Lands and the Origins of the Public Domain," *Agricultural History,* 20 (1946): 8–18; Jerry O'Callaghan, "The War Veteran and the Public Lands," *ibid.,* 28 (1954): 163–68; Treat, *The National Land System,* 230–46; William Thomas Hutchinson, "The Bounty Lands of the American Revolution in Ohio" (Unpublished doctoral dissertation, University of Chicago, 1927).
6. 2 Stat. 728–30 (May 6, 1812).

that of the year 1811," the commissioner advised Alexander J. Dallas, Secretary of the Treasury. Meigs estimated the expense of surveying the bounty lands alone at $40,000.[7]

Dallas promised the funds. Under the bounty land act the President was ultimately responsible for the surveys of the land, and Meigs now checked with Madison. "I have lately had several conversations with the President relative to the surveys of public lands," Meigs advised Edward Tiffin, the Surveyor General Northwest of the Ohio. "It is his wish & I am particularly instructed to cause the six millions of Acres of military lands . . . to be surveyed . . . as speedily as possible—It is desirable that you should, *without loss of time take every necessary preparatory step* for the execution of this important work." Detailed instructions followed, and Tiffin was soon fully informed of the President's wishes, as interpreted by the commissioner. The surveyor general was to locate the two million acres in Michigan at the far southeastern corner of that territory, bordering the Ohio boundary and the western edge of Lake Erie; the tract in Illinois should lie between the Illinois and Mississippi rivers; the third block should be placed between the St. Francis and Arkansas rivers in the southeastern part of the Missouri Territory.[8]

Everywhere along the western frontier men were eager to get on with the business of the public lands. With the close of hostilities their thoughts turned to land, to the great quantities available, and how to spy out the best tracts. In such a vast region as the Old Northwest, information about the public lands was scarce. Deputy surveyors had great advantages in this respect. The necessity for an immediate survey of the bounty lands offered them an excellent opportunity to see the lands of various territories. "I am much pestered with applications for surveying in the Military bounty lands," wrote Edward Tiffin. Letters from prospective surveyors came from every part of the Union. Two of the most determined applicants were Congressmen Samuel McKee and Thomas Montgomery from Kentucky. McKee was the chairman of the House Committee on Public Lands. Since Congress would not be in session during the surveying season, these gentlemen proposed to survey some two million acres for Tiffin—a request "in

7.   NA: Treasury Department, Ltrs. Recd. from Comm. GLO to Sec. Treas., 4: Feb. 24, 1815 (this depository cited hereafter as TD).
8.   Meigs to Tiffin, NA: GLO, Ltrs. Sent, SG, 1: March 23, 13, 24, 27, 1815.

which they cannot be gratified to anything like their wishes." Other applicants included "several Gentⁿ of the first respectability & talents. . . ." The surveyor general concluded, "In short I have perhaps ten applicants for every township I have to let out." Meigs was delighted with the prospect of so many surveyors. He believed that small contracts to several deputy surveyors would insure a rapid job without the dangers of subcontracting.[9]

Tiffin found that he had far more to do than simply survey some military bounty lands. The federal government intended to hold sales soon throughout the Old Northwest in order to meet the demands for land of those moving to the West at the end of the war. And at the very moment when all of these enterprises demanded the attention and full duty of all those connected with the survey of the public lands, the Indians of the Northwest threatened to ruin the entire system. They had not acquiesced in the peace treaty between the United States and their former ally, and they were not at all disposed to see executed the various treaties of cession to which tribes or factions of tribes had agreed in the previous decade. The surveyors in the Illinois and Indiana territories were particularly vulnerable to Indian raiding parties. Viewing the situation in the spring of 1815, Tiffin thought the threat of the Indians would retard the survey of the bounty lands in Michigan and Illinois at least one year.[10]

From his desk in the General Land Office, Josiah Meigs thought this view unduly pessimistic. The war was over, he wrote; the treaties were legal and binding. The commissioner had "no disposition to countenance any thing like yielding to the insolence of the Savages. . . . In a very short time the Savages will lower their tone along the whole Frontier, and you will be able to do much this year in the Great Business of Surveying the Military Bounty Lands." Tiffin pointed out, with all due respect, that the Indians did not subscribe to this kind of logic. The deputies agreed and refused to go into the field. The surveyor general reported with "the greatest degree of pain, mortification and regret" that a general Indian outbreak along the frontier was imminent. For the moment at least, his "ardent expecta-

9.   Tiffin to Meigs, *ibid.*, Ltrs. Recd., SG, NW, 5: late March, 1815; Meigs to Tiffin, *ibid.*, March 27, 1815; Meigs to Dallas, Sec. Treas., NA: TD, Comm. GLO to Sec. Treas., 4: March 19, 1816.
10.   Tiffin to Meigs, NA: GLO, Ltrs. Recd., SG, NW, 5: April 25, May 16, 1815.

tions . . . are at present blasted." Meigs was unhappy, but he accepted the delay and reported the reasons to the President.[11]

In order to diminish the possibility of an Indian uprising along the northern frontier, territorial authorities called a conference to meet in early August of 1815 at Detroit. Pending the outcome of this meeting, Tiffin decided to push ahead with the survey of other military bounty tracts, and he issued detailed instructions for the survey of two million acres in Missouri to William Rector, the principal deputy surveyor for the Missouri Territory. Tiffin intended that the surveys should begin in both the Illinois and the Missouri territories in October 1815. Before that time "the Inundations, the undergrowth, weeds & Flies of various descriptions," would keep out even the toughest surveyors, for "no mortal man could take the woods before October either North of the Illinois or in Missouri. . . ." If Rector put every available man into the field in early fall, and if the Detroit conference satisfied the Michigan Indians, completed surveys of the bounty lands would arrive at the General Land Office before "the rising of the next session of Congress" or by the spring of 1816. These possibilities became more likely with the rumors of peace from Michigan, and the surveyor general rejoiced at the prospects of quickly surveying the military bounty lands "for the brave men who have contributed to exalt the Nation to its present enviable and high rank amongst the Goliaths of the earth." Meigs was delighted and asked once more that "no reasonable exertion be spared to complete the Surveys of the Military Lands."[12]

The surveyors went into the field as scheduled, only to encounter another obstacle. Their instructions followed the law in directing that the lands chosen for military bounties be "fit for cultivation," but Tiffin's surveyors in Michigan thought that the land they viewed did not meet this requirement. "From what I have seen this country is no ways inviting," wrote one of the deputies. "It is true there is some good spots, but a large proportion is either useless swamps, or poor and barren."[13] Tiffin's observations to Washington left no room for doubt: "The whole of the two millions of acres appropriated in the

---

11. Meigs to Tiffin, *ibid.*, Ltrs. Sent, SG, 1: June 1, 1815; Tiffin to Meigs, *ibid.*, Ltrs. Recd., SG, NW, 5: June 12, 1815; Meigs to the President, *ibid.*, Ltrs. Sent, Misc., 6: June 20, 1815.
12. Tiffin to Meigs, *ibid.*, Ltrs. Recd., SG, NW, 5: July 26, 31, 1815; Meigs to Tiffin, *ibid.*, Aug. 8, 1815.
13. Benjamin Hough, deputy surveyor, to Tiffin, *ibid.*, 5: October 12, 1815.

Territory of Michigan will not contain any thing like one-hundredth part of that quantity, or is worth the expense of surveying it. Perhaps you may think with me, that it will be proper to make this representation to the President of the United States, as he may arrest all further proceedings, by directing me to pay off what has been done and abandon the country." In a subsequent letter he noted that later reports from his deputies made "the country out worse (if possible) than I had represented it to be." [14]

The commissioner called the attention of Congress to the information forwarded by Tiffin and also notified the President. In early February 1816 the President sent a special message to Congress in which he recommended the approval of additional lands outside the Michigan Territory. Congress agreed and authorized "lieu" bounty lands, located in the areas already set aside: 1,500,000 additional acres in Illinois and 500,000 acres in Missouri.[15]

Meigs continued to hope that the bounty lands in Illinois and Missouri could be prepared for distribution in 1816. The surveyor general promised "all that men can do shall be done." The deputy surveyors suffered severe winter losses of horses and hands, and the spring was uncommonly wet. The men would be late beginning work, Tiffin wrote, and they might refuse to work through the summer months.[16]

Congress determined to achieve more results in the survey of the military bounty lands. In April 1816, acting on the assumption that the administrative organization had too far-flung a surveying district for efficiency, it created a third surveying district, consisting of the Illinois and the Missouri territories. The President appointed William Rector to the new post. Rector immediately advised that the deputies would not go into the field before fall. Of the fifteen deputies, he reported that only one would begin work before September. The reasons were obvious to all experienced deputies: "All the Surveyors & others . . . with whom I have conversed say that it would be impracticable to Survey between the St. Francis and Arkansas [rivers] in the

14. *American State Papers, Public Lands*, 3: 164–65.
15. Meigs wrote to Jeremiah Morrow and Thomas B. Robertson, chairmen of the Senate and House Committees on Public Lands, NA: GLO, Ltrs. Sent. Misc., 6: December 19, 1815; James D. Richardson, ed., *A Compilation of the Messages and Papers of the Presidents, 1789–1908* (11 vols., Washington, 1909), 1: 570–71 (Feb. 6, 1816); 3 Stat. 332 (April 29, 1816).
16. Meigs to Tiffin, NA: GLO, Ltrs. Sent, SG, 1: April 15, 1816; Tiffin to Meigs, *ibid.*, Ltrs. Recd., SG, NW, 5: March 14, 1816.

Summer time on account of heat of the weather. The vast number of musquitoe flies & other insects, & reptiles, that would greatly annoy both men & horses. And in the heat of Summer, much of the water becomes putrid which they will be obliged to drink." Everything considered, the survey of the military bounty lands in Missouri could not begin until the fall of 1816.[17]

Rector had more success in Illinois. Work went forward steadily through the summer months, in spite of harassment from discontented Indians. A treaty between the Potawatomi Confederation and the United States Government on August 24, 1816, settled the Indian problem to the temporary satisfaction of all parties. It was a productive summer for clerks as well as deputies; and by the early part of November, Rector had prepared a map of the partially surveyed Illinois bounty lands. In general, he thought well of the Illinois tract: it was fertile, well watered, easily accessible, much superior to the "low & marshy or hilly, Stony, & poor" area between the St. Francis and Arkansas rivers. Meigs was indifferent to such news. His only interest was a completed plat to satisfy aggressive veterans, a pressing Secretary of the Treasury, and an insistent Congress.[18]

In response to repeated pleas from the Commissioner of the General Land Office, Rector finally set May 1817 for the completion of the Illinois tract. At last Meigs had something definite to show Congress, and he happily notified the Secretary of the Treasury of the near completion of the surveys. Rector came close to meeting the target. In mid-June 1817 he reported, "The field work of the whole of the Surveys of the Military Bounty Lands in the Illinois Territory is now done." Unfortunately no final plats were yet available, for "several of the Surveyors who are good workmen in the woods are extremely slow in making out returns." But the moment was close at hand.[19]

Meigs now turned his attention to the distribution of the bounty lands. Congress had dictated much of the system. The Secretary of War issued warrants to all eligible veterans upon application. The

17.   3 Stat. 325–26 (April 29, 1816); Rector to Tiffin, NA: GLO, Ltrs. Recd., SG, NW, 5: March 14, 1816.

18.   Theodore L. Carlson, *The Illinois Military Tract: A Study of Land Occupation, Utilization and Tenure* (Illinois Studies in the Social Sciences, Vol. 32, no. 2, Urbana, 1951), 4–5; Rector to Meigs, NA: GLO, Ltrs. Recd., SG, Mo., 61: Nov. 25, Dec. 30, 1816.

19.   Rector to Meigs, *ibid.*, June 16, 1817.

land warrant was not transferable. When the lands were ready for distribution, the veteran took or mailed his warrant to the General Land Office, indicating in it the territory where he wished to locate his tract, which was then drawn by lot. Eventually the warantee received a patent for his bounty.[20]

With the war's end, the westward migration of large numbers of settlers increased the value of unsettled western lands. The bounty lands formed a new opportunity for wealth, for both settlers and speculators. Amidst the rising interest of veterans, speculators, lawyers, and Congressmen, Meigs prepared the office to meet a flood of applications. In February 1817 the commissioner requested three additional clerks to increase his staff to fifteen. As justification he cited the increased sale of land and the mass of business certain to accompany the distribution of the military bounty lands. The department provided no additional assistance. In August the commissioner issued an urgent appeal, this time to the Secretary of the Treasury: "About 10,000 warrants have been issued from the War Depart. about 8,000 lottery tickets have been prepared from the surveys already received. . . . I anticipate such a demand for patents for three or four months that I apprehend it will be necessary for the Clerks of the Office to write patents & record them in extra hours. . . ."[21]

There was a new Secretary of the Treasury, William H. Crawford of Georgia. An acknowledged leader of the southern Republicans, he assumed the office in 1816. Time would prove him an aggressive and confident administrator. Like Hamilton and Gallatin before him, Crawford took an active and eager interest in all aspects of the Treasury Department, including the administration of the public lands. The indifference of Wolcott, Campbell, and Dallas to anything except the creation of fiscal policy—in most of which they deferred to Congress—was gone. And as the importance of the public lands increased, so did the interest with which he observed proceedings in the General Land Office, and the frequency with which he himself entered into its affairs. Crawford was an old-style Republican. He believed in honest, simple, frugal government. He believed that his department and its bureaus should set an example for the rest of the

20. 2 Stat. 729 (May 6, 1812); Meigs to Rep. Thomas Fletcher (Ky.), NA: GLO, Ltrs. Sent, Misc., 7: March 8, 1817.
21. Meigs to Joseph Nourse, Register of the Treasury, *ibid.*, Feb. 28, 1817; Meigs to Sec. Treas., NA: TD, Ltrs. Recd., Comm. GLO to Sec. Treas., 4: Aug. 4, 1817.

administration of the government. The fact that Crawford was an avowed candidate for the Presidency during his years in the Treasury Department only served to spur his interest in the proper function of the department and its efficiency at low cost.[22]

The Secretary was unsympathetic to Meigs's plea for additional assistance. "The persons employed in the public offices ought so far to imitate the example of prudent individuals in the management of their private affairs, by making temporary exertions to meet temporary presses of business, so as to prevent its accumulation from such causes," he replied.[23] By the end of September, Meigs was desperate. Eleven thousand warrants were in circulation, and the War Department issued an additional forty each day; fifteen hundred warrants had already been presented at the General Land Office, and the lottery had not even begun. A final appeal for additional help also fell on deaf ears.[24]

Meigs also requested that the Secretary of the Treasury set a date for the distribution of the bounty lands. He first asked for a decision in early August 1817, but without result. Six weeks later he again appealed for a firm date. "The tickets for the whole of that [Illinois] tract will be in the wheel to-morrow—this office is teazed daily by Soldiers, some of them are so insolent & abusive that it is necessary to turn them out; were the day fixed & notice thereof given their minds would probably be quieted & the office be free from disturbance," he wrote. Crawford hesitated. The President, who was legal superintendent of the distribution, was out of town. Finally, under the badgering of Meigs, the Secretary chose the first Monday in October. The commissioner announced the date in the press.[25]

In order to meet the anticipated rush, Meigs reorganized his office staff. He selected three clerks and an office boy to handle the applications of the veterans, while others prepared patents. Upon receipt and validation of a warrant, the boy drew a ticket from the lottery wheel, and a clerk gave the soldier a slip with his name and the location of the tract. The veteran might return for his patent the next day. Other

22. White, *The Jeffersonians*, 137.
23. Crawford to Meigs, NA: TD, Ltrs. Sent, Misc., 1801–33: Aug 16, 1817.
24. Meigs to Crawford, *ibid.*, Ltrs. Recd., Comm. GLO to Sec. Treas., 4: Sept. 30, 1817.
25. Meigs to Crawford, NA: GLO, Ltrs. Sent, Misc., 7: Sept. 24, 1817; *Daily National Intelligencer*, Sept. 26, 1817.

clerks handled mail applications after satisfying the needs of those who appeared personally. In order to facilitate the whole operation, Meigs ordered the printing of form letters.[26]

At nine o'clock on the morning of Monday, October 6, the door of the General Land Office swung open, and the veterans swarmed in. The small office force was engulfed by crowds of pushing, shoving, demanding warrant holders. All administrative arrangements proved inadequate. In response to a desperate plea, Crawford sent reinforcements of six clerks from the Treasury Department, a sure sign that a state of emergency prevailed. The crowds of land seekers persisted for some weeks, but the crush gradually subsided. The problem of selection and distribution was followed immediately by the issue of patents. In early December, Meigs admitted, "For some days past the demands of Military patents has been such, that [with six extra clerks] instead of reducing the quantity of business it accumulates on our hands." Many veterans had sent warrants to their Congressmen, and legislators continually complained of the delay in acquiring patents for their constituents. Meigs demanded that his clerks work three extra hours at their homes each evening. He "hoped" that a suitable reimbursement would be provided "that next month the mass of business on hand may be got through, and the extra work discontinued."[27] As the arrears continued to mount and the complaints increased in proportion, the commissioner raised his demands for additional clerk hire from $6,000 to $8,500.[28] In spite of his pleas, the Treasury Department offered no relief.

Finally Meigs appealed directly to Congress. "Five clerks have been withdrawn from their current business for four months past, and placed on the business of locating and patenting military bounty land warrants. . . . Four more clerks are necessary for the purpose of dispensing with extra services in future," he wrote. Soon afterward the commissioner referred to a need for ten extra clerks. In early 1818, Congress passed a new act fixing the number of clerks in the General Land Office at twenty-three, an increase of five over the previous max-

26. Meigs to Crawford, NA: TD, Ltrs. Recd., Comm. GLO to Sec. Treas., 4: October 2, 1817.
27. Meigs to Crawford, NA: GLO, Ltrs. Sent, Misc., 7: December 3, 1817.
28. Meigs to Crawford, NA: TD, Ltrs. Recd., Comm. GLO to Sec. Treas., 4: Dec. 18, 1817.

imum, which partially relieved the burden of administering the bounty land act.[29]

In spite of a clause that forbade their transfer, bounty land warrants soon became the object of speculation. As early as 1815, before serious plans for the survey and distribution of the land had been formulated, Meigs warned the Secretary of the Treasury that "I have heard of $200 having been given for 160 acres." The speculation increased as the time for distribution of the lands approached. Veterans, in increasing numbers, wrote and entered caveats to prevent the issue of patents to land attorneys who claimed to be acting for soldiers. Crawford finally decreed that no patents would be issued to attorneys, a decision that drew loud protests from members of the legal profession.[30]

The press reported large purchases of bounty land warrants. The veteran apparently suffered grievously at the hands of the speculator, partially through need and not a little through ignorance. "It is to be regretted that the brave and faithful soldier is not taught to estimate, *properly*, the value of the reward which his country has given him for his courage and fidelity," wrote the editor of the *National Intelligencer*. Of equal significance were the vast distances between many warrantees and their properties and the countless hardships that awaited them there.[31] Alarmed by the increasing evidence of speculation, Representative Cave Johnson, chairman of the House Military Committee, introduced a bill to commute veteran's land bounties to cash at the rate of $1.40 per acre—a sum to be paid in four annual installments. The sale of the land would produce sufficient revenue to defray the expense of the bill; and "the measure, he hoped, would have the effect of cutting off all speculation, of which there was so much complaint, and by which the soldier was deprived of his rights under the influence of his necessities." The bill lost in a close vote.[32]

29. Meigs to Rep. William Loundes (S.C.), NA: GLO, Ltrs. Sent, Misc., 8: March 25, 1818; 3 Stat. 446 (April 20, 1818).
30. Meigs to Sec. Treas., NA: GLO, Ltrs. Sent, Misc., 6: April 28, 1815; same to same, *ibid.*, 7: Aug. 30, 1817; Meigs to James Berrien, attorney-at-law, New York City, *ibid.*, Nov. 5, 1817.
31. *Daily National Intelligencer*, Dec. 2, 9, Nov. 20, 1817. The *Intelligencer* estimated that the veteran received about $50 for his 160-acre bounty.
32. *Annals of Congress*, 15 Cong., 1 Sess., 31: 461, 460–62, 468–75, 479–86, 522, 808–14, 816–17.

The bounty land act did little to settle the military tracts, but it created endless work for the General Land Office.[33]

Amid questions of administrative procedure, speculation, and an insufficient work force, the commissioner still had to prepare the bounty lands in Missouri for distribution. While making arrangements to parcel out the Illinois lands, he announced that veterans who preferred lands in Missouri must wait another few months for their lottery. In December his estimate was three to six months. This second lottery did not begin until late 1818.[34] Its beginning was delayed by the continuing demand for lands in the Illinois military tract and resulting problems. The annual report of the General Land Office for 1818 called attention to the constant demand for patents to military lots, noted that thirty volumes of military patent records had been filled, and identified six of the twenty-four office clerks as laboring full time on "military business."[35] More than any other individual, the commissioner felt the pressure. In May 1818 he estimated that he had officially written his name fifty thousand times in the previous six months, principally in connection with the business of the military bounty lands. He confided at the time, "The business of Military Land Bounties, superadded to the ordinary business is almost too much for me."[36]

The "ordinary business" of the General Land Office was extensive. The administration of the military bounty lands was only one of its functions. Of far more significance for the nation was the survey and sale of the public domain to the great floods of people who were moving west in the years immediately after the war.

33. Carlson, *The Illinois Military Tract*, 25.
34. Meigs to Crawford, NA: TD, Ltrs. Recd., Comm. GLO to Sec. Treas., 4: August 4, December 13, 1817; November 5, 1818.
35. John Gardiner to Meigs, NA: GLO, Ltrs. Sent, Misc., 8: January 6, 1819.
36. Quoted in Meigs, *Life of Josiah Meigs*, 88.

The Land Office Business, 1815–1819: Preparation

5

The years immediately following the War of 1812 saw the greatest westward migration in the history of the young nation. From the hills of New England and the valleys of Virginia and North Carolina, men left their exhausted lands and headed toward the setting sun. For two hundred years the American people had clung to the seaboard and the lands east of the Appalachians. Suddenly they were on the move. The war had broken the grip of the Indian on the western lands. Andrew Jackson's exploits in the field and around the conference table had freed a large section of the Southwest from Indian claims, and his decisive victory over the Creeks at Horseshoe Bend squashed further organized military resistance. North of the Ohio, Tecumseh's death and Harrison's Purchase had done the same for the Northwest. The war had broken the confidence of the Indian and his faith in a British ally. The Indians now faced the advancing white settler alone. Although they remained east of the Mississippi for another generation, raiding isolated settlements and interfering with surveyors, Indian resistance henceforth was sporadic.[1]

Caught in the restlessness that engulfed the nation in 1815, the pioneer put his family, livestock, and belongings on a raft or a flatboat and headed down one of the great avenues to the interior of the continent. Swarms of these craft floated down these rivers—down the Ohio, the Mississippi, the Cumberland, and the Tennessee. Once ashore at a likely spot, the emigrant found himself in a new world. On all sides stretched the wilderness, as all-encompassing, frightening, and exhilarating as it had been for the first settlers on the continent.

1. For the extent of postwar Indian removal, see Charles C. Royce, comp., *Indian Land Cessions in the United States* (18th Annual Report of the Bureau of American Ethnology, 2 vols., Washington, 1899) 2: 678–82.

The most important thing about the new world was the land. It lay all around him, often hidden by great forests, sometimes visible for several miles on the prairies of Indiana, but always rich and fertile with the mold of centuries, in seemingly inexhaustible quantities, and waiting to be taken. Occasionally a new arrival found the surveyor's blazes and made his way to the land office for a down payment on his homestead tract. But more frequently men simply settled down to grow a crop at the expense of the government. The fascination of the land never ceased. Each spot seemed more inviting than the last, the timber of better quality and easier to clear, the streams smoother, the water more pure and sweet, the soil more fertile. In their quest, men moved steadily west. Gershom Flagg wrote to his father of this phenomenon:

Altho you say the Ohio feever is abated in Vermont—the Missouri & Illinois Feever Rages greatly in Ohio, Kentucky, & Tennessee and carried off thousands. When I got to Ohio my Ohio feever began to turn but I soon caught the Missouri feever which is very catchin and carried me off. I think most probable I shall return if my life & health is spared a year from next spring but it is very uncertain whether I stay in that country. Surely nothing except my friends would tempt me ever to se[e] Vermont again.[2]

Even the distant settlements in the Illinois and the Missouri territories attracted large numbers of settlers. "Missouri and Illinois exhibit an interesting spectacle at this time," commented a St. Louis paper. "A stranger to witness the scene would imagine that Virginia, Kentucky, Tennessee, and the Carolina's had made an agreement to introduce us as soon as possible to the bosom of the American family. Every ferry on the river is daily occupied in passing families, carriages, wagons, negroes, carts, &c. &c. —respectable people, apparently able to purchase large tracts of land."[3] Those who came to St. Louis fanned out along the Mississippi and often ventured up the Missouri River toward the fertile center of the territory.

The same symptoms affected the people of the Old South. Here lands that had produced tobacco for almost two centuries without respite could no longer compete with the new lands of the Southwest.

2. Flagg to his parents, Feb. 1, 1818, Solon J. Buck, ed., "Pioneer Letters of Gershom Flagg," *Transactions of the Illinois State Historical Society*, 15 (1910): 154–55.
3. St. Louis *Missouri Gazette*, Oct. 26, 1816.

The war brought a sharp drop in the price of tobacco and the loss of the British West Indian markets. Peace brought competition from the fertile lands of the Southwest. Scientific agriculture had so far indicated no way to replenish the worn-out lands of the upper South. New lands seemed the only solution, and in the West they were available practically for the taking. The Old South responded. Planters left Virginia and the Carolinas. The large numbers of families on the move taxed the capacity of the river ferries, and often migrants camped by the sides of the rivers for days awaiting their turn in the crush. The presence of large gangs of slaves indicated that it was not only the poor and dispossessed who chose to cast their lot with the Southwest. It was also the wealthy Virginian and Carolinian, whose roots had lain for generations in the soils of the Tidewater, but whose eyes rested on the fertile lands of the West.[4] They were looking to the lands of the Mississippi Territory and the so-called Alabama country, from which the recent Treaty of Fort Jackson had removed the Indian claims. One North Carolina planter wrote of the impulse to migrate:

> The *Alabama Feaver* rages here with great violence and has *carried off* vast numbers of our Citizens. I am apprehensive, if it continues to spread as it has done, it will almost depopulate the country. There is no question that this *feaver* is contagious . . . for as soon as one neighbour visits another who has just returned from the Alabama he immediately discovers the same symptoms which are exhibited by the person who has seen the allureing Alabama. Some of our oldest and most wealthy men are offering their possessions for sale and desirous of removing to this new country.[5]

The force behind the impulse to move was cotton. The reopening of the European trade and the expansion of the British textile industry brought an enormous demand for cotton immediately after the war. The price of that staple doubled in slightly more than a year to reach 32½ cents a pound by June 1815. The dramatic impact of this phenomenon was increased by the opening to occupation of great quantities of the public lands in the Southwest, which were admirably suited to cotton culture. Cotton continued to bring 24 cents a pound through 1819, and people rushed to take the cotton lands of Alabama and Mississippi. Cotton production followed rising prices. Between 1800 and

4. Adam Hodgson, *Letters from North America* (2 vols., London, 1824), 1: 113.
5. James Graham to Thomas Ruffin, Nov. 9, 1817, J. G. de Roulhac Hamilton, ed., *The Papers of Thomas Ruffin* (4 vols., Raleigh, 1918–20) 1: 198.

1830 cotton production doubled every decade. Indeed it increased more than twofold between 1814 and 1816. The great sales of public lands between 1815 and 1819 in the Southwest laid the basis of the Cotton Kingdom.[6]

At the same time, the prices of other southern staples rose in almost like proportion. Sugar, tobacco, wheat, corn, and rice found a ready market in New Orleans at high prices.[7] The price index of wholesale agricultural products in the Ohio Valley also rose rapidly. No period in the history of the young Republic, even the prosperous years immediately prior to the embargo of 1808, had been more remunerative to the farmer.[8]

Land was the immediate or ultimate object of the people moving west. Heretofore the government's apparatus to administer the public lands had been of modest proportions, and so had the land business itself. Gallatin's had been a small and orderly enterprise, concerned with the establishment of precedents in method and procedure. The settlement of private land claims and other preparatory exercises were more important than the actual sale of the public domain. A growth in the land business apparent in 1810 and 1811 was cut short by the outbreak of the War of 1812. The war did not diminish interest in the land, but the physical danger posed by the English and their Indian allies held migration and purchase within bounds.

With the end of the war this restraint disappeared. The Treasury Department began a desperate race to prepare the public lands for sale. While the government was committed to orderly disposal of the public domain, the rapid advance of settlement and the attendant rise in squatting over vast tracts of the public lands threatened its careful plans. District land offices in Indiana and Illinois reported intruders in increasing numbers. Thomas Sloo, land officer at Shawneetown, wrote, "There are nearly a thousand improved places in this District that are not Located—And if the Government does not adopt some energetic

6.   On the rise of cotton culture and the great migration to the Southwest in the years immediately after the war, see Paul Wallace Gates, *The Farmer's Age: Agriculture, 1815–1860*, Henry David *et al*, eds., *The Economic History of the United States*, Vol. 3 (New York, 1960), 7–10, 59–60; Thomas P. Abernethy, *The South in the New Nation, 1789–1819*, Wendell H. Stephenson and E. Merton Coulter, eds., *A History of the South*, Vol. 4 (Baton Rouge, 1961), 444–75.
7.   Lewis C. Gray, *History of Agriculture in the Southern United States to 1860* (2 vols., Washington, 1933), 2: 1030, 1034, 1038, 1039.
8.   Thomas S. Berry, *Western Prices before 1861: a Study of the Cincinnati Market* (Harvard Economic Studies, Vol. 74, Cambridge, 1943), 563.

Measures to nip this Conduct in the bud—it will retard the sale of all those places. . . ." [9] The experience was the same in the South. As settlers moved onto the public lands, they chose the wooded regions. The great forests began to go down, as men cleared their squatter sites, constructed a few wooden improvements, did a little fencing, and sold what timber remained to their neighbors or passing steamboats. [10]

Some men moved frequently; others made extensive improvements and then refused to relinquish their tracts. Those whose lands were forfeited for nonpayment joined them in maintaining possession of their lands. The presence of occupants intimidated prospective purchasers. Occasionally squatters banded together in defense of their rights, and they were a formidable force. Thomas Freeman, the Surveyor General South of Tennessee, considered that the large number of militant intruders in his district threatened orderly public sales. He thought that even if the lands in the district west of Pearl River could be marketed, the sales "cannot with safety, or propriety, be opened & conducted in that District. It is very evident to me that no gentleman would be safe in that District who would bid for, or purchase any of those squatters' settlements." [11] The report from northwest of the Ohio was much the same. "Since my return from Cincinnati several persons have called on me as the public agent to give them Peaceable possession of their Lands," wrote Thomas Sloo from Shawneetown. "Persons who are residing on them now & were previous to the sale refuse to give them up—and the rightfull owner is kept out of possession who thinks his case a hard one to be compelled after paying the Government for a tract of land to be reduced to the Necessity of Commencing a Suit at Law to obtain his Just right." [12]

The problem of trespass became so serious that President Madison

9. Sloo to Meigs, NA: GLO, Ltrs. Recd., Reg. & Rec., Shawneetown, 14: March 11, 1815; Nathaniel Ewing, Vincennes, to Tiffin, *ibid.*, SG, NW, 5: Jan. 24, 1815; Michael Jones and Shadrach Bond to Meigs, *ibid.*, Reg. & Rec., Kaskaskia, 13: Nov. 14, 1815.
10. Meigs to Sec. Treas., *ibid.*, Ltrs. Sent, Misc., 6: Dec. 6, 1815; Nehemiah Tilton, Register, to Tiffin, *ibid.*, Ltrs. Recd., Reg. & Rec., Washington, 30: July 1, 1814; John Read, Register, to Tiffin, *ibid.*, Huntsville, 4: Nov. 18, 1814; Thomas Sloo, Register, to Meigs, *ibid.*, Shawneetown, 14: Aug. 11, 1816.
11. Meigs to the President, *ibid.*, Ltrs. Sent, Misc., 6: Aug. 8, 1815; Freeman to Lewis Sewall, Register, St. Stephens, quoted in *ibid.*, Ltrs. Recd., Reg. & Rec., St. Stephens, 6: Dec. 8, 1815; Freeman to Meigs, *ibid.*, SG, Miss., 53: Dec. 9, 1815.
12. Sloo to Meigs, *ibid.*, Ltrs. Recd., Reg. & Rec., Shawneetown, 14: March 11, 1815.

himself intervened. He had observed the activities of settlers on the public domain since 1789. It is doubtful that he expected the new breed of pioneer to have more respect for the declarations of the federal government than the previous generation of frontiersmen, but nonetheless he resorted to a proclamation—unsuccessful during the Confederation and under Thomas Jefferson, but still a traditional solution. In this case his proclamation of December 12, 1815, was in part a substitute for the prompt administration of the public domain. Since the government could not place the lands on sale, some measure must be taken to protect them until they could be sold. The President addressed himself to the "many uninformed or evil-disposed persons" who held the public lands, specifically those on lands not previously "sold, ceded, or leased by the United States" or on lands without recognized or confirmed claims. He demanded these individuals "forthwith to remove therefrom" or face the use of "such military force as may become necessary. . . ."[13]

The proclamation "produced much alarm," in the words of the register at St. Stephens; and some squatters even inquired when lands would come on the market.[14] The apprehension was short-lived. The West now had a growing population to match its vast spaces. Large numbers of "intruders" had no intention of removing or of being removed from the public lands. Jonathan Jennings, the delegate from the Indiana Territory, served as their spokesman. He reminded Congress of the services rendered and the sufferings endured by those on the Indiana frontier at the hands of the hostile Indians during the recent war, the very same settlers about to be evicted by Presidential decree. The proclamation of 1807 had at least permitted temporary occupancy. Furthermore, Jennings told Congress, the blame lay not with the settler, but with the government for failing to put the lands on the market. Settlers would purchase, he affirmed, but the government must do its part.[15] Jennings's contention that the settlers would purchase lands was doubtful, but it clearly pointed up the fact that nearly a year after the close of the war the government was not prepared to auction the lands and test the intentions of the occupiers.

13. Richardson, ed., *Messages and Papers of the Presidents*, 1: 572 (Dec. 12, 1815).
14. Lewis Sewall to Meigs, NA: GLO, Ltrs. Recd., Reg. & Rec., St. Stephens, 6: Jan. 26, 1816.
15. *Annals of Congress*, 14 Cong., 1 Sess., 29: 452–53.

A more traditional defense came from John McLean, Congressman from Ohio. He wrote the Secretary of State, James Monroe, that "not one in fifty of these persons, were conscious of infracting the laws of their country. . . ." McLean was probably right; in the settler's view the public domain was the property of the citizens of the nation and was to be used for their benefit. The pioneers, continued McLean, were "actuated by the same hardy enterprize which has always characterized our Western settlements," and the government would benefit at any public sale from the improvements made by these occupiers. He closed with an impassioned appeal for the simple creatures of the wilderness:

They have fought, and some of them have bled, in defense of their homes. Does policy require that the arm of the Government should be lifted against them? Shall they, with their Wives and Children, at an inclement season of the year, by military force, be driven from their possessions? This, to them will be more terrible, than the whoop of the remorseless enemy, with which they have so lately been accustomed. In the hour of attack, their bravery secured them from savage destruction. Shall their government, now, visit them with more certain ruin.[16]

Petitions added weight to individual appeals, and Congress responded to this pressure by passing a law to permit settlers to remain on the public lands prior to their sale. Its provisions followed closely those of the act of 1807. The task of executing the law fell to the General Land Office. Already swamped by the duties of surveying and administering military bounty lands, Meigs did not act on the new law for five weeks. He eventually issued a circular making district land officers and marshals responsible for advertising the law and for receiving applications from squatters for permission to remain on the public lands.[17]

Although reports indicated that the squatters received news of the new law "with *much rejoiceing,*" few showed their thanks by bothering to obtain the necessary permission from the government. In the traditional manner of their predecessors on this and other frontiers,

16. McLean to Monroe, Jan. 19, 1816, Carter, ed., *Territorial Papers*, 8: 373–74. Cf. *Daily National Intelligencer*, Dec. 16, 1815, upholding the Administration's position but admitting the necessity of marketing the public lands rapidly.
17. 3 Stat. 260–61 (March 25, 1816); Circular to land officers and marshals, NA: GLO, Ltrs. Sent, Misc., 6: April 30, 1816.

they did nothing, "calculating I suppose," wrote one land officer, "on the lenity of the government in keeping them in possession." Thomas Sloo estimated that from 500 to 750 settlers illegally occupied lands available from private sale; and to assist them in registering, he "proceeded in person to Every principle part of the District in the Months of July & August, without Receiving a single application, the Reason Generally assigned me for not applying for permissions, Were that they were Apprehensive that Speculators would be able to designate their tract and bid against them at the public Sales. . . ." The register at Vincennes (Indiana) issued fourteen applications; the register at Washington (Mississippi), thirty-one; and the Marshal of Louisiana a total of two.[18]

The important first step in the preparation of the attractive new Indian cessions for public sale was their survey. When Josiah Meigs took office, he found the public domain divided into two surveying districts: North of the Ohio, under Edward Tiffin, and South of Tennessee, under Thomas Freeman. Along with the postwar interest in land and the rush to the West went the race for deputy surveyor jobs. An energetic surveyor could survey from four to five miles a day. At the rate of four dollars a mile (three in the northern district), and generally about thirty miles a week (surveyors worked on Sunday), the venture was profitable. Although the surveyor had to hire several hands, chainmen, foresters to cut down brush and timber along the line of survey, and a hunter to provide meat, the occupation was lucrative for a man who would work long hours under difficult conditions. Large contracts that might be subcontracted were even more attractive. The possibility of such rewards and the large tracts of new lands to be surveyed immediately after the war led to fierce competition for surveying jobs. Moreover, in a vast wilderness where no man knew much about the lands, no one knew more than the surveyors. It was not surprising that most surveyors connected themselves in one way or another with the buying and selling of lands.[19]

18.   Lewis Sewall to Meigs, *ibid.*, Ltrs. Recd., Reg. & Rec., St. Stephens, 6: March 8, 1816; Samuel Gwathmey, Jeffersonville, to Meigs, Nov. 7, 1816, Carter, ed., *Territorial Papers*, 8: 447; Thomas Sloo to Meigs, NA: GLO, Ltrs. Recd., Reg. & Rec., Shawneetown, 14: Nov. 17, 1816; Meigs to Crawford, NA: TD, Ltrs. from Comm. GLO to Sec. Treas., 4: Dec. 20, 1816; same to same, NA: GLO, Ltrs. Sent, Misc., 7: Jan. 15, 1817.
19.   Thomas Freeman to Meigs, *ibid.*, Ltrs. Recd., SG, Miss., 54: June 23, 1821. An analysis of the relation between surveying and speculation in public lands is

By the autumn of 1815, Thomas Freeman had ten applications for every available position. Josiah Meigs had recommended a friend, and the commissioner's brother, Colonel Return Jonathan Meigs, asked preferment for an old army acquaintance. There were many more. Every mail brought letters in favor of former officers. Freeman adopted the policy of employing deserving officers whom he knew to be qualified—men such as "Col^{nl} Anderson of the Regulars from Tennessee—and General Coffee tho' of the Militia.—a meritorious *officer* & old acquaintance & friend too, whom I knew to be well qualified. . . ." General Andrew Jackson wrote "in favor of two of his Tennessee Militia Officers who accompanied him thro' all the Creek War, & did not part from him 'till after Peace—A long & intimate acquaintance, and respect for General Jackson, in addition to his late fortunate successes would involuntarily draw attention to his application." The surveyor general continued:

The Governors of Tennessee, North Carolina & Georgia have each written to me in favor of individuals for several appointments—To these may be added at least one hundred individual applicants whom it would be a pleasure to serve [but] few, very few of them, are sensible of the difficulties, privations & hardships, unavoidably connected with the Surveying of Public lands in a wilderness. [Instead,] their avowed object is to obtain a large District, & *only superintend* the survey of it—That is, employ such novices in the business, to do the drudgery, as they could procure for little or nothing, without their requisite Talents, Character, or responsibility, whilst they themselves legally appointed and responsible, by Examination, Bond & Oath, would amuse themselves in viewing & exploring the country at public expence for Speculative purposes. . . .[20]

These numerous applicants sought employment as surveyors in the Creek Cession: the 14,284,800 acres of central Alabama lands ceded by the Creeks at the Treaty of Fort Jackson on August 9, 1814. These lands included all of the Creek territory west of the Coosa River and the Alabama-Tombigbee basin, nearly three-fifths of the present state. Andrew Jackson continued his treaty-making work after the war, and by 1816 he had concluded other agreements with the Choctaw, Chickasaw, and Cherokee tribes. The area opened to settlement was

Gordon T. Chappell, "John Coffee; Surveyor and Land Agent," *Alabama Review*, 14 (1961): 180–95, 243–50.
20. Freeman to Meigs, NA: GLO, Ltrs. Recd., SG, Miss., 53: Nov. 17, 1815; Freeman to Tiffin, *ibid.*, Oct. 7, 1815.

to be the heart of the Cotton Kingdom.[21] Congress responded by establishing a land district in the Creek Cession and directing the immediate survey of these lands. Members of the southern delegations went home convinced that the Creek Cession would be prepared for public sale forthwith. When they returned to Washington in December 1815, they found the surveying of the cession not yet begun. They promptly indicated their displeasure to the Commissioner of the General Land Office. Meigs responded with a peremptory letter to Thomas Freeman. "The President of the United States directs that a portion of the lands acquired from the Creek Indians . . . shall be surveyed and prepared for sale *forthwith*," he wrote. Freeman shifted his attention from the complexities of Mississippi's private claims to the new enterprise. He sent word to the deputies who organized their hands and trekked to Washington (Mississippi Territory), the headquarters of the surveyor general. Freeman dispatched to Meigs a plan of survey, interspersed with misgivings about the size of the project and the danger from Indians. In the spring of 1816 he shouldered a pack himself and led twelve surveying parties into the wilderness to begin the survey of the Creek Cession.[22]

Troops from near-by Fort Montgomery kept the Indians sufficiently cowed to permit work to proceed, but Freeman and his deputies encountered other difficulties. The summer was particularly hot, and in the canebrakes of the Creek Cession the heat was oppressive. Swarms of insects plagued the surveyors, and the stagnant water often made them sick. Many of the gangs operated at less than full strength for the entire summer. When conditions became intolerable, the chainmen, axmen, and hunters often left the deputies and returned to the settlements. Operations then ceased while the deputy made the rounds of the squatter settlements and recruited replacements. This conduct and the attendant delays outraged Freeman. "Whilst I was with the Surveyors last summer, I discovered an Idle, lazy, restless & Turbulent Disposition, amongst the hands that were employed by the Surveyors in that District, and I took some pains to correct their bad

21. *American State Papers, Public Lands,* 3: 462; Thomas P. Abernethy, *The Formative Period in Alabama, 1815–1828* (Montgomery, 1922), 17–19; Royce, comp., *Indian Land Cessions in the United States,* 2: 678, 680, 682.
22. Meigs to Freeman, NA: GLO, Ltrs. Sent, SG, 1: Dec. 28, 1815; Freeman to Meigs, *ibid.,* Ltrs. Recd., SG, Miss., 53: Jan. 31, March 4, 1816; Meigs to Freeman, *ibid.,* Ltrs. Sent, SG, 2: May 15, 1816.

disposition and conduct," he wrote. "Yet several of the scoundrals abandoned the surveyors after a few days of service, or on the first difficulty they met with either in swamps or canebrakes. . . ." [23]

Freeman had optimistically predicted the survey and platting of one hundred townships by the spring of 1817. Yet the winter brought added problems. Sickness continued to hamper the deputies and their hands, horses were in short supply, and provisions were scarce and expensive. Freeman wrote that the deputies "have for sometime past been obliged to pay, three dollars a bushel for Indian Meal & $16—for a barrel of bad flour, provisions are so scarce in that country that a large portion of the present Intruders will be compel'd to abandon their Improvements, and seek existence in the older settlements to prevent starvation, yet there are hundreds of families arriving there daily." [24] Soon provisions could not be obtained at any price. Surveying parties sent foraging groups to Tennessee, Georgia, and even Louisiana in search of supplies. Several deputy surveyors retired from the field and went home. Another hot and miserable summer further depleted the ranks. The postwar flood of applicants receded. Those interested had already seen the land to their satisfaction or made other arrangements. Freeman begged the commissioner to send him "a few good Surveyors or even those well acquainted with the Theory. . . ." [25]

At the time that Freeman faced great difficulty in hiring surveyors, the pressure for the rapid survey and sale of the Creek Cession increased in Washington. The principal spokesman for an immediate public sale was Andrew Jackson himself. The general had in mind more than the nation's welfare. He himself was a land speculator of experience and skill, and he saw that the lands of the Alabama country offered the opportunity for a perceptive and intelligent man with proper financial backing and sufficient information to reap a fortune. Jackson favored a new surveying district to speed operations, and as its surveyor general he nominated his old friend and fellow speculator, John Coffee. Coffee had commanded the Tennessee militia at the battle of New Orleans, had cooperated in many business ventures with Jackson, and was one of his most trusted friends. Of the appointment, Jackson wrote to Secretary of State James Monroe, "should the Gov-

23. Freeman to Meigs, *ibid.*, Ltrs. Recd., SG, Miss., 53: Dec. 9, 1816.
24. Freeman to Meigs, *ibid.*, Nov. 11, 1816; 54: Jan. 29, 1817.
25. Freeman to Meigs, *ibid.*, Oct. 10, 1817.

ernment divide the survayors District as proposed, and place Genl Coffee as survayor of the northern District, his Energy and industry will bring it into markett in all June next. . . ." [26] Immediately before adjournment in 1817, Congress acceded to the wishes of Jackson and divided the Creek Cession into two surveying districts. At the head of the northern district President James Monroe placed John Coffee.

Josiah Meigs immediately dispatched special "directions of the President" to the new surveyor general. Coffee's most important task was the rapid survey of fifty townships on the north side of the Great Bend of the Tennessee for immediate sale. Commissioner Meigs wrote, "Considering the solicitude that exists on the part of the Govern't as well as with Individuals wishing to remove to that territory, to bring the public Lands in that District as early as possible into the Market, the President expects that every exertion will be made by the Surveyor of the public Lands to effect that object." Coffee immediately engaged thirty deputy surveyors. "At present [I] have no hesitation in believing I shall complete the survey of 100. townships as directed in all the month of July . . . ," he replied. He did indeed make splendid progress, and by November of the year he took office his strenuous efforts made possible a sale of lands in the Huntsville office. He also continued his rapid surveying in the next months. In 1818 through January 1819, Coffee supervised the survey of 240 townships.[27] His was an integral part of the land office business.

Meigs also had extensive responsibilities north of the Ohio, where Edward Tiffin struggled to survey six million acres of military bounty lands and, at the same time, to prepare the lands of his surveying district for public sale. Tiffin had numerous volunteers to assist in the work of surveying as the war closed. Governor Lewis Cass of the Michigan Territory sent a brother with suitable letters of recommendation. Meigs also interceded for friends.[28]

Tiffin expressed doubt about the resilience of several of the commis-

26. Jackson to Monroe, Nov. 12, 1816, John S. Bassett, ed., *Correspondence of Andrew Jackson* (6 vols., Washington, 1926–33), 2: 264. On Coffee's life and cooperative speculative ventures with Andrew Jackson, see Gordon T. Chappell, "The Life and Activities of General John Coffee," *Tennessee Historical Quarterly*, 1 (1942): 125–46.
27. Meigs to Coffee, NA: GLO, Ltrs. Sent, SG, 2: March 18, 1817; Coffee to Meigs, *ibid.*, Ltrs. Recd., SG, Ala., 49: May 5, 1817; July 25, 1819.
28. Cass to Tiffin, *ibid.*, NW, 5: Oct. 26, 1815; Tiffin to Meigs, *ibid.*, Feb. 14, 1818; March 10, 1819; April 11, 1820.

sioner's appointees. "I am sure if those Gentlemen who are often times desirous of engaging in Surveying . . . were acquainted with the nature of the work—the hardships they wou'd be exposed to—an the sure consequences of sinking their funds from want of a knowledge of the hands they wou'd be obliged to hire and other unavoidable losses & impositions they would kindly thank their friends to cool their ardour and advise them to other pursuits," he commented to Meigs. The task of surveying made severe demands upon the individual, Tiffin continued.

None but Men as hard as a Savage who is always at Home in Woods & Swamps can live upon what they afford (if occasions so require) who can travel for Days up to the knees in mud & mire, can drink any fluid he finds while he is drenched with water also—and has a knowledge of the lands who are equally patient & persevering under similar hardships can make anything by surveying the kind of Country we have to Survey.[29]

When in April 1816 Tiffin's responsibilities for the military bounty lands were transferred to William Rector to relieve the work load, the task of first importance in the Northwest became the survey of Harrison's Purchase: 2,800,000 acres of southwestern Indiana that Governor William Henry Harrison had acquired from the Indians in 1809. While still in office, Jared Mansfield had let the contracts for most of this tract, but the outbreak of war in 1812 completely halted surveying operations. Interest in the Harrison Purchase remained lively. In the fall of 1814 the office of the surveyor general in Cincinnati was subjected to "very frequent and anxious enquiries . . . for information when the Sales of Lands in Harrison's Purchase would commence." The surveyor general continued, "The Lands in that Purchase are said to be of great value, and probably would, *at this time,* command a higher Price than at any future Period of moderate length." The entire purchase "would have been surveyed long ago, had not the Surveyors been interrupted by Indian hostility, either *actual* or *reasonably apprehended.*" [30]

The close of hostilities enhanced the attractions of this tract, and settlers immediately began moving in. Even as word of peace spread

29. Tiffin to Meigs, *ibid.,* Oct. 9, 1817; cf. Freeman to Meigs, *ibid.,* Miss., 53: Sept. 17, 1815.
30. Meigs to Tiffin, *ibid.,* NW, 4: Oct. 10, 1814.

across the frontier of the Northwest, Nathaniel Ewing, receiver at the Vincennes land office, reported that "this part of the Territory is now full of people who are waiting to purchase in that part of the district." Meigs did spur on his surveyor general, but in June 1815, Tiffin noted that most of the Harrison Purchase remained unsurveyed. Furthermore, the hostile disposition of the Indians who threatened the completion of the military bounty surveys also upset the Indiana surveys.[31] Tiffin had success in this enterprise during the summer months, however, and reports became more optimistic. In response to an enquiry from Meigs about the completion of the Harrison Purchase, the surveyor general could reply in August, "I hope to have it all completed before Winter sets in." Meigs was delighted to have something to show an increasingly impatient Congress and Secretary of the Treasury.[32]

The commissioner anticipated success and reported the completion of the Harrison Purchase surveys in his annual report for 1815. Actually Indian threats in the fall prevented their finish. Meigs had to be content with emphasizing that "at least *five sixths* of the *whole* has been surveyed. . . ."[33] At last he had a large body of attractive land ready for the market.

The Michigan Territory now claimed Edward Tiffin's attention. Here he found an interested governor in Lewis Cass, a man determined that Michigan should enjoy the same postwar growth as other areas of the West. Tiffin pushed forward a modest surveying effort in Michigan, but he found the area as unattractive as he had described it to the President earlier. The surveyors had "serious difficulties" with a swampy surface that turned into a quagmire with heavy rains. The result was "sickness and hardships" among the deputies and their hands to a degree that "really excited pity." By March 1818, Tiffin had prepared plats of sixty-eight townships for public sale. He now recommended a suspension of further surveys. Michigan's small population, the reported poor quality of the soil, the apparently swampy nature of the territory, the small demand, and the large quantity of land available for sale all entered into his opinion. Cass vehemently protested.

31.   Ewing to Tiffin, *ibid.*, 5: Jan. 24, 1815; Tiffin to Meigs, *ibid.*, June 20, 1815.
32.   Meigs to Tiffin, *ibid.*, Ltrs. Sent, Misc., SG, 1: Aug. 2, 1815; Tiffin to Meigs, *ibid.*, Ltrs. Recd., SG, NW, 5: Aug. 9, 1815.
33.   Meigs to Cong. Jeremiah Morrow (Ohio) and Thomas B. Robertson (La.), *ibid.*, Ltrs. Sent, Misc., 6: Dec. 19, 1815; Meigs to Sec. War, *ibid.*, April 1, 1816.

The Secretary of the Treasury supported Meigs, who endorsed Tiffin's recommendation, and the surveys ceased.[34]

One hundred townships also had to be prepared for sale in Missouri. Here another problem presented itself. Deputies were to "lay down all the private claims in each township," a task much easier set than accomplished, for "the private claims in that Territory are scattered over an immense extent of Country, and will require a great deal of surveying in order to embrace them." [35] In 1816, Tiffin relinquished this task to William Rector, the new surveyor general for Illinois and Missouri. For the next three years Rector struggled through the thicket of private claims and disputes over pre-emptions. By cutting corners and employing large numbers of surveyors, he managed to have plats prepared for a public sale in 1818.

Postwar problems in the Missouri Territory began with the Preemption Act of April 12, 1814. Pre-emption legalized settlement on the public domain and assured the settler of the right to purchase later at the minimum price. The previous year Congress had given the same right to settlers in the Illinois Territory. With such examples the settlers throughout the Northwest stuck fast to their tracts, fired by "the delusive hope of obtaining pre-emption rights," as John Badollet wrote from Vincennes. Periodic grants of pre-emption did much to undermine Madison's proclamation against squatters and trespassers on the public lands. Pre-emption was also one of the most vexing pieces of legislation encountered by administrators, in local or national office, for it raised problems of interpretation about the act itself and of determining what was public land fit for sale. All of these aspects developed in heightened form in the Missouri Territory, as westward expansion inflated the value of public lands.[36]

For nearly three years neither the Secretary of the Treasury nor the Commissioner of the General Land Office made any effort to execute the Missouri pre-emption law. As the time for public sales approached, the territorial delegate, John Scott, pointed out the over-

34. Tiffin to Meigs, ibid., Ltrs. Recd., SG, NW, 5: Oct. 4, 1817; Meigs to Crawford, ibid., Ltrs. Sent, Misc., 8: March 20, May 27, 1818; Meigs to Cass, ibid., May 29, 1818.
35. Tiffin to Meigs, ibid., Ltrs. Recd., SG, NW, 5: Aug. 29, 1815; Meigs to Tiffin, ibid., 6: March 6, 1816.
36. Badollet to Tiffin, ibid., 5: Dec. 20, 1815. The Illinois Pre-emption Act of February 5, 1813 (2 Stat. 797–98) became the model for subsequent laws conveying this right.

sight; and the commissioner hastily instructed the recorder of land titles, the surveyor general, and the officers of Missouri's only land office at St. Louis.[37] Meigs ordered the register to receive pre-emption claims as soon as the general plat became available from the surveyor general. Alexander McNair wrote that suddenly "the right of pre-emption has become a subject of great importance in this Terri-tory—Daily applications are made at this Office for the entry of pre-emption claims. . . ." Outcries arose over the lack of sufficient land offices. Pre-emptioners must travel to St. Louis to give evidence of their rights and locate their tracts. Meigs advised that the register should spend several days taking pre-emption evidence in Howard County to accommodate the many pre-emption claims in the Boon's Lick area. Congress quickly established another land office at Franklin in the Boon's Lick settlement. After these elaborate preparations few settlers bothered to come forward with their claims, or at least so the land officers thought.[38]

Before it could take effect, the Missouri pre-emption law needed an interpretation of its effective date. Although President Madison signed the act on April 12, 1814, Meigs ruled that since the Missouri law had reference to the Illinois law of 1813, it applied only to those citizens on the land before February 5, 1813.[39] A storm of protest followed. The Secretary of the Treasury, William H. Crawford, at the urging of delegate Scott, promptly reversed the decision and granted pre-emption rights to those who were on the land and cultivating before April 12, 1814, the date of the Missouri law.[40] In 1819, more than five years after the signing of the act, an interpretation approved by the Secretary of the Treasury made its way to the Missouri land offices.

Secretary Crawford also found his decisions concerning the Pre-emption Law criticized. The issue arose over the expansion of popula-tion into central and western Missouri Territory and the extension of civil government to the new region. By a treaty of September 13,

37.   Scott to Meigs, NA: GLO, Ltrs. Recd., Misc., S: Jan. 27, 1817; Meigs to Scott, *ibid.*, Ltrs. Sent, Misc., 7: Jan. 30, 1817.
38.   Alexander McNair to Meigs, *ibid.*, Ltrs. Recd., Reg. & Rec., St. Louis, 33: June 16, 1817; Meigs to McNair, *ibid.*, Ltrs. Sent, Misc., 7: July 14, 1817.
39.   Meigs to Thomas A. Smith, Franklin, *ibid.*, 8: Sept. 8, 1818; Smith to Meigs, *ibid.*, Ltrs. Recd., Reg. & Rec., Franklin, 31: Aug. 1, 1818.
40.   Scott to Crawford, May 17, 1819, Carter, ed., *Territorial Papers*, 15: 538–39; Meigs to Charles Carroll and Thomas A. Smith, Franklin, NA: GLO, Ltrs. Sent, Misc., 9: June 30, 1819.

1815, the federal government extinguished Indian claims to a large section of the interior of the territory. The territorial legislature then organized Howard County in 1816, a vast area which included the Boon's Lick settlements.[41] Congress responded by establishing new land offices at Franklin (Howard County) and Jackson (Cape Girardeau). When news of forthcoming sales of public lands reached the territory, citizens of Howard County flocked to the new land office and demanded pre-emption rights under the law of 1814. Charles Carroll, the Franklin register, denied them on the ground that at the time of the passage of the Pre-emption Act Howard County was Indian territory and not within the legal boundaries of the Missouri Territory. Meigs passed the problem to Crawford, and the Secretary upheld Carroll's view.[42]

Crawford's interpretation loosed a storm of protest. A St. Louis land officer noted "much feeling excited by the decision of the Secretary of the treasury on the subject of Preemption Claims in the Boons Lick Country or Howard District." Travelers in the Boon's Lick region commented on the bitterness of feeling there. A protest memorial from the territorial legislature scored the judgment and asked that the citizens of Howard County not "be frustrated by the ignorance or neglect of *Territorial Authorities,* nor the illegal, arbitrary, and officious intermeddling of *Speculative land jobbing Executive officers.*" [43] John Scott quickly asked Congress to extend the right of pre-emption to citizens of Howard County. For this suggestion he won the praise, and Crawford the scorn, of the *St. Louis Enquirer,* whose editor wrote, "It will be shown that Mr. Scott was neither seduced nor awed from his duty at Washington City, but spoke out with Republican firmness, arraigned the judgment of Mr. Crawford to his face, and brought him to reflect upon the difference between a ministerial and a judicial officer." [44] A paper supporting Crawford explained away the

41.   Meigs to Crawford, *ibid.,* 8: Nov. 17, 1818; Royce, comp., *Indian Land Cessions in the United States,* 2: 680.

42.   Carroll to Meigs, NA: GLO, Ltrs. Recd., Reg. & Rec., Franklin, 31: Oct. 15, 1818; Meigs to Crawford, *ibid.,* Ltrs. Sent, Misc., 8: Nov. 17, 1818; Crawford to Meigs, Nov. 27, 1818; Carter, ed., *Territorial Papers,* 15: 463–64.

43.   Samuel Hammond to Meigs, NA: GLO, Ltrs. Recd., Reg. & Rec., St. Louis, 33: Dec. 27, 1818; Rufus Babcock, ed., *Memoir of John Mason Peck, D.D.* (Philadelphia, 1864), 147–48; "Memorial to Congress by the Territorial Assembly," Jan. 22, 1819, Carter, ed., *Territorial Papers,* 15: 502–06.

44.   *Annals of Congress,* 15 Cong., 2 Sess., 33: 385 (Dec. 10, 1818); *St. Louis Enquirer,* March 31, 1819.

decision as "an oversight, which ought to have been attended to by the Commissioner of the General Land Office." The battle raged on, even after Crawford's apology and the passage of a law to give citizens of Howard County pre-emption rights.[45] Thus, in an attempt to formulate a suitable system of land disposal in Missouri Territory, Secretary Crawford had on one occasion overruled the commissioner's decision, and Congress had overridden the Secretary's on a second occasion, all within the space of a year. Such activity only further confused and delayed the most pressing problem, that of placing the lands of the territory on sale.

Adding to the confusion were the presence of numerous "New Madrid claims" throughout the territory. New Madrid County, located in the far southeastern part of the territory, was the site of an earthquake in 1812. To relieve the settlers who suffered loss, Congress granted tracts of land "on any of the public lands of the said territory." Unfortunately the law failed to make the claims inalienable, to circumscribe their location to a certain part of the territory, or to limit the time for the location. Enterprising speculators quickly bought up these "floating claims" and located them on town and village lots, common fields, and town and village commons; and one individual claimed the sandbar between the town of St. Louis and the low-water mark of the Mississippi River. The struggle between New Madrid claimants and pre-emptioners was bitter. From St. Louis, Samuel Hammond wrote,

New Madrid Claims have been layed upon several of the best improved farms in that [Howard] District as I am informed—One location has been made to include Franklin Town and another upon Boons Ville both of which are flourishing Villages and have many Respectable inhabitants on lotts well improved & Titles derived from Preemption Claims: The holders of Madrid Claims are all upon the alert several have entered upon the same improved Spots & have been Drawing for preference & I have no doubt that most of the preemption Claims will be Covered by them before their next sales take place.[46]

Settlers were quick to resort to force in defense of their improvements. Strangers in the Missouri Territory encountered open hostility as they

45. St. Louis *Missouri Gazette*, March 10, May 5, 1819; *St. Louis Enquirer*, May 5, 1819.
46. 3 Stat. 211–12 (Feb. 17, 1815); Hammond to Meigs, NA: GLO, Ltrs. Recd., Reg. & Rec., St. Louis, 33: Dec. 27, 1818.

wandered about. At every point on their travels, settlers accosted them, "Got a new Madrid claim? Are you one of these land-speculators, stranger?" [47] Meigs judged that the pre-emption claimants had precedence because of the earlier act, but the commissioner admitted that "I am not perfectly satisfied with this construction. . . ." The Secretary of the Treasury upheld his decision but uncertainty remained.[48]

The necessity of incorporating the private claims in the general plats delayed the opening of land sales in the Missouri Territory until 1818. On the publication of the President's proclamation directing the long-awaited sale, more difficulties arose. Territorial delegate Scott pointed out that under the act of 1811 no claim properly registered with the recorder of land titles could be sold until acted upon by Congress. Scott noted that Congress had confirmed a large number of claims but had not considered those disallowed by the land commissioners and the recorder of land titles. Under his interpretation of the law these, too, must be reserved from sale. Commissioner Meigs disagreed and pronounced all claims denied by the land commissioners as "invalid, & subject to Sale. . . ." Crawford, perhaps smarting still from his experience with Howard County pre-emptions, overruled the commissioner and directed the reservation from sale of all land claims "presented and registered under the different acts of Congress" whether confirmed by Congress or not.[49] The Secretary's decision resulted in the reservation from sale of more than 1,500,000 acres; and the receiver at St. Louis estimated that this figure was only "about one third or perhaps a little more than One third of the Claims within those Limits which are yet unprovided for by Law." [50] The task of separating private from public lands was almost impossible. Of the confirmed and unconfirmed claims, the *Missouri Gazette* commented, "it would take Endor's witch to designate what is or what is not public lands." [51]

The operation of the land system suffered from the host of individuals engaged in interpreting Congressional legislation. After the war

47. Babcock, ed., *Memoir of John Mason Peck, D.D.,* 147.
48. Meigs to Scott, NA: GLO, Ltrs. Sent, Misc., 7: Feb. 4, 1817; Crawford to Meigs, March 13, 1819; Carter, ed., *Territorial Papers,* 15: 525–26.
49. Meigs to Crawford, NA: GLO, Ltrs. Sent, Misc., 8: May 11, 1818; Crawford to Meigs, June 10, 1818, Carter, ed., *Territorial Papers,* 15: 399–400.
50. Samuel Hammond to Meigs, NA: GLO, Ltrs. Recd., Reg. & Rec., St. Louis, 33: July 20, 1818.
51. St. Louis *Missouri Gazette,* March 2, 1816.

Congress had given responsibility for the public lands to a separate bureau of the Treasury Department, the General Land Office, created for that prupose; but such was the importance of the enterprise and its political repercussions that superiors were constantly interfering and reversing the decisions of subordinates. Congressmen, district land officers, and interested citizens were understandably confused.

In the years after the war the swiftly advancing tides of population generated great pressure on the land system and the administrators of the public domain. The President, the Secretary of the Treasury, Congressmen, and private citizens demanded that public lands be placed on the market as fast as possible. Yet a myraid of problems had to be resolved. The lands had to be surveyed, the issue of private claims had to be solved, and the various land laws had to be phased into the land system. In spite of the contradictions and confusions that resulted, the land system steadily established itself over the public domain. Surveyors let contracts, the deputies and their gangs surveyed the lands and returned the field notes, the clerks and draftsmen prepared the plats and sent them to the General Land Office and the district land offices. The system did not work so promptly or uniformly as either the public or the Treasury Department would have liked, but it did succeed in making possible the great sales of the public domain that took place in these years. Sales in the Old Northwest continued with the close of the war. John Coffee and Thomas Freeman prepared the Creek Cession for the great Alabama sales by late 1817. William Rector and Frederick Bates did the same for the Missouri Territory by 1818. The land was at last ready to sell.

The Land Office Business, 1815–1819: Fulfillment

6

The burden of the great westward migration of 1815–1819 fell with great severity on the Treasury Department, on the General Land Office, and especially on the several district land offices. Some thirty district land offices served the citizens of the Republic, including twelve offices established in these five years to meet the demands of a westering people. They ranged over the western country from Steubenville (Ohio) to Franklin (Missouri) and Little Rock (Arkansas), from Detroit to New Orleans. To these centers of the land business came hordes of men bent on a single object: the acquisition of land. The dimensions of the land office business, its impact on the land system, and its influence in the settlement of the West are best understood by examining the experience of the land offices at St. Stephens, Washington, Cahaba, and Huntsville in the Southwest; those of the Old Northwest; and those at St. Louis and Franklin in the Missouri Territory.

The land district east of Pearl River, with its office at St. Stephens, contained a number of tracts acquired in the Choctaw Purchase of 1805. These lands, which lay north of the Florida border and west of the Tombigbee River, were already occupied by numerous squatter settlements by the outbreak of the War of 1812. The Creek uprising of 1813 laid waste much of this region, and after the massacre at Fort Mims the land office at St. Stephens, on the Tombigbee just above its confluence with the Alabama, was the center of military activity. With the pacification of the Indians by Andrew Jackson and the coming of peace, however, settlers appeared in large numbers, and the public lands became the paramount concern of all men.[1]

1. Royce, comp., *Indian Land Cessions of the United States*, 2: 672–73; James F. Doster, "Land Titles and Public Sales in Early Alabama," *Alabama Review*, 16 (1963): 115.

The register at the land office since 1810 had been Lewis Sewall, who at the war's end took an active role in persuading Josiah Meigs to place the Choctaw lands on the market. Sewall noted the rising immigration in the spring of 1815 and the promise of even greater crowds of land seekers in the autumn. Among the prospective purchasers were the soldiers brought to the region by the late war. Sewall wrote that these troops had "been the means of throwing a considerable sum of money into circulation," and many might return their funds "into the United States Treasury, by a sale of public lands East of the Tombigbee if it was *early announced* that a sale would take place in the *course of the present year.*" Commissioner Josiah Meigs arranged for a public sale in November 1815.[2]

The older squatter settlements in the district greeted the news with dismay and anger. They had served as buffers in the recent war against the Indians, and their sacrifices had assured the safety of the towns and larger plantations in the eastern part of the territory, or so they felt. The surveyor general warned Sewall to expect trouble at the sale from "intruders who threaten with assassination, any person who will dare to bid for the lands they, those Intruders, occupy."[3]

In order to guard against what he called "approaching disorder, and disturbance," Sewall called in the territorial marshal. It was well that he did so. As the date for the sale of the district lands approached, the little town of St. Stephens swarmed with squatters, who bullied or begged indulgence from prospective purchasers. When the sales began, it was only with the greatest difficulty and the aid of the marshal that the register could preserve order. Few of the large crowd intended to purchase, but the bulk of the onlookers intended to prevent the sale of squatter tracts. The hostility of the impecunious settlers focused on the district land officers. Sewall described the scene in which "civil officers, in ye discharge of their *official duties;* among whom I was one, were *grossly insulted,* and the *laws disregarded.* . . ." But reports that short staple cotton would bring more than 25 cents a pound on the New Orleans market strengthened the determination of men to bid. In spite of the hostility of the crowd, several buyers ventured to cry off choice tracts of bottom lands from $4 to

2.   Sewall to Meigs, NA: GLO, Ltrs. Recd., Reg. & Rec., St. Stephens, 6: March 8, 1815.
3.   Thomas Freeman to Sewall, quoted in Sewall to Meigs, *ibid.*, Dec. 8, 1815.

$13.25 per acre. The high prices and the determination of some of the purchasers to have the lands in the face of physical violence indicated the attractions of the Alabama country.[4]

With the end of the public sale, the crowds dispersed; but many individuals remained, and others hastily returned to the land office. Perhaps the President's proclamation against trespassers made them uneasy, or fear of the growing competition for lands had resolved them to purchase. Whatever the reason, private sales were unusually heavy. "Since the *commencement* of the late Land-sales, till the present time, we have been incessantly occupied. The office has been almost continually throng'd," the register reported, "Applications for land have been numerous, and they Still continue." [5]

In response to the rush, the receiver issued 880 receipts in December and January 1816, and the officers were "incessantly interrupted by applicants for lands while making out our returns." The arrival of spring brought a flood of pioneers to the region, and the land office business grew during the summer and fall. Sales in October alone reached $50,000. The location, price, and fertility of land became the principal topic of conversation in the Alabama country. Men came to the district land office in swarms. They hung around the register's log cabin, visiting with one another, inspecting the plats innumerable times, interrogating the land officers, everywhere seeking information about choice tracts. Sewall complained:

Often six, or eight men from the Woods enter the Office at the Same time: an examination of the Maps follows of Course; applications are then to be written, many unnecessary questions ask'd; and while they stay, it is useless to attempt doing any business which requires attention and accuracy. —Scarce have one Set of these people left the office, before another arrives; and the whole Scene of interruption and hinderance is acted over again: and this has been the case for months past.[6]

The administrative system soon felt the strain of the land office business. The record of sales for December 1815 reached the General Land Office in March of the following year, and with the spring sales

4. Sewall to William Lattimore, Territorial Delegate, *ibid.*, Dec. 11, 1815; Sewall to Meigs, *ibid.*, Dec. 8, 1815.
5. Sewall to Meigs, *ibid.*, Jan. 12, 1816.
6. Sewall to Meigs, *ibid.*, Feb. 23, Nov. 10, 1816.

the gap between the month and the appropriate account widened.[7]

The accounts of Samuel Smith, the receiver of public monies and a former Congressman from Pennsylvania, suffered similar delays. With the extended use of credit, many transactions demanded complex calculations of principal and interest. From the first sale in the autumn of 1815, Smith employed "one of the most active and experienced clerks" to be found in that frontier region. The clerk wrestled with the account books, while the receiver himself had to "devote my time to receipt of money and calculations necessarily connected therewith. . . ." Both men worked from daylight to sunset "and from one to two hours by candlelight. . . ." And still the accounts fell further into arrears with each passing day.[8] In the face of harsh criticism from the commissioner and the Secretary of the Treasury, and hampered by failing eyesight, Sewall resigned with the bitter comment, "I don't think there is a man in the United States who can; alone, discharge the duties of this Office *regularly as they occur,* and a competent Clerk can't be got here for less than *Six hundred dollars per annum.*" [9] Both Smith and Sewall had reason to feel aggrieved. Figures for the land sales in the St. Stephens office reflected the rise of the early land office business:[10]

	ACRES	
1814	1,463.48	$ 2,926.97
1815	48,756.94	107,664.91
1816	191,116.81	383,778.47
1817	212,241.22	450,504.02

To the district west of Pearl River, with its land office at Washington near Natchez, the close of the war also brought an influx of settlers and demands for the sale of public lands. Meigs heard of these developments from Parke Walton, the receiver. Walton had been a clerk in the Washington land office from 1805 until his appointment as

7. Sewall to Meigs, *ibid.,* April 12, 1816; Meigs to Sewall, *ibid.,* Ltrs. Sent, Misc., 7: Nov. 13, 1816.
8. Meigs to Smith, *ibid.,* Nov. 13, 1816; Smith to Meigs, *ibid.,* Ltrs. Recd., Reg. & Rec., St. Stephens, 6: Dec. 1, 1816.
9. Meigs to William H. Crawford, *ibid.,* Ltrs. Sent, Misc., 7: Jan. 16, 1817; Sewall to Meigs, *ibid.,* Ltrs. Recd., St. Stephens, 6: March 7, 1817.
10. *American State Papers, Public Lands,* 5: 384.

receiver in 1810, and he had observed the land business in the Mississippi Territory for several years. "As applications are daily made by
persons to purchase," he recommended an immediate sale of all available public lands within the district. Walton also suggested a sale of
forfeited tracts, some of which had been continually under cultivation
since 1799.[11]

Meigs arranged for a sale of public lands in Washington in October
1815. On the appointed day the village was overflowing with men interested in the land business, and numerous citizens had to find accommodations at Natchez. The public auctions were noisy, but bidding was controlled, apparently by prior agreement. Then with the
offering of the forfeited lands toward the end of the sale, the reserve
of the crowd evaporated, and "every man appeared to be only waiting
for opportunity to help himself to his neighbours settlement." [12] Enthusiasm for the cotton lands of the Southwest had broken down a
time-honored custom of the frontier. Other more formal regulations
also appeared in jeopardy. The crowd demanded that Nicholas Gray,
the recently arrived register, permit private entries of lands before the
formal close of the public sale. The inexperienced register vacillated,
unsure of himself and uncertain where to turn for advice, and finally
consented. He reasoned that with the great "clamour" raised by the
crowds, the land officers "thought it wisest to gratify them, having
come from a distance and complaining of the expense of waiting—
more especially as the practice had been adopted in other Land Offices; there then did not appear to be a single individual dissatisfied, all
appeared to be pleased and expressed themselves so publickly." His
was a clear case in which sales were conducted under rules laid down
by the purchaser rather than the federal government. Men crowded to
the platform to make their private entries at the minimum price.
Others who had bid for lands during the sale sought the right to alter
their purchases, a demand that Gray resisted with the greatest difficulty.[13]

Gray's conduct of the sale provoked a storm of protest and many

11. Walton to Meigs, NA: GLO, Ltrs. Recd., Reg. & Rec., Washington, 30: May
30, 1815.
12. Nicholas Gray to Meigs, *ibid.*, Dec. 30, 1815.
13. Gray to Meigs, *ibid.*, Dec. 30, 1815; Meigs to Gray, *ibid.*, Ltrs. Sent, Misc.,
6: Dec. 4, 1815.

charges against his official conduct. Josiah Meigs entered into a long correspondence in order to straighten out the affairs of the Washington land office. Gray was an outspoken man, full of confidence, and inclined to ignore those whose opinions did not agree with his. He defended himself in spirited fashion against the charges of misconduct; and while the commissioner sought the details of the case (on which few could agree), relations among the conflicting parties in Mississippi worsened. The register saw himself surrounded by "a desperate gang of Villains here," and he regretted the lack of official protection. In the middle of the investigation Gray's chief adversary assaulted him in the office.[14]

Meigs's attitude toward the illegal sales was ambivalent. He was anxious to let affairs quiet down around the Washington land office, but should he ignore the obvious illegality of the transactions? Gray wanted to forget the whole affair. "Should these tracts be advertized for Sale I have no doubt of the revival of old animosities and troubles Which have now all subsided . . . ," he wrote. Finally the commissioner concluded not to resell the lands *unless a clamour is to be apprehended from Persons who wished to have a chance of Purchasing at public Sale.* The commissioner could also bend official regulations to meet the situation of the moment.[15] Gray's experience was a clear case where the citizens of the western country brought pressure to bear in the most democratic fashion to determine the conditions under which the public lands would be sold, to the total disregard of the rules and regulations laid down by administrators in the nation's capital. Later the Commissioner of the General Land Office concurred in the violation of department regulations.

In spite of the controversy over Gray's conduct, sales increased. By July 1816 only seven townships in the district remined unoffered, and these were "nearly covered with Claims," Gray wrote, "the demand for lands since the 1st July seems as great as ever; all payments are made in the Mississippi Stock—which is sold at $25 p ct discount." Several applicants appeared for most of the tracts, which Gray disposed of by lot. He concluded that "the demand for lands is so great I have not

14.   Meigs to Gray, *ibid.,* Jan. 23, 1816; Gray to Meigs, *ibid.,* Ltrs. Recd., Reg. & Rec., Washington, 30: Feb. 1, March 7, 1816.
15.   Gray to Meigs, *ibid.,* May 24, 1816; Meigs to Gray, *ibid.,* Ltrs. Sent, Misc., 7: Sept. 2, 1816.

time within office hours to attend to my returns or books." [16] The rise
in sales at the Washington office was indeed dramatic: [17]

	ACRES	
1814–15	2,833.20	$ 5,666.40
1816–17	175,609.37	352,213.06

The land sales in the two older districts of the Mississippi Territory
at St. Stephens and Washington were an interesting but minor part of
the land office business in the Southwest. Private claims were numerous; there were few sizable tracts in these districts; and much of the
land was occupied by long-settled squatters: all these factors made
the sales in the districts east and west of the Pearl River primarily a
local phenomenon, however vital and significant they may have been
for those concerned. The magnet of the Southwest was Jackson's
Creek Purchase—a region of vast proportions, fertile beyond all belief,
ideally suited to the cultivation of cotton. The attraction of the lands
of central Alabama was well known even before the end of the war.
One observer could scarcely control his enthusiasm. "Should the Alabama lands fall into the hands of our Gov't & I will not doubt it, you
must come out & select you a tract of land & bring all our friends with
you if possible," he wrote in 1814. "The Alabama will be the garden of
America ere many years." [18]

The end of the war and the subsequent rise of cotton prices set off a
spirited movement of people to this region. Even before the last Indians disappeared or the surveyors ventured into the wilderness, spec-

16.   Gray to Meigs, *ibid.*, Ltrs. Recd., Reg. & Rec., Washington, 30: July 15,
Sept. 10, 1816. Mississippi Stock had its origins in the Yazoo Land Company
frauds. An act of March 31, 1814 (3 Stat. 116–20) appropriated $5,000,000 to
be divided among the claimants. Companies involved received payment in non-
interest-bearing stock receivable in payment for public lands sold in the Mississippi Territory in the ratio of $95 in stock and $5 in cash for each $100 of land.
This flood of paper, which generally circulated at a discount, greatly increased
speculation in lands in the Mississippi Territory. A good account of the Yazoo
frauds is Abernethy, *The South in the New Nation*, 136–68.
17.   *American State Papers, Public Lands*, 5: 385; the figures cover sales from
Oct. 1 to Sept. 30.
18.   George S. Gaines to James Taylor Gaines, Feb. 8, 1814, "Letters From
George Strother Gaines Relating to Events in South Alabama, 1805–1814," *Transactions of the Alabama Historical Society*, 3 (1898–99): 189; Royce, comp., *Indian
Land Cessions in the United States*, 2: 682–85.

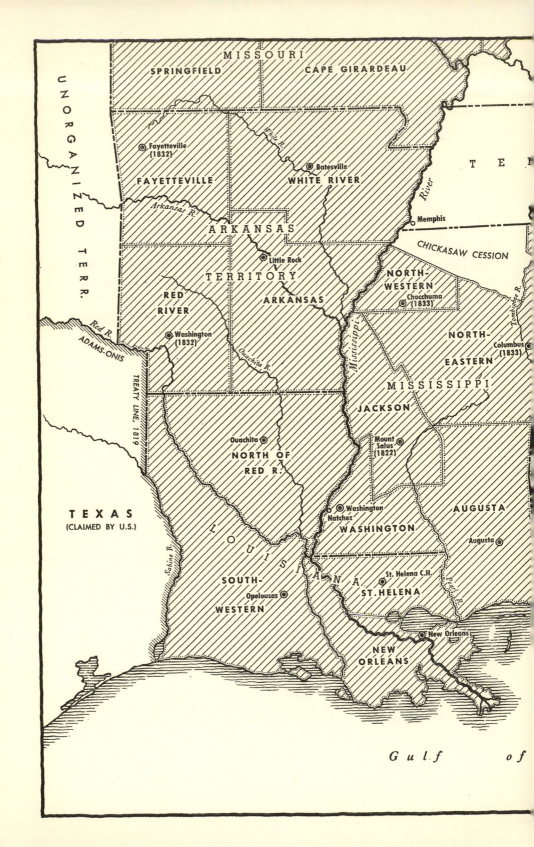

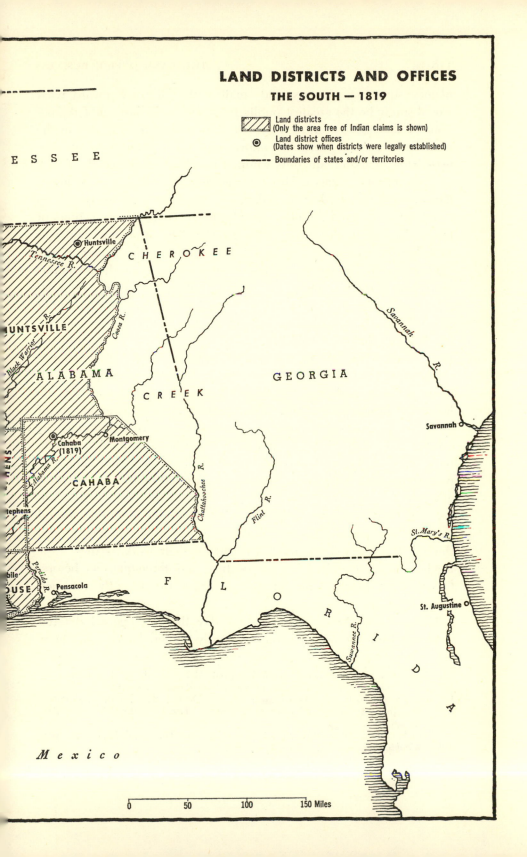

LAND DISTRICTS AND OFFICES
THE SOUTH — 1819

Land districts
(Only the area free of Indian claims is shown)

Land district offices
(Dates show when districts were legally established)

Boundaries of states and/or territories

ESSEE

CHEROKEE

Huntsville

Tennessee R.

HUNTSVILLE

Coosa R.

ALABAMA

Black Warrior R.

CREEK

GEORGIA

Savannah R.

Cahaba
(1819)

Montgomery

Alabama R.

CAHABA

ENS

Chattahoochee R.

Flint R.

Savannah

tephens

St. Mary's R.

ble

Perdido R.

Pensacola

USE

F   L   O   R   I   D   A

St. Augustine

Suwannee R.

Mexico

| 0 | 50 | 100 | 150 Miles |

ulators, squatters, planters, and small settlers hurried toward what would surely be the greatest public land sale in the history of the nation. By the spring of 1816, when the war was scarcely a year in the past, and the lands were still unprepared for a public sale, an estimated ten thousand squatters camped on choice tracts of the Creek Cession. Primitive towns with taverns, general stores, and an abundance of attorneys-at-law specializing in the land business sprang up to meet the needs of the new arrivals. These villages were centers of information about the tracts in the interior. The most important was Milledgeville (Georgia), created by Congress as the center of the land district for the Creek Cession. To this region came the adventurous spirits of the Southwest. The sales of public lands would be a national spectacle; they intended to take part in them and to profit largely. The constant meeting of old friends in the new cession reminded men that the Old South was breaking up. The creation of the new awaited the sale of the public lands in the Creek Cession.[19]

The first great land sale in the Creek Cession took place at Milledgeville in August 1817. The thirty-one townships advertised for sale lay at the headwaters of the Alabama River near the present city of Montgomery. The entire area consisted of choice river bottoms, "its fertility is inexhaustible . . . it will produce for almost an indefinite term of years, in constant cultivation, 100 bushels to the acre," reported Hezekiah Niles. "This assertion is repeated by so many respectable persons who know the land, that great as the product may appear, we cannot suppose there is any exaggeration."[20] For several weeks before the sale, land "viewers" moved singly and in groups through the selected sections, as intent on their work as their New England namesakes had been a century and three-quarters before. Others tried to purchase information from the recently returned surveyors.

The crowd at Milledgeville on the day the sale opened differed markedly from the motley group generally gathered for such affairs.

19. The most important accounts of the great Alabama sales of this period are Gordon T. Chappell, "Some Patterns of Land Speculation in the Old Southwest," *Journal of Southern History*, 15 (1949): 461–68; Doster, "Land Titles and Public Land Sales in Early Alabama," 115–23; Abernethy, *The Formative Period in Alabama*, 50–56.
20. Proclamation, dated May 24, 1817, Carter, ed., *Territorial Papers*, 6: 791; *Niles' Weekly Register*, 13: 16 (Aug. 30, 1817).

Everywhere gentlemen were in evidence, with their carriages and Negro servants. They came with funds to do business at the land office, and many took the precaution of using the register's strong box: both land officers accepted large advance deposits of cash and Mississippi Stock from "several Gent^n Who intended to purchase largely. . . ." The sales were remarkable for their order and decorum, with no hint of the mob scenes that engulfed the land offices at St. Stephens and Washington. The register, Alexander Pope, or his crier offered a township each day between 9 A.M. and 2 P.M. From then until dark he and the receiver, John Taylor, settled up the accounts of the day's sales. Pope recognized that this system departed from the rules of the Treasury Department that a deposit should be given at the end of each individual sale; but "if it should be required to give deposite receipts for every tract as sold during the day and make all entries in the books as contemplated by the forms sent us I am persuaded that without five or six competent clerks not more than 12 or 15 Sections could be conveniently sold in a day." From the beginning, large speculators dominated the sale, with the main emphasis on choice tracts that would be useful for speculation or the development of town sites. Spirited bidding on the best tracts resulted in the sale of more than 121,000 acres at an average price of $5.35 per acre, or a total sale of $647,371.94.[21] With the sale over, the register and the receiver sat down to prepare their accounts, despite ill health, and plagued by "the impossibility of procuring competent Clerks at any price. . . ."[22]

The great sales at Milledgeville continued in the autumn of 1818. Two public sales in October attracted large crowds. Alexander Pope auctioned thirty townships, and several tracts brought as much as $50 per acre; others, only the minimum price. Pope himself fell victim to the urge to buy. "I have bidden off several tracts," he wrote. Purchasers bought 267,580.91 acres for a reputed $700,000 at the two October sales. Sales for the entire year at Milledgeville were 292,525.75 acres, and the total purchase money $1,222,780.94.[23]

21. Alexander Pope to Meigs, NA: GLO, Ltrs. Recd., Reg. & Rec., Cahaba, 1: Oct. 14, 1817; Niles' Weekly Register, 13: 62 (Sept. 20, 1817).
22. John Taylor to Meigs, NA: GLO, Ltrs. Recd., Reg. & Rec., Cahaba, 1: Oct., 1817; Pope to Meigs, ibid., Jan. 7, 1818.
23. Pope to Meigs, ibid., Oct. 31, Nov. 22, 1818; Daily National Intelligencer, Nov. 9, 1818; American State Papers, Public Lands, 5: 385.

In the summer of 1818 the Secretary of the Treasury directed the removal of the land office to Cahaba, an undeveloped town site at the confluence of the Cahaba and the Alabama rivers. Pope and Taylor complained bitterly of the primitive conditions, but the lack of roads, accommodations, mail routes, and banks did not seem to affect the size of the crowd that came in January 1819 for the public sales. The weather was excellent, sunny and cool, and the prospective purchasers transformed the clearing into a vast campground. On the opening day of the sale the register announced that all the plats had not arrived from the office of the surveyor general. He expressed doubt about holding the public sale with only ten of the thirty townships available. The assembled multitude did not hesitate: with a single voice it demanded the sale proceed as scheduled. When rumors spread that the trunks with the missing plats were only forty miles away, the register wrote, "some Gentlemen volunteered to have them produced at my Office in Four and twenty hours provided I would promise to go on with the sale of them. . . ." Pope declined. He believed that "a great many purchasers had gone off and that the interest of the U. S. would be compromitted thereby I posted up a notice here declaring that none other but the ten already recd would be offered here during the present sales. . . ."[24]

The great sales continued in 1819. Some of the frantic competition waned, and at first speculators were better organized. Prices for lands were much closer to the minimum level. Alexander Pope auctioned several desirable tracts in March until the collusion of purchasers forced him to suspend the sales. Another sale came in May, with results "rather more favorably to the United States than those of March." Yet the sales were large. In the first six months of 1819 men bought lands at the Cahaba land office in unheard-of quantities. In the spring, choice tracts of cotton lands produced wild bidding and high prices to the government. Stimulated by cotton prices, by the flexible credit system, and by the air of prosperity that filled the Southwest, a land office business of staggering proportions developed. Sales for the first two quarters of 1819 at Cahaba reached 568,328.40 acres, with returns to the government of almost $2,000,000.[25] Ala-

24. Pope to Meigs, NA: GLO, Ltrs. Recd., Reg. & Rec., Cahaba, 1: Jan. 14, 1819.
25. Pope to Meigs, *ibid.*, March 19, April 2, May 22, 1819; *American State Papers, Public Lands,* 5: 385.

bama newspapers saw the land office business as visible evidence of the territory's growing prosperity. "At the last sales of public lands at Cahaba, we understand, the prices, pretty generally, were at their former high rates," commented the *Halcyon*. "What better evidence can be given of the immense wealth continually flowing into our country, than the high price of land and town lots? nay of the progressive state of every species of improvement in all parts of the Territory." [26]

The center of the land mania that gripped the Cotton Kingdom was in Madison County, at the Great Bend of the Tennessee; its land office was at Huntsville. Madison County had long been a region of great agricultural promise, but for several years the growing white population had remained confined behind a well-defined and ably defended Indian boundary. The barrier was now down. The lands in the surrounding countryside had been inspected and proved as fertile and attractive as hearsay had made them.[27] In 1817, Congress and the President met the demands of the large influx of population by creating a special surveying district under John Coffee.

The prospective land sales generated enormous excitement, as the land officers were well aware. John Brahan, the receiver, wrote, "If the lands are sold in Huntsville (which I presume will be the Case) I have no doubt but they will Command a better price than any body of land of the same extent ever heretofore sold in the United States. . . ." New arrivals strained the facilities of Huntsville and the surrounding country, provisions were scarce, prices for lodging and food were exorbitant, and famine became a possibility. Yet so great was the attraction of the lands that men would not leave. The register, John Read, wrote at length of the situation:

I hope for the interest of Government, that the Big Bend of Tennessee, or lands on the North side of Tennessee river, will be surveyed & brought into market first, great numbers of people in this Country are desirous to buy lands there, & many gentlemen from the Eastern States (very considerable capitalists too) have arriv^d in this Country & have hired their negroes . . . until those lands are ready for market, giving a decided preference to this part of the country,—The lands on the North side of Tennessee river, is in

26. St. Stephens *Halcyon & Tombeckbe Public Advertiser*, June 14, 1819.
27. On the early history and settlement of Madison County, see Francis Cabaniss Roberts, "Background and Formative Period in the Great Bend and Madison County" (Unpublished doctoral dissertation, University of Alabama, 1956).

my opinion much better than any other in the new district, & if brought into market during the very high price of Cotton & other produce, & while such a Spirit of emigration from the East to the west, prevails, (for the price of produce measurably regulates the price of lands) would sell generally as high & perhaps higher than any lands of the united States ever sold. . . .[28]

The President designated February and March 1818 for the public sales. The waiting period was over. Settlers, squatters, planters, and capitalists began to lay firm plans. The sales were crowded and tense, but orderly. Men had ranged themselves into groups long before the crier announced the first tract. At first only a few bid competitively; but when choice tracts came up for sale, collusion was forgotten, and the bidding was spirited. Prices reached extraordinary levels. In the first flush of the great sales John Brahan wrote, "Never did lands sell better in the United States, the amount of sale of the six ranges on the north side of Tennessee River amounts to near two and a half millions of Dollars. . . ." John Read echoed that "the lands Sold will probably average higher than any lands of the United States ever did. Many tracts brought 35 to $40 per acre & some 70 to $78." The first Monday in March, the officers began the sale of the remainder of the lands on the north side, and Brahan predicted "that the land will sell for a good price. . . ." It did. If prices were not as high as those in February, "entries have been much more numerous. . . ." Returns for February and March "will be a little upwards of four million dollars," the receiver reported.[29]

No sooner had the public sales ended than men rushed to enter at the minimum price the tracts passed over in the public auction. On March 30, the first day for receiving private entries, "about two Hundred tracts were applied for, & for that number there was upwards of one thousand applicants, for many tracts ten to forty applicants at the same time. . . ." Read added that "people are now anxiously enquiring when the lands on the south side of Tennessee River, will be sold, many wealthy planters of this neighbourhood are desirous to purchase & settle there, & I am told there will be an immence emigration from the East. . . ." From his log cabin, which served as office and living

28.   Brahan to Meigs, NA: GLO, Ltrs. Recd., Reg. & Rec., Huntsville, 4: April 18, 1817; Read to Meigs, *ibid.*, April 17, 1817.
29.   Brahan to Meigs, *ibid.*, Feb. 18, 1818; Read to Meigs, *ibid.*, Feb. 21, April 10, 1818; Brahan to Meigs, *ibid.*, March 31, 1818.

quarters in the little village of Huntsville, the register wondered at a phenomenon in the American experience that others had observed at various times in previous centuries. "There appears to prevail something like a land mania," he explained.[30]

The "land mania" left chaos in the district land offices. During the hectic sale weeks of February and March the receiver could "do but little more than make Calculations & receive money." He wrote to Meigs, "I have now four Clerks in my office, and shall have my books kept up, I hope next mail to have my Returns for Feby & March ready to send you. . . ." In June the register reported that clerk hire and office rent had consumed his entire annual stipend of $3,000, and half the year remained.[31]

The land business grew, and the land mania continued unchecked. Large crowds appeared once more in July to watch the officers auction the first five ranges south of the Tennessee River. Bidding was again lively, with lower prices the rule. The whole sale was over in two weeks. Lands brought from $2 to $21 per acre, with the total sale in excess of $400,000. Read commented, "although the prices are small when compar^d to those obtain^d for lands sold in Feby & March, it is believed that they *sold equally high* in *proportion to quality,* for the lands in the last five Ranges South of Tennessee river, are *decidedly* the *poorest in the district.* . . ."[32]

Numerous private sales followed, and the land officers did not have sufficient time to prepare their accounts before the public sales in September. The returns for the sales in September were $2,249,249.36. In October, Read auctioned the lots at Marathon, and private entries brought in another $125,267.97. The land officers sold 730 tracts in two weeks at another public sale in November. The sale had attracted "an immense crowd of purchasers," many of whom noted the favorable location of the lands on sale, for they lay just below Muscle Shoals on the Tennessee, and so gave the occupant "at all times a free and uninterrupted access to market. . . ." Final figures for the No-

30.   Read to Meigs, *ibid.,* April 10, 1818.
31.   Brahan to Meigs, *ibid.,* March 31, 1818; Read to Meigs, *ibid.,* April 10, 1818; Meigs to Crawford, *ibid.,* Ltrs. Sent, Misc., 8: June 27, 1818. An act of April 20, 1818 (3 Stat. 466), limited the income of land officers to $3,000 per year.
32.   Read to Meigs, NA: GLO, Ltrs. Recd., Reg. & Rec., Huntsville, 4: July 23, 1818.

vember sales were $1,598,937.92. After such figures December private sales of $103,595.38 were an anticlimax.[33]

The sales of land at Huntsville in 1818 inflamed the imagination of the most hardened speculator. They dismayed the district land officers charged with their execution and alternately delighted and terrified the administrators in Washington. When the public sales closed on November 14, the land officers had offered more than 2,200,000 acres of public lands. Citizens had purchased more than 4,000 separate tracts. Each transaction had to be calculated, recorded, and transcribed, and the full record sent to Washington. The burden on the land officers and the total expense of hiring additional clerks were enormous. John Read appealed to Congress for additional compensation. The accounts of the Huntsville office lay six months in arrears. The size and suddenness of the "great land boom" in Madison County were remarkable. The figures for the two years were:

	ACRES	
1817	5,610.37	$ 11,220.74
1818	973,361.54	7,225,204.00

Secretary Crawford continued to remind the harassed land officers that he was "extremely dissatisfied on account of your neglecting to settle your accounts, that no longer delay is admissable. . . ." Read was furious. The sales were unparalleled in the history of the nation—in fact so much larger than any other public sale that there was no basis of comparison. "I hope when the Hon[ble] Secretary examines well the reports of the business done here during the Public Sales, & for some time after, that it will serve as some sort of an apology for my suppose neglect of duty. . . ." Read noted that in the last six months of 1818 sales at the Huntsville office came to $4,610,427.85. He felt any additional apology unnecessary.[34]

The great land sales at Huntsville in 1818 had attracted nationwide

33. Huntsville *Alabama Republican,* Sept. 19, 1818, quoted in the *Daily National Intelligencer,* Oct. 9, 1818; Read to Meigs, NA: GLO, Ltrs. Recd., Reg. & Rec., Huntsville, 4: Oct. 22, Nov. 26, 1818; April 22, 1819; *Daily National Intelligencer,* Nov. 30, 1818.
34. *Daily National Intelligencer,* Dec. 4, 1818; Read to Meigs, NA: GLO, Ltrs. Recd., Reg. & Rec., Huntsville, 4: Oct. 29, Nov. 26, 1818; April 22, 1819; Meigs to Read and Brahan, *ibid.,* Ltrs. Sent, Misc., 8: March 16, 1819; *American State Papers, Public Lands,* 5: 384.

attention. The large sales, high prices, speculative schemes, all became national news, noted and digested in St. Louis, Pittsburgh, Baltimore, and Washington alike. The Territory of Alabama soon achieved a national reputation as the most fertile, wealthy, and rapidly growing region in the nation. The publicity undoubtedly increased the numbers of immigrants to the Territory.[35] The *Alabama Republican* summarized the feelings of the territorial editors when it affirmed, "Notwithstanding the high prices of land heretofore given the current of emigration has set to Alabama Territory, in a continued and rapid stream, unparallelled in the History of the world." [36] Rarely has an area been settled with such rapidity. In 1810 the population of Mississippi's eastern counties was 9,046; ten years later Alabama counted 144,317 within her borders. Statehood came in 1819.

Slowly the great speculative impulse that engulfed the Southwest spent itself. Four public sales at Huntsville in July, September, and November of 1819 and in January 1820 aroused only mild interest or none at all. Private sales continued strong, however, at the minimum price. Sales for the entire year 1819 at Huntsville totaled 221,763.77 acres. At Cahaba, sales in December 1819 and January 1820 followed the activity of March and May. Here, in a final burst of activity, the first-quarter sales in 1820 reached 233,925.90 acres, as particularly attractive tracts came on the market. Alexander Pope once more wrote of the "continued press of business ever since the sales passed over . . . ," and his records were far behind. Everywhere, he reported "the people continuing still to enter daily." But it was a last flurry. By the second quarter, sales had also dropped at Cahaba. Statistics at this office demonstrate the dramatic shift:

		ACRES	
1820	1st Quarter	233,925.90	$801,029.37
	2nd Quarter	16,380.72	37,724.64
	3rd Quarter	1,956.55	6,051.97

35. *Niles' Weekly Register*, 14: 64 (March 21, 1818); 15: 64 (Sept. 19, 1818), 125–26 (Oct. 17, 1818), 198–99 (Nov. 14, 1818); St. Louis *Missouri Gazette*, Oct. 9, Nov. 30, 1818; Kaskaskia *Western Intelligencer*, Oct. 2, 1817; *Detroit Gazette*, May 22, 1818; *Daily National Intelligencer*, April 15, Oct. 9, Nov. 9, 30, Dec. 4, 1818.
36. Huntsville *Alabama Republican*, April 17, 1819.

In October the *Alabama Republican* reported that "the spirit of high bidding for public lands has very considerable abated." The land office business in the Alabama Territory had ended.[37]

The land office business of the Alabama Territory generally benefited the capitalist and investor rather than the small settler. Men did not intend to bid competitively for tracts: that they did so in numerous cases showed the attractions of the land and the land mania that gripped even the coolest operator. For the most part, competing groups reached agreements beforehand. Interested individuals organized into joint-stock companies or partnerships; every possible arrangement was employed. Most of the organizations made a quick resale, frequently within sight of the government's crier, for investors wished to disband as quickly as they had joined forces. Usually the government officials could do little about such activities. The operations of one such company were described in the following terms: interested investors each deposited $1,000; land was purchased for the company at the minimum price; and the tracts thus acquired were immediately resold at auction. These well-financed combinations of influential citizens were beyond the control of individual purchasers and of the land officers themselves, and elicited the comment: "We presume that the gentlemen speculators formed their plans on the commonly received principle, that the public is a goose, and that while its enchanting plumage offered so many temptations to pluck a few feathers, no other danger was to be apprehended than that of being *hissed at!*"[38]

The register and the receiver at St. Stephens offered another description of such cooperative enterprise. At the sales of land in April 1819 the officers noticed "the prevalence of a system of combination at the public sales, which it rests with the Government either to counteract or permit." They viewed the operation as completely successful at this particular sale. "This combination had been formed and was in operation several days before it was discovered by the Superintendents," they wrote, "and in this manner Competition was in a consid-

37. Huntsville *Alabama Republican*, July 3, 1819, quoted in the *Daily National Intelligencer*, Aug. 6, 1819; *American State Papers, Public Lands*, 5: 384, 385; Pope to Meigs, NA: GLO, Ltrs. Recd., Reg. & Rec., Cahaba, 1: Feb. 15, 1820; Huntsville *Alabama Republican*, Oct. 9, 1819.
38. *Fort Claiborne Courier*, reprinted in the Huntsville *Alabama Republican*, May 1, 1819.

erable degree silenced." [39] The Treasury Department responded slowly to collusion at the public sales. While Crawford approved the decisions of individual land officers to close sales or to bid against the speculators, he declined to take any general action against the threat. When the St. Stephens officers described the operations of a company formed to stifle competition at the public sales, Commissioner Meigs sent their letters to the Secretary of the Treasury. Crawford returned them with the notation "needs no attention." Eventually he changed his mind. In July 1820 he directed the issue of a circular to land officers and advised them to "counteract combinations by bidding" against them.[40]

North of the Ohio, individuals and families moved to take the fertile lands that the war had opened up in the Old Northwest. "Old America seems to be breaking up, and moving westward," wrote Morris Birkbeck. "We are seldom out of sight, as we travel on this grand track, towards the Ohio, of family groups, behind and before us, some with a view to a particular spot; close to a brother perhaps, or a friend, who has gone before, and reported well of the country. Many, like ourselves, when they arrive in the wilderness, will find no lodge prepared for them." The pilgrims struggled over rutted roads until they reached the Ohio. Almost all traveled light. The common equipage was a small wagon, bedding, livestock, and "a swarm of young citizens." The migrants also carried "a little store of hard-earned cash for the land office of the district; where they may obtain a title for as many acres as they possess half-dollars, being one-fourth of the purchase money." [41] One observer counted 260 wagons passing down the Allegheny in the space of nine days, plus a large number of

39. Israel Pickens and William Crawford to Meigs, NA: GLO, Ltrs. Recd., Reg. & Rec., St. Stephens, 6: May 2, 1819. Pickens, the new register, was a former Congressman from North Carolina, president of the Tombeckbe Bank of St. Stephens, and later Governor of the State of Alabama. Hugh C. Bailey, "Israel Pickens, Peoples' Politician," *Alabama Review*, 17 (1964): 83–101.
40. Crawford to Meigs, NA: GLO, Register of Ltrs. Recd., Ltrs. from Sec. Treas., July 31, 1820. Alabama newspapers denied that the sales did not benefit the settler and constantly stressed that "practical farmers" paid from $40 to $70 per acre for tracts "calculated only for cultivation," and that "no artificial value has been put upon the lands by the competition of visionary speculators," and even that "purchases have been made for the most part with a view to actual settlement." *Daily National Intelligencer*, April 15, 1818; Huntsville *Alabama Republican*, March 20, 1819.
41. Morris Birkbeck, *Notes on a Journey in America from the Coasts of Virginia to the Territory of Illinois* (London, 1818), 25–26.

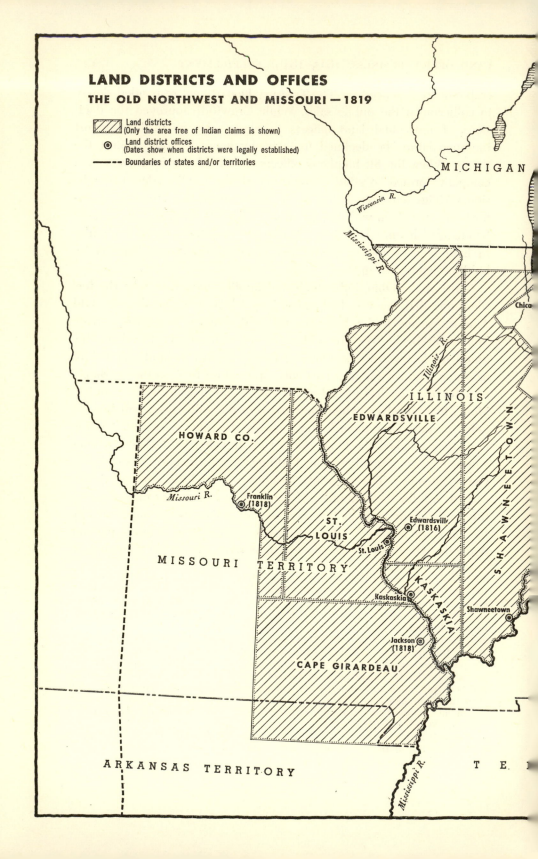

LAND DISTRICTS AND OFFICES
THE OLD NORTHWEST AND MISSOURI — 1819

Land districts
(Only the area free of Indian claims is shown)

Land district offices
(Dates show when districts were legally established)

Boundaries of states and/or territories

MICHIGAN

Wisconsin R.

Mississippi R.

Illinois R.

ILLINOIS

EDWARDSVILLE

HOWARD CO.

Missouri R.

Franklin
(1818)

ST.
LOUIS

Edwardsvill·
(1816)

St. Louis

MISSOURI TERRITORY

Kaskaskia

KASKASKIA

SHAWNEETOWN

Shawneetown

Jackson
(1818)

CAPE GIRARDEAU

Mississippi R.

ARKANSAS TERRITORY

T E

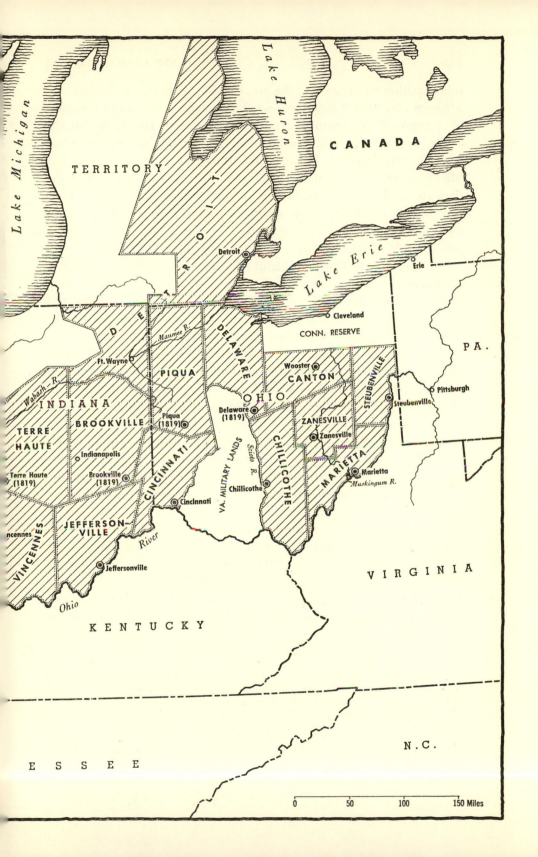

other families on horseback. "So great is the emigration to *Illinois* and *Missouri* also, that it is apprehended that many must suffer for want of provisions the ensuing winter," commented Hezekiah Niles.[42]

The rush into the Old Northwest filled the State of Ohio, reached into the territories of Indiana and Illinois, and largely bypassed Michigan. Occupation and sale of public lands in Ohio lacked the dramatic quality of Alabama or Mississippi, as corn and wheat did not promise the quick and easy wealth of cotton. Instead, there was a strong and steady demand for land. There were substantial sales of public lands in Ohio before 1815. Between July 1814 and July 1815 the Canton and the Cincinnati land offices sold more than a quarter of a million acres each, and Steubenville and Zanesville, more than 200,000 acres between them. In the postwar rush the western and southwestern parts of the state received a heavy influex of settlers, and sales at Cincinnati reached 272,340 acres in 1817 and 168,144 acres in the first nine months of 1818. By 1819, Congress had established new land offices in the central and western parts of the state, at Delaware, Bucyrus, Piqua, Wappakonnetta, Lima, Tiffin, Upper Sandusky, and Defiance. This expansion of the land system was evidence of the demand for lands in the interior and western part of the state. Between 1812 and 1821, Ohio land offices sold more than 3,750,000 acres of public lands, a figure not exceeded anywhere in the nation. By 1820, Ohio had more than 581,000 people, and substantial manufacturing had developed. The state was settled, with the exception of the far northwestern corner.[43]

Many pioneers headed west passed through Ohio to Indiana. Indiana Territory was known for its large tracts of rich and fertile lands; the most renowned were the well-watered valleys of the Ohio, White, Whitewater, and Wabash rivers. Although the Indians were a menace for several years after the war, people came and settled in river valleys. In 1816, Indiana won statehood. By 1820 the land in the lower third of the state was taken, and settlement was moving up the eastern border along the line of the Greenville Treaty.[44]

42. *Niles' Weekly Register*, 13: 224 (Nov. 29, 1817). On the postwar migration into the Old Northwest, see R. Carlyle Buley, *The Old Northwest, Pioneer Period, 1815–1840* (2 vols., Bloomington, 1951), 1: 1–57.
43. *American State Papers, Public Lands*, 3: 420; *ibid., Finance*, 3: 284–85; Utter, *The Frontier State*, 130, 145, 391–93, 229–31.
44. Waldo F. Mitchell, "Indiana's Growth, 1812–1820," *Indiana Magazine of History*, 10 (1914): 369–95; Chelsea L. Lawlis, "The Great Migration and the Whitewater Valley," *ibid.*, 43 (1947): 125–39.

The chief attraction was Harrison's Purchase (ceded by the Treaty of Fort Wayne in 1809), a tract of about 2,800,000 acres, lying north of Vincennes and intersected by the Wabash and the eastern and western branches of the White River. When this tract came on the market in the autumn of 1816, purchasers flocked to the land offices at Vincennes and Jeffersonville. In December, John Badollet, the Vincennes register, wrote that his accounts would be delayed because of "the extraordinary quantity of lands sold at the public sales. . . ." More sales of the Harrison Purchase in 1817 had the same result. Private sales were numerous. John Badollet called attention to "the number of persons daily thronging in the office," and he continued, "for a considerable time the applications were so numerous that it was impossible to record them as rapidly as they came in." Nathaniel Ewing, the receiver, noted, "The Public sales taking place so near the end of the year and the great quantity of land sold, more than could have been calculated on in the time allow'd by Law, occationed a hundred mistakes in our books, which has taken nearly all winter to correct." The Vincennes officers had reason to complain. In 1817 their land district led the nation in sales.[45] At the same time the demand for public lands in the eastern part of the state was equally heavy. The land officers at Jeffersonville wrote of "the increase in business in the Register & Receivers Office within the last 12 months, and the probability of its continuance. . . ." Sales in 1817 reached 286,558.36 acres at Vincennes for $570,923.52; at Jeffersonville, 256,350.92 acres for $512,701.78.[46]

In 1815 the northern two-thirds of the Territory of Illinois was still controlled by the Indians. The peace with the tribes so recently allied with the British seemed shaky. Many people thought another Indian war was imminent. Under such circumstances, wrote the Kaskaskia land officers, Michael Jones and Shadrach Bond, land sales "will in a great measure depend on the political state of our country and our relations with the indians. . . ." [47] Diplomacy was successful, the In-

45. Badollet to Meigs, NA: GLO, Ltrs. Recd., Reg. & Rec., Vincennes, 20: Dec. 12, 1816; July 5, 1817; Ewing to Meigs, *ibid.*, March 1, 1817.
46. Gwathmey and Taylor to Meigs, *ibid.*, Jeffersonville, 19: Oct. 11, 1817; *American State Papers, Finance*, 3: 284. On the operation of the land system in Indiana following the war, see Charles J. Bayard, "The Development of the Public Land Policy, 1783–1820, with Special Reference to Indiana" (Unpublished doctoral dissertation, Indiana University, 1956).
47. Jones and Bond to Meigs, NA: GLO, Ltrs. Recd., Reg. & Rec., Kaskaskia, 13: Jan. 11, 1815.

dians were pacified, and by 1817 the land office business was a powerful force in the Illinois Territory. A correspondent of the *Western Intelligencer* declared that "almost every person has in a greater or less
degree, become a dealer" in the public lands.[48] Sales during the first
nine months of 1818 increased enormously. The land officers at
Shawneetown sold more than 200,000 acres in that period—a figure
that placed that office in a class with Vincennes and Huntsville. The
flood of settlers in these years sufficed to propel the infant territory to
statehood in 1818; but thereafter immigration slowed and land sales
dropped. Money became tight, credit disappeared, and the land office
business faded. The great Kickapoo Cession of 1819 freed a large portion of the central part of the new state from Indian ownership, but
old and new settlers greeted the treaty with indifference. Illinois concluded this period of the land office business with statehood but with
a society and an economy still oriented toward the frontier. Land was
plentiful and, for the most part, empty. The great rush to the center
and north would wait until the 1830's.[49]

Large numbers of settlers moving west after the war went to the
Territory of Missouri and gave that region its own land office business—later than in the South or the Old Northwest, but considerable nonetheless. New arrivals squatted on the public lands and
waited. The Treasury Department responded to this influx of settlers
by opening the St. Louis land office, authorized by Congress in 1811
but never organized. President James Madison appointed as register,
Alexander McNair, one of the leading citizens of the city, and as receiver the equally influential Samuel Hammond of Virginia and
Georgia.[50]

During the war, men had sought lands close to St. Louis. Now
wagons and settlers—a "current of population," in the words of the
new register—pointed the way toward the interior of the territory,
particularly along the banks of the Missouri River. The greatest postwar attraction was the Boon's Lick settlement, a region synonymous
with lush fertility. Timothy Flint wrote of it:

48. Kaskaskia *Western Intelligencer*, Feb. 28, 1818, Carter, ed., *Territorial Papers*, 17: 581.
49. Solon J. Buck, *Illinois in 1818* (Illinois Centennial Publications, Springfield,
1917), 43–58.
50. Walter B. Stevens, "Alexander McNair," *Missouri Historical Review*, 17
(1922): 3–21; Stella M. Drumm, "Samuel Hammond," *Missouri Historical Society Collections*, 4 (1923): 402–22.

For some cause, it happens that in the western and southern states, a tract of country gets a name, as being more desirable than any other. The imaginations of the multitudes that converse upon the subject, get kindled, and the plains of Mamre in old time, or the hills of the land of promise, were not more fertile in milk and honey, than are fashionable points of immigration. During the first, second, and third years of my residence here, the whole current of immigration set towards this country, Boon's Lick . . . Boon's Lick was the common . . . point of union for the people. Ask one of them whither he was moving, and the answer was, "To Boon's Lick to be sure. . . ." [51]

Toward the Boon's Lick country, migrants "poured in a flood, the power and strength of which could only be adequately conceived by persons on the spot." The stream of settlers, "like a mountain torrent, poured into the country faster than it was possible to provide corn for breadstuff." Many came during the war, others in the following year, "but in the winter, spring, summer, and autumn of 1816, they came like an avalanche." A missionary familiar with the greater part of the western country wrote of the movement to Boon's Lick in terms reminiscent of those used to describe the great migration to the Southwest: "It seemed as though Kentucky and Tennessee were breaking up and moving to the 'Far West.' Caravan after caravan passed over the prairies of Illinois, crossing the 'great river' at St. Louis, all bound to the Boone's Lick. The stream of immigrants had not lessened in 1817." [52]

New arrivals—"respectable people, apparently able to purchase large tracts of land," according to the *Missouri Gazette*—eagerly awaited the sales of the public lands. The register of the St. Louis land office, Alexander McNair, surveyed the territory's prospects and concluded, "In fact all it wants to be the first country in the western world, is, its Lands to be in market." [53] The problem of private land claims, the satisfactory adjustment of pre-emption rights, and a rapid and accurate survey delayed the first public sales until 1818. At last the President issued a proclamation directing the public sale of thirty townships in each of four sales at St. Louis in August and October of

51. McNair to Meigs, NA: GLO, Ltrs. Recd., Reg. & Rec., St. Louis, 33: Jan. 27, 1816; Timothy Flint, *Recollections of the Last Ten Years* (Boston, 1826), 203.
52. Babcock, ed., *Forty Years of Pioneer Life: Memoir of John Mason Peck, D.D.*, 146.
53. St. Louis *Missouri Gazette*, Oct. 26, 1816; McNair to Meigs, NA: GLO, Ltrs. Recd., Reg. & Rec., St. Louis, 33: June 16, 1817.

1818 and February and April of 1819. Modest crowds responded in-
differently to the long-awaited sales. During the August sale of
700,000 acres, only about 35,000 acres were bought. The average price
was three dollars per acre.[54] The October sales followed the pattern
set in August. Hammond thought them "rather dull" and "limited." [55]

To serve the needs of the Boon's Lick country, Congress established
a land district for Howard County, with its land office at Franklin.
The register was Charles Carroll, a New Yorker, and the receiver was
Brigadier General Thomas A. Smith, a native Virginian who had
served in the army from 1800 until his discharge in 1818. Four public
sales in the Franklin office in the first six months of 1819 saw a strong
impulse to purchase. The auctions were well attended, the bidding
was competitive and active, and the sales were heavy. During the
January sale numerous purchasers ignored the inclement weather to
seek lands, and almost every good quarter-section brought from $4 to
$12 per acre, and one section brought $26.25. The next month, land
officers sold choice tracts covered with pre-emption claims; the sales
totaled 320,000 acres in the three-week period at an average price of
nearly $4 per acre. The large sales indicated the prosperity of the
region, while the generally moderate prices were an invitation to other
settlers.[56] The Franklin land officers reported that the official figures
of the February sale were 249,347.185 acres sold, at an average of
$3.85 per acre.[57]

Sales at St. Louis in February and March inspired the same sort of
enthusiasm. The February auction disposed of 69,883 acres at an
average price of $2.52—"a sum considerably lower than had been an-
ticipated." On the other hand, the prices must "be encouraging to
emigrants; as the price is very low when compared with that of lands
not more fertile in other parts of the southern and western sections of
the union." Large crowds at the March sales bought more than
107,000 acres in two weeks, at an average price of $2.91 per acre.[58]

54. Proclamation dated April 30, 1818, Carter, ed., *Territorial Papers,* 15: 385–
86; St. Louis *Missouri Gazette,* Aug. 28, 1818.
55. Hammond to Meigs, NA: GLO, Ltrs. Recd., Reg. & Rec., St. Louis, 33: Oct.
17, 1818.
56. St. Louis *Missouri Gazette,* Jan. 27, March 10, 1819; *St. Louis Enquirer,*
March 31, 1819.
57. Smith and Carroll to Meigs, NA: GLO, Ltrs. Recd., Reg. & Rec., Franklin,
31: May 13, 1819.
58. St. Louis *Missouri Gazette,* March 3, June 9, 1819; Hattie M. Anderson,
"Frontier Economic Problems in Missouri, 1815–1828," *Missouri Historical Review,* 34 (1939–40): 49.

As the territory moved into the second half of 1819, prosperity appeared on every hand. "Rivers were covered with commerce, every day respectable heads of families, or enterprising young men arrive in the country, by land or by water," noted the *St. Louis Enquirer.* "Gold and silver is more abundant than in any other part of the Union; the demand for money less pressing; and the whole community animated with the consciousness, that all the comforts of life lay within the reach of every industrious man." Land sales in the territory in 1819 reached 892,047.04 acres for $2,447,335.82.[59]

Enthusiasm for lands was widespread. "Land-claims, settlement-rights, preemption-rights, Spanish grants, confirmed claims, unconfirmed claims, and New Madrid claims . . . made up the burden of the song in all social meetings," wrote Timothy Flint. "They were like the weather in other countries, standing and perpetual topics of conversation." An active demand developed for military bounty warrants; New Madrid claims brought top prices; "and a great and fortunate land-speculator and land-holder was looked up to with as much veneration by the people, as any partner in the house of Hope in London, or Gray in America." The itinerant preacher John Mason Peck noted "a terrific excitement about getting land." [60]

Despite optimistic statements, Missouri's land business was dull in the first half of 1820. Sales of the public lands continued in regular fashion, but few purchasers appeared. The effects of the panic of 1819 reached Missouri by the autumn of 1820, later than elsewhere but with the same destructive effect. Statistics indicate the change:[61]

ACRES

1819	892,047.04	$2,447,335.82
1820	75,791.96	137,188.04

The land office business of the postwar years closed on a jarring note, as economic crisis and subsequent depression dampened the op-

59. *St. Louis Enquirer,* June 25, 1819; *Senate Public Documents,* 27 Cong., 3 Sess., #246: 5.

60. Flint, *Recollections of the Last Ten Years,* 199, 198; Babcock, ed., *Memoir of John Mason Peck, D.D.,* 147. The dominance of land in Missouri Territory in this period is described in Marvin R. Cain, "Edward Bates: The Rise of a Western Politician, 1814–1842" (Unpublished master's thesis, University of Missouri, 1957); Donald J. Ambramoske, "The Public Lands in Early Missouri Politics," *Missouri Historical Review,* 53 (1959): 295–305.

61. Dorothy B. Dorsey, "The Panic of 1819 in Missouri," *Missouri Historical Review,* 29 (1935): 79–91; *Senate Public Documents,* 27 Cong., 3 Sess., #246: 5, 8.

timism of the nation. Yet one of the greatest migrations in history had brought five new public land states into the Union: Indiana in 1816, Mississippi in 1817, Illinois in 1818, Alabama in 1819, and eventually Missouri in 1821. The western country had generated political power that made it a section to be reckoned with in the councils of the nation. The economic impact was no less dramatic. The land office business of the Southwest provided the royal domain for the Cotton Kingdom. North of the Ohio the fertile lands of the Old Northwest became the basis of commercial agriculture in the Mississippi Valley and opened up the great postwar trade down the Mississippi to New Orleans.

The failure of the federal government to react to the collusion of purchasers at the land sales (particularly in the South) indicated a curious inability on its part to understand the attitude of the frontier toward the public lands. For the settler, the planter, the squatter, and the speculator alike, land always belonged to those who were there. These individuals accepted the hazards of competing against one another for profits from the public lands, but they did not accept the right of the government to be unreasonably stringent or exacting about the conditions or terms under which lands should be distributed. Untrammeled individualism and competition without interference from the government were the accepted standards on the frontier.

PANIC
AND
RELIEF

7

The panic of 1819, which had a devastating effect on the western portion of the nation and brought a sudden end to the land office business, was the result of several forces. An important one was the postwar banking system. Prosperity and the demand for additional credit, the confused state of the currency, the failure to resume specie redemption—which had been suspended during the war—and the acknowledged profitability of banks had led to the rise of a large number of new banking institutions. "Wherever there is a 'church, a blacksmith's shop and a tavern' seems a proper scite for one of them," commented Hezekiah Niles in 1816. The Secretary of the Treasury, William H. Crawford, wrote, "Banks have been incorporated, not because there was capital seeking investment; not because the places where they were established had commerce and manufactures which required their fostering aid; but because men without active capital wanted the means of obtaining loans, which their standing in the community would not command from banks or individuals having real capital and established credit." From 1813 to 1819 the amount of bank capital increased from $65,000,000 to more than $125,000,000.[1]

The notes of these banks aided in creating the prosperity of the postwar years in the West and the South, along with the rush to new lands and speculation in the public domain. Two Alabama institutions, the Planters and Mechanics Bank of Huntsville and the Tombeckbe Bank of St. Stephens, were chartered to meet the needs of

1. *Niles' Weekly Register*, 11: 130 (Oct. 26, 1816); *American State Papers, Finance*, 3: 494–95. Postwar banking developments in two western states with heavy land sales are analyzed in William H. Brantley, *Banking in Alabama, 1816–1860* (Birmingham, 1961), 3–51; John R. Cable, *The Bank of the State of Missouri* (Columbia University Studies in History, Economics and Public Law, Vol. 102, New York, 1923), 47–74.

men for credit and currency to use at the Alabama land sales. Even the little village of St. Stephens had its own bank, and the founder and president was Israel Pickens, register of the land office in that town. Pickens suggested the importance of the bank to the land office business in a letter to the Secretary of the Treasury. "On the new surveys coming into market, and after the land office is brought from Milledgeville into the heart of the country, the effect produced on the land market by the facility of procuring loans in the country may be easily imagined," he wrote. Pickens's bank and others in the Old Northwest and the Missouri Territory helped to finance the great sales of public lands.[2]

In 1816 the Second Bank of the United States (the First Bank of the United States expired in 1811) was chartered to stabilize the nation's currency. Initially, however, it did nothing to control the large volume of paper money circulating in the West and South, for it immediately entered upon a period of ill-advised and uncontrolled expansion. It extended credit easily, expanded its loans substantially, and helped swell the inflation that was felt in every section of the country by the middle of 1817.[3]

In the summer of 1818 the Bank of the United States reversed its policy of expansion, curtailed discounts, and ordered that balances due it must be settled forthwith. Confusion quickly followed, and the state of the paper money in circulation, already uncertain, became everywhere suspect. In the autumn the Secretary of the Treasury wrote to John Taylor at Milledgeville, "The doubtful state of the currency, in most parts of the country resulting from the excessive multiplication of banks by the States renders it extremely difficult to discriminate between those that are really solvent, from those that are not so." [4]

The sudden change of direction by the Bank of the United States was initially felt in the East, where the stronger banks stood fast and called in loans from the West. The region of greatest expansion and inflation suffered severely. Between July 1818 and January 1819, from western Pennsylvania to Missouri, from Illinois to Alabama, an eco-

2.   Pickens to Crawford, Aug. 9, 1818, Carter, ed., *Territorial Papers,* 18: 396.
3.   Ralph C. H. Catterall, *The Second Bank of the United States* (Chicago, 1903), 22–67; Bray Hammond, *Banks and Politics in America from the Revolution to the Civil War* (Princeton, 1957), Ch. 10.
4.   Crawford to Taylor, NA: TD, Ltrs. to Land Officers, 1801–33: Oct. 26, 1818.

nomic crisis developed. The Second Bank of the United States even took the unprecedented step of refusing to receive the notes of any of its branches except "at a discount proportioned to the distance from the place at which it is payable. . . ." The state banks immediately followed suit and discredited the paper of their branches.[5] The conclusion of observers in the West: "The United States' branches are drawing the cord tighter and tighter; they are limiting the number of banks whose notes are receivable for lands. . . ." [6]

The tightening of money and credit in the West heightened the dilemma of William H. Crawford who, as Secretary of the Treasury, was responsible for designating the bank notes receivable for public lands at the various land offices of the nation. Crawford sought desperately to mitigate the financial crisis and at the same time to protect the receipts of the Treasury. By July 1819 the scarcity of "land office money" had begun to affect the land business in Alabama. The spring sales brought only modest prices, and the *Alabama Republican* commented that Crawford's decision to limit land office money to specie or notes of specie-paying banks "begins to operate with great severity upon the people of this country. . . . All confidence in the paper currency of the country appears to be lost by the people at large." [7] Elsewhere the story was the same. From Ohio came word that "such money, as will be received in the Branch Bank of the United States, and in the Land Office here is really not to be had." Edward Coles wrote from Edwardsville (Illinois), "Little or no land, except immediately in the vicinity of the scite of the New Seat of Govt of this State, has sold above two dollars per acre; and I will further add, if the list of Land Office Money be not enlarged much of the little that has been sold will be forfeited." Throughout the Edwardsville district, Coles continued, "as all the notes of the Banks of the District of Columbia, and to the North and East of it, bear a premium in this country, they are immediately bought up by the merchants and sent to the Eastward to purchase goods; so that they are seldom seen in circulation. There is now in circulation scarcely any land office money." From St. Louis the surveyor general, William Rector, asked that instead of pay-

5. *Daily National Intelligencer*, Sept. 5, 1818.
6. Ohio *Western Herald,* quoted in the *Daily National Intelligencer,* Sept. 24, 1818.
7. Huntsville *Alabama Republican,* July 3, 1819, quoted in the *Daily National Intelligencer,* Aug. 6, 1819.

ing deputy surveyors from the receipts of the district land offices, the
government send funds to the Bank of Missouri. "Much of the money
that has been received in payment for public Lands is not now Bank-
able," he commented.[8]

The failure of the nation's currency system and its growing impact
on the West was accompanied by a dramatic slump in the prices of
agricultural products, which was most severe among the staple export
commodities. In 1818 cotton brought 21.5 cents in New Orleans;
within a year the price was 14.3 cents a pound; and in 1820 it was
only 15.2 cents. Corn, tobacco, rice, and wheat lost value in the same
proportion. The price of wheat fell from $1.45 a bushel in 1818 to 91
cents in 1819, to 72 cents, in 1820. In 1820 prices of export products in
the Ohio Valley dropped to half their value of a year earlier.[9] Nathaniel
Ewing, president of the Bank of Vincennes (Indiana), wrote, "The
present situation of the western people is distressing; they cannot get
for their produce one dollar of the kind of money that will be received
in payment of their debts due to the United States." The Secretary of
the Treasury commented, "In the early part of 1819, the price of all
articles produced in the Western States fell so low as scarcely to defray the expense of transportation to the ports from whence they were
usually exported to foreign markets." [10]

The economic crisis provoked a sharp debate over the terms under
which public lands should be sold. The credit system had persuaded
the sturdy settler to assume obligations that went beyond his power to
fulfill. While Secretary of the Treasury, Albert Gallatin had come to
favor a cash system of purchase, but he had received little support.[11]
As the full extent of the depression became apparent, his earlier views
prevailed. Observers who had exalted the credit system in the midst of

8.   Samuel Finley, Chillicothe, to Meigs, NA: GLO, Ltrs. Recd., Misc., F: June
2, 1819; Coles to Meigs, ibid., Reg. & Rec., Edwardsville, 12: Aug. 5, 1819; Rector to Meigs, ibid., SG, Mo., 61: Oct. 18, 1819.
9.   Gray, History of Agriculture in the Southern United States to 1860, 2: 1027,
1030, 1038, 1039; Berry, Western Prices before 1861, 585.
10.   Ewing to Crawford, Jan. 9, 1819, American State Papers, Finance, 3: 735;
Crawford to Speaker of the House, Feb. 14, 1822, ibid., 718. The connection
between land sales and depression is examined in Arthur H. Cole, "Cyclical and
Sectional Variations in the Sale of Public Lands, 1816–1860," Review of Economic
Statistics, 9 (1927): 41–53.
11.   American State Papers, Public Lands, 1: 286–87; Gallatin to Senator Jeremiah Morrow (Ohio), Jan., 1809, ibid., 910; Gallatin to John Eppes, Feb. 26,
1810, ibid., Finance, 2: 413–14; Gallatin to Andrew McGee, NA: Legislative
Division, Rpts. of the House Committee on Public Lands, 1: March 28, 1806.

optimism, speculation, and 30-cent cotton felt that the cash system would abolish the evil of speculation and work to the interest of the settler and the cultivator. All agreed that in the future "human virtue must not be the basis of the system" for the sale of the public lands. The government must protect the purchaser from himself.[12]

Congress passed a new land law to meet these criticisms. The act of April 24, 1820, accomplished several things. It established cash sales after July 1, 1820; it provided for the sale of tracts as small as eighty acres and reduced the minimum price to $1.25 per acre.[13] It also required important changes in the administrative system: new instructions must be issued to the district land officers concerning their accounts, new forms must be drawn up and sent to the western country, and plans must be made to accomplish the change from the credit to the cash system of entry on July 1. Josiah Meigs supervised these accommodations to the new land law and soon dispatched suitable instructions and forms. The transition from the old to the new system took place without noticeable confusion.[14]

The Land Law of 1820 provided only for the future, however, and a land debt of some $23,000,000 remained. With the sharp fall in prices and the tightening of credit, purchasers "found that they, in common with the community around them, had been deceived by the *mere* appearance of prosperity," in the words of the chairman of the House Committee on the Public Lands; and he continued, "the price of cotton continued to fall, till, finally, it did not bring one-third of the price upon which their calculations to pay their land debts had been based."[15] At Huntsville, site of the huge speculative sales of only two years before, "the hardness of the times and the extreme difficulty of getting land office money, which is now 15 per cent above the currency of the country, no doubt depress the price of land." The *Alabama Republican* added, "The settlers never dreamed that cotton would be reduced from 25 to 10 cents per pound, or that the common

12. *Kentucky Herald*, quoted in the *Daily National Intelligencer*, April 15, 1819; Huntsville *Alabama Republican*, May 15, 1819; St. Stephens *Halcyon & Tombeckbe Public Advertiser*, June 14, 1819.
13. 3 Stat. 566–67 (April 24, 1820); an account of the debate and passage of the law is in Treat, *The National Land System*, 139–42.
14. Meigs to Crawford, NA: GLO, Ltrs. Sent, Misc., 10: April 22, 1820; circular to land officers, *ibid.*, May 29, June 7, 1820.
15. Rep. Jacob Isacks (Tenn.) to the House, Jan. 17, 1828, *American State Papers, Public Lands*, 5: 377.

currency of the country would become so depreciated that $100 would only pay $85 debt at the land office. . . ." [16]

Loud pleas for assistance also came from north of the Ohio and from Missouri. The large debt and its universality—embracing every class and every section of the Republic—were a powerful force. The *St. Louis Enquirer* spoke of "the government debtors become too numerous and too powerful to be controlled by the government." [17] From the Ohio country the astute politician-surveyor Edward Tiffin wrote:

> I cannot forbear saying, that, I much fear a Spirit of disaffection & & & towards the general government is arising in the West sufficient to alarm its fast friends and certainly requires vigilence in watching its Officers among us, some of whom it is feared are helping it on, at least it is enough to admonish the government to make no more Debtors, but change the system of disposing of the public lands. State Sovereignty is the cry, the Lobby now—and ridiculous as it is many have got mounted on it at the late elections who have scarcely understanding to know the tail from the ears of the Ass they are upon.[18]

Even the sanguine Secretary of the Treasury spoke of the "most serious distress of the moment" and the "alarming apprehensions for the future." [19]

In his State of the Union message to Congress in December 1820, President James Monroe viewed public affairs "with great satisfaction" and rejoiced "in the felicity of our situation." But at the end of his long and optimistic message Monroe alluded to the nearly $23,000,000 that purchasers of the public lands owed the government. "In bringing this subject to view I consider it my duty to submit to Congress whether it may not be advisable to extend to the purchasers of these lands, in consideration of the unfavorable change which has occurred since the sales, a reasonable indulgence. It is known that the purchases were made when the price of every article had risen to its greatest height, and that the installments are becoming due at a period of great depression." [20]

16. Huntsville *Alabama Republican,* Oct. 20, Dec. 1, 1820.
17. *St. Louis Enquirer,* Sept. 1, 1819.
18. Tiffin to Meigs, NA: GLO, Ltrs. Recd., SG, NW, 5: Oct. 31, 1819. Utter notes, "Probably half the men living in Ohio were indebted to the Government for land purchases, and the fortunes of the other half were closely bound to theirs." *The Frontier State,* 290.
19. *American State Papers, Finance,* 3: 718.
20. Richardson, ed., *Messages and Papers of the Presidents,* 2: 73, 78 (Nov. 14, 1820).

The government had long been a most generous creditor. Between 1808 and 1820, Congress had passed a series of laws extending the time for payment of debts on public lands. The most recent of these accompanied the Land Law of 1820 and suspended forfeitures until March 21, 1821.[21] When it met in the winter of 1820, Congress could look back on a history of leniency. The editorials of newspapers across the nation, letters from constituents, and memorials from states and territories urged a continuation of this policy.[22]

On March 2, 1821, after twelve weeks of debate on whether to grant relief to the land debtors, Congress adopted a law under which a debtor might give up part of his land to complete payment on the rest. The law also extended credit to debtors for four, six, or eight years, depending on the amount of the purchase money a debtor had paid. The smaller the payment made, the longer the credit. Debtors who completed cash payment for their lands before September 30, 1821, were given a discount of 37½ per cent—the difference between the old minimum price of $2 per acre and the new one of $1.25. Thus, the law offered some incentive to those who could complete payment for their land; but by granting additional credit for periods up to eight years, it encouraged debtors to hold onto large tracts and to seek further indulgence.[23]

The West applauded the passage of the Relief Act. The *Liberty Hall* noted that it was "hailed with much satisfaction by the people of the western country," and the *Western Herald* of Steubenville concluded that "whatever may be said as to the conduct of Congress in other respects, the people of the West cannot but feel grateful for the attention that has been paid to their interests." [24] Elsewhere in the Northwest the law was described as "just and generous," and every purchaser "must feel entirely satisfied with them, and find his mind relieved from many disagreeable forebodings, which the low price of the products of the earth and the pressure of the times had engen-

21.   3 Stat. 555 (March 31, 1820). For a summary of the earlier relief measures, see Treat, *The National Land System,* 129–37, and esp. 143.
22.   *Liberty Hall and Cincinnati Gazette,* Nov. 8, 1820; *Senate Public Documents,* 16 Cong., 2 Sess., #18 (Dec. 11, 1820), #40 (Jan. 8, 1821).
23.   3 Stat. 612–14 (March 2, 1821). On the debate and passage of the Relief Law, see Treat, *The National Land System,* 147–51; Hugh C. Bailey, *John Williams Walker, A Study in the Political, Social and Cultural Life of the Old Southwest* (University, Alabama, 1964), 151–67.
24.   *Liberty Hall and Cincinnati Gazette,* May 9, 1821; *Western Herald & Steubenville Gazette,* March 17, 1821.

dered." To the man who had come to the land with high hopes for a just reward and shelter in his old age, "this heart-cheering succor, comes like a welcome plank to the wearied and drowning swimmer. . . ." The law's individual provisions were invariably described as "most liberal and humane." [25]

The Relief Act of 1821 posed a complex and enduring problem of administration. Before September 30, 1821, purchasers who wished to take advantage of its provisions had to file written "relinquishments" of their lands and "declarations" for further credit. They had to make these arrangements at the district land office where they originally purchased the land. Under the terms of the law, the registers and the receivers of the sixteen district land offices where land was sold under the credit system, had to keep "full and faithful accounts and records" of the act in accordance with the "forms and instructions which shall be given in that behalf by the Treasury Department, to assist in carrying this act into execution. . . ." Since the privileges of relinquishment and declaration expired on September 30, the effective period on the law was only seven months. Although the forms for carrying out the law should have been prepared by the Comptroller of the Treasury, Commissioner Josiah Meigs decided to prepare them himself. He and his clerk spent more than four weeks creating the preliminary drafts of forms and instructions. When the Secretary of the Treasury complained, Meigs replied that "it was found impossible to require fewer particulars and at the same time to be able to meet every probable requisition of the Treasury Department relative to the Proceedings under this Act." Meigs was a natural bureaucrat in his desire to fulfill the law and to protect the administrator. Because of the Secretary's criticisms, Meigs reconsidered the forms, at the cost of additional valuable time. [26]

Meanwhile land debtors throughout the nation waited with mounting irritation. The act was generous, but the time for its operation was limited. By the first week in May the silence from Washington had aroused anger. "This law, the passage of which was hailed with so much satisfaction by the people of the western country, is likely to be

25. *Detroit Gazette,* March 30, 1821; Franklin *Missouri Intelligencer,* Aug. 7, 1821; *Edwardsville Spectator,* Sept. 11, 1821.
26. 3 Stat. 612–14 (March 2, 1821); Meigs to Crawford, NA: GLO, Ltrs. Sent, Misc., 10: March 29, 1821; April 6, 1821; Crawford to Meigs, NA: TD, Ltrs. Sent, Misc., 1801–33; April 6, 1821.

inoperative for the want of instructions from the Secretary of the Treasury respecting the construction which is to be given to it," commented the *Liberty Hall*.[27] When no instructions or forms had reached Alabama by the end of June, the *Alabama Republican* of Huntsville advised that the Relief Act had brought forth "nothing but promises" from Washington, and noted that "only three months from this date are allowed for arranging the certificates of about 10,000 tracts." Debtors besieged the district land offices in search of information, but without result.[28]

Meigs continued to be undecided about the final wording of the forms and instructions. At the end of May, nearly three months after the passage of the law, he wrote Crawford that the forms would soon be mailed, and the delay "is solely attributed to their complexity and magnitude, and not to the want of any watchful diligence or laborious activity." The forms were indeed involved and numerous. Meigs had determined that each register should receive an abstract of the land relinquished, which was designed to show each debtor's account with the government in terms of lands relinquished and lands retained. The land officer also received a form for "an abstract of further credits," to show the debtor's balance on every tract, and the amount due, the amount paid, and so forth. Or if the debtor chose to pay at the discount of 37½ per cent, a third form transcribed this information. Meigs intended that these three forms should serve as a "day-book" and provide the data for a final journal, to be written up at a future time "when the press of business shall have subsided so as to allow you leisure for that purpose." Another form listed the names of eligibles who did not take advantage of the Relief Act by September 30, and involved a search through the complete record of sales under the credit system. And the register also had forms for "certificate of further credit" in case of relinquishment and another where no lands were relinquished. With each relinquishment the register had to open a new account between the government and the purchaser. There were two forms of final certificates: one for tracts paid for in cash; another

---

27. *Liberty Hall and Cincinnati Gazette*, May 9, June 18, 1821. Also note the *Edwardsville Spectator*, June 5, 26, 1821; Huntsville *Alabama Republican*, June 29, 1821.
28. E.g., Peyton S. Symmes to Meigs, NA: GLO, Ltrs. Recd., Reg. & Rec., Cincinnati, 37: June 8, 1821; Wyllys Silliman to Meigs, *ibid.*, Zanesville, 43: June 23, 1821; Reasin Beall to Meigs, *ibid.*, Wooster, 41: July 7, 1821.

for lands with payment completed by relinquishment of other tracts of lands. Meigs enclosed detailed instructions to solve the mysteries of these stacks of printed blanks. The receivers received an equally abundant and bewildering set of forms. The commissioner reminded his land officers that by January 1, 1822, they should submit to Washington a report of lands relinquished, the quantity of lands fully paid for—both by transfer of land and by cash at the discount—and the quantity of lands on which further credit had been taken.[29]

Meigs and his clerks committed the first batch of forms to the mail on June 28, almost four months after the passage of the Relief Act and slightly more than three months before its expiration. The mails were slow, the schedules were unreliable, the large crates of forms were bulky and difficult to handle. Land offices in Ohio acknowledged the receipt of their parcels the second week in July; those in Indiana, a week later. The largest number of debtors were in regions most remote: Alabama, Illinois, and Missouri. The forms reached Cahaba (Alabama) on August 14; Franklin (Missouri) officers had forms on August 2 but no instructions until August 16.[30]

Land officers immediately expressed dissatisfaction about the complexity and numbers of the forms and doubted the feasibility of carrying out the law in the few weeks before its expiration. Edward Coles, the register at Edwardsville, wrote Meigs, "I have found it difficult to understand some of the forms, and have already experienced considerable embarrassment in disposing of cases which have occurred, agreeably to my understanding of the forms prescribed." Coles voiced "apprehension that there will not be sufficient time now left to complete the business, in the manner prescribed, in the time limited by law." Another register expressed admiration for the procedures and forms adopted and added, "There is nothing wanting but sufficient time to carry it into complete effect." David Hoge of Steubenville viewed the problems as "insurmountable, considering the shortness of time . . . the calculations alone could not be done in the time allowed." Sheer numbers made compliance impossible. Samuel Gwath-

29. Meigs to Crawford, *ibid.*, Ltrs. Sent, Misc., 11: May 31, June 6, 1821; circular to land officers, *ibid.*, June 1, 15, 1821.
30. Reasin Beall to Meigs, *ibid.*, Ltrs. Recd., Reg. & Rec., Wooster, 41: July 14, 1821; David Hoge to Meigs, *ibid.*, Steubenville, 39: July 17, 1821; Samuel Gwathmey to Meigs, *ibid.*, Jeffersonville, 19: July 9, 1821; Alexander Pope to Meigs, *ibid.*, Cahaba, 1: Aug. 14, 1821; Charles Carroll to Meigs, *ibid.*, Franklin, 31: Aug. 2, 1821; Thomas A. Smith to Meigs, *ibid.*, Aug. 16, 1821.

mey of Jeffersonville calculated that if he and his clerks worked constantly in the time remaining, they could meet the needs of only half the debtors in the district.[31]

When Meigs called for information on how many forms were needed, the numbers of debtors became evident. The receiver at Chillicothe estimated that twelve hundred purchasers in his district fell under the Relief Act, but that three or four hundred of that number would not attend to their tracts "in time to derive any benefit from the law." From Steubenville, "one of the oldest land districts," with "innumerable" open accounts, came a similar story. At Jeffersonville the register and the receiver needed "at least twice as many Abstracts of Land relinquished as have been recd"; while the Cincinnati office required another six hundred relinquishment forms and two thousand more declarations.[32] In the South the situation was even worse. Charles Carroll wrote from Franklin, "You may judge the mass of business to be done at this Office, as we have issued 4000 certificates & they are held by nearly two thousand Individuals & were they to come in regularly every day, we have barely enough time to receive them & can attend to nothing else." At Cahaba, one of the centers of the land office business, the receiver estimated that of the "8300 Certificates granted here for Land sold prior to 1st of July 1820 . . . it is presumed however that no more than ⅓ will be surrendered. . . ."[33]

In spite of their objections, land officers worked diligently to carry out the provisions of the Relief Act. By newspaper, broadside, letters, and word of mouth, they spread the news that their offices were ready to give assistance under the law. Soon debtors began to appear: squatters, speculators, bona fide settlers. All had purchased at a time of great prosperity and unfounded optimism. Now they sought to save what they could. The scene repeated itself again and again at the land offices scattered throughout the West.

Just as Huntsville had been the center of the most active sales, now

31. Coles to Meigs, *ibid.*, Edwardsville, 12: Aug. 6, 1821; Hoge to Meigs, *ibid.*, Steubenville, 39: July 14, 20, 17, 1821; Samuel Gwathmey to Meigs, *ibid.*, Jeffersonville, 19: July 9, 1821.
32. Alexander Bourne to Meigs, *ibid.*, Chillicothe, 36: July 14, 1821; David Hoge to Meigs, *ibid.*, Steubenville, 39: July 16, 1821; Samuel Gwathmey to Meigs, *ibid.*, Jeffersonville, 19: July 17, 1821; Peyton Symmes to Meigs, *ibid.*, Cincinnati, 37: July 25, 1821.
33. Carroll to Meigs, *ibid.*, Franklin, 31: Aug. 2, 1821; Alexander Pope to Meigs, *ibid.*, Cahaba, 1: Aug. 14, 1821.

it offered perhaps the most dramatic example of men seeking to divest themselves of their lands and their debts. From the moment the forms and instructions arrived, the *Alabama Republican* reported, "the Register's Office in this town, has at all times of the day from sun rise till dark, exhibited one of the most bustling scenes we have ever witnessed." Men came from everywhere, continued the account, "from Georgia, North and South Carolina, Virginia, Tennessee and Kentucky, besides the immense crowds from every county, and indeed every neighbourhood in this district. . . ." They stood in long lines waiting for the land office to open in the morning, then surged inside,

all struggling for precedent in filing their declarations, and relinquishments of certificates in conformity to the provisions of the act. [The forms completed,] it is amusing to see the impetuous anxiety of some and the patient forbearance of others in presenting their papers to the examination of the Register, who stands at his desk from morning till night and with a scrutinizing glance decides on the accuracy or informity of the documents offered for his inspection and either silently folds them up and receives the fees or returns them to the half-distracted applicant with a laconic and heart-rending sentence, *"Take them back, they are wrong."*

Benjamin Pope, the register, had no time for explanations and "neither entreaties or promises can induce him to say another word on the subject. . . ." Many debtors failed to understand "the endless intricacies and perplexing forms prescribed at the General Land Office in Washington City. . . ." These sought assistance from their friends or the numerous lawyers who quickly set up shop and did their own land office business in making out the forms for a substantial fee. That "the time specified for doing this business was altogether inadequate to the magnitude of the transactions of this office" was obvious to all observers. Sadly embarrassed as were the debtors, the land officers suffered even more; and "from the appearance of the immense heaps of papers filed in the Register's Office, we should judge there was employment for years to come, to record the applications, make out the quarterly returns and issue the new certificates." [34]

The Cahaba land office was also one of the busiest, and its officers were among the most sorely tried. Alexander Pope, the receiver, wrote Meigs, "Scarcely a day has passed since we commenced doing busi-

34. Huntsville *Alabama Republican*, Sept. 28, 1821.

ness but what I have stood up at my desk from 8 or 9 OClock in the morning until 9 OClock in the evening receiving and examining the papers handed in for record and this too in a crowd frequently of 20 or 30 persons asking questions at the same time." But Pope had more to complain about. The late summer was a time of sickness in Alabama, and "many persons have taken up the idea that a Contagious disease prevailed and to prevent their being affected have prepared themselves with some Asafitida-Garlic Onions and all sorts of noxious and strong smelling things not a little to my annoyance or my comfort." [35]

Petitions for relief under the law had to be filed by September 30, and Josiah Meigs expected to have complete reports on the operation of the Relief Act by January 1, 1822. He was disappointed. "It will not be practicable to complete the whole of the returns by the 1st of January," wrote Samuel Gwathmey from Jeffersonville. "You may judge of the Mass of business that has resulted from the Relief law, when I tell you that at least 800 final Certificates and upwards of 2500 Certificates of further credit will issue under the law." The register of the land office at Cahaba presided over the relinquishment of 308,790.45 acres, final payment for 118,845.45 acres, and further credit for 78,360.25 acres.[36] When Meigs attempted to spur his officers to promptness, he aroused only bitterness. Obadiah Jones wrote from Huntsville:

Untill the Books can be brought up, under the *small matter* Call'd the *Relief Bill*, I cannot see it possible for me to send you a transcript, & altho', I presume there is not more (on the average) than 30 times as much to do in this Office, as there is in the other Offices of the Un. States, I am fearful it will be a tedious time before I can possibly do it, or even (at great expense) *have* it done, for we, in the *back woods* Country, can only One write in the Book at the same time.[37]

As the district land officers struggled with their work, Congress considered supplementary relief measures. Some persons had not taken

35. Alexander Pope to Meigs, NA: GLO, Ltrs. Recd., Reg. & Rec., Cahaba, 1: Sept. 18, 1821.
36. Gwathmey to Meigs, *ibid.*, Jeffersonville, 19: Oct. 10, 1821; *Cahawba Press and Alabama State Intelligencer*, Feb. 25, 1822.
37. Obadiah Jones to Comm. GLO, NA: GLO, Ltrs. Recd., Reg. & Rec., Huntsville, 5: Oct. 3, 1823.

advantage of the first law. Debtors frequently lacked information or did not hear of the law. In some cases the distance to the land office made compliance impossible, or so it was claimed. Moreover, the tardy and complicated administration of the first law had denied to some the benefits that should have been theirs. No sooner had Congress met in December 1821 than Representative William B. Rochester of New York asked the Secretary of the Treasury for a report on the operation of the relief law. Josiah Meigs "regretted" the lack of information. He presented a partial report composed of returns from seven land offices in the Old Northwest. The total relinquishments of public lands at these seven offices were fewer than the numbers of acres relinquished at the Huntsville office alone. From the states of Alabama, Missouri, and Illinois, where most of the land office business had taken place, and where resided most of the debtors, only one land office (Shawneetown) had forwarded returns.[38]

Some members of Congress were determined to offer additional relief. Early in the session two Senators from debtor states, John Williams Walker of Alabama and David Barton of Missouri, introduced a bill to extend the Relief Act of 1821 to September 30, 1822.[39] It made rapid progress through the Senate. The sponsors declared:

> Shortness of the time allowed, after the passage of the late act, for the purchasers to make the necessary application to the land offices, the injustice of excluding a great portion of them, who were actually unable to make application in time, after the necessary instructions and forms reached the different land offices, in preparing and forwarding which much of the time allowed by the act was consumed, and leaving very little for a compliance with the law, by those for whose relief it was intended, &c.

The *Western Herald* of Steubenville commented, "The bill is of much importance to those who, owing to their distance from the Land Office, ignorance of the law, or the inability of the officers to transact their business in consequence of the shortness of time, were unable to take advantage of the law of last session." Some land officers also urged indulgence on the same grounds, emphasizing those debtors

38. *Annals of Congress,* 17 Cong., 1 Sess., 38: 587–88; *House Executive Documents,* 17 Cong., 1 Sess., #19: 5.
39. *Annals of Congress,* 17 Cong., 1 Sess., 38: 371; *Western Herald & Steubenville Gazette,* April 20, 1822; Thomas Smith and John Miller to Meigs, NA: GLO, Ltrs. Recd., Reg. & Rec., Franklin, 31: Feb. 1, 1822.

who lived at a distance or suffered from legal obstacles.[40] The bill was passed by both houses of Congress with little opposition.

In spite of the news circulated by the district land officers, the debtors showed little interest in the extension of relief. The new indulgence brought no reduction in the land debt comparable to the $8,778,505.27 lopped off by the first law. Considering the liberal discount and the small sums received, the *Alabama Republican* concluded that "but few who have taken further credit on their lands, ever intend paying for them." Land officers suggested that those who desired to take action had done so under the first law.[41]

In 1823, Congress passed another extension of the Relief Act, but it too, drew little response.[42] Two acts in 1824 dealt only with those debtors who had taken further credit under one of the earlier relief acts, and one offered inducements for them to close their accounts with the government.[43] Debtors responded in large numbers to this offer of government amnesty, and the laws of 1824 reduced the debt for public lands by another $3,300,000. On June 30, 1825, the entire debt stood at $6,322,765.64½. The Commissioner of the General Land Office reported that the provision permitting relinquishment was the greatest single factor in reducing the debt. He wrote, "The lands thus relinquished are, for the most part, those which were purchased at the highest prices. . . ."[44] The whole relief experience seemed to show that the ultimate purpose of the administration of the public lands and the laws laid down by Congress was to distribute the public domain to the citizens of the nation as rapidly and with as little cost to them as possible. In these respects, the relief laws passed between

40. 3 Stat. 665–66 (April 20, 1822); *Annals of Congress,* 17 Cong., 1 Sess., 38: 581.
41. *Brookville Enquirer,* July 30, 1822; Huntsville *Alabama Republican,* Oct. 18, 1822; Gwathmey to Comm. GLO, NA: GLO, Ltrs. Recd., Reg. & Rec., Jeffersonville, 19: Dec. 8, 1822; Jesse Spencer to Meigs, *ibid.,* Chillicothe, 36: May 16, 1822.
42. 3 Stat. 781 (March 3, 1823); Circular to Registers, NA: GLO, Ltrs. Sent, Misc., 12: July 14, 1823; Alexander Pope to George Graham, *ibid.,* Ltrs. Recd., Reg. & Rec., Cahaba, 2: Aug. 30, 1823.
43. 4 Stat. 24–25 (May 18, 1824); 4 Stat. 60 (May 26, 1824).
44. *American State Papers, Public Lands,* 4: 482; 790–95. Two further acts extended indulgence to the debtor until the close of the decade: 4 Stat. 158–59 (May 4, 1826); 4 Stat. 259–60 (March 21, 1828). Even then Congress was not finished. Additional laws in 1831 and 1832 extended the relief business until 1833: 4 Stat. 445–46 (Feb. 25, 1831); 4 Stat. 567–68 (July 9, 1832).

1821 and 1832 were a great success, despite difficulty and confusion of administration.

Another class of purchasers now appeared to demand relief—those whose lands had been forfeited for failure to meet payments. By 1828 a movement to reimburse the victims of forfeitures had gained substantial support in both houses of Congress. The commissioner viewed the whole idea as absurd. The passage of such a law would negate the effect of the relief laws. He could see no reason why "those persons who have had an opportunity to liquidate their debt by relinquishment and have failed to do so, should be reimbursed the money paid and forfeited." [45] Congress compromised and granted relief in the form of certificates good as payment for public lands in the amount of the forfeited sum, but it excepted those who had taken further credit under the act of 1821.[46] Whatever the explicit exceptions, the law gave the impression that additional legislation would soon include those who had taken advantage of the Relief Act of 1821, and debtors felt no urgency to discharge their obligations. Writing a year later, the commissioner commented that the terms of the early relief acts were "liberal," and that

> there is no doubt that the purchasers would have very generally closed their accounts but for the premature passage of the Act of 23d May 1828 authorizing Certifs to be issued for the money forfeited on Lands that had not been further credited and the purchasers of which were not entitled to the benefit of the relief laws, waive[d] that relief under the expectation that the money paid & forfeited would be refunded & particularly those who purchased at high prices and who expected to obtain the Land on a resale for less money than the amount forfeited.[47]

The extension of further credit undermined the provisions of the Relief Act of 1821; by removing the threat of financial loss by forfeiture, the new law of 1828 thwarted any attempt to reduce the public land debt.

The administrative burden of the laws fell heavily on the district land officers, and their compensation soon became a vital issue. Under

45.   George Graham to Senator David Barton (Mo.), NA: GLO, Ltrs. Sent, Misc., 20: Jan. 15, 1828.
46.   4 Stat. 286–88 (May 23, 1828).
47.   Graham to Samuel Ingham, Sec. Treas., NA: TD, Ltrs. from Comm. GLO to Sec. Treas., 8: Aug. 1, 1829.

the act of 1821 registers received 50 cents for each relinquishment or declaration of further credit they recorded; receivers collected fees only for relinquishments. As early as July 9, 1821, Samuel Gwathmey of Jeffersonville complained to Meigs about the pay, "If the fee stated in the law shall be considered all the pay to which we shall be entitled, the most favourable construction which can possibly be put upon the act will not give more than a reasonable compensation for carrying into operation a System, the perplexity & labour of which you can hardly conceive when reduced to practice." The Relief Act, "when reduced to practice," became even more taxing than the most pessimistic officer had expected. The central issue was clerk hire. From the relatively quiet district of Steubenville (Ohio), David Hoge commented, "Other registers may judge for themselves; but I must declare my decided conviction that the law cannot be executed without allowing clerk hire for one year, at least at the rate of not less than seven hundred and fifty dollars, or giving the register a salary that will enable him to procure the necessary assistance." [48] Meigs responded that such relief was the prerogative of Congress, and the Treasury Department had no latitude to meet the unusual expenses of land officers. Nonetheless, he wrote, "There is every reason to expect at the next session of Congress some suitable provision will be made in favor of the land officers for the additional trouble caused by the late act." [49]

When the rush to the land offices began in mid-July and early August, land officers could no longer wait for Congressional action. In part because of Meigs's promise and to a larger degree out of sheer necessity, the district land officers everywhere employed clerks, impressed their families and relatives into service, and even worked themselves. From Kaskaskia, Michael Jones wrote, "I have had for some time four clerks, and never less than three, employed in my office; the duties are very arduous, and will require much labour and time to complete the whole accurately, and I trust the government will allow the registers compensation commensurate with their service, a per centum on all land relinquished would, in fact, not amount to an adequate reward for the additional services required of them."

48. Gwathmey to Meigs, NA: GLO, Ltrs. Recd., Reg & Rec., Jeffersonville, 19: July 9, 1821; Hoge to Meigs, *ibid.*, Steubenville, 39: July 14, 1821.
49. Meigs to Hoge, *ibid.*, Ltrs. Sent, Misc., 11: Aug. 15, 1821; Meigs to Beverley R. Grayson, *ibid.*, Aug. 30, 1821.

Another thought that the "compensation allowed is by no means adequate to the labor performed." At Vincennes, John Badollet employed five extra clerks, many of them for nearly two full years. Other land officers faced the same situation. "The relief act crowded an immense mass of business within a small space of time, and has increased the labor and expense of the office two-thirds," explained George Strother, the St. Louis receiver.[50]

Several land officers considered the operation of the Relief Act part of their usual duties and charged the government 1 per cent commission in their accounts. Edward Coles thought this justifiable. George Strother, the St. Louis receiver, did also. In Washington, Mississippi, Joseph Dunbar arbitrarily charged the government $500 for an assistant because of the "excessive labour necessary to the completion of the duties prescribed under the act of March 2, 1821. . . ."[51] The Comptroller of the Treasury disallowed the commission charges of Coles and Strother, as well as the special compensation of Dunbar. Relief must come through an act of Congress. Yet Congress in 1822 tabled a bill that would have provided supplementary compensation.[52] The next year a similar measure also failed. Land officers were understandably angry. William Christy of St. Louis wrote:

If Congress have thought proper to pass laws, the effect of which has been to bring five times the labour & expense into this Office which otherwise would not have occurred, I hope they have also left sufficient discretionary power in the Treasury Department to compensate the Officers of the Department for all extra services, at least to shield them from loss & oppression. I have now three clerks employed in my office & have had from one to three since the commence of the relinquishment business, I have received about $1000—fees by Relinquishment and I can readily show that $2000 would not reimburse the amount which I have paid and shall have to pay before all the business created by the Relinquishment system shall be finished.[53]

50.   Jones to Meigs, *ibid.*, Ltrs. Recd., Reg. & Rec., Kaskaskia, 13: Nov. 2, 1821; Badollet to Albert Gallatin, Sept. 10, 1823, Gayle Thornbrough, ed., *The Correspondence of John Badollet and Albert Gallatin, 1804–1836* (Indiana Historical Society Publications, Vol. 22, Indianapolis, 1963), 259–60; Strother to Comm. GLO, NA: GLO, Ltrs. Recd., Reg. & Rec., St. Louis, 34: Dec. 4, 1823.
51.   Coles to Meigs, *ibid.*, Edwardsville, 12: Feb. 12, 1822; Strother to Meigs, *ibid.*, St. Louis, 34: Dec. 4, 1823; Dunbar to Meigs, *ibid.*, Washington, 30a: Jan. 2, 1823.
52.   *Annals of Congress*, 17 Cong., 2 Sess., 40: 362–63.
53.   William Christy to Comm. GLO, NA: GLO, Ltrs. Recd., Reg. & Rec., St. Louis, 34: March 23, 1824.

The land officers at Washington, Mississippi, threatened to resign and, only with the pleas of the commissioner and the Secretary of the Treasury, could be persuaded to remain at their posts.[54]

In 1826, Congress finally passed by a narrow margin a bill to compensate the registers and the receivers for their services in executing the Relief Act of 1821. Under the law, the next to the last one signed for the session, the Secretary of the Treasury had the power to fix compensation, but the figure should not exceed the cost of clerk hire and ½ per cent of the amount of payments made by relinquishments and discounts, with the value of the relinquished lands computed at two dollars per acre. The limit on compensation was $3,000 per year. Land officers rejoiced in the recognition of their services and the "liberal" provisions of the law.[55]

But it was not easy for district land officers to collect what they thought was owed them. The Comptroller of the Treasury honored no claims without receipts. Many of the land offices had new officers; the incumbents of 1821 and 1822 had long since departed, as had many of those who had served as clerks in time of need. Others had done the work themselves or with the aid of members of their families, for which they had issued no receipts. In cases where vouchers could not be found, the commissioner recommended the submission of the best possible evidence of the amounts paid and the services rendered by the clerks. In setting the rate of clerk hire, the Secretary of the Treasury turned to the commissioner for recommendations. In general, the latter felt that the duties of the register were "very pressing & arduous involving more details than those of the Recr & that altho both officers keep similar books as to the general and individual accounts yet the labor of the Register exceeded that of the Receiver from two causes one of which was the greater variety of books kept by the former & the other from the circumstance of his having to act on all cases in the first instance & to prepare documents for the Recr as authority for his action."[56] For an official interpretation of the law, the Secretary of the Treasury appealed to the Attorney General, who defined the act

54. Beverley R. Grayson to Graham, *ibid.*, Washington, 30a: Jan. 1, March 30, 1824; Joseph Dunbar to Graham, *ibid.*, June 28, 1824.
55. 4 Stat. 193 (May 22, 1826); Peyton Symmes to Comm. GLO, NA: GLO, Ltrs. Recd., Reg. & Rec., Cincinnati, 37: Aug. 8, 1826.
56. George Graham to Alexander Pope, *ibid.*, Ltrs. Sent, Misc., 18: Dec. 5, 1826; Graham to Sec. Treas., NA: TD, Ltrs. from Comm. GLO to Sec. Treas., 7: April 28, 1827.

narrowly and authorized no compensation "except where there has been an expenditure actually incurred in clerk-hire by the register or receiver." The Secretary followed this decision.[57]

The Relief Act of 1821 has been called "a combination of statesmanship and political expediency. . . ."[58] It displayed little statesmanship. Its avowed purpose was the rapid and efficient reduction of the large debt that had grown out of the land office business in the years before the panic of 1819; it achieved this purpose by means of an administrative nightmare. The most notable accomplishment of the act was the introduction of the principle of further credit. Innumerable purchasers in the "flush times" refused to relinquish their lands in hopes of a continuing indulgence from the government. For a dozen years, until 1833, Congress met their expectations and passed ten supplementary relief acts. Yet the Relief Act was good politics. It managed to keep much of the land that had been sold between 1815 and 1820 in the hands of the purchasers, and to this extent it probably served the national purpose.

57.   William Wirt to Rush, *ibid.*, Opinions of the Atty. Genl., March 20, 1828; Graham to Sec. Treas., *ibid.*, Ltrs. from Comm. GLO to Sec. Treas., 8: March 13, 1829; Graham to John Badollet, NA: GLO, Ltrs. Sent, Misc., 19: May 16, 1827.
58.   Bailey, *John Williams Walker*, 167. Senator Walker of Alabama was one of the principal authors and supporters of the measure.

During the 1820's the flow of population to the West slowed but did not cease. Settlers moved farther up the Wabash River and by 1830 covered the southern two-thirds of the State of Indiana. They pushed up the Illinois River, filled in the bounty land tract, and occupied much of the Sangamon River country. In Missouri they reached west from Boon's Lick to the Missouri River at its junction with the Kansas. By 1825 sizable numbers had settled along the Mississippi both above and below St. Louis, especially in the vicinity of the Salt River. In the South they pushed up the Arkansas River as far as Fort Smith. The lands of the Jackson's Creek Purchase in Alabama, which had attracted so much attention at the public sales in 1818 and 1819, were heavily settled, but formidable Indian tribes prevented expansion of white settlement into western Alabama and the northern half of Mississippi. The settlement of Louisiana continued slowly, hampered by confusion over private claims and the failure of the government to prepare the public lands for sale. The West also was expanding in other respects: in political power and in economic strength.[1]

The two dominant characteristics of the land business were the uncertainty of its administrators and the parsimony of Congress. Along with the modest land sales and diminished migration, confusion and chaos plagued the land business in the 1820's. The Treasury Depart-

1. On the advance of population into the West in the 1820's, see Buley, *The Old Northwest*, 2: 43–57; Esarey, *History of Indiana*, 1: 310–15; Arthur Clinton Boggess, *The Settlement of Illinois, 1778–1830* (Chicago Historical Society's Collection, Vol. 5, Chicago, 1908), 139–45; Hattie M. Anderson, "Missouri, 1804–1828; Peopling a Frontier State," *Missouri Historical Review*, 31 (1937): 171–74; Frederick Jackson Turner, "The Colonization of the West, 1820–1830," *American Historical Review*, 11 (1906): 303–27; Frederick Jackson Turner, *Rise of the New West, 1819–1829*, Albert Bushnell Hart, ed., *The American Nation: A History*, Vol. 18 (New York, 1906).

ment and the General Land Office, amidst changing personnel, struggled with a variety of problems such as the continuing issue of private land claims, and the endless questions presented by a growing and moving people whose interest was centered on the public domain.

Adding to the confusion and disorder in Washington and in the various district land offices was a drive for retrenchment in Congress. The financial problems of the federal government that had begun with the War of 1812 and the postwar policies of the Second Bank of the United States were intensified by the financial crisis of 1819 and the subsequent depression. In 1820, Congress forced major retrenchments on the military establishment, and, at the next session a standing Committee on Retrenchment was established to investigate the expenses of administering the government. The *Illinois Gazette* of Shawneetown commented that Congress had begun to display "an extraordinary zeal for investigation and retrenchment."[2]

During this decade personnel changes also unsettled the land business. On September 4, 1822, Josiah Meigs, the conscientious Commissioner of the General Land Office, died after a short illness. President James Monroe spoke of the late commissioner as an "admirable man" and expressed concern "more particularly by the distressed state in which he leaves his family." Hezekiah Niles added that Meigs was "one of the best of men and most faithful of officers."[3] Josiah Meigs was a Republican bureaucrat of the old school, more at home in the rational world of Albert Gallatin than the hectic political struggles of William H. Crawford. He had indeed rendered valuable service by his longevity in office, but he was not equipped by temperament or tradition to handle the great stresses placed on the administrative system by the postwar land office business.

After considering a number of candidates for Commissioner of the General Land Office, President Monroe chose John McLean, then a justice of the Supreme Court of Ohio and, in Monroe's words, "so useful in the late war."[4] McLean was born in Morris County, New Jersey, in 1785. In the remaining years of the century his family went to

2. White, *The Jeffersonians*, 119–25; Shawneetown *Illinois Gazette*, May 25, 1822.
3. Monroe to Crawford, Sept. 7, 1822, Monroe Papers (microfilm), Princeton University Library; *Niles Weekly Register*, 23: 32 (Sept. 14, 1822).
4. Monroe to Crawford, Sept. 7, 1822, Monroe Papers (microfilm), Princeton University Library.

Virginia, Kentucky, and finally to Ohio. He was self-educated; and in 1803 he settled in Cincinnati, where he read law with Arthur St. Clair. After admittance to the bar in 1807, McLean married and moved to Lebanon, where he founded the *Western Star* and quickly established himself as a leading lawyer. In 1811 and 1812 he served as inspector of the Cincinnati land office. During his two terms in Congress (1813–1816), McLean supported the Administration and served on the House Committee on Public Lands. He resigned in 1816 to become an associate justice of the Supreme Court of the State of Ohio, a post that he filled with distinction for the next six years. For Josiah Meigs the commissionership was a final reward in a life of disappointment and frustrated ambitions; for John McLean it was a temporary office in a career of distinguished public service that would eventually lead to the Supreme Court of the United States.[5]

Within nine months of taking office John McLean resigned to accept an appointment as Postmaster General. He had made no significant impact on the administration of the public lands. This time President Monroe turned to George Graham, who had been a leading candidate for the position on the death of Josiah Meigs, but he had removed himself from consideration on the grounds that "the appointment ought to be conferred on some person in the western country." Graham was from an important and influential Virginia family. He graduated from Columbia in 1790, became a lawyer, and served in the Virginia Assembly, where he knew both Madison and Monroe. After brief military service at the outbreak of the War of 1812, between 1813 and 1823 Graham served as chief clerk in the Department of War, where he also carried out diplomatic missions for the Department of State.[6] In experience and outlook Graham was a career civil servant. He became Commissioner of the General Land Office on June 26, 1823, and served until his death in the summer of 1830.

The influence of the Treasury Department in the administration of the public lands waned noticeably in the 1820's. The strong hand of William H. Crawford was gone. In August 1823, Crawford suffered a

5. Francis P. Weisenburger, *Life of John McLean: A Politician on the Supreme Court* (Columbus, 1937), Chs. 1–2.
6. White, *The Jeffersonians*, 520; Walter Prichard, ed., "George Graham's Mission to Galveston in 1818: Two Important Documents Bearing Upon Louisiana History," *Louisiana Historical Quarterly*, 20 (1937): 619–50; George M. Stafford, ed., "The Autobiography of George Mason Graham," *ibid.*, 43–46.

stroke that left him blinded and bedridden, with his mental faculties impaired. Until his retirement from office on March 4, 1825, his work in the Treasury fell to a trusted clerk, Asbury Dickens, who transacted the routine business in a satisfactory manner but made no effort to influence Treasury policy in the manner of his strong-willed chief. Crawford's removal from the scene left a gap in the decision-making machinery of the land business and thrust wide authority into the hands of the Commissioner of the General Land Office.[7]

In 1825 the new President, John Quincy Adams, offered the Treasury Department to Crawford, who had the good sense to refuse and retire to his plantation. Adams then approached Albert Gallatin without success and finally turned to Richard Rush, the son of the illustrious physician-scientist Benjamin Rush. The younger Rush had chosen a career in law. He emerged on the public stage shortly after the turn of the century and became in succession Attorney General of Pennsylvania (1811), Comptroller of the Treasury (1811), Attorney General of the United States (1814–1817), and Ambassador to the Court of St. James's (1817–1825). Rush's career in government service had given him experience in a variety of fields. From his work in the comptroller's office he understood the operations of the Treasury Department and the government's finances. His years in London gave him a rich knowledge of English life and institutions, which he admired with a tinge of distrust, and provided him with a certain reputation as a diplomat. But the new Secretary of the Treasury had been out of the country between 1817 and his assumption of office in 1825. Indeed, Rush did not leave London until May 1825. He was orientated by temperament and experience more to the drawing rooms of London and Philadelphia than to the western country. To Richard Rush the public lands were simply another source of revenue for the nation, and a small one at that. He did nothing to diminish the power that had passed to the Commissioner of the General Land Office after Crawford's illness.[8]

One of the most confused and disorderly problems that plagued the land business in the 1820's was the management of the public domain

7. Philip Jackson Green, *The Life of William Harris Crawford* (Charlotte, 1965), 201–02, 213, 227. Green's study is an inadequate consideration of Crawford's career as Secretary of the Treasury.
8. John H. Powell, *Richard Rush, Republican Diplomat, 1780–1859* (Philadelphia, 1942), Chs. 1–6.

in Louisiana. A large number of private claims had to be judged, approved, confirmed, surveyed, and integrated into the general plat before the remainder of the public domain could be sold. The original grants made by the Spanish and French officials had passed from hand to hand, had been broken into smaller tracts, or had been sold to other parties. In the course of years the original documents had been lost or stolen or had yielded to the Louisiana climate. In Spanish Louisiana ownership had rested on a surveyed grant; the concept of a patent issued by a central government was unknown. Under the purchase treaty the United States Government had recognized these claims; but when it called for the presentation of claims for confirmation, numerous citizens would not bring forward their claims, fearful of being cheated by a new land system and alien officials. Language problems and the broken terrain further complicated the task. At the same time many settlers and Representatives in Congress demanded quick action on claims that covered some of the most attractive land in the state. A constant stream of Congressional legislation concerned with the Louisiana claims spoke eloquently of the confusion in the public domain there.[9] As late as the autumn of 1823 the Commissioner of the General Land Office disclosed that "there has never yet been a private claim from the State of Louisiana presented to this Office in shape on which a patent could issue." This was an astonishing confession of the degree and duration of the problem with the Lousiana claims, for the state had been under the jurisdiction of the United States for more than twenty years. The "wise, beautiful and perfect" land system of the Republic had not worked satisfactorily when imposed on the Franco-Spanish system.[10]

To facilitate settling the private claims, Congress had divided Louisiana into three districts; each had its own board of commissioners and its own principal deputy surveyor, who was under the supervision of the Surveyor General South of Tennessee. The St. Helena district was typical. On May 8, 1822, after more than fifteen years of work, the commissioners submitted their report to Congress, which confirmed three thousand claims.[11] Under the law the responsibility for locating the approved claims in the district, "spread over a

9. *Ante,* p. 40, n. 34.
10. George Graham to Levin Wailes, NA: TD, Sec. Treas. to Comm. GLO, 1821–27: Nov. 14, 1823.
11. 3 Stat. 707–08 (May 8, 1822).

great extent of country, and necessarily interfering with each other in all those parts of the district where the lands were valuable," fell to the register of the St. Helena land office, whose stipend was $500 per annum and a few minor fees. The incumbent was James M. Bradford, a lawyer and planter with some experience in the land business. "From having practiced law in all the parishes of the district for the last nine years, the situation of the land claims, the quality of the soil, and the general face of the country, is familiar to me . . . ," he wrote. But Bradford's experience in land and law did not prepare him for his first encounter with the papers of his new office: "a mass of confusion, which I am incompetent to describe." In the dark, humid room of the former clerk of the office he discovered "from 12 to 18 bundles of papers, wrapped in old newspapers, except the ends, which were exposed without order or method; and the balance of the papers of the office carelessly thrown into two trunks, rumpled, twisted and pressed down, as of no value." His predecessor had kept no record of the certificates issued, "nor is there an index to a single Book in the Office." In short, he concluded, "More confusion could not be imagined." [12] The new register predicted, "I feel convinced, from the knowledge I now possess, that a longer time will be required to complete the adjustment of the Land Claims in this district, than was contemplated by Congress, and that much that has been done, will have to be done again." [13]

Bradford was an efficient, energetic, able public officer, and he soon recognized that the salary and remunerations of the post were not commensurate with his talents. Like other skilled officers in the Louisiana tangle, he resigned within a year, his determination, enthusiasm, and sense of responsibility eroded by the impossibility of the task, the parsimony of the government in providing machinery for its solution, and the paucity of his own reward. In his parting letter he advised the government of the needs in the St. Helena district. Three years work remained, he wrote; and in order to procure the services of a suitable officer, the government should pay a good salary for the period. On the frontier, such as the St. Helena district, an honest man's talents were highly prized: "At St. Helena court-house a man

12. Bradford to Comm. GLO, NA: GLO, Ltrs. Recd., Reg. & Rec., St. Helena, 24a: Oct. 22, Nov. 5, 1822.
13. Bradford to Comm. GLO, *ibid.*, Nov. 15, 1822; June 14, July 8, Oct. 29, 1823.

can pursue nothing to make a living, and must consequently depend entirely on the salary. However humble a man's talents may be, if he can discharge the mechanical part of the duty of Register, and is trustworthy, he can make more than $500 in any of the parishes on the Mississippi in one year." The office called for high skills: its incumbent should be fluent in Spanish and French, for more than half the claims involved one or both of these languages; and he should be knowledgeable in law and have a good reputation in the community. The government should not expect to acquire the services of such a man for less than $1,500 to $2,000 per year. With these parting words Bradford went back to his plantation and the practice of law, and the three thousand unsurveyed claims lay unattended.[14]

Commissioner Graham used the same arguments in describing the situation to Congress:

It is evident that the act of 8th May, 1822, has imposed duties on the Register and Receiver more arduous, and having a greater tendency to bring them into collision with their neighbors and fellow-citizens, than those required under the general provisions of the law in relation to officers of that description [he wrote]. It is not, therefore, to be expected that, in a section of the country where labor is high, and talent can be profitably employed, the Government can command the services of individuals qualified by their independence of character and discriminating powers of mind, to adjust these claims speedily and satisfactorily, unless a more adequate compensation for their services shall be given.[15]

Commissioners of land claims were supposed to observe the laws, usages, and customs of the Spanish government, but confirmed claims had to be surveyed under the rectangular system—adopted by the Government of the United States—by a United States surveyor. The old Spanish and French claims specified frontage and depth on a given watercourse. As for the rectangular surveying system, "nothing like Townships, Ranges & Sections being known in this Country, it being totally unsusceptible of such divisions," the register, Samuel Harper, wrote from New Orleans. The reason was the topography of the land. Henry Bry, receiver at Ouachita, wrote that the land lent it-

14. Bradford and William Kinchen to Comm. GLO, Oct. 29, 1823, *American State Papers, Public Lands,* 3: 636; Bradford to Comm. GLO, Jan. 5, 1824, *ibid.,* 636–37.
15. Graham to Senator John Gaillard (S.C.), Dec. 22, 1823, *ibid.,* 632.

self to the old system: "Nature did not make our water courses in a Straight line and we must do the best we can with the meanders of our rivers." [16] Upon recommendation of the Surveyor General South of Tennessee, John McLean advised Secretary Crawford that the traditional rectangular system must be modified to meet the special needs of Louisiana. He wrote: "From the slight examination which I have given to the subject, I am inclined to believe, that the best plan would be, to run the township and range lines, without regards to those claims, and in issuing patents, each tract may be designated by its number, in a certain township and range. . . ." [17] In 1824, Congress passed a law directing the President, at his discretion, to modify the rectangular system. [18]

The responsibility for the survey of the confirmed claims in Louisiana rested with the Surveyor General South of Tennessee. The three principal deputies gave an initial inspection to the surveys made in their districts, but the surveyor general appointed the principal deputies, hired the deputy surveyors, and signed all the surveys made within his district as evidence of his approval. After serving in this critical post for eleven years, Thomas Freeman died in 1821. Although some complaints had arisen over his failure to prepare the Creek Purchase for a quick public sale, and Congress had provided for a separate surveyor general for the Alabama Territory, Freeman had accomplished much. As his successor, President Monroe appointed Levin Wailes. Born into an influential Maryland family, Wailes moved to Georgia in 1792 and there represented Robert Morris's North American Land Company. It was in this capacity that he learned how to survey. His skills were many, and within a few years he was judged one of the best surveyors on the early frontier of the Southwest. Lured by the promise of the new lands in Mississippi, he moved his family there to Washington in 1807. Seth Pease found him to be a trustworthy, skilled surveyor and gave him steady employment. In 1810, Wailes accepted an appointment as register of the Opelousas land office, where he served continuously until his appointment as surveyor general. [19]

16. Harper to Meigs, NA: GLO, Ltrs. Recd., Reg. & Rec., New Orleans, 23: Sept. 4, 1822; Bry to Meigs, *ibid.*, Ouachita, 24: Aug. 17, 1822.
17. McLean to Crawford, *ibid.*, Ltrs. Sent, Misc., 12: June 19, 1823.
18. 4 Stat. 34 (May 24, 1824). Congress had modified the rectangular survey in Louisiana as early as 1811. 2 Stat. 662–66 (March 3, 1811).
19. Charles S. Sydnor, *A Gentleman of the Old Natchez Region: Benjamin L. C. Wailes* (Durham, 1938), 32–40.

Commissioner Graham's instructions to the new surveyor general emphasized that the object of the work was "to secure the prompt, uniform, and economical survey of private confirmed claims and pre-emptions in the several land districts." Graham also suggested that the success of the operation depended in large part on the ability of Wailes to establish pleasant but firm relations with his three principal deputy surveyors: Silas Dinsmoor, east of Orleans; John Dinsmore, southwestern district; and John Wilson, southeastern district.[20] Within a few weeks of taking office Wailes had alienated the principal deputies by his arrogant, unsympathetic manner and aroused the animosity of the deputy surveyors by his exalted standards of accuracy. "There is not one Deputy in my employ, who has received more than part payment for work return to, and examined & approved in this office," complained Silas Dinsmoor. The "unseasonable Delay" wrought great hardships on men who had borrowed money at 20 per cent in order to outfit their parties. By mid-1824, Wailes's stringent requirements had brought the surveying business in Louisiana to a complete halt.[21] When Graham's letters grew sharp and admonished Wailes that "the gentlemen who compose the delegation from Mississippi & Louisiana are very much dissatisfied with the state of the Surveying Department in your District particularly as it respects the situation of the private claims," Wailes refused to answer his mail. He would not even acknowledge receipt of letters from the General Land Office. Graham sent fifteen letters in the first three months of 1824, and "to no one of these letters has a direct answer been given, so far as I recollect, by Mr. Wailes." [22] At Graham's urging, President Monroe finally removed Levin Wailes.

The next Surveyor General South of Tennessee was George Davis. Davis came to the job after a long and interesting frontier career in which he had frequently been associated with men and enterprises of importance but had himself never risen above quarrelsome mediocrity. He appeared on the stage in 1805, when he recommended himself to President Thomas Jefferson as a proper person to accompany an expedition up the Red River. Jefferson was impressed with Davis's mathematical accomplishments and suggested that he would be "the fittest person to take the direction of the expedition. . . ." William

20. Graham to Wailes, NA: GLO, Ltrs. Sent, SG, 3: July 27, Sept. 12, 1823.
21. Dinsmoor to Graham, *ibid.*, Ltrs. Recd., SG, Miss., 54a: Sept. 28, 1823.
22. Graham to Wailes, NA: TD, Sec. Treas. to Comm. GLO, 1821–27: Nov. 14, 1823; Graham to George Davis, NA: GLO, Ltrs. Sent, SG, 3: June 30, 1824.

Dunbar of Natchez received this news unhappily, for he knew of Davis and wanted no part of him. "Mr. Briggs and myself have both discovered that he is a very improper person; he is of so unhappy a disposition that we cannot think that any harmony would exist in the party where he might be placed only as a subordinate character, much less would he be fit to exercise any authority," Dunbar wrote to the President. "He is of a most jealous temper & seems continually upon the watch to take offence which he scruples not to express in rude terms." [23] Davis did not make the trip, but he continued to work as a deputy surveyor in Louisiana and Mississippi, alternately quitting and then returning to seek employment. He was an accomplished technician and mathematician in a profession and place where physical courage and stamina counted for more than scientific achievement. In appointing him surveyor general, President Monroe was either ignorant of or inclined to overlook Dunbar's advice that Davis was not "fit to exercise any authority." Davis took the oath of office on June 1, 1824, about a year after Graham became Commissioner of the General Land Office.

The administration of the surveying district South of Tennessee by George Davis and his correspondence with various public officials was a bizarre fantasy in which one absurdity followed another until the responsible bureaucrat George Graham was driven to distraction. Such was the confidence and even arrogance of George Davis, and such was the indecision of the General Land Office and the President, that Davis held office for almost four full years. He was an indefatigable correspondent, and during these years his letters to the Secretary of the Treasury, the Commissioner of the General Land Office, the principal deputy surveyors, and the deputies ran to more than three thousand pages. Of Davis, one of his deputies wrote, "It will then be asked how does he employ his time let the Voluminous correspondence (and wholly useless) around the country answer. . . ." Davis was also an unbounded egotist with sufficient mathematical skills to make him a pedant. In the course of his administration he ignored instructions from the Commissioner of the General Land Office, the Secretary of the Treasury, the Comptroller of the Treasury, the first Auditor of

23. Jefferson to Dunbar, May 25, 1805, Mrs. Dunbar (Eron) Rowland, ed., *Life, Letters and Papers of William Dunbar* (Jackson, 1930), 174–75; Dunbar to Jefferson, July 6, 1805, *ibid.*, 154.

the Treasury, and the Attorney General. He also became paranoid. He
saw himself surrounded by a series of plots, whose instigators were
district land officers, principal deputy surveyors, deputy surveyors,
and the Commissioner of the General Land Office. The optimistic and
even-tempered Graham concluded at last, "Mr. Davis was certainly an
unfortunate appointment. . . ." When the President finally removed
him, Davis carried off all the official correspondence of his office for
use in protecting himself against attacks from newspapers—or so he
alleged.[24]

The fourth Surveyor General South of Tennessee during the 1820's
was James Turner, a former deputy surveyor and brother of an influential Adams supporter in Mississippi. To his new surveyor general,
Graham gave great authority. He directed that Turner should supervise the survey of the private claims and the back concessions, connect
these with the township lines, arrange them in order, and return them
to the General Land Office for patenting. For holders of confirmed
claims who would not come forward and designate the land for survey, Graham told Turner to advertise, set a deadline, and then survey
the land as public domain. Turner should pay off the deputies wherever possible. Graham also took the unprecedented step of raising the
fee under certain circumstances. He directed Turner to endorse additional charges where the deputies encountered special hardships or
would not work for the allowed price. After Turner's certification the
President himself would approve the accounts, but the system must be
used only where the deputy suffered "actual loss, after allowing him
for his services at least $3. a day while actually engaged in the sur-
vey."[25] That Graham and the President should agree to such a policy
in the midst of the greatest retrenchment campaign in the history of
the nation and with the Adams administration under fire for extravagance was ample evidence of the desperate situation in Louisiana and
Mississippi. Congress provided support by voting $87,185 for surveys
south of Tennessee in 1829, the largest sum for surveying since the
bonanza days of the Creek Purchase. Graham was pleased with the

---

24. James Turner to Graham, NA: GLO, Ltrs. Recd., SG, Miss., 57: Feb. 14,
1828; Graham to Richard Rush, *ibid.*, Ltrs. Sent, Misc., 19: June 23, Nov. 13,
1827, Feb. 15, 1828. Davis's correspondence with the General Land Office can
be found in *ibid.*, Ltrs. Recd., SG, Miss., 54a, 55, 56, and 57, *passim.*
25. Graham to Turner, *ibid.*, Ltrs. Sent, SG, 4: April 24, July 29, March 18,
1829.

work of his new surveyor general and commented that the "industry and exertions of Mr. Turner have . . . placed the business of the Office in a train. . . ."[26] Eight years had been squandered in finding a suitable man.

Surveying in Illinois, Missouri, and Arkansas was also in an uneasy condition. In the autumn of 1824, President Monroe removed William Rector because of nepotism and appointed in his place William McRee, a former colonel in the Army Corps of Engineers, who assumed the duties of office in the spring of 1825.[27] McRee handled the deputy surveyors well, sympathized with their difficulties, and at the same time demanded reasonable standards of accuracy. He was strongly impressed with the difficulties imposed by the laws. He wrote, "Under the present system the [illegible] Surveyor is exposed, nay subjected, to unavoidable impositions. . . . Conditions are prescribed without furnishing the means to fulfill them."[28]

The obligations and facilities of McRee's own office were a case in point. Under its present force and organization, he wrote, the staff "is wholly inadequate to the correct performance of a fourth part of the duties that have devolved on it, and are required of it, by the express terms of the law; independent of those who are incidental, including a large portion of the requisitions of the General Land Office." The three clerks in the office were not equal to the daily business of supervising the annual surveys of the public domain and recording them; and what of the private claims ("from which there is no escape") and the calls from the old land offices in Illinois for a renewal of their plats, more than four thousand of which lay in the St. Louis office awaiting the attention of the harassed clerks. "But these are mere items," commented McRee as he warmed up to his subject. "There is near ten years arrearages of other work on hand; which must be performed before either accuracy or promptness can characterize the operations of this office—until then I am working in the dark, and the correctness of my intentions affords no guaranty to the Government for that of my performance." Always McRee returned to the same point: the government had established a perfect land system, but the means

26.   Graham to William S. Hamilton, *ibid.*, Sept. 25, 1829.
27.   Graham to McRee, *ibid.*, 2: Oct. 18, Nov. 15, 1824; Little Rock *Arkansas Gazette*, Feb. 8, 1825.
28.   McRee to Graham, NA: GLO, Ltrs. Recd., SG, Mo., 63: Jan. 16, 1826.

provided to implement that system were completely inadequate. "In relation to all these duties; and to others not enumerated: the Law, is positive with its injunctions; while it withholds the means of executing them: and is at once imperative,—and impossible to obey.—" Under the present condition the office could handle in routine fashion the different kinds of business in order of relative importance, but the surveying business of the Missouri, Illinois, and Arkansas regions could never be placed in the perfect order visualized in the system established by Congress. And, of course, on the accuracy of the surveys depended perfect title to the land the government was offering to purchasers. McRee concluded, "I can assure you, that so far as it regards *merely the labour* to be performed here, it is a matter of very great indifference at which end of the mountain we may begin: the requisite quantum of daily drudgery being pretty nearly the same at all points." [29] The work of his office dominated the surveyor general's every waking moment. "I came here with hopes of being able to write to you frequently and at large, on whatever I supposed might be of any interest," he recalled sadly to Graham, "but I have not had time to write to any person—and have not removed from the spot on which myself & baggage were first deposited, on landing from the Steam boat." [30]

Graham responded by calling on Congress to support the surveyor general with additional clerical funds. He referred to the unfortunate St. Louis situation in the annual report on the state of the public lands. The commissioner even appealed to Thomas Hart Benton, head of the Missouri Congressional delegation. Under Benton's spur the Senate approved a $1,700 increase, but the House was opposed, and the appropriation failed. Successive Congresses also remained indifferent to the problem. Finally, in early 1828, Graham appealed directly to the Secretary of the Treasury in half a dozen letters detailing the condition of the St. Louis office. The whole affair drifted, as Congressmen from all sections of the nation called for parsimony and retrenchment. It was not until the end of the first session of the Twenty-second Congress, in the spring of 1829, that Congress provided for an additional $2,000. Both McRee and Graham agreed that the sum was

29. McRee to Graham, *ibid.*, Jan. 11, May 2, 1826.
30. McRee to Graham, *ibid.*, Nov. 29, 1826.

hardly more than a token recognition of the problems and would do little to solve them.[31]

The same uncertainty and confusion characterized other areas. The land business in Alabama suffered a severe dislocation with the destruction of John Coffee's office by fire in December 1827. The office of the surveyor general of Alabama was closed, and the land business of the state had to be carried on by way of the General Land Office. Clerks in the Washington office laboriously copied the innumerable plats and field notes from the duplicates and sent them to Coffee. Three years passed before Coffee once more assumed responsibility for supplying the district land offices of Alabama with returns in time for public sales.[32]

Farther south, the newly acquired lands of the Florida Territory demanded attention. Private claims once more posed a barrier to the public sale of lands. Among the sources of private grants under the Spanish regime were the King, the Intendant of Cuba, the laws of the Indies, the Royal Order of 1790, and the grant for military service under the Royal Order of 1815. Two boards of commissioners (one for East Florida, the other for West Florida) established land offices, listened to evidence, examined written documents, and passed judgment. They did their work with dispatch. The commission in West Florida finished its business early in 1826; that in East Florida, four years later.[33]

For the orderly disposal of the public domain the proceedings of the boards of commissioners were equal in importance to the surveys of the confirmed claims. The new surveyor general of the terri-

31. Graham to McRee, Nov. 8, 1826, *American State Papers, Public Lands*, 5: 463; *Senate Public Documents*, 19 Cong., 2 Sess., #1 (pt. 4): 137; Graham to Benton, Feb. 15, 1827, *American State Papers, Public Lands*, 5: 465–66; Graham to McRee, NA: GLO, Ltrs. Sent, SG, 3: March 17, 1827; Graham to Rush, *ibid.*, Ltrs. Sent, Misc., 21: Feb. 13, 1828; Graham to McRee, *ibid.*, SG, 4: March 30, 1829.
32. Graham to Coffee, *ibid.*, Jan. 11, 1828; Coffee to Elijah Hayward, *ibid.*, Ltrs. Recd., SG, Ala., 50: Jan. 11, 1831.
33. The complete reports of the commissioners are in *American State Papers, Public Lands*, 4: 561–748; *House Executive Documents*, 19 Cong., 1 Sess., #115; *Senate Public Documents*, 21 Cong., 1 Sess., #25. Two secondary accounts are Sydney W. Martin, "The Public Domain in Territorial Florida," *Journal of Southern History*, 10 (1944): 174–87; and, a more detailed treatment, Joseph F. Page III, "The Private Land Claims in Florida" (Unpublished bachelor's thesis, Princeton University, 1964).

tory was Robert Butler, a former Army officer on the staff of Andrew Jackson. Graham determined to profit from earlier costly errors. "By surveying & sectioning large quantities of Land in Louisiana & Mississippi, before the private claims were finally acted upon, & including much barren piney land, the Government & individuals have been put to great inconvenience and much money has been unnecessarily expended," he wrote Butler. "The object of the Government, is for the present to bring into market, the lands in Florida, which are entirely exempt from private claims; & which may be most in demand for the accommodation of actual settlers—You will, therefore, take care to have no township sectioned in which there are private claims." By heeding the commissioner's advice, Butler quickly prepared lands for sale at Tallahassee.[34] But the private claims had to be surveyed and platted so that they could be patented. Graham was optimistic. He knew that the claims were few and "generally well defined and well known" and thought that they could be "completed in a reasonable time and without much difficulty." Butler was far less sanguine. He saw instead a scene of "vague and clashing interests." Butler's deputies encountered problems in the indefinite nature of the claims ("the word *about* appears to be a common commencement, and running *about* N. NE. (or some other mariner's point) to a picket, so many Parisian perches, &c., but never closes"), and in lack of cooperation on the part of claimants.[35]

In the Northwest, Edward Tiffin, who was semiretired in the pleasant surroundings of Chillicothe, Ohio, supervised the surveys in Ohio, Michigan, and Indiana with his customary efficiency. Only in this district did the administration of the land business resemble in fact the model system created by Congress. Each spring the surveyors disappeared into an ever-receding wilderness, returned in the fall, and received payment; and Tiffin forwarded their returns almost mechanically. Tiffin did express great dissatisfaction about the reduction of the surveying fee from $3 to $2.50 per mile, noting that as the surveyors moved ever farther from civilization, the task of transporting supplies

34.   Graham to Butler, NA: GLO, Ltrs. Sent, SG, 2: Aug. 20, 1825.
35.   Graham to Butler, Feb. 26, 1827, *American State Papers, Public Lands*, 6: 522; Butler to Graham, July 3, 1827, *ibid.*, 539; John W. Exum, deputy surveyor, to Butler, enclosed in Butler to Graham, July 24, 1827, *ibid.;* Exum to Butler, July 10, 1827, *ibid.*, 539.

grew more difficult. The lower figure prevailed, however, and surveyors could always be found to take government money, whatever the
price. Nothing disturbed the calm efficiency with which Tiffin directed
the field force and office staff; and Graham had the sense to leave a
successful operation without much direction, except for an occasional
letter suggesting that fewer townships be surveyed in Michigan, for reports to the House of Representatives already showed that there was a
constant increase in the quantity of surveyed lands unsold there.
Tiffin's accuracy in transcribing the surveys and his promptness in
conveying them to the proper land offices in time for sales prevented
the slightest complaints from district land offices—a rare situation indeed, which even drew the praise of the commissioner himself.[36]

In the 1820's the affairs of some of the district land offices were also
badly deranged. The accounts of the land office at Washington (Mississippi), for example, were virtually nonexistent. Between 1815 and
1820 there were three registers: Nicholas Gray (1815–1818), Samuel
Winston (1818–1820), and Louis Winston (1820–1821). When Beverley R. Grayson became register in 1821, he discovered that of the
three the only one who had kept any records was Samuel Winston,
who received $1,500 for bringing up the arrears of his predecessor,
while neglecting his own work. As for Louis Winston, "He left the
Journal and Ledger just as he found them—he did not make an entry
in either," wrote Grayson. Congress would not appropriate extra funds
to bring up the books, the commissioner had no authority to make the
expenditure, and the affairs of the office lay in confusion throughout
the decade.[37]

Other land officers did not understand the system under which they
administered and accounted for the public lands. J. S. C. Harrison, receiver at Vincennes, was one. He confessed an ignorance of the department's whole accounting system. "True it is, I have regularly received from your Office, and also from the Comptroller, quarterly
statements of the manner in which my accounts have been adjusted,"
he wrote to Graham, "but I never could understand them, nor have I
ever been able to meet with anyone, who could give me such information as to enable me to comprehend them." In general, Harrison did

36.   Tiffin to Graham, NA: GLO, Ltrs. Recd., SG, NW, 6: Jan. 2, May 12, 1824;
Sept. 22, 1823; Graham to Tiffin, *ibid.*, 12: Aug. 24, 1826.
37.   Grayson to McLean, *ibid.*, Reg. & Rec., Washington, 30a: Jan. 21, 1823.

"not understand your mode of doing business . . . as it respects accounts of this character." [38]

Parsimony hampered the administration of the land business, and among the foremost of the several Congressional targets were the contingent expenses of the district land offices and the compensation for the registers and receivers. Members of the Retrenchment Committee inquired into the costs of printing, books, stationery, advertising, examinations of the land offices, clerk hire, superintendents of the sales, auctioneers, and even postage. The salaries of the registers and receivers had fallen in proportion to the decrease in sales. Even Secretary of the Treasury Crawford agreed that not only had the salary of the land officers "fallen far short of the maximum allowed by law, but that at only one office has it amounted to $2,000, and that, including the allowance for attending public sales, it has averaged but about $850." Yet Congress refused to increase the compensation and even cut $1,700 in additional clerk hire from the office of the Surveyor General South of Tennessee. [39]

Crawford's figure of $850 by no means met the high costs of carrying on the government's business on the frontier. Recent appointees, Richard Call and George Ward, wrote in detail of their problems in the new Tallahassee office. After two years in office both knew "that the Compensation falls very far Short of all reasonable expectation both there and here . . . the time is very near at hand that we shall actually Sink money by them and that at the best they have very little (if any) more than met the actual expenses attending them. . . ." Both the offices of register and receiver "require Clerks of the very first accuracy and respectability and it is well Known that Such clerks in Orleans Mobile and other Southern cities are getting from 700 to $1200 Pr. annum." If one added to the minimum figure board at $20 per month ($240), rent at $10 ($120), and $100 for incidentals such as candles, firewood, and paper, the cost of maintaining the office for a year was $1,160 cash. [40] Along with their regular duties, land officers performed additional tasks and administered special acts without extra

38. Harrison to Graham, NA: TD, Ltrs. Recd., re Public Lands at the Office of the 1st Comptroller, 1: Jan. 29, 1829.
39. *House Executive Documents*, 17 Cong., 2 Sess., #65, #79; *ibid.*, 18 Cong., 2 Sess., #92: 3.
40. Call and Ward to Graham, NA: GLO, Ltrs. Recd., Reg. & Rec., Tallahassee, 11: Jan. 23, 1827.

compensation. These included gifts of land to individuals or organizations, judging pre-emptions, adjudicating donations, for all of which "the Executive Government have not deemed themselves authorized to allow compensation for any extra duties imposed upon the Land Officers by law." [41]

Congress ignored the low salaries and additional duties and called instead for the statements of the annual incomes of the registers and receivers. The Retrenchment Committee noted that in five district land offices expenses exceeded sales between 1822 and 1825. Observant members of the Congress also noted that more than twenty-five million acres of the public domain had been surveyed but not offered on the market to prospective purchasers.[42] It was against this background of parsimony, retrenchment, high surveying expenditures, and the large bulk of unsold surveyed land that in 1829 Senator Samuel A. Foot of Connecticut offered his resolution calling for temporary restrictions on the quantity of public lands placed on the market, and abolishing the office of surveyor general.[43] Foot's resolution brought on a general debate. The spokesman for the South, Senator Robert Y. Hayne of South Carolina, seized the opportunity to castigate Foot's resolution as part of a consistent New England policy to stunt the growth of the West and reduce its influence in the national councils. Senator Daniel Webster of Massachusetts replied that New England was the traditional friend of western interests. In the uproar that accompanied the clash between Webster and Hayne and the rising sectional antagonism, Congressmen and historians have ignored the fact that Foot's resolution was perfectly consistent with the policies of Congress during the previous eight years.

Members of Congress also attacked the large number of district land offices. Senator Rufus King of New York told his colleagues that "the land offices under the authority of the United States, had already increased to about thirty; and he suggested whether, at a time when the contributions to the public Treasury were daily diminishing, it was

41. Graham to Rep. William Haile (Miss.), *ibid.*, Ltrs. Sent, Misc., 21: Feb. 9, 1828.

42. *House Executive Documents*, 19 Cong., 1 Sess., #170, #89; *American State Papers, Public Lands*, 4: 533–34.

43. *Register of Debates in Congress* (29 vols., Washington, 1825–37), 21 Cong., 1 Sess., 6: 3–4.

expedient to multiply channels to drain it." [44] But not even King's strictures could restrain interested Congressmen. In 1822 and 1823, Congress created new land offices in Fort Wayne (Indiana), Springfield (Illinois), Lexington and Palmyra (Missouri), Augusta (Mississippi), Monroe (Michigan), and at Tallahassee and St. Augustine (Florida). Commissioner Graham opposed the establishment of other new offices on the grounds of limited demand for public lands; and Congress established no land offices between 1823 and 1831. [45]

Congressional retrenchment touched the operations of the General Land Office in a period of severe need. Owing to the Relief Act the western country spewed forth a large volume of final certificates ready for patents. Already, by the middle of 1821, the delay in the issue of patents had become severe enough to necessitate a circular to the land offices on the reasons for the delay. The commissioner listed, among others, the urgent demand for military bounty land patents ("the demands of the *needy soldier* for his recompense of his country"), the burden of the Relief Act, and the administrative difficulties of procuring suitable parchment, engraving, and preparation. [46] By the beginning of 1823 a backlog of twenty thousand patents awaited the attention of the patent clerks; the commissioner also estimated that within a year another twenty thousand would be ready for issue. [47] Under George Graham the business of issuing patents assumed new efficiency. By the time he had been in office for a year, the patent clerks were issuing patents at the rate of thirty thousand a year. Congress provided no additional assistance in this task. Indeed, the contingent expenses of the offices were reduced to a point where Graham lacked copies of Congressional laws to send to his land officers, the men charged with the execution of these laws. [48]

The congestion in the General Land Office, with its fixed clerical staff, was increased by the constant demands of Congress for information. For reasons ranging from the public interest to personal and political profit, members of Congress called constantly on the General

44. *Annals of Congress,* 17 Cong., 1 Sess., 38: 364; *House Executive Documents,* 17 Cong., 1 Sess., #94: 3–4.
45. Graham to Rep. John Scott (Mo.), NA: GLO, Ltrs. Sent, Misc., 16: Jan. 12, 16, 1826.
46. Circular to the land officers, *ibid.,* 11: Sept. 5, 1821.
47. McLean to Crawford, *ibid.,* 12: Feb. 14, 1823.
48. Graham to Obadiah Jones, Huntsville, *ibid.,* Oct. 28. 1823.

Land Office for information: the salaries of registers and receivers, annual sales of land at the various offices, an estimate of the time that various classes of land by quality (first, second, third class, and so forth) had been on the market and where they were located, the transmission of extended correspondence relevant to various matters, explanations for failures to solve certain problems associated with the management of the public domain. Some legislators sought patents for their constituents, information on various tracts, special favors in the management of the land business.

Josiah Meigs had labored under these "ill-considered" solicitations. On a Congressional request for a statement of the net proceeds of the sale of public lands in the State of Illinois, he commented, "The tedious operation necessary to extract this information will create delay—as it can only be obtained by paging the Ledgers and extracting all the monies paid on the lands sold since the 1st Jany 1819— from the accounts of purchasers scattered throughout upwards of one hundred volumes." On another occasion Meigs passed on to the various district land offices a Congressional request for a statement of the land sold at each land office from its opening to March 31, 1822. Benjamin S. Pope, register at Huntsville, called the request "utterly impossible to comply with, unless all other business under the relief act is suspended. . . ." Peyton Symmes wrote from Cincinnati, "This task . . . one of the most tedious undertaken (twice as much as in this District as any other on account of the *State Lines* running through it)—I have not been able to complete, either so soon as was expected . . . or, perhaps, so accurately as could be desired." Many land officers had to employ extra clerks at their own expense.[49]

Every Commissioner of the General Land Office struggled against the determination of Congress to reduce the costs of administering the public lands. No sooner had John McLean arrived in Washington in 1822 than he found a note from the House Committee on Retrenchment requesting that he identify those clerks of the office who might be termed "unnecessary, inefficient or engaged in other pursuits in nowise relating to the public Office." With his bags still packed and

49.   Meigs to Crawford, NA: GLO, Ltrs. Sent, Misc., 11: Oct. 25, 1821; Pope to Meigs, *ibid.*, Ltrs. Recd., Reg. & Rec., Huntsville, 5: Aug. 4, 1822; Symmes to Meigs, *ibid.*, Cincinnati, 37: Nov. 2, 1822; John Miller to Meigs, *ibid.*, Franklin, 31: Aug. 6, 1822.

every clerk a complete stranger with the exception of John M. Moore, whom he knew only by correspondence, McLean parried the request with that combination of pleasant openness and quiet sagacity that made him a perennial candidate for office. "I find some of the clerks more efficient than others, but I might do injustice by saying that any of them are inefficient," he replied.[50] After familiarizing himself with the duties and the responsibilities of the office, McLean was far less pleased. "The business of the Office is much more behind that I supposed, and I find the general labour, much greater than I anticipated," he wrote Crawford.[51] John McLean left the office in the same condition as he found it. He did feel that "the Office stands much higher now in the estimation of the members of Congress generally, than it did sometime since," and he was probably right. John McLean was far more skillful in his dealings with Congress than his predecessor had been. But the burden of labor remained.[52]

George Graham was a new kind of administrator. Unlike the early commissioners, Graham was an old bureaucrat who had held jobs within the government for more than a decade. He was accustomed to serving Congress, and he acted on Congressional requests without question. He was also a Virginia Republican, a man who believed devoutly in a small government with only minor administrative machinery, and he was retrenchment-oriented even about his own organization. Graham drove his clerks hard, reminding them that lack of assiduity would be grounds for dismissal. By the spring of 1826 "the great press of business, which for the last four years had arisen in this office, in consequence of the several acts for relief of the purchasers of the Public Lands . . . having in a measure subsided," he recommended that "the number of the Clerks in this office, may, with a due regard to the public interest, be diminished." His plan called for a cut in the number of clerks from twenty-three to seventeen, "seven of those being good and efficient Book Keepers, would be adequate to execute the business assigned to this office." In so doing, the commissioner won the unbounded gratitude of the Committee on Retrench-

50. *Annals of Congress,* 18 Cong., 1 Sess., 41: 891; Crawford to McLean, NA: TD, Ltrs. from Sec. Treas. to Comm. GLO, 2: Nov. 26, 1822; McLean to Crawford, Nov. 28, 1822, *American State Papers, Misc.,* 2: 981–82.
51. McLean to Crawford, NA: GLO, Ltrs. Sent, Misc., 12: Feb. 14, 1823.
52. McLean to John M. Moore, *ibid.,* Ltrs. Recd., Misc., M: March 3, 1823.

ment, as well as the undying irritation of his successors. The House
hastily accepted his recommendations.[53] Graham found other ways to
conserve funds, too. One of the biggest items in the contingent expenses was the purchase of parchment. Graham canceled the contract
with the traditional suppliers and opened the parchment purchase to
competitive bidding. The winner "bid considerably lower than any
other and lower than the price we had been giving." Unfortunately
the quality of the parchment was so poor that President John Quincy
Adams complained he could scarcely sign his name to the patents.[54]

For the administrators of the public domain, the decade of the
1820's was a period of uncertain relations with Congress. Many Congressmen thought that the commissioner intruded on Congressional
prerogative. The commissioner and even the district land officers did
vary the application of legislation, particularly in Louisiana, Mississippi, and Arkansas, where distance made uniformity difficult and the
force available was not equal to the task. Senator Thomas Hart
Benton of Missouri once demanded the issue of a land patent. Commissioner Josiah Meigs refused. Benton pointed out that Meigs's duties
were administrative not judicial. "How far the duties of the Commissioner of the General Land Office are merely 'Ministerial and not
Judicial' is not, perhaps for him to judge," Meigs replied, "but, until
the connected Plat is before him, he ventures to exercise his Judgment." When George Graham began to issue detailed instructions for
each act of Congress, he assumed great powers of interpretation. The
office of commissioner was certainly no longer purely "ministerial."
Graham further decentralized authority by expressing doubts about
the binding effect of his instructions on the registers and the receivers
of the district land offices. "Such instructions are not paramount to the
law, it becomes the duty of every Officer to compare the instructions
which he may receive with the law and with his previous instructions
and to give such a construction to them as shall be compatible with
positive law; and if he can not do this, then ask for explanation before
he acts . . . ," Graham once wrote. The district land officers obviously had a right to question the interpretations of law given by the

53.   Graham to Shadrach Bond, Kaskaskia, ibid., Ltrs. Sent, Misc., 17: March 7,
1826; Senate Public Documents, 19 Cong., 2 Sess., #1 (pt. 4): 138–39.
54.   President to Graham, NA: GLO, Register of Ltrs. Recd., President, 1: Aug.
22, 1826; Graham to the President, ibid., Ltrs. Sent, Misc., 17: Aug. 26, 1826;
Graham to Wilson & Bruner, Parchment Makers, ibid., Aug. 28, 1826.

Commissioner of the General Land Office and, after suitable thought, to act as they saw fit, within the framework of "positive law." No one questioned the authority of the Secretary of the Treasury, but his interest and influence were minimal.[55]

Thus in the 1820's, owing to a succession of Secretaries of the Treasury who were occupied otherwise and to a strong commissioner, George Graham, the responsibility for the interpretation of Congressional legislation was diverted into the General Land Office and from there by degrees into the western country. Even in a period of relative quiet and reduced westward migration, at least before 1825, the administrators of the public domain were unable to prevent disorganization, confusion, uncertainty, favoritism, fraud, and exploitation from permeating the land business. "There are but two ways for the Surveyor here to 'get along,'" wrote William McRee, in a statement that applied in many other cases, "first by having sufficient means placed at his disposal to perform the duties of his Office According to law—and secondly (and which is much the most convenient for him who chooses to have recourse to it) to receive the work, without examining it—And sign his name, without Knowing what is above it." McRee concluded, "It would almost appear that apprehensions were entertained lest Knavery should become extinct in the Community, when the laws offer premiums for its exhibition, or practice." [56]

55. Meigs to Benton, NA: GLO, Ltrs. Sent, Misc., 10: Jan. 20, 1821; Graham to Joseph Wood, Marietta, *ibid.*, 12: Sept. 27, 1823; Wood to Graham, *ibid.*, Ltrs. Recd., Reg. & Rec., Marietta, 38: Sept. 15, Oct. 13, 23, 1823.
56. McRee to Graham, *ibid.*, SG, Mo., 63: Nov. 29, 1826.

The Private Uses of the Land Business: The Republicans and Others

9

The growth of the bureaucracy of the Republic stimulated concern about who should enjoy the emoluments of office and about the problem of ethics in the public service. In the first quarter of the nineteenth century the land business became a big business. The Land Law of 1800 established four district land offices in the territory northwest of the Ohio; by 1823 purchases from Indian tribes and the movement of population to the West had increased this number to forty-two, scattered from Steubenville (Ohio) to Lexington (Missouri), from New Orleans to Detroit. Also, to the single surveying district Northwest of the Ohio, Congress added surveying districts for Alabama, Florida, South of Tennessee (Mississippi and Louisiana), and a surveyor general for all of Illinois, Missouri, and Arkansas. The new offices needed new men to staff them. Each district land office required a register and a receiver, clerks; and at a period of public sale, additional clerks, a crier, and often a marshal or other officials joined the government payroll. Every new surveying district meant a large number of new deputy surveyors. Each deputy employed a gang of men to assist him in the wilderness: axmen, chain carriers, a cook, and occasionally a hunter. Official notices and proclamations of public sales were advertised in large numbers of newspapers and so provided income for the frontier editors of the period.[1] In a region of uncertain and scarce currency the land business provided ample quantities of sound money. The gentlemen engaged in the land business also had prestige, for their office indicated an official trust and might be taken as a sign of political preferment.

From the time of the organization of the government under the

1. The cost of publicizing a land sale was $200 to $300 per proclamation. See Meigs to Crawford, NA: GLO, Ltrs. Sent, Misc., 8: March 20, 1819.

Constitution, President George Washington had been concerned with the selection of proper men to run the new enterprise, and the search for able public servants became one of his most constant duties. Although the issue of party gradually intruded, his dominant criterion was fitness for office. Washington maintained a high standard of selection in spite of the growing factionalism around him.[2] John Adams was less successful in maintaining this freedom from political bias, but his administration was largely free of removals for political reasons. The slender political support Adams commanded made him more responsive to the wishes of Congressional delegations in matters of appointments. Intertwined with the rise of politics and the division among the Federalists were the rising importance of political appointments, the increased interest and power of Congressional delegations and individuals, and Adams's own elevated standards of public service and his strong personal prejudices.[3]

Under President Thomas Jefferson, who took office in 1801, the domain of the nation was enlarged, the territorial system was expanded, and migration to the West increased. The land business expanded accordingly. New offices in Illinois, Indiana, Mississippi, and Louisiana needed men to staff them. Candidates were not lacking. "In this part of the country no other qualifications, except perhaps a little Law knowledge, are deemed necessary for filling any office, under the State, or even General Government," wrote Jared Mansfield from the Ohio country. For every opening ten candidates appeared, and "there is perpetual competition for office." The surveyor general concluded, "Office hunting in the State of Ohio, & Indiana Territory is most barefaced & ridiculous. Those who obtain places, are considered only as more fortunate, not more meritorious than others of the *Corps*."[4] To distinguish among the hordes of office seekers, Thomas Jefferson depended on the recommendations of influential state and national fig-

2.   Leonard D. White, *The Federalists*, 253–66; Carl Russell Fish, *The Civil Service and the Patronage* (New York, 1905), 6–16; Gaillard Hunt, "Office-Seeking during Washington's Administration," *American Historical Review*, 1 (1896): 270–83.

3.   White, *The Federalists*, 267–90; Fish, *The Civil Service and the Patronage*, 16–26; Gaillard Hunt, "Office-Seeking during the Administration of John Adams," *American Historical Review*, 2 (1897): 241–61. On the increasing Congressional influence in appointments, see White, *The Federalists*, 82–87.

4.   Mansfield to Gallatin, Jan. 24, 1812 (a letter marked "private & confidential"), Gallatin Papers (microfilm), Princeton University Library.

ures. Letters on appointments in the land business went to Secretary of the Treasury Albert Gallatin, who sorted them out, suggested a priority list, and passed the information on to the President.[5]

Amidst the rush for office and Jefferson's determination to base his administration on talent and integrity, the President increasingly relied on his own judgment and that of Albert Gallatin. An excellent example was the appointment of John Badollet to the registership at the new Vincennes (Indiana) land office. Badollet, who had migrated to the United States in 1786, was a native of Geneva and a childhood companion of Gallatin's. Through the influence of his well-known sponsor Badollet held a series of minor appointments in western Pennsylvania. In 1804, Gallatin nominated his friend, whom he termed "a tried Republican," as register of the land office at Vincennes. It was a good choice. Badollet became a center of Republican strength in Indiana Territory and an important source of information on the West and Indiana politics, and he conducted his office with the utmost integrity.[6]

Jefferson began the practice of sending deserving members of the Republican party out to administer the land business in the territories. In choosing four land commissioners for the newly established Mississippi Territory, for example, the President ignored the earnest solicitations of the Georgia delegation in favor of deserving Georgians. Instead, he appointed Thomas Rodney of Delaware, Robert Williams of North Carolina, Ephraim Kerby of Connecticut, and Robert Nicholas of Kentucky. All were meritorious Republicans from the East. Rodney was the son of Caesar Rodney, Republican leader and Congressman from Delaware; Kerby was a leading Connecticut Republican; Williams was a close relative of the second territorial governor of the Mississippi Territory.[7] The Georgia delegation went home empty-handed. Within individual states, however, Jefferson traditionally consulted the state delegation to Congress on appointments to the land business. Aside from the influence of the Executive and Congress, governors of territories in which the offices were vacant also exerted

5.   E.g. Gallatin to Jefferson, Feb. 25, 1805, Carter, ed., *Territorial Papers,* 5: 385.
6.   Thornbrough, ed., *The Correspondence of John Badollet and Albert Gallatin,* 9–22.
7.   James Jackson *et al* to the President, March 4, 1803, Carter, ed., *Territorial Papers,* 5: 205n.

influence on appointments.[8] As the experience of the appointments in the Mississippi Territory suggested, politics was never far removed from the issue of appointments to the land business. Thomas Jefferson believed in selecting men on the basis of fitness, but he also believed that, because of their philosophy of government, Republicans tended to be more "fit" than Federalists.[9]

What should Jefferson do about the Federalists appointed by his predecessors? The President's supporters clamored for office, he himself doubted the ability of the opposition to support a government that their political principles seemed bent on destroying, and the issue of their competence became less and less important. Few appointments had been made in the land business before Jefferson's accession to power. Aside from the eight district land officers in the Northwest Territory (of which at least three were Republicans), only Rufus Putnam, the Surveyor General Northwest of the Ohio, remained from the Adams administration. Jefferson removed Putnam from office in early 1804, ostensibly for cause. Putnam was equally convinced "that *no want of ability, integrity,* or *industry* was the cause of my removal from office. no. it was don because I did not Subscribe to the Measures of him whom I have called, *Arch* enemy to Washingtons Administration." [10]

When Putnam raised the cry of political proscription, Jared Mansfield, his replacement, replied that the Republicans kept in office the fittest men. "Genl Putnam is wholly incompetent to the business for which I was selected," explained Mansfield. "The Surveyor General's office was dead in these parts. The Only circumstance, which to him is disagreeable, is that of his not being permitted to resign. This he would have done, in 2 or 3 months, as he told me." [11] The Republicans in Ohio also urged the President to dismiss—on grounds of incompetence—Zaccheus Biggs, the Steubenville receiver and sole Federalist appointment of John Adams. Charges multiplied that Biggs "cannot give satisfaction" and that his "politics are strongly federal,"

8. E.g. Thomas Freeman to Edward Tiffin, NA: GLO, Ltrs. Recd., SG, Miss., 53: Feb. 21, 1815.
9. Senator James Wilson (N.J.) to the President, May 16, 1804, Carter, ed., *Territorial Papers*, 7: 193–94; Thomas Worthington to the President, June 17, 1804, *ibid.*, 202; Alexander Balmain to Sec. State, Feb. 4, 1807, *ibid.*, 427.
10. Buell, comp., *Memoirs of Rufus Putnam*, 125–26.
11. Mansfield to William Lyon, Feb. 20, 1804, Mansfield Papers, Ohio Historical Society Library, Columbus.

but Jefferson retained Biggs in office for another five years.[12] In at least one case Jefferson actually appointed a Federalist to an office in the land business. The man was Benjamin Tupper, the son of General Benjamin Tupper, a close friend of Rufus Putnam. In 1804, with the support of Mansfield, Jefferson appointed the younger Tupper receiver of public monies at Marietta.[13]

In his determination to have the appointments of his administration reflect his own high standards, Jefferson did not hesitate to remove Republicans from office, even though such a dismissal would cause political dissension within Republican ranks. On December 15, 1803, Jefferson named Edward Turner register for lands lying west of the Pearl River in the Mississippi Territory, an appointment that he made over the objections of the surveyor general, Isaac Briggs. Briggs argued that Turner was not qualified for office.[14] The register was one of the three commissioners passing judgment on the large land claims in the territory. Turner was an ambitious Republican with a Virginia background, and he assisted his young political career by marrying Mary West, the daughter of Cato West, leader of the territorial Republicans. The appointment was a good one politically for Jefferson. West was the leader of a faction opposed to the President's territorial governor, Robert Williams. Here was a fine opportunity to split the opposition and attract the support of one of the leading younger men in the territory. Within a year the President found Turner derelict in the performance of his duties, and removed him. Turner had advised claimants "that their claims should have a legal form & exactness to which themselves are inadequate, that therefore they must employ a lawyer to draw them up; that he himself is a practising lawyer & does that business, & will do it if desired. . . ." Jefferson also recorded that the register left the business of the office to his clerks (while he spent his time in the practice of law), that he advised

12.   Tiffin to Worthington, Dec. 29, 1803, Worthington Papers, The Ohio State Library, Columbus; Return Jonathan Meigs to Worthington, Dec. 30, 1803, *ibid.;* Worthington to Gallatin, June 12, 1804, Carter, ed., *Territorial Papers,* 7: 201; Tiffin to Gallatin, May 26, 1808, Gallatin Papers (microfilm), Princeton University Library.
13.   Mansfield to Gallatin, July 9, 1804, *ibid.;* Albert Gallatin to Jonathan Russell, Sept. 25, 1805, "Letters to Jonathan Russell, 1801–1822," *Massachusetts Historical Society Proceedings,* 47 (1913–14): 294–95.
14.   Gallatin to Turner, Dec. 15, 1803, Carter, ed., *Territorial Papers,* 5: 296–97; Briggs to Jefferson, Sept. 8, 1803, *ibid.,* 297n.

"claimants not to give in certain claims, but others on which they will get more," and that "his family connections are deeply interested in a great number of claims." [15] The removal of Turner stirred the West faction to strong protest. Governor Robert Williams wrote that "the dismissal of Edward Turner—West's son in law from the office of Register roused all their resentment." [16] West attempted to engineer Turner's election to Congress as the territorial delegate, but he failed to muster sufficient votes. The President's decision to remove Turner in spite of the political consequences reflected credit on his policy of appointments to the land business.

The continuity and efficiency that Albert Gallatin brought to the conduct of the land business vanished with the end of the War of 1812. Gallatin himself went to Europe on diplomatic business, and a new group of Republicans came to power. They were a generation removed from those who had fought the Revolution and engaged in the ideological struggles of the 1790's. Henry Clay, John C. Calhoun, John Quincy Adams, Daniel Webster, and Andrew Jackson were among the leaders, and they would guide the nation for a generation. This group would be primarily concerned with domestic affairs, as its predecessors had never quite been able to divorce themselves from the pressing involvement of the new nation in foreign affairs. Part of this internal orientation meant greater interest in the public domain, a universal interest that in part caused and in part reflected the rush to the West in the years immediately after the war. Rising land sales, a speculative mania, more district land offices, more machinery necessary to prepare the lands for sale and to administer the nation's public domain were all part of the new scene. All these changes reflected the quickening pace of westward expansion everywhere.

The movement to the West in part stemmed from the readjustments that American society commonly undergoes after a military conflict. Thousands of men returned to civilian life, and many of them sought government employment. Some of these veterans had suffered wounds or distinguished themselves in battle, and they thought that they had a right to a government job. The next decade saw a frantic search for government offices. " 'The avidity for office is of the highest grade of Mania here,' " commented Josiah Meigs on the press for clerkships in

15. Undated memorandum in Jefferson's handwriting, *ibid.*, 375n.
16. Williams to Jefferson, May 17, 1805, *ibid.*, 402.

the General Land Office. He went on, "'I have at least 100 applicants for a single clerkship in the G. L. Office of the lowest grade of compensation—viz: $800—and I am confident I could raise in ten days a Regiment of 800 clerks at $400.'" [17] With the large number of applicants, influence became far more valuable than talent. Competition for appointments to district land offices became extremely severe. "You know some thing of the effort for appointments in Indiana," wrote a friend to John Tipton, an unsuccessful applicant. "They are much greater & perhaps much more extensive than you are aware of Vice Presidential influence is enlisted in favor of some applicants." For the office that Tipton sought, there were "perhaps fifty or sixty applicants." [18] First to be served were the relatives of those in high places. Edward Tiffin made his son a clerk in the General Land Office; Josiah Meigs found a place for his brother-in-law. When he became Secretary of State, John Quincy Adams found himself overwhelmed by men seeking offices throughout the government. His New England soul rebelled. "There is something so gross and so repugnant to my feelings in this cormorant appetite for office . . . ," he wrote.[19]

Many of those whose lives were upset by the war intended to go west, and they sought to do so with a government job. Perhaps they wished to launch a political career, but more likely they wanted the fertile lands appearing on the market with increasing regularity. Everyone sought what Captain James Riley of Connecticut, a friend of Josiah Meigs's, wanted—"an uncommon job" that would be "well paid for." [20] Those who desired to speculate in land or script first sought to tour the vast wilderness of the West at government expense as deputy surveyors. The postwar demand for surveying contracts far exceeded the supply, and rank and influence were used on every hand.[21] The rewards were large. To meet the demand for land created by postwar settlers, Congress voted large sums for surveying. From $47,083.98 in 1815, the first year of peace, to $232,408.43 in

17.   Meigs to Dr. Daniel Drake, April 8, 1822, quoted in Meigs, *Life of Josiah Meigs*, 108.
18.   Rep. William Hendricks (Ind.) to Tipton, March 4, 1820, Nellie A. Robertson and Dorothy Riker, eds., *The John Tipton Papers* (3 vols., Indiana Historical Collections, Indianapolis, 1942), 1: 187–88; Waller Taylor to Tipton, March 11, 1820, *ibid.*, 189.
19.   Charles Francis Adams, ed., *Memoirs of John Quincy Adams* (12 vols., Philadelphia, 1874–77), 5: 24 (March 18, 1820).
20.   Riley to Meigs, NA: GLO, Ltrs. Recd., Misc., R: Aug. 25, 1820.
21.   *Ante*, pp. 96–7, 100–101.

1817, the year that the Creek Purchase in Alabama received full attention, appropriations reached $175,034.51 in 1818 and $237,418.49 the
following year.[22]

Surveying became an extremely profitable business. The most adept
practitioner was William Rector, a forerunner of surveying entrepreneurs such as James Clymer and Abraham Lincoln. He had begun
surveying in the western country shortly after the turn of the century,
and in 1813, Josiah Meigs called him "the most skilful and able *practical Surveyor* in the United States." Rector ran some of the first surveys
in Indiana Territory, and it was to him that Edward Tiffin entrusted
responsibility for the military bounty lands at the close of the war. In
1816, William Rector became the surveyor general of a new surveying
district covering Illinois and Missouri.[23] After years in the field, the
mire and mud of spring, the stifling heat of summer, the drenching
rains of fall, and the clouds of mosquitoes, Rector had reached a position of power and profit. He gratefully seized it. Immediately he engaged his five brothers as deputy surveyors. He recognized that their
profits were limited by the amount of ground that a deputy could
cover in a season. He solved this problem by subcontracting. The
wandering Vermonter, Gershom Flagg, heard of this ruse as early as
1818. "There is now considerable surveying to be done but the Surveyor General, Rector, has so many connections that are Surveyors
that it is not possible for a stranger to get any Contract of any importance," Flagg wrote from Illinois. "Some who are not Surveyors (but
favorites) make Contracts for surveying and then hire it done." [24] But
in a period of the greatest pressure for preparation of the military
bounty lands and of lands for public sales in Missouri to meet the
hordes of citizens headed for the Boon's Lick country, Rector got results. He surveyed bounty lands, public lands, private claims, and
donations. In short, William Rector surveyed anything that did not
move. He put eighty companies of surveyors into the field, and he returned the desired plats to the General Land Office on time. The
volume of his work continued unquestioned (and perhaps unknown)
throughout the period of the land office business and the general prosperity that followed the war.

22. *American State Papers, Public Lands*, 3: 459.
23. Meigs to Tiffin, NA: GLO, Ltrs. Recd., SG, NW, 5: Nov. 21, 1813.
24. Flagg to Artemas Flagg, Sept. 12, 1818, Buck, ed., "Pioneer Letters of Gershom Flagg," 160.

With the panic of 1819 and the subsequent depression, however, Rector's enthusiasms came to the attention of the retrenchment-minded Crawford in the Treasury Department. In 1821 the surveyor general proposed to survey 559 townships in Illinois, Missouri, and Arkansas, at a total cost of more than $120,000, a figure that nearly equaled the amount appropriated for all surveying in the nation that year. "It is apparently not in obedience to any instructions which have been given by me that such a quantity of land is to be surveyed," commented the Secretary. "At a time when there is but little demand for the public lands even when first brought into market it is peculiarly unfortunate that such an effort should be made." Crawford directed that Rector "stop this extraordinary effort and if practicable reduce the contemplated expenditure at least one half." When Commissioner Meigs corresponded with Rector, however, he discovered that the surveyor general had already let contracts worth $120,000 for surveying, and that the work appeared to have progressed too far to halt.[25]

Rumors circulated in Congress that William Rector's accounts were in arrears, and that his plentiful returns were inaccurate, but a thorough investigation failed to uncover any irregularities. Rector came to Washington for a personal visit and made a convincing defense. He returned to St. Louis with additional clerk hire and a letter from the President reappointing him for another four years. The friends of the surveyor general honored him with a testimonial dinner at the best hotel in St. Louis. Guests included Representative John Scott of Missouri and "several officers of the U.S. Army," and the toastmaster was William Christy, register of the St. Louis land office. A man who controlled hundreds of thousands of dollars of government funds had many friends.[26]

At the very moment when General William Rector was listening to the flowery phrases of his devoted followers, further attacks on his conduct were in the offing. From information gathered to support the surveyor general's request for additional clerk hire, the great quantity of surveying done under him became evident for the first time. Between April 1818 and the end of December 1822, Rector had

25. Crawford to Meigs, NA: TD, Ltrs. Sent, Misc., 1801–33: May 25, 1821; Meigs to Crawford, NA: GLO, Ltrs. Sent, Misc., 11: Aug. 1, Nov. 3, 7, 1821.
26. *Edwardsville Spectator*, May 11, 1822; Shawneetown *Illinois Gazette*, May 4, 1822; Rector to Meigs, NA: GLO, Ltrs. Recd., SG, Mo., 61: June 28, 1822.

supervised the survey of 98,299 miles, 59 chains, and 43 links. It was a startling figure. In the same period three other surveying districts recorded combined surveys of 123,240 miles. Senator David Barton of Missouri, an archenemy of Thomas Hart Benton and no friend to the surveyor general, rose in the Senate to ask the General Land Office for copies of Rector's contracts with his deputies.[27] A long recitation of charges against the surveyor general appeared in the *Missouri Republican,* and violence flared. Frederick Bates, who was a former recorder of land titles and was soon to be elected governor of the state, called for Rector's removal; and Senator Barton wrote the President a series of letters accusing Rector of subcontracting much of the surveying done in Missouri.[28]

Rector's defense of his conduct of the business in St. Louis had something to recommend it. He had done his work promptly in an area where delays were all too common. His work on the military bounty lands was particularly noteworthy for its promptness under duress from Washington. Rector nowhere denied that he had employed his brothers, but his brothers were competent surveyors and, with their extensive experience, probably more competent than most. He had the largest and the most remote surveying district in the nation; it should not be surprising that he had done more surveying than any other. The surveys were correct, and in their execution he had received and fully accounted for more the $450,000 without the slightest grounds for the charge of misappropriation. This last was a significant achievement, particularly since the accounting system of the federal government traditionally refused anything but the most careful accounts.

Success was Rector's greatest enemy. The huge sum of money that had passed through his hands was indicative of the opportunities for profit. A full list of the contracts let—made up in response to the resolution of David Barton—showed that General Rector had given nearly one contract in four to his brothers. Also prominent were his nephews, Henry W. Conway, then deputy surveyor and receiver of the land office at Little Rock, and James S. Conway, later first surveyor general of the Arkansas Territory. Commissioner Graham noted

27. NA: GLO, Ltrs. Recd., SG, Mo., 60: March 27, 1823; *Annals of Congress,* 17 Cong., 2 Sess., 40: 286.
28. St. Louis *Missouri Republican,* June 25, July 23, Aug. 27, 1823; Barton to the President, NA: GLO, Ltrs. Recd., Misc., B: Aug. 21, 1823.

numerous cases in which the plats of survey specified "an assistant surveyor acting for the deputy surveyor who made the contracts." [29] The list of relatives by blood and marriage who shared in the contracts that Frederick Bates had recited in the *Missouri Republican* remained unchallenged. The most determined accuser, David Barton, refuted point by point the defense of the surveyor general. The question was not whether the contractors were "honorable men," in Barton's own words, but rather whether they were "skillful surveyors," under the meaning of the act of April 1816. And if they were "skillful surveyors," this fact in itself did not "prove that they could sit in St. Louis, and superintend the running of lines and marking of trees, at a distance of several miles, at Arkansas on the right, and Lake Michigan on the left, with sufficient accuracy to certify the execution upon their official oaths!" Were such indeed the case, "the more appropriate certificate would have been, that they were men of extraordinary optick powers, and regularly descended from Argus." Barton concluded that "Gen: Rector had forfeited all claim to this office he holds, by a course of official misconduct and abuses." [30]

President James Monroe also found the evidence conclusive and removed Rector. The President's decision was widely supported.[31] Rector wrote a bitter letter to George Graham and then retired to a position as elder statesman in the land business, to which his former experience gave him full title.[32] Edward Tiffin, the shrewd observer from Chillicothe, wise in the way of the land office business, offered his benediction. "I am [illegible] to observe by the public papers that General W. Rector is determined to show the public (if he can) that he has been unjustly treated (as he says) by a removal from Office, silence becomes him best," he wrote to Commissioner Graham. "I will only add—That if I have been correctly informed of his general conduct and that of his numerous needy relatives, he has been mercifully born with too long." [33]

29. *American State Papers, Public Lands*, 4: 19–25; Graham to Rector, NA: GLO, Ltrs. Recd., SG, Mo., 60: April 26, 1824.
30. Barton to Graham, *ibid.*, May 8, 1824. The act of April 29, 1816 (3 Stat. 325), specified that the surveyor general should employ "skillful surveyors as his deputies."
31. Shawneetown *Illinois Gazette*, July 10, 1824; Franklin *Missouri Intelligencer*, July 31, 1824; *Evansville Gazette*, Aug. 26, 1824.
32. Rector to Graham, NA: GLO, Ltrs. Recd., SG, Mo., 62: Sept. 19, 1824.
33. Tiffin to Graham, *ibid.*, NW, 6: July 19, 1824.

General William Rector's case demonstrated the profits to be made from the land business and the opportunities for power available to those who could control appointments. John Quincy Adams once referred to Josiah Meigs as a man with "extensive patronage scattered all over the Union."[34] Adams might have been right in the years immediately after the war, but thereafter the appointment power of the commissioners of the General Land Office was taken over by the Treasury Department. From 1816 until August of 1823 the Treasury Department lay under the firm hand of William H. Crawford. Crawford was also a constant candidate for the Presidency—quietly before Monroe's second election, openly thereafter. Many thought that he used his power over patronage to advance his Presidential ambitions. In his seven active years as Secretary, every appointment in the administration of the public domain went over his desk. Candidates were not all loyal to him; they were not even necessarily men that he liked; but directly and indirectly he exercised great influence in their appointment; and once appointed, they were under his jurisdiction.

In 1820, Congress passed a law fixing at four years the terms of a large number of officers closely connected with the collection or disbursement of government funds (including registers and receivers). Secretary Crawford's political enemies did not doubt that he had fashioned and forced the act through Congress in order to vacate offices that might be filled with his partisans. Of the so-called Tenure of Office Act, John Quincy Adams wrote that its

real and immediate object was to promote the election of W. H. Crawford as President of the United States in 1825. . . . It was drawn up by Mr. Crawford, as he himself told me. It was introduced into the Senate by Mahlon Dickerson, of New Jersey, then one of his devoted partisans, and its design was to secure for Mr. Crawford the influence of all the incumbents in office, at the peril of displacement, and of five or ten times an equal number of ravenous office-seekers, eager to supplant them.

Adams said that the act "succeeded so far as to enlist a multitude of the most active electioneering partisans in Crawford's cause . . . Registers of the Land Offices, Receivers of Public Moneys . . . were ardent Crawfordites."[35] General Andrew Jackson also suspected the

34. Quoted in Meigs, *Life of Josiah Meigs*, 89.
35. Adams, ed., *Memoirs*, 7: 424 (Feb. 7, 1828).

Secretary of the Treasury: "I . . . am fully aware how he uses his cunning, in the appointment of the officers in his department." [36]

Crawford strongly supported Senator Jesse B. Thomas in the struggle with Ninian Edwards for political control of the State of Illinois. Both men were Senators, but Thomas had the advantage of Crawford's patronage. In 1821, Crawford named Thomas inspector of land offices in Missouri, Illinois, Indiana, and part of Ohio. It was a lucrative appointment. Adams bitterly denounced "Crawford's electioneering practices at the public expense," which made it possible for Thomas to travel "from land office to land office, over all those States, everywhere canvassing for Crawford and reviling me." [37] Representative Daniel Cook of Illinois saw the rival faction benefit from government patronage, called for information on the Thomas trip, and suggested that such employment at government expense violated the law forbidding members of Congress to have a public contract. A select committee of the House cleared Thomas of wrongdoing, and Crawford further stated that the Illinois Senator had neither demanded nor received compensation for this service to the nation. The Secretary's enemies found the reply evasive. The records showed that Thomas had received payment for examining land offices. Andrew Jackson spluttered over Crawford's treachery and the absurdity of the suggestion that Thomas did his work "pro bono publico" instead of for six dollars per day.[38] Illinois newspapers took up the issue, and opinion was divided along factional lines. Whatever his reasons for sending Thomas to the western country, Crawford had used his power over the land business to benefit a key ally.[39]

William H. Crawford was not the only political figure of national stature to find support among the administrators of the land business. John C. Calhoun's good friend John McLean was a Commissioner of

36. Jackson to Calhoun, May 22, 1821, Bassett, ed., Correspondence of Andrew Jackson, 3: 59. White discusses Crawford's appointments, removals, and ethics in The Jeffersonians, 386–90.
37. Adams, ed., Memoirs, 5: 482–83 (Jan. 6, 1822).
38. Annals of Congress, 17 Cong., 1 Sess., 38: 635–37; House Committee Reports, 17 Cong., 1 Sess., #81: 2; Memorandum of Andrew Jackson, Feb., 1822, Bassett, ed., Correspondence of Andrew Jackson, 3: 151. An act of April 21, 1808 (2 Stat. 484–85) forbade members of Congress to have public contracts.
39. Edwardsville Spectator, Jan. 29, Feb. 26, 1822; Vandalia Illinois Intelligencer, May 18, 1822.

the General Land Office.[40] Josiah Meigs and his nephew Return Jonathan Meigs, Jr., then Postmaster General, attended dinners in support of Henry Clay.[41] At the same time Andrew Jackson actively sought offices in the land business for his friends. Indeed, the desire to reward his supporters was one of the principal reasons that he accepted the governorship of the Florida Territory. He was notably successful. Surveyors general Coffee of Alabama and Robert Butler of Florida and land officers Richard Keith Call, George Ward, and Samuel Overton (all of the Florida Territory) owed their places to the general.[42] Even President James Monroe found places for his friends and relatives. To his brother John J. Monroe went a job as inspector of land offices in Missouri and Arkansas in 1822. Henry Clay described George Graham, the Commissioner of the General Land Office, as "a favorite of the President. . . ." For his former private secretary, Edward Coles, the President found a post as register of the land office at Edwardsville (Illinois). Coles used this office as a springboard to the governor's office.[43]

In spite of the anguished cries of his rivals, William H. Crawford was never able to create a great patronage machine built around the many appointive offices within the Treasury Department. Undoubtedly his illness handicapped him. Part of his failure arose from President Monroe's determination to reappoint officers whose commissions expired under the Tenure of Office Act. Certainly Crawford and Monroe differed on appointments; and upon at least one occasion, it was rumored, the Secretary and President had a bitter quarrel over the subject and nearly came to blows.[44] A more fundamental reason was

40. Harry R. Stevens, *The Early Jackson Party in Ohio* (Durham, 1957), 40–41, 69–70.

41. James F. Hopkins, ed., *The Papers of Henry Clay* (3 vols. to date, Lexington, 1959–), 3: 69n.

42. Jackson to Dr. James C. Bronaugh, June 9, 1821, Bassett, ed., *The Correspondence of Andrew Jackson*, 3: 65. For the dominance of the Jacksonian appointees in the Florida land business, and their influence and interest in politics, see Herbert J. Doherty, "Andrew Jackson's Cronies in Florida Territorial Politics," *Florida Historical Quarterly*, 34 (1955–56): 3–29.

43. Josiah Meigs to John J. Monroe, May 27, 1822, Carter, ed., *Territorial Papers*, 19: 433; Clay to Charles Hammond, Aug. 21, 1823, Hopkins, ed., *The Papers of Henry Clay*, 3: 471–72; E. B. Washburne, *Sketch of Edward Coles* in Clarence W. Alvord, ed., *Governor Edward Coles* (Collections of the Illinois State Historical Library, Vol. 15, Springfield, 1920), 48–49.

44. Adams, ed., *Memoirs*, 7: 424–25 (Feb. 7, 1828); *ibid.*, 80–81 (Dec. 14, 1825).

the growing power of Congressional delegations over appointments. If the clerkships in the Treasury Department and the inspectorships of land offices were controlled by the Secretary, more and more survey-ors general and district land officers were nominated by interested Congressmen. By Monroe's second term the appropriate Congressional delegation was invariably consulted before appointments to land offices. Patronage remained the life blood of political success, and the land business provided lush offices. Congressmen demanded a voice in their distribution.[45]

During the Presidency of John Quincy Adams these trends contin-ued and intensified. Adams himself was a man of principle, and never was this more clearly displayed than in his attitude toward appoint-ment to office. He began his term by appointing the same officers who had served under Monroe. To his diary, he confided, "Registrars of the Land Offices and Receivers of public moneys, renominated." He con-tinued, "Efforts had been made by some of the Senators to obtain different nominations, and to introduce a principle of change or rota-tion in office at the expiration of these commissions; which would make the Government a perpetual and unintermitting scramble for office. A more pernicious expedient could scarcely have been de-vised." [46] The President was also extremely reluctant to dismiss men from office. Upon at least one occasion, the case of Andrew P. Hay, receiver at Jeffersonville (Indiana), Adams's determination to observe due process and to conduct an exhaustive investigation led to a finan-cial loss.[47]

Adams met strong opposition to his administration in both Houses of Congress; and, not surprisingly, the growth of Congressional power over appointments continued. This growth resulted in part from the determination of influential men in Congress to prevent Adams from using appointments to strengthen his position, in part from the de-termination of Congress to increase the power of its own members through the dispensation of suitable patronage, and in part from Adams's indifference to matters of appointment. Decisions of the Gen-eral Land Office and the President on the future of land officers were

45. White, The Jeffersonians, 126–29.
46. Adams, ed., Memoirs, 6: 520–21 (March 5, 1825); Fish, The Civil Service and the Patronage, 72–74.
47. Graham to Richard Rush, NA: GLO, Ltrs. Sent, Misc., 22: Dec. 16, 1828; American State Papers, Public Lands, 7: 560.

always taken in consultation with "the Delegation in Congress"—in the words of Commissioner George Graham.[48] In case of resignation or death the Secretary of the Treasury and the President made a temporary appointment to last until the next convening of Congress, when, Graham continued, "the Senators and Reps will be prepared to recommend proper persons to fill these offices permanently." [49] The appropriate Congressional delegation or territorial delegate more and more often defined the "proper persons." President Adams went along with this general policy.[50]

George Graham, commissioner for most of the decade, was well aware of the increasing use of the land business for political purposes, and he tried to raise the administration of the public lands above political strife. This attempt brought him into conflict with Congressmen and territorial delegates such as Austin Wing of Michigan. Wing worked energetically for the establishment of a separate surveyor general for the Michigan Territory, and Graham blocked him at every step. When the commissioner successfully opposed the separate administrative unit in 1826, Wing charged that the surveys in the Michigan Territory were inaccurate and badly numbered. Edward Tiffin denied that the responsibility lay with his deputy surveyors. Errors in numbering sections, running lines, and measuring were possible, he admitted, but he suspected that those "engaged in the same business" use this method to cast aspersions on the surveying of the Territory in hopes of benefiting from the creation of a separate surveying district. Of the gentlemen so involved, "some of them have been disappointed applicants for surveying. Others wish to obtain the new Office of Surveyor General (if created) or to profit from its patronage; therefore these clamours are raised by them and enlisted into their cause. . . ." [51] Wing grudgingly accepted defeat on the issue of a separate surveying district and demanded instead that Edward Tiffin employ only deputy surveyors from Michigan for surveying in that territory. Graham acquiesced on this point and recommended that the surveyor

48. Graham to Richard Rush, NA: TD, Ltrs. from Comm. GLO to Sec. Treas., 7: June 23, 1827.
49. Graham to Rush, NA: GLO, Ltrs. Sent, Misc., 17: July 22, 1826.
50. E. g. Adams, ed., *Memoirs*, 7: 85–86 (Dec. 17, 1825).
51. *American State Papers, Public Lands*, 4: 483; Graham to Tiffin, Jan. 31, 1826, Carter, ed., *Territorial Papers*, 11: 939–40; Tiffin to Graham, NA: GLO, Ltrs. Recd., SG, NW, 7: Feb. 11, 1826.

general give "preference" to Michigan applicants. Tiffin replied that only one of the seven deputies engaged in Michigan was from Ohio, but he agreed to replace him.[52]

During the administration of John Quincy Adams a parsimonious Congress failed to create additional district land offices. Instead, battles erupted over the location of the existing offices. The President had the authority to change the site of a district land office. Selection of a town for a land office meant the fulfillment of every town promoter's dream: an influx of men with capital to develop the village, the construction of overnight accommodations for travelers, transportation facilities, a supply of capital that might lead to a bank, and a constant flow of land purchasers with funds to spend. The extreme concern of interested men over the location of land offices appeared in the struggle over the removal of the Delaware (Ohio) office to the little village of Tiffin. "I called on the proprietor of Tiffin, and his son informed me, that he had, some time since, recd intelligence of the location of the Land Office there," wrote Horton Howard, the receiver. "He had not expected to have got it to his town, but he gave the credit of it to a good friend of his in Congress, and he should now use all his influence to have him elected again." As the deadline for the transfer of the office came near, letters poured into the General Land Office protesting the decision. Among the leading objectors were the land officers, who must follow the land office or lose their offices. Other writers included the governor of the state, a judge, "& other Gentn of high standing in the State of Ohio," all of whose views "are entitled to a due consideration. . . ."[53] The Secretary of the Treasury suspended the transfer in the face of such determined opposition and passed this affair on to the President. Adams now "read a multitude of papers . . . about the removal of a land-office from Delaware to Tiffin, in the State of Ohio—a distracting question of state, upon which perhaps depend the political standing and election of two or three members of Congress." The President sifted through all the correspondence on the matter and felt that Tiffin was poorly located, unhealthy, and isolated from the major transportation networks. Commissioner Graham re-

52.   Wing to Graham, *ibid.*, Misc., W: Feb. 11, 1826; Graham to Tiffin, Feb. 13, 1826, Carter, ed., *Territorial Papers*, 11: 953; Tiffin to Graham, NA: GLO, Ltrs. Recd., SG, NW, 7: March 2, 1826.
53.   Howard to Graham, *ibid.*, Reg. & Rec., Delaware, 40: May 27, 1826; Graham to Rush, *ibid.*, Ltrs. Sent, Misc., 18: Oct. 24, 1826.

ported the President's views to the Ohio Congressman whose district was most vitally affected, and requested his reactions. Mordecai Bartley was determined that the land office should go to Tiffin. The President acquiesced, and after eighteen months of debate and delay, the land office moved in the spring of 1828. "This subject is contested as if the fate of the Union depended upon it," concluded Adams with the asperity of a New Englander who never sought his fortune in town site speculation.[54]

The concept of the land business as a service to the citizens of the Republic had vanished, to be replaced by the idea of the land business as a means of profit. By the end of the Adams administration the change was complete. The land office had become a fief, a species of personal property that imparted to its holder a vested right. This attitude was openly displayed in a letter from the receiver of the Monroe, Michigan, office on hearing of the creation of a new land district to the west. He would lose the "fairest portion of the District," he wrote, and concluded that such an act of Congress was "an infringement of the rights, which the Act establishing the Southern District of this Territory gives and intended to give, to the officers connected with it." [55]

The public domain affected every aspect of life in early nineteenth-century America. In the period of the land office business after the War of 1812, the line between public and private in terms of the public lands gradually merged. Because of the all-pervasive influence of land, everyone dealt in it, especially on the frontier; and it was fatuous to think that a public officer would forego this activity because of his official duties. Land officers bought freely at the public sales, with the understanding that they should do so in competition with other purchasers. The Treasury Department recognized the existence of land transactions among its officers by making special provision to handle their purchases. The problem of public service ethics increased with the growth of the influence of land. Several early officials under the Republicans had been concerned with land, of course. Albert Gallatin was a speculator in Ohio tracts, Rufus Putnam had close connections with the Ohio Company, other minor officials also indulged.

54. Adams, ed., *Memoirs*, 7: 220–21 (Feb. 4, 1827); Graham to Bartley, NA: GLO, Ltrs. Sent, Misc., 19: May 21, 1827; Adams, ed., *Memoirs*, 7: 340 (Oct. 18, 1827); *ibid.*, 374 (Dec. 8, 1827); *ibid.*, 407 (Jan. 17, 1828).
55. Charles J. Lanman to Graham, NA: GLO, Ltrs. Recd., Reg. & Rec., Monroe. 27: Nov. 24, 1828.

But Gallatin himself brought to the land business much of his own integrity. In truth, he came as close as any man to placing the officials of the land business above reproach.

In the years after the war this purity was tarnished. Business relations between land officers and western banks were all too common. Israel Pickens (the Tombeckbe Bank), Samuel Hammond (the Bank of St. Louis), and Nathaniel Ewing (the Bank of Vicennes) were only the obvious examples of a tendency to use land office funds to finance banking establishments, either illegally through loans and diversion of funds, or by having the new bank made a government depository and so given custody, and use, of the funds of the land office. The speculations of the great land office business took its toll, and a few receivers defaulted for large sums. Others who remained solvent and prosperous used their official position for their own profit in dealing in lands. Additional ethical puzzles appeared. William L. D. Ewing, the receiver at Vandalia (Illinois) ran a land agency and actively solicited "all business of the Agency nature that non-resident owners of Land lying either in this or the State of Missouri, may entrust him with." [56] The clerks of the Treasury Department and the General Land Office often performed special services for clients, for which they received fees. Eventually William H. Crawford forbade them to carry on such agency work or to act in the employ of land agents. The commissioners of the General Land Office, especially George Graham, habitually recommended letters of inquiry concerning land services to a leading Washington land agency run by a Colonel J. Watson. Graham and the others did not profit from such a referral; they simply found Watson and his agency a convenience. Watson's organization paid taxes for absentee land owners and purchased military bounty land warrants. Yet the problem remained. As Secretary Crawford commented, "It is not fair to presume that in the case of Col. Watson the benefit of the soldier is the principal object. . . . It is in fact the duty of the officers to prevent, indirectly, the employment of agents as such employment is not credible to the Govt." [57] In 1829, Watson was an inspector of land offices. Whether he achieved this post through the recommendation of Graham is unknown. There remained the ethical question of

56. Vandalia *Illinois Intelligencer*, Aug. 17, 1822.
57. Crawford to Comm. GLO, NA: TD, Ltrs. Sent, Misc., 1801–33: June 28, 1821.

whether a man in the land business might look through the records of the district land officers, whatever the recommendations that brought him the post. Even more delicate was Commissioner George Graham's own speculation in public lands. Through the medium of Alexander Pope, the register at Cahaba, Graham bought and sold tracts of land in Alabama, with the aim of making a profit. The commissioner appeared distressed when the profits were embarrassingly large, but he continued to deal in public lands with Pope as his agent.[58]

The growth of the "business" aspect of land management paralleled the growth of the land business itself. Under Thomas Jefferson and Albert Gallatin, land officers handled the modest business in their spare time; it was one of a series of duties; and their emoluments were low. The end of the war brought not only an explosion of interest in land but a commensurate rise in the possibilities of profit. Offices now became extremely desirable, and as they did, politics entered into the selection process. Gradually the administration of the public domain became simply another cog in the patronage machine of various political factions. By the end of the term of John Quincy Adams the cycle had come a full half-turn. The service to the government and public had long since been forgotten in favor of the vested interest that the office holder received with his office, an interest that bowed neither to public welfare nor to the wishes of his fellow citizens. The land office business had become very businesslike indeed, and businessmen supervised the distribution of the public domain to the citizens of the Republic.

58. Graham to Pope, NA: GLO, Ltrs. Sent, Misc., 17: April 26, June 7, 1826; Pope to Graham, *ibid.*, Ltrs. Recd., Reg. & Rec., Cahaba, 2: May 8, 1826.

Administering the General Pre-Emption Acts of 1830, 1832, and 1834

10

The complexities of administering the public domain were nowhere more apparent than in the general pre-emption acts. Pre-emption was a response to continued trespassing on the public lands. From the time of the earliest English settlements, men had settled illegally on the land. After the Revolution this concern of the colonial landowners passed to the new government of the United States. Under the land system established in 1785 and modified thereafter, the lengthy settlement of private claims in the several states and territories, the failure of the surveyors to keep abreast of the great rush west after the War of 1812, the confusion attending the various relief acts and their administration, and the delay in the issue of patents, all contributed to squatting on the public domain. Some men sought to purchase land and found themselves blocked by administrative delay. Others had no intention of purchasing and defied the federal government, as their ancestors had flouted Governor Arthur St. Clair, the British Proclamation Line, and the land agents of the Penns. Daniel Ashby settled in Howard County (Missouri) in 1815 and wrote, "I drove out three hundred and seventy-five head of stock hogs, and squatted in the west part of the settlement of Howard County. There I lived as happy as Lord Selkirk on his island. I was monarch of all I surveyed. My rights—there were none to dispute." [1]

The federal government was well aware of these illegal acts, and periodically the Congress or the President acted to reassert its authority. Troops dispatched to the Ohio Valley burned settlers' dwellings and destroyed their improvements in 1788 and 1789. Responding to

1. "Anecdotes of Major Daniel Ashby," *Glimpses of the Past* (Publications of the Missouri Historical Society), 8 (1941): 105; another example in the same vein is "Autobiography of Gideon Lincecum," Mississippi Historical Society, *Publications*, 8 (1904): 443–519.

the growing spread of squatting in the early nineteenth century, Thomas Jefferson considered a proclamation against illegal settlement, and Congress passed a law making trespassers subject to fines and imprisonment. After the first shock had worn off, settlers went about their business, and the law was honored only in the most desultory fashion. With the surge to the West and the rise of illegal settlement that marked the end of the war, James Madison also ordered intruders off the public domain.[2]

Far surpassing the number and strident tone of the government directives against illegal settlement were the petitions, memorials, remonstrances, resolutions, and letters from citizens and legislatures of the West who demanded pre-emption: the right to settle, to improve, and subsequently to purchase a tract of public land at the minimum price. Congress received these expressions of the popular will but persistently refused to sanction general pre-emption. The House Committee on Public Lands made a resolute statement of that policy in 1815, declaring

that from the year 1785 to the [present] laws to prevent the unauthorized individuals from settling on the public and unappropriated lands of the United States have been in constant operation . . . that the policy and wisdom of such laws appear to be undeniable if those by whom they have been violated have in some instances been vested with rights of pre-emption, yet it seems clearly impossible to hold out invitations to a further disregard of them, the committee are not aware that the system in this respect requires alteration or amendment. . . .[3]

As the committee report suggested, there were certain exceptions. From the beginning of the century Congress had given pre-emption rights in a limited number of cases. The most important and far-reaching of these laws were the pre-emption acts of 1813 for citizens in Illinois (a prototype for later special pre-emption laws), for pioneers in the Missouri Territory (later extended to Howard County in western Missouri), and finally for the settlers of the Florida Territory.[4] Among those citizens outside the benefits of the special pre-emption acts, this favoritism produced a bitterness that was exacerbated by the

2. 2 Stat. 445–46 (May 3, 1807); Richardson, comp., *Messages and Papers of the Presidents,* 1: 572–73 (Dec. 12, 1815); 3 Stat. 260–61 (March 25, 1816).
3. National Archives, Legislative Division, Reports of the House Committee on Public Lands, 1: Dec. 22, 1815.
4. Special pre-emption acts are listed in 4 Stat. 420n.

feeling that the land belonged to all the citizens of the Republic, and the government should not stand in the way of distributing it to those who had broken the trails to the West and improved it.[5]

The administrators of the public lands had long opposed a general pre-emption act. Albert Gallatin had felt that revenue from the public domain would be seriously jeopardized by the grant of lands at the minimum price.[6] Josiah Meigs was also outspoken on this issue. Pre-emption laws "rather *encourage* than forbid *intrusion*," he wrote. "It is not improbable that the occupants indulge a hope that they may hereafter obtain a pre-emption right to the same lands which they illegally occupy." Meigs lent himself to the prevailing philosophy of the expanding America of his day and made an exception for "peaceable, bona-fide settlers, who are only waiting for an opportunity to become legal proprietors of the soil they now *harmlessly* occupy . . . nor is it the wish of the government *under such Circumstances* to molest them."[7] In spite of his interest in the "bona-fide settler," the Commissioner of the General Land Office was well aware that the growing number of illegal settlers on the public lands threatened the orderly distribution of the public domain.

The decade of the 1820's brought hard times and a stagnant economy, particularly in the western country. Congress abolished the credit system and demanded immediate cash payments for the public lands. Few purchasers could comply. Settlement on the public lands continued and subsequently grew when the confusion of the relief acts further muddied the question of who resided legitimately on the public domain. With the hard economic conditions came the renewed cry for pre-emption and the continued resistance of the administrators and others who felt "the gift made would soon only swell the monopolies of heartless speculators," in the words of Hezekiah Niles.[8] The election of Andrew Jackson in 1828 seemed to hold out the promise of

5. Ford, *Colonial Precedents of Our National Land System as It Existed in 1800*, 123–42; Roy M. Robbins, "Preemption—A Frontier Triumph," *Journal of American History*, 18 (1931): 331–42; Treat, *The National Land System*, 384–88; Hibbard, *A History of the Public Land Policies*, 144–47; a detailed analysis is Henry Tatter, "The Preferential Treatment of the Actual Settlers in the Primary Disposition of the Vacant Lands in the United States" (Unpublished doctoral dissertation, Northwestern University, 1933).
6. *American State Papers, Public Lands*, 1: 184.
7. Meigs to Crawford, NA: GLO, Ltrs. Sent, Misc., 11: May 14, 1821; Meigs to Edward Coles, *ibid.*, Sept. 25, 1821.
8. *Niles' Weekly Register*, 37: 274 (Dec. 26, 1829).

land for the landless. At least many of his supporters thought so. One of his Illinois followers wrote, "There are thousands of people in this country who have families to support, and have not the means of procuring a piece of land for homes, who are waiting with great anxiety in expectation that you will recommend to Congress to make some provision whereby the industrious poor may become the owners, each of a piece of land, by actual settlement on, and improving the same." [9] President Jackson was a grave disappointment. He made no such recommendations to Congress, and in 1830, to the consternation of western squatters and the general's political supporters, he issued a proclamation against the "many uninformed or evil-disposed persons" settled on the public lands in the Huntsville land district. He threatened those who did not immediately remove with military force, in accordance with the provisions of the act of March 3, 1807.[10] The Jacksonian supporters hastened to repair the damage by reassuring citizens of the western country that the President would enforce the proclamation in lenient fashion and permit those who wished to remain as tenants-at-will.[11]

At the very moment that Jackson moved against illegal settlers in Alabama, Congress responded to the demand for general pre-emption. In 1828 the House Committee on Public Lands for the first time endorsed a general pre-emption act. The committee wrote, "It is right and proper that the first settlers, who have made roads and bridges over the public lands at their expense and with great labor and toil, should be allowed a privilege greater than other purchasers." [12] That bill failed, but in the early months of 1830 the Senate Committee on Public Lands reported favorably on another such measure. David Barton of Missouri spoke for the committee. He told the Senate that

Congress had on various occasions deemed it necessary to depart from the provisions of the act of 1807, and grant pre-emption rights to actual settlers on the public lands. Inasmuch, then, as these various grants, made at different periods, in different sections of the country, together with the operations of the old law above alluded to, created general inequality in the con-

9. William Kenney to Jackson, Oct. 8, 1829, Jackson Papers (microfilm), State Historical Society of Wisconsin.
10. Richardson, comp., *Messages and Papers of the Presidents*, 2: 494 (March 6, 1830).
11. Cincinnati *Republican and Ohio Political Register*, April 23, 1830.
12. *American State Papers, Public Lands*, 5: 401.

ditions of the various settlers on the public lands, the object of the committee was to destroy that inequality, and place all the new States and Territories on the same footing.

Barton concluded by reminding the Senate that "a source of revenue
is by no means the most important view of our public lands," and by
recommending that they be used as "a fund, with which to elevate the
numerous non-freeholders of our country to the proud rank of free-
holders. . . ." [13]

The pre-emption bill passed the Senate and went to the House.
There the House Committee on Public Lands asked the Commissioner
of the General Land Office for his "*views* and *opinions* of the probable *operations* and *effects*" of the Senate bill.[14] George Graham
responded that a general pre-emption law would threaten the orderly
sale and administration of the public domain by necessitating a removal of public lands from the market for the duration of the law.
Scheduled sales of lands already advertised would have to be postponed or suspended. As for the lands now subject to entry at private
sale, "it would be unsafe for a purchaser to enter any portion of this
land until the occupants had entered and paid for his preemption." A
second objection was the unlimited time for payment proposed by the
Senate bill, for "if the poorer occupants have not the present means of
paying for 80 Acres of Land, it is not to be expected that in twelve
months they would generally have the means of paying for *160* or *320*
Acres as the case may be. . . ." Such a law would also encourage illegal settlement on the public domain in expectation of another pre-
emption act. It should not be surprising, wrote Graham, that the settler of 1830 should feel himself entitled to the rights accorded the
settler in 1829. In short, he concluded, a system for the disposition of
the public domain founded on the bill under consideration would soon
"arrest the regular Sales of the public Lands, and throw those Lands
into the hands of the occupants who would pay for them only when
convenient, if at all." [15] The House amended the bill to provide for
continued sales of the public domain. The commissioner did not

13. *Register of Debates,* 21 Cong., 1 Sess., 6: 8.
14. Rep. Samuel Vinton (Ohio) to George Graham, NA: GLO, Ltrs. Recd.,
Misc., V: March 5, 1830.
15. Graham to President Andrew Jackson, *ibid.,* Ltrs. Sent, Misc., 25: March 5,
1830.

change his mind and remained "opposed in principle to the whole bill." [16]

But Graham could not block general pre-emption. Under the terms of the act of May 29, 1830, settlers on the public lands "now in possession" who had cultivated the land in 1829 might purchase up to 160 acres at the minimum price. If two or more settlers claimed the same quarter-section, the tract should be divided between the two, and each would be entitled to "a pre-emption of eighty acres of land elsewhere in the said land district. . . ." These grants became known as "floats," because they could be located anywhere in the district. The act should not delay the sale "of any of the public lands of the United States, beyond the time which has been, or may be, appointed for that purpose, by the President's proclamation. . . ." The Commissioner of the General Land Office was to prescribe the "rules" of what would constitute "proof of settlement or improvement" which was to be "made to the satisfaction of the register and receiver of the land district in which such lands may lie. . . ." Assignments and transfers of pre-emption rights were illegal until the patents were issued. The act would remain in force for one year from the date of its passage.[17]

Citizens on the distant western frontier hailed the measure enthusiastically. The *Arkansas Gazette* commented, "This is unquestionably a most important law for Arkansas, and will tend more to promote her interest, than any other law that has been passed for some years." [18] In the midst of the rejoicing the Tallahassee *Floridian* commented that the bill extended only to "those who occupy lands which have already been surveyed but not yet offered for sale. We have no doubt that Congress will be induced to extend its provisions to all present occupants of public lands, as they shall be brought successively into market." [19] And so it would be.

Graham's failing health prevented his attendance at the office, but with the support of John M. Moore, his chief clerk, he drafted a circular designed to implement the act that he had so vigorously opposed. "The Fact of *cultivation* in 1829, and that of the *possession* of

16. John M. Moore to Rep. Clement C. Clay (Ala.), *ibid.*, May 28, 1830.
17. 4 Stat. 420–21 (May 29, 1830). On the passage of the act, see Hibbard, *A History of the Public Land Policies*, 151–53.
18. Little Rock *Arkansas Gazette*, June 16, 1830.
19. Tallahassee *Floridian and Advocate*, July 13, 1830; *Pensacola Gazette and Florida Advertiser*, June 26, 1830.

the land applied for on the 29th of May, 1830, must be established by the affidavit of the occupant, supported by such corroborative testimony as may be entirely satisfactory to you both," he wrote the land officers. Evidence must be taken before a justice of the peace, and the land officers must be present to question the applicant. The commissioner's instructions endowed the district land officers with great powers in the execution and administration of the law—a necessary step in view of the volume of business and the distance of the General Land Office from the various districts. While the Relief Act of 1821 had presented problems with the sheer volume of business and the limited amount of time for its execution, the pre-emption law led to an endless series of legal cases, each one with its evidence, oaths, witnesses, affidavits, and decision.[20]

Land offices already swarmed with settlers anxious to take advantage of the Pre-emption Act, and the circular provoked a storm of questions. Minor details must be clarified. "Every day, almost, brings with it some new difficulty in relation to the *Celebrated* act of the 29th of May relative to pre-emption," wrote William Wright from Palmyra.[21] Land officers differed as widely in their interpretation of the act's general intent as they did in their administration of it. Some registers and receivers followed the circular rigidly; others made their own rules. A few consulted with local "experts" on land matters. The Springfield officers adopted a most stringent interpretation of the law until they conversed with their Congressman, Joseph Duncan, who changed their minds and persuaded them to give the act "the most liberal construction." [22] The conditions under which a man might successfully claim a pre-emption under the act of May 29, 1830, depended in part upon his location and the chance that placed him in one land district rather than another.

Members of Congress raised strenuous objections to the General Land Office's interpretation of the Pre-emption Act. The most influential objector was Representative C. C. Clay of Alabama, a member of the important Committee on Public Lands and one of the principal architects of the Pre-emption Act. Clay termed "objectionable" Gra-

20.   NA: GLO, Circular to Reg. & Rec., June 10, 1830.
21.   Benjamin S. Pope to Graham, *ibid.*, Ltrs. Recd., Reg. & Rec., Huntsville, 5: June 20, 1830; William Wright to Graham, *ibid.*, Palmyra, 33: Aug. 13, 1830.
22.   William Wright to Graham, *ibid.*, Aug. 3, 1830; William May and John Taylor to Graham, *ibid.*, Springfield, 15: Aug. 5, 1830.

ham's decision that the right of pre-emption was limited to two settlers on any quarter-section. The Alabaman held instead that the term "said settlers" meant all the settlers on the quarter, not simply the first two who made improvements. And he felt that all settlers should be entitled to eighty-acre floats. According to John M. Moore, Graham had surmised that "the two first settlers would occupy the land for agricultural purposes only. . . ." To reverse this interpretation, Moore continued, would mean that "all the settlers on the public lots in the Towns laid out by the U. States as well as those in the Villages & Towns which have been formed by unauthorized settlements on the other lands of the Government will each receive a floating right to 80 acres of the public domain in any part of the Land District. . . ." These floats would quickly engross the most valuable portions of the lands still open to the public. Graham's interpretation continued in effect.[23]

The problem of administering the Pre-emption Act was further complicated by the death of George Graham on August 7, 1830. Graham had presided over the office since 1823; and although some Congressmen and the Executive branch disagreed with his interpretation of various Congressional laws, he had brought continuity to this important post. Congress had adjourned, and the President and his Cabinet had wisely deserted the capital during this hottest month of summer. In their absence and surrounded by the multiplying questions and issues concerning the interpretation of the act of May 29, 1830, the chief clerk, John M. Moore, felt it necessary to issue another general circular on the law. The most important question was whether the grant of pre-emption for a year necessitated the suspension of private sales for that period, "or whether the ordinary private entries can proceed at the hazard of interfering with the occupant within the year." The act of May 29, 1830, merely stated that sales should continue without creating machinery to assure that conflicts would not arise between pre-emptions and private entries. In order to guard against such a possibility, Moore directed that the applicant for a tract of land by private purchase take an oath, "that, to the best of his knowledge and belief, no claim exists to the same land, as a pre-emption, under the act of 29th May, 1830." The chief clerk specified no form for the

23. Moore to Samuel D. Ingham, Sec. Treas., NA: TD, Ltrs. from Comm. GLO to Sec. Treas., 8: Aug. 12, Sept. 7, 1830.

affidavit, but he must have been aware of the difficulties that his requirement would pose for the purchaser and the land officers.[24]

The settler who wished to take advantage of the law first had to identify his tract and then go with his witnesses to a district land office. There he and his supporters would be interrogated by the register; evidence would be presented, depositions taken, and a decision handed down. Those who wished to make private purchases from the government had to make an oath before a justice of the peace or other officer authorized to take depositions, that the tract he sought to enter did not have a pre-emption claimant, and that no conflict would result from his action. Only upon taking this legal document to the land office would he be permitted to enter his land. Thus, the interpretations of Graham and Moore greatly complicated the operation of the Pre-emption Act, for citizen and land officer alike. The settlers, Congressmen, and squatters who had so vociferously supported a general pre-emption act now loudly objected to its administration.

While land officers, private citizens, and Congressmen in the western country were criticizing Moore's directions, Andrew Jackson appointed a new Commissioner of the General Land Office, Elijah Hayward. Hayward was a leading Jackson supporter from Ohio and, at the time of his appointment, a justice of the Ohio Supreme Court.[25] He settled in Washington just in time to receive the protests about Moore's circular. Visiting Congressional delegations from Ohio, Indiana, and Illinois called to register formal objections. The land officers added to the din. Their views were summed up in the words of Joseph Kitchell: "Should the instructions issued by the acting commissioner be confirmed difficulties will multiply. We cannot believe but that these instructions are at war with the letter and spirit of the law." [26] Hayward finally took the issue of the oath to the Secretary of the Treasury, who judged that no alteration could be made in the instructions from the General Land Office without an act of Congress.

24.   NA: GLO, Circular to Reg. & Rec., Sept. 14, 1830; Elijah Hayward to Martin Van Buren, Jan 26, 1835, *Senate Public Documents*, 23 Cong., 2 Sess., #87: 1–4.
25.   Francis P. Weisenburger, "The 'Atlas' of the Jacksonian Movement in Ohio," *Bulletin of the Historical and Philosophical Society of Ohio*, 14 (1956): 283–95.
26.   Hayward to Van Buren, Jan. 26, 1835, *Senate Public Documents*, 23 Cong., 2 Sess., #87: 3; Kitchell to Hayward, NA: GLO, Ltrs. Recd., Reg. & Rec., Palestine, 16: Oct. 31, Nov. 30, 1830.

Hampton L. Boon, the register at Franklin, Missouri, wrote that Moore's circular of September 14 "takes a very different view of the law to that given as the opinion of the Register and Receiver. They regret exceedingly that they cannot reconcile the instructions with the law; and they do say with candor & sincerity that it is extremely painful for them to depart in any instance from the mandates of those placed above them." Boon doubted the wisdom of granting preemption to settlers on public lands open to private entry, and he expressed strong reservations about the oath. Boon also reminded the commissioner that the land officers had the sole authority to grant preemption, and he intended to grant pre-emptions according to his own interpretation of the law.[27]

For the next year Hayward answered endless questions about the Pre-emption Act. The inquiries dealt with such divergent problems as occupation, floating rights, proof of cultivation, and the expiration of the act.[28] He also handled complaints from those who did not accept the decisions of land officers on their pre-emption rights. One settler announced that he had a family of eleven children (which certainly entitled him to sympathy), "one of which I have named Andrew Jackson," which in Hayward's eyes did not entitle him to anything more.[29] Hayward continued to support the independence of his land officers in deciding pre-emption claims.

Dissatisfaction over the law grew with the volume of its operations. The Pre-emption Act of 1830 created a land office business of its own, and the procedures prescribed by the General Land Office for adjudicating each case consumed much time and caused great inconvenience to both officers and claimants. The burden of bringing witnesses as far as one hundred miles to a district land office was immense; the oath required for private entry was a nuisance; and everywhere innumerable questions arose over what could and could not be done under the act. A veteran of the land business, Gideon Fitz, wrote for all land officers, "the inconvenience in this office in answering thousands of

27.   Boon to Hayward, *ibid.*, Franklin, 32: June 13, Sept. 26, 1831.
28.   Hayward to William Wright, *ibid.*, Ltrs. Sent, Reg. & Rec. (New Series), 2: March 19, 1831; Charles F. Morhouse to Hayward, *ibid.*, Register of Ltrs. Recd., Ouachita, July 21, 1831; William May and John Taylor to Hayward, *ibid.*, Ltrs. Recd., Reg. & Rec., Springfield, 15: Dec. 1, 1831.
29.   T. S. Smith (Mich. Terr.) to Hayward, *ibid.*, Misc., S: May 8, 1831.

questions as to what may, or what may not be done with this act, is beyond anything you can imagine." [30] Elijah Hayward found the law a burden to the General Land Office, and he so stated in his annual report for the year. "The execution of the act of the 29th May, 1830 . . . has been attended with considerable difficulty, and some embarrassment to this office and at the several land offices," he wrote. The commissioner defended the oath on the grounds that since the law obviously did not intend to bring about a complete suspension of public sales, "precautionary regulations" must be taken to avoid conflict. Hayward found the entire law objectionable, and he wrote:

The expediency of granting such privileges may well be questioned, when it leads to a course of speculations founded exclusively upon the gracious liberality of the government, inconsistent with the public interest. In numerous cases, the occupants dispose of the advantages thus acquired by law to less fortunate individuals, at a profitable advance, with a view of making a settlement elsewhere, in anticipation of another similar speculation at a future day.

A far better policy, concluded the commissioner, would be to make a rapid survey of the public lands and sell those lands in demand. As for "intruders and trespassers," they should be left "to the local tribunals of justice for such relief as they may be entitled to on any principles of legal right or equitable jurisdiction." [31] The rush to act under the Pre-emption Law was especially great in the spring of 1831, when citizens "thronged" to land offices to make good their claims just before its expiration.[32] A measure of the business occasioned by the act of 1830 appeared in the figures for the land annually secured under pre-emption laws: [33]

	ACRES
1828	5,507.56
1829	2,623.03
1830	242,979.78
1831	557,840.34

30. Valentine King to Hayward, *ibid.*, Opelousas, 23: Nov. 17, 1830; Fitz to Hayward, *ibid.*, Mount Salus, 29: Nov. 28, 1830.
31. *American State Papers, Public Lands*, 6: 192.
32. Little Rock *Arkansas Gazette*, May 25, June 1, 1831.
33. *Senate Public Documents*, 24 Cong., 1 Sess., #376: 3–4.

From the moment of its passage, the Pre-emption Act of 1830 invited fraud. The abuses under the law were most clearly outlined by Gideon Fitz. Fitz had begun in 1806 as a deputy surveyor, then had served for fifteen years as the principal deputy surveyor for the western district of Louisiana, had followed with four years as commissioner for the adjustment of private claims in that district, and since that time had served as register of the Choctaw district in the State of Mississippi. "The law exposed men on the frontier to the greatest of all temptations, a bargain in land," he wrote. "The temptation is so great to get land worth five to ten dollars an acre, in many instances, at the Government price for the poorest land, that witnesses will be found to prove up the occupancy of the land." Unprincipled men will claim pre-emptions simply to "get the labor and improvements of innocent and honorable purchasers." The law of 1830 had already brought about "the most odious schemes of extensive speculation." It will end

with heart-burning litigation and bloodshed, if not something like a civil war. Swarms of speculators will be out to get floating rights as they are called from every part of the district, which floating rights will be scattered along the banks of the Mississippi, and other valuable lands, leaving small intervals which could not suit other persons, and thus secure all the best land at the Government price, and deprive the greater part of the community of all chance to purchase, but at second hand, and at a high price.

Fitz described in detail how speculators engrossed the most attractive tracts of land:

At present it is customary for the leader of a party of speculators to agree with a number of dealers, with their witnesses, men, women & children, to meet on a certain day at the Register's Office,—They come like the locusts of Egypt, & darken the office, with clouds of smoke & dust, and an uproar occasioned by whiskey and avarice, that a Register at least can never forget. . . . The speculator tells the settler that he cannot get his money without proving, and if the claim is not so clear as it might be, that it is as good as others that have been allowed: that he had as well have the land as another. —In this way sometimes, three hours are consumed, before one claim is got through. I believe I should have quit the office ere this, but for the expectation of being relieved by my successor. I am distressed and my health is fast sinking under this dreadful system. I cannot hold out long, and no price would induce me to act under such another pre-emption law.[34]

Fitz was one of the few to note the difference between legislation and administration. "I think it is to be regretted that there is so much feverish anxiety to make alterations in the land System by members of Congress who have not the practical experience necessary to enable them to avoid confusion and endless difficulties," he continued. A case in point was the Pre-emption Act. Fitz described the law of May 29, 1830, as "the most unguarded & in all respects the worst land law that has ever been passed in the United States." Good reasons might exist to extend pre-emption to forfeited lands or to tracts improved under the credit system, or to give the whole community an equal chance to make settlements on the public lands, "but that a general sweep should be made of the most valuable lands of the United States by intruders, at as low a price as that which the poorest person in the nation, would have to pay for the poorest pine barren, is unreasonable in the extreme." Congress displayed appalling innocence in the creation of the "floating eighth." Fitz wrote, "I find there is a great anxiety among claimants to get out these *floating half quarters,* which can be placed on other valuable places, leaving strips of vacant land between, as to prevent the sale of the intermediate lots, to any but those who hold the preemption claims." Congress had passed this act ostensibly "to favor poor people; but it is a fact, that the rich are the persons benefitted in the end; because the poor . . . cannot pay for the land, and all they can do, is to sell their claims and remove to some other place. It is also a fact that, many of the very wealthy inhabitants, send overseers & slaves, or hire men to make improvements on the most choice places for the purpose of getting preemptions." If the law were for the benefit of the poor, Congress should have limited its benefits to the poorer class of citizens. Half a quarter-section or a quarter-section might be donated to them, and "their inability to buy might be proven to the Registers & Receivers on the plan that pensions are obtained by revolutionary soldiers." [35]

34.   Fitz to Graham, NA: GLO, Ltrs. Recd., Reg. & Rec., Mount Salus, 29: July 5, 1830; Fitz to Hayward, March 20, 1831, *House Executive Documents,* 24 Cong., 1 Sess., #211: 46–48; Fitz to Graham, NA: GLO, Ltrs. Recd., Reg. & Rec., Mount Salus, 29: May 8, 1831.
35.   Fitz to Hayward, *ibid.,* Jan. 16, 1831.

When Congress met in late 1831, a bill was offered that made additional concessions to the small settler. It would provide forty-acre tracts for sale to actual settlers who would use the land "for cultivation." District land officers were aghast at the thought of twice as many records and transactions in the land business. "The project proposed by some, to cut up the Sections into 40 acre tracts, would be attended with endless difficulty," wrote Gideon Fitz on hearing of the proposal. "It would destroy the use of all the tract books at present in use in the land offices, and would make it so difficult for purchasers to describe the lots, for the tracts could not be designated any other way, that erroneous entries would continually occur." Fitz was not alone in his dismay. "What under Heaven is Congress passing a 40 acres entry bill?" cried Samuel Gwin from Mount Salus. "Had they not better at once give the land to the poor. . . . It has always been the theme of certain politicians to take care of the poor—the poor, & every move they have made has had directly the reverse effect." A case in point was the Pre-emption Act, "passed for the poor—but not one honest man could obtain its advantages, if any there was, for the speculators could hire men to swear anything for $30. In fact men were in attendance at this office for months to prove up preemptions the price of swearing was $30 . . . & mark if this 40 acre scheme will end as to the poor much like the pre-emption law." Congress should give more attention to the problems of administrators. Should the law pass we shall have to make an entire new set of tract books & the errors will be immense. To describe each 40 acres contained in a 640 acre tract carefully will require the knowledge of a member of Congress, who studies alone the interest of the poor." [36]

Neither district land officers nor the commissioner himself could stem the tide of sentiment carrying the "forty-acre law" through Congress.[37] The President signed the bill on April 5, 1832. For the first time the government would sell forty-acre tracts. The law specified that the tract must be intended "for cultivation," and created administrative obstacles to insure this distinction. The person applying under the act must file an "affidavit under such regulations as the Secretary of the Treasury may prescribe, that he or she makes the entry in his or

36. Fitz to Hayward, *ibid.*, Jan. 16, 1831; Gwin to Hayward, *ibid.*, April 7, 1832.
37. Hayward's views and several suggested amendments (not incorporated into the final law) are in Hayward to Rep. Clement C. Clay (Ala.), *ibid.*, Ltrs. Sent, Misc., 27: Jan. 12, 1832.

her own name, for his or her own benefit, and not in trust for another." All "actual settlers" received the right of pre-emption on a quarter-quarter or a half-quarter section provided that the entry was made within six months.[38] The Secretary drew up the appropriate "affidavit," and Elijah Hayward sent it to the district land officers with a circular directing that the affidavit be taken before a justice of the peace or other officer authorized to administer oaths. The Secretary's affidavit was only the beginning of the swearing. The settler who hoped to exercise the pre-emption privilege must present proof of his claim in the form of a second deposition, also made before a suitable magistrate and setting forth that "he or she is an actual settler and housekeeper on *public* lands, (*not on lands already purchased from the Government,*) and that the half quarter section applied for includes his or her improvements, which affidavit is to be sustained by the affidavits of one or more *disinterested* persons, substantiating the fact to your entire satisfaction." And in order "to prevent collision" between ordinary entries and pre-emption claimants, all purchasers during the entire operation of the act (six months) must affirm that the land applied for was not subject to any pre-emption claims. The commissioner also noted that suitable provision must be made for twice as many entries in a tract book. Where "practicable," entries might be interlined, but generally this might be done only where the handwriting of the officer was "small and neat." Where interlining was impossible, entries of the quarter-quarters should be made in a "miscellaneous tract book" by the date of application.[39]

The forty-acre law was received happily on the frontier as another sign of government interest. "Its benefits will be felt in every part of Arkansas; and we have no doubt the Government will realize many thousand dollars from the sale of hundreds of small tracts which never would have sold under the former laws restricting locations to tracts of 80 acres and upwards," affirmed the *Arkansas Gazette*.[40] The administrators of the public lands were far less enthusiastic.

The purchase of public land had become extremely complex and burdensome, even for the settler who claimed neither quarter-quarters nor pre-emption. Did the commissioner's instructions intend "that all

38.   4 Stat. 503 (April 5, 1832).
39.   NA: GLO, Circular to Reg. & Rec., May 8, 1832.
40.   Little Rock *Arkansas Gazette,* May 9, 1832.

purchasers of public Lands are to be put under oath before they are permitted to make an entry?" inquired Biddle and Kearsley from Detroit. "Last year there were upwards of two thousand entries of land in this District; and during the present year the number may be as great. Under the provisions of the former pre-emption law not a single sale took place at this office, and there may not be under the present." Commissioner Hayward replied that "it is to be regretted that a necessity for adopting the rule should exist as it must be troublesome in its operation & frequently prove of no utility," but he directed that it be obeyed.[41] Throughout the land districts the commissioner's instructions underwent modification to meet a local situation. In some districts the scarcity of magistrates and suitable officials led to informal oaths and affidavits.[42] Congress had neglected to specify the date when settlers must have resided on the public domain in order to be eligible for pre-emption privileges. Numerous inquiries on this matter necessitated a circular by the commissioner, who announced that settlers must have been on the land at the date of the act's passage. Hayward admitted that "on this point neither the law itself nor the first instructions appear to be explicit." [43] He also concurred that the act was sufficiently vague in its wording to permit a man who claimed a pre-emption under the act of 1830 to claim another under that of April 5, 1832, provided, of course, that he had made a new settlement.[44]

While officials in Washington and in the western country debated the meaning and execution of the forty-acre law, settlers hastened to take advantage of its opportunities. Much depended on the interpretation given the law by district land officers. Some were stringent. "You will no doubt be surprised at the few preemptions proven up under the act of the 5th Apl. 1832—out of fifty or sixty only five were approved and allowed complaints will be made of the strict manner with which I have required the proof to be made of *actual settlement prior* to the *approval* of the Law—and the bonafide settlement," wrote

41. Biddle and Kearsley to Hayward, NA: GLO, Ltrs. Recd., Reg. & Rec., Detroit, 26: June 4, 1832; Hayward to Biddle and Kearsley, *ibid.*, Ltrs. Sent, Reg. & Rec. (New Series), 3: June 23, 1832.
42. Hampton L. Boon to Hayward, *ibid.*, Ltrs. Recd., Reg. & Rec., Franklin, 32: July 28, Sept. 29, 1832.
43. *Ibid.*, Circular to Reg. & Rec., July 28, 1832.
44. Hayward to Archibald Yell, July 31, 1832, Carter, ed., *Territorial Papers*, 21: 526–27.

one officer. The settlers were a determined lot where the public domain was at issue. Refusals to grant pre-emptions often brought a visi-
tation "by a [illegible] eye lawyer, or two, armed with a string of non-
descript depositions, setting forth the claim in bold relief." Others
were, of course, less vigorous in their requirements. Reports that "the
press of business" and "the office was overflowing by business" indicated that the act of 1832 produced great interest and activity.[45] And
evidence of corruption and fraud appeared just as rapidly. Valentine
King commented from Louisiana, "I think it proper to apprise you
that men women and children almost, are in motion to make such settlement on the Choicest of the public lands as will enable them to
Swear and prove that they are Settlers & housekeepers—tho', it may
not be their intention to be so one hour after they may have made
entry." [46]

Congress and the President also extended the provisions of the act
of May 29, 1830, to those eligible who had not taken advantage of its
provisions within the time limit because the surveys had not been
completed or the lands had not been attached to any land district.
They could now do so within a year after survey. If the President proclaimed the land for sale by public auction within the year, then the
claimant must enter the pre-emption before the public sale.[47] Upon
inspecting the signed law for the first time, Hayward concluded that
the Treasury Department must bend its administrative efforts "to
guard the vested right of pre-emption" and to permit sales to proceed
under "precautionary regulations." The result was another oath and
more controversy. Hayward did express satisfaction about the omis-
sion of a provision for "floating rights." A circular from the General
Land Office outlined the commissioner's views on these major points
and answered a large number of specific questions about smaller matters.[48]

Meanwhile citizens settled on the public lands since 1829 also de-

45.   Breckenridge to Hayward, NA: GLO, Ltrs. Recd., Reg. & Rec., Fort Wayne,
17: Sept 1, 1832; Rogers to Hayward, *ibid.*, Opelousas, 23: Oct. 22, 1832.
46.   King to Hayward, *ibid.*, July 20, 1832.
47.   4 Stat. 603 (July 14, 1832).
48.   Hayward to Louis McLane, Sec. Treas., NA: TD, Ltrs. from Comm. GLO
to Sec. Treas., 9: July 14, 1832; Circular to Land Officers, July 28, 1832. Among
the minutiae were such critical points as what rights accrued and where when a
claimant's house spread over the corner of a section. Hayward's answer: the
pre-emptor was entitled to the quarter-section on which the largest part of the
dwelling lay.

manded pre-emption rights. The case of these settlers was just as meritorious as that justifying the first law. By an act of June 19, 1834, Congress extended pre-emption for two years to all those who were occupying and cultivating a tract of land in 1833. The fact of cultivation and possession must be established by affidavit, supported by the customary testimony of "disinterested witnesses."[49] Discussing the problem of defining cultivation, Hayward wrote that land officers should demand as the minimum "the cultivation of a crop of grain, esculent roots, or other vegetable, or ordinary culture in the peculiar section of the country . . . together with the ordinary fence or other suitable enclosure. . . ." To these general instructions the commissioner added an administrative innovation. "Evidence adduced in support of the pre-emption rights admitted under this act, and also the oaths required of purchasers at ordinary private sale, are to be carefully enclosed in the appropriate certificates of purchase, and transmitted therewith to this office, accompanied by your joint certificate *as to the credibility of the witnesses.*"[50] Land sales were rising rapidly in the western country. The commissioner's directive that land officers must forward evidence and oaths to Washington imposed an additional burden on an over-taxed administrative system. It also infringed on the right of land officers to make decisions in cases of pre-emption by subjecting them to the scrutiny of a higher authority.

Widespread protest greeted the circular. At the center of the land officers' protests was the issue of the transmission of evidence and oaths to the General Land Office. Land officers also constantly emphasized how difficult it was for purchasers to comply with the commissioner's instructions on oaths.[51] There were frequent requests that notary publics be permitted to administer the oaths.[52] To mitigate the growing criticism, the commissioner finally issued a supplemental circular, which modified the oath requirement to permit oaths formerly taken before a justice of the peace to be sworn to before a notary public or other officers qualified to administer oaths.[53]

The most important and influential protesters were members of

49. 4 Stat. 678 (June 19, 1834); *Register of Debates,* 23 Cong., 1 Sess., 10: 4469–80.
50. NA: GLO, Circular to Land Officers, July 22, 1834.
51. E.g., William B. Slaughter and Arthur St. Clair, Jr., to Hayward, *ibid.,* Register of Ltrs. Recd., Indianapolis, Aug. 14, 1834.
52. William Wright to Hayward, *ibid.,* Register of Ltrs. Recd., Palmyra: Aug. 14, 1834; A. Saltmarsh to Hayward, *ibid.,* Cahaba, Feb. 4, 1834.
53. *Ibid.,* Circular to Reg. & Rec., Oct. 23, 1834.

Congress. They demanded that Hayward present copies of the oath and of the act of Congress that authorized such oaths. Commissioner Hayward replied that the practice of requiring oaths began in 1830 with the first pre-emption act in order that "the ordinary sales should not be discontinued for one year," and that the instructions of 1834 were simply a continuation of this principle. Hayward admitted that the law did not specify an oath, but he went on, "in its execution, and to conform to its manifest intent and object, which was to protect the actual settler and occupant against the interference of the script locator, the only effectual means suggested, and which I am happy to say has been attended with great success, was the oath prescribed." [54]

The general Pre-emption Act of June 19, 1834, revived once more the "floating claims" found first in the law of 1830. A flood of letters from the western country showed the high level of interest in the float, and land officers expressed their grave misgivings about this loophole through which choice tracts of the public domain might be engrossed. "In some instances [applicants] proving up their claims to preemptions & floating rights have brought their sons & daughters of all ages 10 years & upwards, to testify &c," wrote Thomas L. Sumrall from Mount Salus. Everywhere speculators produced hordes of witnesses in favor of their claims. Rumors of extensive fraud became so widespread that the Treasury Department took official notice of them. The Secretary wrote the Commissioner, "It is represented that associations of men are engaged in speculating in the purchase of floating rights under the late preemption law & by means of facilities afforded by Deputy Surveyors acting as Agents in their location much valuable lands in Louisiana is thus engrossed, & that these rights are multiplied by the recognition of separate preemption rights in the parents, children & hired men of each family & fictitious persons." The commissioner sought to block these loopholes, but others continued to appear; and the overriding authority of land officers meant that the General Land Office had no clear jurisdiction (nor could it have because of sheer numbers) to grant or deny pre-emptions.[55] Gideon Fitz of Mis-

54. Hayward to Martin Van Buren, Jan. 26, 1835, *Senate Public Documents*, 23 Cong., 2 Sess., #87: 1–4.
55. Sumrall to Hayward, NA: GLO, Register of Ltrs. Recd., Mount Salus, Nov. 5, 1834; John T. Cabean to Hayward, *ibid.*, Sept. 17, 1835; Levi Woodbury, Sec. Treas., to Comm. GLO, NA: TD, Ltrs. Sent, Misc., 1833–39: Dec. 1, 1835; Ethan Allen Brown to Louisiana land officers, NA: GLO, Ltrs. Sent, Reg. & Rec. (New Series), 6: Dec. 17, 21, 1835.

sissippi added to the general indictment of pre-emption legislation. He wrote:

It is believed by many that the law itself was intended for fraud, because if it had been the object of him who drew it, to give the Settler his improvement only, it was wholly unnecessary to give him floating rights, contrary to the very object of all such laws, and if the object of Congress was to prevent any land from being sold for more than a dollar & a quarter an acre, then it would only be necessary to let the lands be entered without offering them at public sale.

If Congress intended to distribute the land as widely and rapidly as possible, concluded Fitz, why not do it at the minimum price "without killing the public officers to write volumes of preemption lies or truths?" [56]

By 1834 the sudden spurt of movement west, the rising commodity prices, and the growing speculation in real estate led to a dramatic rise in the sale of public lands. The Pre-emption Act provided a welcome opportunity for men to escape the public auction and acquire choice tracts at the minimum price; and they took advantage of it, as the acreage of land secured under the various pre-emption acts indicates: [57]

	ACRES
1832	49,971.17
1833	31,756.79
1834	637,597.59
1835	574,936.85
1836	112,842.93

The figures reflect the westward movement of the nation and the acquisition by its citizens of land at a bargain price. The experience of the administrators of the public domain tells another story: the thankless task of trying to protect the public domain from the rapacious grasp of these citizens and from the ambiguous or deliberately vague wording of Congressional legislation. The pre-emption acts were a continuation of the various relief acts of the 1820's and, like them,

56. Fitz to Graham, *ibid.*, Ltrs. Recd., Reg. & Rec., Mount Salus, 29: May 8, 1831.
57. *Senate Public Documents*, 24 Cong., 1 Sess., #376: 4.

were designed to distribute the public lands to the citizens of the Republic. Unfortunately they were imperfect instruments. While the basic law of 1830 was designed to meet the needs of the restless citizens who were opening the way to the West, most of these individuals could no more pay $1.25 for their pre-emption rights than they could bid at public auction. Traditionally these people put down shallow roots, made improvements, cleared a portion of the public domain, perhaps put up a bit of fencing, built a shelter, harvested a crop or two, sold their improvements, and moved on. Some purchased only after a series of such intermediate pauses; others never did. As interpreted by the administrators of the public domain, the law's requirements of residence, cultivation, affidavits, witnesses, and $1.25 per acre did nothing for a class of citizens who simply meandered over the face of the western country.[58]

Not only did Congress fail to devise a simple system for distributing the public lands to the poorer citizens who needed the freehold, but it drew up a law that threatened to derange the existing land system and to submerge district land officers under piles of new requirements. Even the system of regular public sales was disordered, and applicants for private purchase were forced into legal steps to avoid possible conflict with pre-emptioners. Thus, in their variation in application, their unguarded phrases, the invitations to fraud inherent in the provisions for floats, and the nationwide derangement of the land system, the various pre-emption acts of the 1830's were another administrative nightmare.

58. William McKee and Benjamin Edwards to Hayward, NA: GLO, Register of Ltrs. Recd., Edwardsville, Sept. 18, 1834; James Sloo to Hayward, *ibid.*, Shawneetown, Jan. 31, May 16, 1835; *ibid.*, circular to land officers, Oct. 23, 1834, directing them to grant pre-emption to applicants whom the register and the receiver felt came within the "meaning and intent of the law," even though they could not qualify under the terms of the act or the instructions issued by the General Land Office.

THE LAND OFFICE BUSINESS, 1830–1837: FLOODTIDE

11

Expansion in the 1820's had filled in selected tracts of fertile lands. The next decade saw another dramatic surge to the West. Between 1830 and 1837 the empty portions of the Republic east of the Mississippi were settled, and the frontier thrust against the Indian barrier on the western borders of Louisiana, Arkansas, and Missouri. It was a time of economic prosperity, and once more, the public domain provided a major impetus to the movement west. The statistics of sales of public lands for the early years of the decade demonstrate the change: [1]

	ACRES	
1828	965,600.36	$1,221,357.99
1829	1,244,860.01	$1,572,863.54
1830	1,929,733.79	$2,433,432.94
1831	2,777,856.88	$3,557,023.76
1832	2,462,342.16	$3,115,376.09
1833	3,856,227.56	$4,972,284.84

Several forces joined to stimulate expansion and the land office business. Better transportation facilities, especially the opening of the Erie Canal in 1825, had laid the basis for commercial agriculture in the upper reaches of the Old Northwest and assisted in the settlement of Michigan, Wisconsin, and northern Illinois. Agricultural commodity prices, particularly of cotton, began a slow recovery from the low levels of the 1820's. Banking practices lent support. The loss of regulatory power by the Second Bank of the United States following Jackson's veto of the bill for recharter and the removal of deposits led to

1. *Senate Public Documents*, 27 Cong., 3 Sess., #246: 10. The slump in sales in 1832 accompanied Black Hawk's uprising.

the rise of innumerable state banks which expanded loans at a dizzy rate, while often filling their vaults with public monies deposited by the local receiver. The policies of these banks and their easy lending practices created a cycle of loan, purchase, and deposit that continued unchecked.[2]

The movement to the West and the accompanying development of the land office business in the early 1830's are best illustrated by the experience of the South and the Southwest. When Andrew Jackson became President in 1829, powerful Indian tribes controlled west central Alabama and the largest portion of central and northern Mississippi. An encircling white civilization that rested on cotton culture looked with open envy on these ancient hunting grounds, potentially the finest cotton lands in the world. Jackson was the first President who could claim the title "western man," with all its connotations, and he and his supporters did so with pride and enthusiasm. In many respects it was not misplaced. The general had long been a land speculator, interested in the public domain as a field of profitable investment and as the principal instrument of the Jeffersonian agrarian ideal. He also had a profound dislike for Indians. The Choctaw, the Cherokee, and the Chickasaw tribes, who occupied large tracts of land suitable for white cultivation and engaged in a running legal battle with intruders and state legislatures, could expect little sympathy from the new Great White Father in Washington.

The United States had promised Georgia to remove the Indians from her borders as part of the state cession of western claims in 1802. Years passed, the Indians remained, and the territorial governors of Mississippi and Alabama joined the Georgia government in demanding Indian removal. At the time of President Jackson's inauguration the Choctaw tribe claimed the east central and northwestern section of the State of Mississippi and a slice of western Alabama. A long series of negotiations had produced no land cession. With the passage of the Indian Removal Act of May 28, 1830, which made the removal of Indians west of the Mississippi official government policy, Jackson re-

2. The relevant state banking studies are C. C. Huntington, "A History of Banking and Currency in Ohio before the Civil War," *Ohio Archeological and Historical Quarterly*, 24 (1915): 352–86; George W. Dowrie, *The Development of Banking in Illinois, 1817–1863* (University of Illinois Studies in the Social Sciences, Vol. 2, Urbana, 1913), 359–540; Logan Esarey, *State Banking in Indiana, 1814–1873* (Indiana University Studies, Vol. 1, no. 15, Bloomington, 1912); Cable, *The Bank of the State of Missouri*, 124–29; and Brantley, *Banking in Alabama*, 292–337.

newed his efforts. He delegated treaty-making powers to his old friends and comrades-in-arms, John Coffee (then surveyor general of Alabama) and John H. Eaton (Secretary of War). Coffee and Eaton were experienced and skilled negotiators, and their tactics of bluff, bargain, and divide brought the affair to a successful conclusion. On September 27, 1830, both parties signed the Treaty of Dancing Rabbit Creek.[3]

The largest portion of the Choctaw Cession lay in the State of Mississippi, and responsibility for its survey would fall on the office of the Surveyor General South of Tennessee. This office had been in a state of embarrassment almost since its establishment in 1803, due to a combination of bad management, bad luck, poor organization, incompetent personnel, and the complexities of private claims. In 1830 the office had a new surveyor general, Gideon Fitz, formerly a deputy surveyor in the district and land officer at Mount Salus. The time involved in the change of command meant that almost ten months elapsed before Elijah Hayward could issue detailed instructions on the survey of the Choctaw Cession. The commissioner emphasized that the correct execution of the surveys was "a momentous concern both as regards the interest of the general government, of the state of Mississippi and its citizens." Speed was also of paramount importance. Hayward constantly reminded Fitz that the President himself took a personal interest in the preparation of the Choctaw lands for sale. Indeed Jackson made weekly and sometimes daily inquiries about the progress of work. Hayward made it clear that whatever the other tasks facing the surveyor general—and there were several—the survey of the Choctaw Cession was to have the highest priority.[4]

Fitz did not lack for volunteers to assist him. No sooner had news of the cession spread than men and applications to the number of two hundred poured into the office from all the southern and southwestern states, particularly from Alabama, Tennessee, and, of course, Mississippi. The fifteen or twenty men selected as deputy surveyors would have an opportunity to view at first hand, at government expense, the lands that excited the whole Southwest. Fitz put surveyors in the field

3. Royce, comp., *Indian Land Cessions in the United States*, 2: 726; Mary E. Young, *Redskins, Ruffleshirts, and Rednecks: Indian Allotments in Alabama and Mississippi, 1830–1860* (Norman, 1961), 22–46.
4. Hayward to Fitz, NA: GLO, Ltrs. Sent, SG, 4: July 27, 1831; *ibid.*, 5: Nov. 12, 18, 1831; Hayward to McLane, Sec. Treas., *ibid.*, Misc., 26: Oct. 27, 1831.

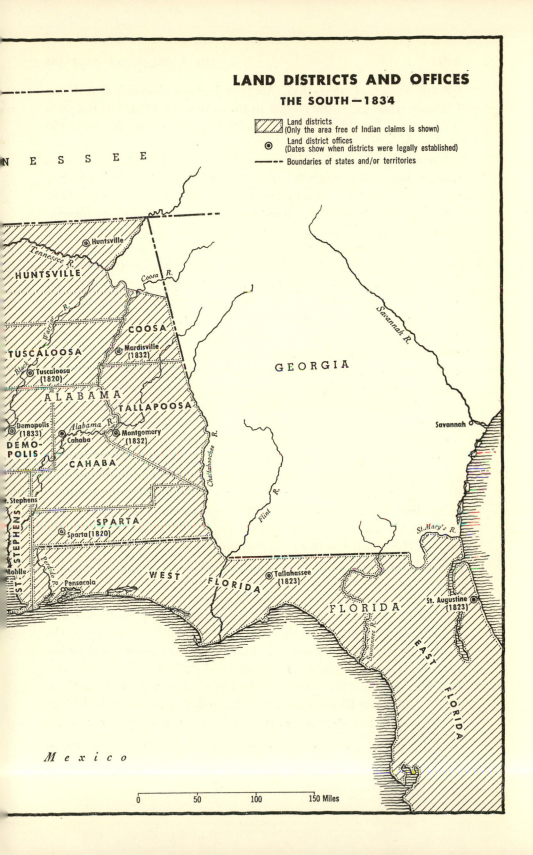

LAND DISTRICTS AND OFFICES
THE SOUTH—1834

Land districts
(Only the area free of Indian claims is shown)

◉ Land district offices
(Dates show when districts were legally established)

—— --- Boundaries of states and/or territories

TENNESSEE

Tennessee R.

Huntsville

HUNTSVILLE

Coosa R.

COOSA

TUSCALOOSA

Mardisville (1832)

Tuscaloosa (1820)

Warrior R.

Black

Savannah R.

GEORGIA

ALABAMA

TALLAPOOSA

Alabama R.

Demopolis (1833)

DEMO-POLIS

Cahaba

Montgomery (1832)

CAHABA

Savannah

Chattahoochee R.

St. Stephens

SPARTA

Sparta (1820)

Flint R.

ST. STEPHENS

Mobile

Pensacola

WEST FLORIDA

Tallahassee (1823)

St. Mary's R.

FLORIDA

Suwannee R.

St. Augustine (1823)

EAST FLORIDA

Mexico

0   50   100   150 Miles

by the winter of 1831–1832. Andrew Jackson demanded that the Choctaw lands go on the market in the autumn of 1832, but not even "Old Hickory" could overcome the administrative incumbrances of the land business.[5]

The long-awaited sales of Choctaw lands took place at Mount Salus, Chocchuma, and Columbus (all in Mississippi) in October and November of 1833, with cotton prices at their highest point in more than a decade.[6] The first sale at Mount Salus was an auspicious beginning. Large crowds of planters, farmers, speculators, observers, and local politicians turned the village into a great tent city. In excellent autumn weather, with its mild days and cool nights, men talked land, its location, its cost, its fertility, and its availability. Tract after tract went for the minimum price. The "very pressing" business of the public sales was followed immediately by an "immense number of applicants at the Office" for private entries. Both land officers engaged additional clerks to meet the rush, and the register employed six extra assistants at a cost of more than $500. "I have had more done in the office than any Register before me ever had done in twice the length of time," he appealed to the Secretary of the Treasury. "The first week for dispatch of business, I was necessarily compelled to have six assistants; one month I had employed three Clerks, and five months two Clerks to do the writing of the office; the first six days the number of applicants was so great that they could not all get near the door; I was therefore necessarily compelled to hire a crier to cry the numbers of the land in each application at the door, that all certificates might be made known." The receiver's experience was much the same. He wrote, "The Office was in all the last Quarter of the last year not only full, but more than full with eager purchasers . . . and such was the Mania that many applied for, and some actually purchased land they had long since paid for & such uneasiness prevailed that the Register informs me, and I believe the fact to be, that many made two and some three applications for the same land hundreds waited for weeks on the office. . . ." Purchasers continued to swarm about the door until well into spring. The receiver continued, "The whole of that business was done under a press, and in a perfect crowd, most of which time I had three Clerks constantly engaged with me in actual office

5.   Hayward to Fitz, *ibid.*, SG, 5: March 26, 1832; *Natchez Gazette*, Nov. 30, 1831.
6.   Gray, *A History of Agriculture in the Southern United States to 1860*, 2: 698–99.

business, much less can be done, when numbers are pressing, than when all would be quiet, and given time, but on the contrary, all was a perfect press." [7]

The land office business was equally dramatic and exciting at Chocchuma. During the first two weeks of the auction, total sales reached $140,000 to $150,000, almost all at the minimum price. After public auctions ended, a great rush took place to claim lands at private entry. "The public Sales were well attended and the press of private entries after the sales closed were immense, at this time I cannot say to you the amount of Sales but I think they are not much short of $300,000," wrote the receiver. So great was the press of the land office business that the land officers "have scarcely slept for many nights in succession. . . ." The register estimated the sales during the public auction and for the first four weeks thereafter at "immense, say $400,000." He continued, "The purchases were immense & during the four weeks of the public sales & up to the last of November the crowd was but slightly diminished, but there was as much business done in the office as we could possibly do. You can form some idea of the business when you see that there were 2116 tracts sold from 21 Oct. to 31 Nov. & that the Sales amounted to $337,199.44 for the same period, up to 1 January 1834 the sales amounted to $356,496.49." The figures accompanying the sales showed that little land changed hands at the public sales. Instead, with the perfect composure born of previous arrangements, men calmly waited for the private sales to make their entries at the minimum price. While he did not see "in direct terms any overt act contrary to law," the register admitted that much took place that "defeated the object of the law. . . ." [8]

Statistics told the story of the great land office business in Mississippi in 1833. The final tabulations showed more than a million acres sold in the state, most of that in the fourth quarter in the sales at Mount Salus, Chocchuma, and Columbus, the land offices where the Choctaw Cession appeared first on the market. With great satisfaction

7. James W. Dickson and Thomas L. Sumrall to Hayward, NA: GLO, Register of Ltrs. Recd., Mount Salus, Dec. 1 (2), 1833; Jan. 31, 1834; Sumrall to Roger B. Taney, Sec. Treas., NA: TD, Ltrs. from Land Officers, 1833–34: May 13, 1834; Samuel W. Dickson to Taney, *ibid.*, May 20, June 6, 1834; Jackson *Mississippian*, Jan. 24, 1834.
8. Samuel Gwin to Hayward, NA: GLO, Register of Ltrs. Recd., Chocchuma, Oct. 11, 12, Nov. 4, 29, 1833; March 11, 1834; R. H. Sterling to Taney, NA: TD, Ltrs. from Land Officers, 1833–34: Nov. 26, 1833; Gwin to Taney, *ibid.*, March 1, 1834; Hayward to Rep. Samuel W. Mardis (Ala.), NA: GLO, Ltrs. Sent, Misc., 28: Feb. 24, 1834.

Commissioner Elijah Hayward noted the rising "tide of emigration to the west and southwest, and the accumulating population of those fertile and extensive regions." He found the reason in the peace and national prosperity of the country and, of course, in the "rapidly accumulating metallic currency, the most powerful stimulus to private enterprise and general industry," and the circulating medium of his patron, President Andrew Jackson.[9]

The Choctaw Cession at Dancing Rabbit Creek was only one of the treaties through which Andrew Jackson evicted the Indians from the cotton lands of the Southwest. On March 24, 1832, federal negotiators concluded a treaty with the Creek tribe under which individual Indians received "allottments" with the understanding that the remainder of the Creek lands would be opened to white settlement. Administrative arrangements quickly followed. The Commissioner of the General Land Office issued hasty instructions for the survey of the new tract. And on the same day that he killed the "monster bank" with a stroke of his pen, President Jackson signed a bill to create two land districts in the new cession, subsequently located at Montgomery and at Mardisville, Alabama.[10]

The task of preparing these lands for market fell to Jackson's old friend, John Coffee. The surveyor general quickly let contracts, and the deputy surveyors scattered over the new cession almost before the President's signature was dry on the treaty. In early fall Hayward inquired about the progress in preparing township plats and descriptive notes. Coffee replied that the survey of the Creek lands was almost completed, and that he expected to receive field notes from the deputy surveyors before the end of the year. His greatest difficulty was the preparation of the township plats. The field notes for 277 townships of Creek surveys made an imposing pile in the surveyor general's office—a quantity of work far beyond the immediate capacity of his small staff.[11] For a full year two clerks and a draftsman labored on transforming the field notes into plats. The death of Coffee in the autumn of 1833 made little difference to the routine of the

9. *American State Papers, Public Lands*, 7: 329, 331; Cole, "Cyclical and Sectional Variations in the Sale of Public Lands, 1816–1860," 51–52.
10. Royce, comp. *Indian Land Cessions in the United States*, 2: 734; Young, *Redskins, Ruffleshirts, and Rednecks*, 35–39, 73–75; 4 Stat. 571–72 (July 10, 1832).
11. Hayward to Coffee, NA: GLO, Ltrs. Sent, SG, 5: Oct. 11, 1832; Coffee to Hayward, *ibid*., Ltrs. Recd., SG, Alabama, 50: Nov. 8, 29, 1832. Coffee estimated the cost of surveying the Creek Cession at $70,000.

office, because his successor was the chief clerk, James H. Weakley. To the new surveyor general, Hayward reiterated the President's great concern for the project, "it being his wish and intention to bring these lands into market as soon as it can be done." [12]

Concern over intrusions on the public lands in the Southwest lent an air of urgency to Jackson's repeated inquiries about the Creek surveys. Trespassing on the public domain had become more widespread and violent in recent years. Bands of squatters and speculators united to threaten prospective buyers, intimidate land-lookers, and deny occupation to legitimate purchasers. Jackson issued a proclamation against the trespassers in the Huntsville district, and the federal troops that attempted to clear the area brought the President into conflict with state authorities. A crisis threatened in August 1833, when federal soldiers shot and killed an intruder on a Creek improvement. Eastern Alabama was quickly transformed into an armed camp.[13]

In the midst of this tension, administration officials suddenly realized that the solution to the problem of trespassing on the Creek Cession lay in the rapid execution of the treaty. Once the lands came on the market, the federal government could let sale and settlement take their course. As soon as Surveyor General Weakley indicated that sufficient plats were available, the President proclaimed a public sale. Dated December 17, 1833, the proclamation gave fewer than four weeks' notice to prospective purchasers. When Senator George Poindexter of Mississippi later asked why so little notice had been given the public, the Commissioner of the General Land Office indicated that issues other than the proper disposition of the public domain had been paramount. "This proclamation did not give so long previous notice of the sales, as is usual, owing to the peculiar circumstances of the case, and an ardent desire not to resort to *coercive* measures, to remove unnecessarily intruders from public lands . . . ," Hayward wrote. He then concluded, "It is believed that these sales, at the time and under the circumstances of the case, have produced the beneficial effects anticipated, so far as to dissipate the popular excitement previously existing in favor of the actual settlers and to render unnecessary, in a great degree, the resort to active and coercive measures to re-

12. Hayward to Weakley, *ibid.*, Ltrs. Sent, SG, 5: Nov. 26, 1833.
13. Edward Harper, Perry County, Ala., to George Graham, *ibid.*, Ltrs. Recd., Misc., H: April 22, 1830; Jabez Curry to Graham, April 9, 1830, and Curry to John H. Eaton, Sec. War, April 14, 1830, *House Executive Documents*, 21 Cong., 1 Sess., #109: 4–6; Young, *Redskins, Ruffleshirts, and Rednecks*, 76–80.

move intruders." The solution was one of form. The sins of the intruders continued. Trespassers continued to occupy public lands as
well as some Indian reservations.[14]

Business at the public sale in mid-January was modest, in part from
the short notice, in part from the agreements between purchasers, and
in part from confusion over currency. Sales at the Montgomery office,
where much of the Creek purchase lands were offered, reached only
8360.83 acres for the public auction period. Once private sales began,
however, purchasers quickly created another land office business.
Throughout the spring, summer, and autumn of 1834, entries increased as speculative interests, cotton prices, and financial arrangements continued to spiral. Alabama sales for the entire year reached
more than one million acres, of which more than half represented
Creek lands offered for the first time.[15]

The techniques for investment in lands on a large scale had been
perfected by this time. Men of capital pooled their resources into
great companies. In order to select the most attractive tracts, these
large investors, as well as smaller speculators, employed "land
hunters," to spy out the length and breadth of the vast Indian cessions. Agents of the company rendezvoused at a local hotel with their
"hunters"; maps appeared, sketches were drawn, and cramped notes
translated into plans. Occasionally information might be purchased
from a clerk in the district land office or a deputy surveyor; such advice was dearly acquired and jealously guarded. At the great land
sales the various companies agreed to avoid competition, bought their
tracts at the minimum price, and then retailed them at a substantial
profit. A subsequent investigation of the sales in Mississippi indicated
that neither federal nor state officials, nor district land officers made
any effort to thwart such combinations and, quite to the contrary, often participated actively in the companies themselves.[16]

---

14.   Hayward to the President, NA: GLO, Ltrs. Sent. Misc., 29: April 7, 1834;
J. W. Bradford and Joab Lawler to Hayward, *ibid.*, Ltrs. Recd., Reg. & Rec.,
Mardisville, Box, Aug. 22, 1834. One result of Poindexter's inquiry was a law
providing that lands must be advertised for at least three months prior to a public
sale. 4 Stat. 702 (June 28, 1834).
15.   Hayward to Rep. Samuel W. Mardis (Ala.), NA: GLO, Ltrs. Sent. Misc., 28:
Feb. 24, 1834; *American State Papers, Public Lands*, 8: 8; Young, *Redskins,
Ruffleshirts, and Rednecks*, 175.
16.   Young, *Redskins, Ruffleshirts, and Rednecks*, 114–60; Chappell, "Some Patterns of Land Speculation in the Old Southwest," 474–77; James Silver, "Land

The government sales at Columbus (Mississippi) in the autumn of 1834 alone brought in estimated receipts of more than half a million dollars. Sales of similar magnitude continued throughout 1835, and speculation reached its height with the marketing of the Chickasaw lands in January 1836. The public sales of these northern Mississippi lands attracted an enormous crowd of speculators and a million dollars in investment capital. A second sale in September produced equal enthusiasm. The ready availability of credit through the generous lending policy of the local Pontotoc bank increased the temptation to buy. In 1836 sales of the public domain in Mississippi exceeded 2,000,000 acres. Alabama sales for the same period were more than 1,900,000 acres.[17] When the "flush times" ended in the spring of 1837, Mississippi's flood of settlement had covered the northern and central parts of the state completely, and only a narrow band along the delta of the River remained unoccupied. Alabama's Creek and Choctaw tracts had filled with settlers, and a frontier line no longer existed in that state.

The enthusiasm for speculation in the public lands in the Southwest during the middle of the 1830's was graphically described by humorist Joseph G. Baldwin: "Marvellous accounts had gone forth of the fertility of the virgin lands; and the productions of the soil were commanding a prize remunerating to slave labor as it had never been remunerated before. Emigrants came flocking in from all quarters of the Union, especially from the slaveholding States. The new country seemed to be a reservoir, and every road leading to it a vagrant stream of enterprise and adventure." The principal attraction was land, and "under this stimulating process prices rose like smoke. Lots in obscure villages were held at city prices; lands, bought at the minimum cost of government, were sold at from thirty to forty dollars per acre, and considered dirt cheap at that." The fever of speculation swept through all those who went to Mississippi. "Great negotiations

Speculation Profits in the Chickasaw Cession," *Journal of Southern History*, 10 (1944): 84–92.

17. *Senate Public Documents*, 25 Cong., 3 Sess., #29: 2; *House Executive Documents*, 25 Cong., 2 Sess., #23: 13; Ethan Allen Brown to Senator Thomas Ewing (Ohio), NA: GLO, Ltrs. Sent, Reg. & Rec., 7 (New Series): April 26, 1836. Chickasaw lands were not technically a part of the public domain in the sense that the receipts from the sale went to the tribal trust fund rather than to the Government of the United States. On the Chickasaw Cession and speculation in these lands, see Young, *Redskins, Ruffleshirts, and Rednecks*, 39–44, 161–68.

for land and negroes among the newcomers," wrote a visiting Virginian. "The operations going on around me excite me, and I cannot help feeling the contagion, and want to be dealing in tens and hundreds of thousands." By 1836 the traveler James D. Davidson could report of the atmosphere at Natchez: "The people here are run mad with speculation. They do business in . . . a kind of phrenzy."[18]

At the same time, across the Mississippi River, the hitherto isolated Territory of Arkansas stood on the threshold of prosperity. By the spring of 1833 the Little Rock land officers reported "the crowded situation of Little Rock at this time from the great number of emigrants continually pouring in upon us. . . ." Cotton prices improved that fall and opened higher the following spring, by which time Arkansas had emerged as an extension of the cotton-land-slave economy already undergoing rapid exploitation across the river in Mississippi and Alabama. By 1834 sales of the public lands in the Territory of Arkansas had reached $213,000, with the largest share in the new land office at Washington, in the southwestern part of the territory adjacent to the fertile lands of the Red River. This trend continued unchecked for the next two years. "We can hardly venture a guess at the amount which has been paid into our Land-office for land, within the last two or three months," commented the *Arkansas Gazette* in 1836, "but it has been large—probably larger than at any former period during the same space of time." Excitement built up before the great spring sales in May. Editors, territorial boomers, and real estate agents rejoiced in the bustle over the great event: the small knots of expectant and excited men discussing land, the jammed hotels and private homes, and the arrival of wealthy strangers in the land office towns. "There are continual arrival here of speculators . . . ," noted the *Advocate*. "Our city is much crowded, and we anticipate large sales." The *Gazette* also singled out numerous "land speculators, who are seeking opportunities for profitable investments of their cash in lands." On the Arkansas frontier the speculator was a welcome sign of prosperity, a harbinger of "a dense and wealthy population." The lands advertised for sale were choice tracts, "of the finest quality for cotton, and it is expected

18. Joseph G. Baldwin, *The Flush Times of Alabama and Mississippi* (New York, 1853), 82–84; William F, Gray, *From Virginia to Texas, 1835* (Houston, 1909), 52; Herbert A. Keller, ed., "A Journey Through the South in 1836: Diary of James D. Davidson," *Journal of Southern History*, 1 (1935): 355.

that there will be great competition for them, and doubtless high prices will be paid—particularly for front lands." [19]

The sales were large. In spite of early reports of "very animated bidding," however, almost all tracts went for the minimum price, and "nearly the whole of the lands were purchased on speculation." After the close of the government sale, private investors auctioned their own purchases at a handsome profit.[20] The Helena office, a district that fronted on the Mississippi River, also had a speculative upsurge that brought out a "number of purchasers . . . unprecedented in this Territory"; and rumor said that "capital to the amount of $1,000,000 was carried there for investment." In the far southwestern corner of the territory, the land office at Washington was also crowded with purchasers, and public sales ran "to near *one hundred thousand dollars*" in a two- or three-week period.[21] The land office business at Helena and Washington reflected the movement of population into the northeastern and southwestern parts of the territory.

Within the state of Missouri, population began to move from the great river valleys to the interior counties. The land office at Palmyra, in the northeastern corner of the state, became the symbol and focus of this movement and accompanying interest in land. In 1835 the Palmyra office alone sold almost half a million dollars of public lands ($482,188.97)—more than half the state's total. "The increase in the receipts of this office, are scarcely exampled in the United States," commented one editor. The reason was clear, he continued: "The whole country is agog for land, and almost every man who can procure money is thus investing in it." [22] Old residents and new arrivals both sought capital for investment in the public lands. One recent emigrant from North Carolina wrote home, "It is my opinion that the man who has money to [in]vest in Missouri lands, that now is the time, and I believe it would be to my advantage to sell 8 or 10

19. Chambers and Smith to McLane, Sec. Treas., NA: TD, Ltrs. from Land Officers, 1833–34: June 7, 1833; Cole, "Cyclical and Sectional Variations in the Sale of Public Lands, 1816–1860," 52; Little Rock *Arkansas Gazette*, May 3, 1836; Dec. 23, 1834; Little Rock *Arkansas Advocate*, May 6, 1836.
20. Little Rock *Arkansas Gazette*, May 10, 17, 1836; Little Rock *Arkansas Advocate*, May 13, 1836.
21. Little Rock *Arkansas Gazette*, May 24, June 28, 1836. The Helena sales had to be postponed because of the absence of the newly appointed register.
22. *American State Papers, Public Lands*, 8: 8, 893; Bowling Green *Salt River Journal*, quoted in the New Orleans *Courier*, July 25, 1836.

negroes at the present high prices and purchase land with the money."
The purchase of land was symptomatic of the movement of people.
"But two or three years since the country in which we live, was the
frontier county, on the west," exclaimed one editor. "At this time, en-
terprize and the spirit of emigration had extended *far* beyond us." [23]
And so it was everywhere.

In the thirty months from the fall of 1834 to the spring of 1837, the
American people generated the largest land office business in the history of the Republic. From the timberlands of Maine to the Cotton
Kingdom of Mississippi, in city lots of Chicago, and in the wilderness
of central Michigan, the dimensions of the land boom touched men of
all stations and locations. Capitalists from New York City, bankers
from Philadelphia, planters from Virginia, land agents in Michigan, settlers in Illinois, and even squatters along the frontier participated. All
expected to profit. The early 1830's had been a period of prosperity.
Farm prices rose, and real estate values soared. Throughout the last
quarter of 1834 enormous quantities of the public domain were
thrown on the market. In July 1834 the Washington *Globe* needed
three full columns to carry notices of the forthcoming fourth-quarter
sales. Seven sales of choice Indian cessions in Alabama, four December sales in Mississippi, three in Michigan Territory, and others in Indiana, Illinois, Missouri, Arkansas, and Florida provided the fuel for
speculative conflagration. Cotton prices improved steadily, expansion
began into new cotton-producing areas, and widespread speculation
developed in cotton, land, and slaves.[24] Fourth-quarter sales of public
lands in 1834 exceeded $3,000,000. Statistics for a four-year period
demonstrate the rapid growth of the land office business: [25]

	ACRES	
1834	4,658,218.71	$ 6,099,981.04
1835	12,564,478.85	$15,999,804.11
1836	20,074,870.92	$25,167,833.06
1837	5,601,103.12	$ 7,007,523.04

23. Walter Raleigh Lenoir to William B. Lenoir, May 1, 1836, Lewis Atherton,
ed., "Life, Labor and Society in Boone County, Missouri, 1834–1852 . . . ,"
Missouri Historical Review, 38 (1944): 303; Jefferson City *Jeffersonian Republican*, March 28, 1835.
24. *Niles' Weekly Register*, 46: 350 (July 19, 1834); Gray, *History of Agriculture
in the Southern United States to 1860*, 2: 898–900.
25. *Senate Public Documents*, 27 Cong., 3 Sess., #246: 10.

Just as the large sales of Indian cessions in 1833 and 1834 dominated the economic development and settlement of the Southwest, so the speculative upsurge from 1835 to 1837 is best observed in the land business and expansion of the old and the new Northwest. The "new" part of the region was the Territory of Wisconsin, a portion of the Michigan Territory which was organized as a territory in 1836. The Mineral Point Land Office, one of two to serve the area, opened in the summer of 1834, but a federal proclamation reserving lead lands from public sales dampened interest. The result was a "very limited sale of Land. . . ." Land officers and speculators settled back to await the marketing of the lead lands.[26]

Across 160 miles of wilderness to the northeast lay the town of Green Bay, the site of a second land district. Its history went back to 1634, when possibly Jean Nicolet landed there, and it was later a French fur-trading post. Green Bay was still a tiny village in the early 1830's, but it was also the center of a wedge of settlement moving down the Fox River Valley. With the creation of the land district in 1834, deputy surveyors fanned out over this vast area of forest, lakes, and rivers, and the reports of the condition of the land were most optimistic. In 1834 and 1835 these deputies surveyed much of the southern half of Wisconsin.[27] The first sale of lands took place at Green Bay in August 1835, and soon the isolated village exhibited the symptoms of the land business: "land, land, town plots and speculations." Nearly one hundred townships containing more than two million acres of land went on the market at Green Bay during the summer and autumn months. Spirited bidding and competition for many of the tracts brought receipts of more than $100,000 during three weeks in August. The pleasant summer weather also brought such floods of population into Wisconsin that the surveyor general recommended a second sale in the early fall. Squatters had settled in all the surveyed townships, he reported, and large numbers had made improvements near the Chicago–Green Bay road. The Commissioner of the General Land Office advised that the sale must take place soon, for in early

26. Carter, ed., *Territorial Papers*, 12: 785–86; John P. Sheldon and Joseph Eneix to Hayward, Nov. 19, 1834, *ibid.*, 817; *The Galenian*, Nov. 24, 1834; Ann M. Keppel, "Civil Disobedience on the Mining Frontier," *Wisconsin Magazine of History*, 41 (1958): 190–91.
27. Joshua Hathaway, Jr., to Micajah T. Williams, SG, Feb. 20, 1835, Carter, ed., *Territorial Papers*, 12: 864–67; *Green-Bay Intelligencer*, March 5, 19, Aug. 2, 1834; April 9, Aug. 22, 1835.

LAND DISTRICTS AND OFFICES
THE OLD NORTHWEST AND MISSOURI—1834

Land districts
(Only the area free of Indian claims is shown)

Land district offices
(Dates show when districts were legally established)

Boundaries of states and/or territories

MICHIGAN

Green Bay
(1834)

WISCONSIN

GREEN
BAY

Mineral Point
(1834)

Galena
(1834)

NORTH-
WESTERN

NORTH-
EASTERN

Chicago
(1834)

TERRITORY

ILLINOIS

DANVILLE

QUINCY

SPRINGFIELD

SALT
RIVER

Quincy
(1831)

Danvill
(1831)

UNORGANIZED

WESTERN

HOWARD CO.

Palmyra
(1824)

Springfield
(1822)

PALESTINE

Fayette
(1832)

Lexington
(1823)

EDWARDS-
VILLE

VAN-
DALIA

Palestin
(1820)

Edwardsville

Vandalia
(1820)

ST.
LOUIS

St. Louis

MISSOURI

KASKASKIA

SHAWNEE
TOWN

SPRINGFIELD

Kaskaskia

Shawneetown

Springfield
(1834)

Jackson

CAPE GIRARDEAU

ARKANSAS TERR.

T E

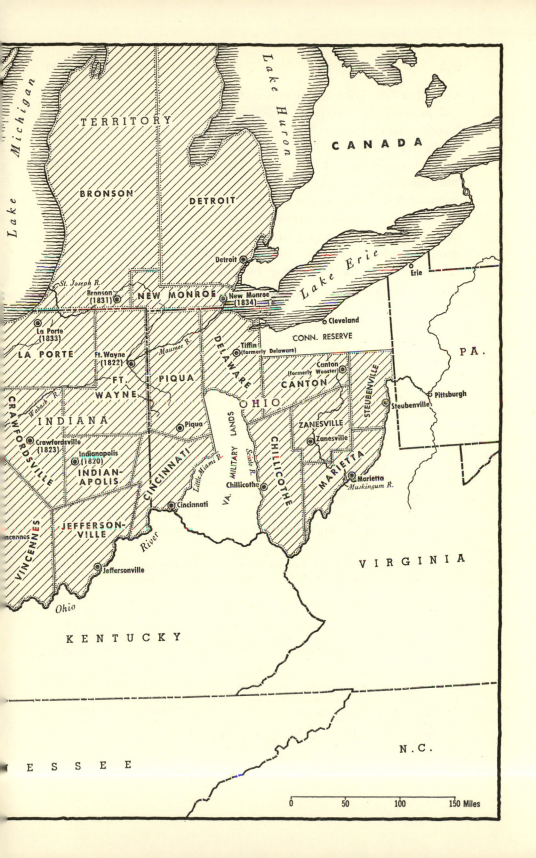

Lake Michigan

TERRITORY

Lake Huron

CANADA

BRONSON

DETROIT

Detroit

Lake Erie

Erie

St. Joseph R.

Bronson (1831)

NEW MONROE

New Monroe (1834)

Cleveland

CONN. RESERVE

PA.

La Porte (1833)

LA PORTE

Ft. Wayne (1822)

FT. WAYNE

Maumee R.

DELAWARE

Tiffin (formerly Delaware)

Canton (formerly Wooster)

PIQUA

CANTON

STEUBENVILLE

Pittsburgh

OHIO

Steubenville

Wabash R.

INDIANA

Piqua

ZANESVILLE

Zanesville

CRAWFORDSVILLE

Crawfordsville (1823)

Indianapolis (1820)

INDIAN-APOLIS

CINCINNATI

Little Miami R.

VA. MILITARY LANDS

Scioto R.

CHILLICOTHE

Chillicothe

MARIETTA

Marietta

Muskingum R.

JEFFERSON-VILLE

VINCENNES

Cincinnati

River

VIRGINIA

Vincennes

Jeffersonville

Ohio

KENTUCKY

ESSEE

N. C.

0   50   100   150 Miles

November "the boistrous Season commences on the lakes . . . there will probably be few persons desirous of encountering the evils of travelling at that season." The November sale was well attended and productive. In spite of the commissioner's warnings, the close of navigation brought no end of activity. The explanation was simply that "the Speculators cannot rest." Investors entered thousands of dollars' worth of land in the Green Bay land office over the winter. "Agents are sent on for companies—monies remitted to the Clerk of the Office, citizens of this place employed to make the entry; and in one way or another the business of entering Public Lands is going on at a brisk rate," explained the *Green-Bay Intelligencer.* "The whole world is bent for Rock River; except some who are by thousands spreading along the west shore of Lake Michigan." [28]

Settlers spread over the southern border of the future territory, and the movement of population into the lake counties quickly necessitated another land district. The land office was located in Milwaukee, the most successful of a large number of pretentious metropolitan centers that sprang up along the lake front in the mid-1830's. The little village quickly became a bustling center of immigration and the land business.[29] Three Wisconsin land districts sold nearly 650,000 acres of public lands in 1836. By the end of that year, surveys had begun in the new Black Hawk Purchase across the Mississippi River, and ten thousand squatters held land in what would become Iowa Territory.[30]

Immigrants to Wisconsin came in part from northern and central Illinois, whose settlement was virtually completed by 1837. Illinois and her settlers had quickly recovered from the effects of Black Hawk's

28. *Green-Bay Intelligencer,* July 20, Sept. 12, 1835; Hayward to the President, NA: GLO, Ltrs. Sent, Misc., 6 (New Series): Aug. 1, 1835; *Green-Bay Intelligencer,* March 2, 1836.
29. *House Executive Documents,* 25 Cong., 2 Sess., #23: 14; *Green-Bay Intelligencer,* March 2, 1836. An account of the settlement of Wisconsin in this period is Joseph Schafer, *Four Wisconsin Counties: Prairie and Forest* (Madison, 1927), 37–64. On land speculators and speculation, note Larry Gara, *Westernized Yankee, The Story of Cyrus Woodman* (Madison, 1956), 20–42; Kenneth W. Duckett, *Frontiersman of Fortune, Moses M. Strong of Mineral Point* (Madison, 1955), 20–48; Joseph Schafer, *The Wisconsin Lead Region* (Wisconsin Domesday Book, General Studies, Vol. 3, Madison, 1932), 110–30, 148–61; Alice E. Smith, *James Duane Doty, Frontier Promoter* (Madison, 1954), esp. 174–208; Joseph Schafer, "A Yankee Land Speculator in Wisconsin," *Wisconsin Magazine of History,* 8 (1925): 377–92.
30. Roscoe L. Lokken, *Iowa Public Land Disposal* (Iowa City, 1942), 13–22, 66–68.

uprising in 1832. By the autumn of 1833 a Galena editor reflected the prevailing sentiment of the times: "The country is desirable and the eyes of thousands are upon it." The spirit of prosperity and settlement continued into the spring of 1834. The Illinois River Valley, the military tract, and the northeastern part of the state were now all rapidly filling. Settlement began to move outward from the river valleys to the inland counties. The center of this expanding population was Springfield, at least to judge by the sales of public lands. The rush to occupy the Black Hawk Purchase, begun in earnest after the end of the Indian uprising, had reached a peak by 1835.[31] The demand for Illinois lands was concentrated at the land offices in Chicago, Galena, and Springfield. Public sales in the spring of 1835 were heavy. Receipts at Quincy in June 1835 alone reached $200,000, with $19,000 taken on a single day. Results at Springfield were equally indicative of the demand for land. Sales on July 1 totaled $30,000. Local boosters reveled in their prosperity: "From this statement, our readers may form some idea of the emigration to this region of country—comment is unnecessary."[32] Business at the Galena office exceeded $80,000 in the three weeks after opening; in seven weeks, $250,000. "The rush for lands in several parts of this district, has been really unparallelled among the actual settlers, not to speak of foreign speculators," wrote one observer. "The greatest day's sale we heard, exceeded $30,000, and three other days sale, each went over $25,000." Sales of public lands in the State of Illinois would reach $3,000,000 in 1835, prophesied Hezekiah Niles. "There is an immense tide of emigration settling into that as well as the other states of the west."[33]

One of the most dramatic manifestations of the growth of northern Illinois was the rise of Chicago. As late as 1830 this future economic center of the nation was nothing more than a clearing of huts and a few hogs. From the close of the Black Hawk War it began to grow,

31. *The Galenian*, Sept. 6, 1833; William V. Pooley, *The Settlement of Illinois from 1830 to 1850* (Bulletin of the University of Wisconsin, Vol. 1, Madison, 1908).
32. White Pigeon *Michigan Statesman*, March 7, 1835; St. Louis *Missouri Republican*, quoted in *Niles' Weekly Register*, 48: 365 (July 25, 1835); Vandalia *Illinois Advocate and State Register*, July 29, 1835.
33. Quincy *Illinois Register*, quoted in the St. Louis *Missouri Argus*, Sept. 25, 1835; *North Western Gazette and Galena Advertiser*, Aug. 29, 1835; *Niles' Weekly Register*, 49: 137 (Oct. 31, 1835). Sales were actually $2,604,698.47. *American State Papers, Public Lands*, 8: 893.

and in spite of its small size in 1834 (probably fewer than 3,400 citizens of all colors), speculation in town lots was already under way. Soon investors began to sense that Chicago was "the germ of an immense city. . . ." Congress added to the town's prospects by locating a land office there. Speculation in real estate, begun as early as 1834, reached hysterical proportions in the summer of 1836 with the sale of canal lands. Visiting at the height of the mania, Harriet Martineau described the scene. "I never saw a busier place than Chicago was at the time of our arrival," she wrote. "The streets were crowded with land speculators, hurrying from one sale to another. A negro, dressed up in scarlet, bearing a scarlet flag, and riding a white horse with housings of scarlet, announced the times of sale." Everywhere crowds of men surrounded him for the latest information. "As the gentlemen of our party walked the streets, store-keepers hailed them from their doors, with offers of farms, and all manner of land-lots, advising them to speculate before the price of land rose higher." [34]

Interest in the development of town sites was not confined to Chicago. Between 1834 and 1837 unborn cities filled the dreams of speculators and developers throughout the Old Northwest. No stream entering Lake Michigan between Chicago and Green Bay lacked its boosters. Scores of paper towns lined interior rivers like the Illinois, the Fox, and the Rock. "Lithograph maps of cities were hung upon the walls of public buildings, in the bar-rooms of hotels, in auction-rooms, and in every place likely to attract the most attention," recalled one participant. On the highways and bypaths of the state, settlers and squatters hoped to sell at a handsome profit. "Everywhere we went on our way home, American farmers offered their land for sale at speculative prices," wrote a traveler. "Speculation in land has become a pestilence throughout the West." A farmer who sought a tract simply for cultivation agreed; "every one is for speculation," he concluded. Federal land offices in Illinois sold more than four million dollars' worth of the public domain in 1836.[35] Transactions in real estate must have reached many times that figure.

34. Patrick Shirreff, A Tour through North America (Edinburgh, 1835), 226; Harriet Martineau, Society in America (3 vols., 2nd ed., London, 1837), 1: 350.
35. John T. Kingston, "Early Western Days," Collections of the State Historical Society of Wisconsin, 7 (1873–76): 340; Fred Gustorf, "Frontier Perils Told By an Early Illinois Visitor," Journal of the Illinois State Historical Society, 55 (1962):

The urge to speculate in real estate also swept through Indiana (sales of over four million dollars in public lands in 1836),[36] but the Michigan Territory was the scene of the greatest speculation. The early unfavorable reports of Edward Tiffin's surveyors had proved erroneous on closer inspection, and the region emerged as a rich and promising agricultural area, as yet comparatively neglected by settlers and speculators alike. As the decade of the 1830's opened, eastern Michigan's population lay in an arc around the shore of Lake Erie with its center at Detroit, while another small outpost of settlement could be found in the far southwestern corner of the territory with its center on the St. Joseph's River. As the new prosperity made itself felt and brought streams of settlers from the East via the Erie Canal and the Great Lakes, settlements began to spread outward from both areas. In June 1831 the Monroe land office, situated south of Detroit on the River Raisin, moved to White Pigeon, more than one hundred miles directly west, in order to meet the needs of the burgeoning population in the southwest. By 1833 four land offices served the territory: the Detroit office, at the principal port of entry to the territory; a new Monroe office, serving the Raisin River area to the south; White Pigeon, strategically placed on the Chicago Road; and Bronson (later Kalamazoo), on the Territorial Road, also connecting Detroit with Chicago. All of these offices had large quantities of excellent lands for sale, the result of years of surveys, few settlers, and fewer purchasers.[37]

A growing population brought rising sales of public lands, more than half a million dollars' worth in 1833. During the first seven months of 1834 sales at the Detroit office alone averaged more than $1,000 each day—evidence that "speaks very emphatically for the increased population, wealth and prosperity of this part of Michigan." The *Free Press* concluded triumphantly, "However rapidly other parts

267 (July 16, 1836); I. M. Wetmore to his wife, May 31, 1836, James Harvey Young, ed., "Land Hunting in 1836," *ibid.*, 45 (1952): 248; *House Executive Documents*, 25 Cong., 2 Sess., #23: 12.

36. On speculation in Indiana, see Paul Wallace Gates, "Land Policy and Tenancy in the Prairie Counties of Indiana," *Indiana Magazine of History*, 35 (1939): 1–26.

37. George N. Fuller, "An Introduction to the Settlement of Southern Michigan from 1815 to 1835, *Michigan Pioneer and Historical Collections*, 38 (1912): 539–79.

of the Territory may be advancing, it is a gratifying fact that this section 'goes ahead.'" The same year the Bronson land office opened, an event that signaled the beginning of the rapid settlement of western Michigan. The full impact of the land office business was felt in the spring of 1835. Receipts at Monroe during June alone were $147,000; Bronson's for the same month, $138,000.[38] Crowds of immigrants discharged from lake craft during the pleasant summer months swelled the demand for lands still further. In October, sales at White Pigeon reached $194,594.17, a figure that prompted one commentator to observe, "But a few years more, and the *State of Michigan* will rise up and take her place side by side with the most powerful of her sister states, in wealth and importance." Reporting that sales in the Monroe land office exceeded $600,000 for the last three-quarters of 1835, the *Free Press* calculated that sales for the entire territory would reach $1,500,000. It was a conservative estimate: the final figure was $2,271,575.17.[39]

These great sales of public lands were obviously not for purposes of cultivation. Speculation was rampant. For citizens of Michigan it was a term to be used with pride and enthusiasm. "Great Speculations—Buying and selling is the order of the day. Our City is filled with speculators who are all on tiptoe," went the cry. "Several snug fortunes of from ten to twenty thousand dollars have already been made." With a shrug of nonchalance that could scarcely suppress excitement came the comment, "Pretty good for a Territory!" The entire nation paused in the middle of buying and selling to gaze at the region where the mania for speculation reached its crest. Hezekiah Niles took careful note. "Michigan must be advancing to prosperity with rapid strides, and Detroit soon become one of the most important cities in that entire section of country," he forecast.[40]

The year 1835 ushered in a rage for town-site speculation that would soon visit other settlements along water transportation routes,

38. Detroit *Democratic Free Press*, Aug. 13, 1834; Fuller, "An Introduction to the Settlement of Southern Michigan from 1815 to 1835," 548; Detroit *Democratic Free Press*, July 15, 1835.
39. White Pigeon *Michigan Statesman*, Nov. 13, 1835; Detroit *Democratic Free Press*, Dec. 30, 1835; *Senate Public Documents*, 24 Cong., 2 Sess., #3: 11.
40. *Detroit Journal*, quoted in the Little Rock *Arkansas Gazette*, July 17, 1835; *Niles' Weekly Register*, 48: 379 (Aug. 1, 1835).

particularly Chicago. Beginning in the spring months and for the rest of the year, far into 1836 and even early 1837, the platting, marketing, buying, and selling of nonexistent future cities continued. It was an enterprise that captured the attention, imagination, and capital of all those within reach. "The walls of the Michigan Exchange, the National hotel, the American hotel, Uncle Ben's, and all the other hotels of Detroit, were papered over with plats, maps and diagrams of new cities, from Lewis Goddard's city of Brest, clear over to Port Sheldon on the shores of Lake Michigan. . . ." Rivals vied with one another in extolling the virtues of their Athenses, and everyone found buyers. "Men bought real estate and did go it blind as the sporting men play poker." These transactions were only outward manifestations of an optimism that captured men of all stations. "Everything seemingly was on the mountain wave of success . . . and one had only to obtain the refusal of a piece of land on Jefferson avenue and to find a purchaser, who was always at hand, to become rich in a single summer." The atmosphere was strong and heady. "Nearly everybody became wild and extravagant on the strength of fancied wealth; at the hotels champagne took the place of water, and bottles popped and cracked like pistols in California." [41]

Some of these cities on air survived; Detroit was a noteworthy example. Most of them disappeared. One of the paper cities that vanished beneath the waves of the panic of 1837 was Allegan. Born in the minds of Michigan entrepreneurs who had the support and financial backing of a Massachusetts judge, it began with the purchase of twenty thousand acres of wilderness on the Kalamazoo River in the western part of the territory. The village of Allegan appeared on paper with a wave of pen and plat, lots were sold, and great plans were laid for its development. "You were not old enough to appreciate the different phases of the inflation, beginning with a gentle breeze in 1834, increasing to a gale in 1835, to a storm in 1836, to a change of wind and an adverse tornado in 1837, leaving wrecks on every hand, succeeded by a dead calm which lasted up to 1844," recalled one founder of the town. Yet it was an activity that called forth universal participation. "The holders of Allegan property and the adjacent wild

41. George C. Bates, "By-Gones of Detroit," *Michigan Pioneer and Historical Collections,* 22 (1893): 379–80.

lands wrote sums in their investories which would occasion a hearty laugh in these days. 'They all did it.' The whole country had lost its balance." [42]

Speculation in real estate came to a climax in 1836. The receipts at Bronson (soon to be Kalamazoo) for January and February averaged $140,000 each month. In March they exceeded $186,000. With the coming of spring, settlers rushed into Michigan Territory in vast numbers. "The emigration westward this season exceeds all bounds of calculation," commented the *Erie Observer,* "though we had before estimated, and so stated, to our readers, that it would equal that of any two previous years, yet we had no conception of the rush that is to be witnessed by every steamboat that passes up the lake." Families, individuals, and baggage waited patiently on the Erie docks for transportation. "Nearly every boat that goes up, (and there are generally three to five a day), is loaded down to the extent of its capacity. In addition to these, large numbers go by schooners and other craft, while the portion that move by land, is without a precedent." [43]

Problems of administering the public domain, already growing, rose in proportion to the sales. The greasy and perspiring hands of countless prospective customers destroyed and dirtied the plats of survey so rapidly that the Bronson register employed an assistant whose sole function was to exhibit the plats and make sketches for whoever wanted one. The spring months wore on, the lines outside the land offices lengthened, voices became more strident, tempers frayed, and records fell into arrears. As early as March men formed lines in the dark to be near the door when the offices opened with the rising sun, and the large March sales at Bronson forced the register to employ another clerk. The task of transporting the government funds to proper depositories became extremely difficult. By the end of the spring the Bronson receiver carried his funds to Detroit "in great bags, as they do wool now, sometimes counting to nearly half a million of dollars." [44]

42. C. C. Trowbridge, "Letter," *ibid.,* 4 (1881): 173–75.
43. Detroit *Democratic Free Press,* March 16, 1836; Comm. GLO to Senator Thomas Ewing (Ohio), NA: GLO, Ltrs. Sent, Misc., 7 (New Series): April 22, 1836; Erie *Observer,* quoted in *Niles' Weekly Register,* 50: 234 (June 4, 1836).
44. Abraham Edwards to GLO, NA: GLO, Ltrs. Recd., Reg. & Rec., Bronson, Register, Jan. 14, March 15, 1836; Bates, "By-Gones of Detroit," 379.

Bronson (Kalamazoo) was the center of Michigan's land office business in 1836. Sales in April reached more than a quarter of a million dollars ($252,834.38). Abraham Edwards, the Bronson register, predicted that "the sales for the present district will amount to three millions, if the business can possibly be done at the Office." Sales for the first quarter reached $467,911.66, and the rush had only begun. With the coming of pleasant summer weather, the commercial craft on the lake began the daily discharge of thousands of settlers through the port of Detroit. These hastened for the western country along the Chicago Road, a route that carried them through the bonanza city of Kalamazoo. Men interested in land filled every corner in the burgeoning village. "We are informed that the village of Kalamazoo is literally thronged with purchasers," reported the Detroit *Democratic Free Press*. "The public and private houses are full, and . . . in some instances, they are compelled to retire to the barns for accommodations in the way of lodging." [45]

The center of interest was the district land office. Neither the system of land distribution nor the staff in the small board building were sufficient to meet the needs of the mob. In February the receiver suggested that the land officers close down the office in order to bring up the books. Lacking firm direction from the General Land Office on this matter, the land officers at Kalamazoo shut down sales from April 1 to 18. This was the first of several forced closings. During this first breathing spell Edwards and Thomas C. Sheldon, the receiver, moved the office to another dwelling constructed especially for that purpose at their own expense. Reopening their doors to business on April 18, the land officers sold land at the rate of $20,000 to $30,000 a day. Sales in May totaled $471,982.05, in spite of a suspension of sales to review work, check accounts, and get some needed rest.[46]

Citizens who had come from great distances and new arrivals with their families resented the closing of the land office. They protested that the register should continue to receive applications for land. Ed-

45. Edwards and Sheldon to GLO, April 5, 1836, quoted in Ethan Allen Brown to Rep. Ratliff Boone (Ind.), Chmn. House Committee on Public Lands, NA: GLO, Ltrs. Sent, Misc., 6 (New Series): April 28, 1836; Detroit *Democratic Free Press*, May 18, 1836. Also see Willis F. Dunbar, *Kalamazoo and How it Grew* (Kalamazoo, 1959), 44–45.
46. Sheldon to GLO, NA: GLO, Ltrs. Recd., Reg. & Rec., Bronson, Register, Feb. 16, April 5, 1836; Edwards to GLO, *ibid.*, May 31, 1836.

wards bowed before public opinion, accepted numerous applications, marked the tracts sold on the maps of the office, and then watched helplessly while the prospective purchasers speculated with the approved applications. In the confusion of the moment, "it was however soon discovered that money could be made by applying for Land the applicant did not want and had no means to pay for. Whole Towns and even Counties were applyed for and then the *chance* of obtaining particular portions was sold from five to fifty Dollars for each half Quarter Section," wrote one land officer. The fortunate winner also paid for the land.[47] Amidst the press of the land office business the land officers had no time to compare accounts and resell the unpaid-for tracts. A large number of tracts never paid for remained "sold" on the maps of the land office. Citizens who had observed the law were now furious. The Commissioner of the General Land Office reprimanded the register and the receiver; and the district land officers issued a public apology, at the same time castigating what they called "nefarious transactions" carried on by "numerous individuals, without capital, and without integrity. . . ."[48]

The extraordinary business of the land offices in the western part of the territory was matched by those in the eastern part. Sales at Detroit in April 1836 reached $141,152. By the middle of May crowds around the land office had blocked off the street and made entrance impossible. The register promptly closed the office and received applications through the window, from which vantage point he conducted business for the rest of the summer. "The scene reminded us forcibly of a contested political election in a country town," noted the *Free Press,* with the expectation that readers recognize that Detroit was no longer a country town. It continued, "The persons were about as numerous, and applications for eighty acre lots were made quite as often, as votes are generally deposited in the ballot box." Receipts for the entire territory for the month of May were rumored to exceed one million dollars.[49]

"The people of the East are buying out by wholesale the Territory

47. Joseph W. Brown to GLO, *ibid.,* Ionia, Aug. 11, 1836; this letter found in the Bronson Box.
48. Edwards to GLO, *ibid.,* Register, Bronson, May 31, 1836; Ethan Allen Brown to Edwards and Sheldon, *ibid.,* Ltrs. Sent, Misc., 6 (New Series): May 12, 1836; *Niles Gazette and Advertiser,* April 30, 1836.
49. Detroit *Democratic Free Press,* May 18, 1836.

of the West . . . ," was the delighted comment. "There are without doubt at least one millions of dollars more now in Michigan, ready to be paid into the land offices as fast as it can be received." The reference to "the people of the East" and their investments in western lands had substantial foundation in fact. Helping to make possible the great sales of public lands and the speculative mania that drove prices steadily upward were a new class of purchasers—at least new in such numbers: men of wealth and station from the eastern communities, who saw in the public lands in Michigan and elsewhere in the West a profitable form of investment for surplus capital. Some—like the Massachusetts judge who financed the founding of Allegan, and Congressmen who invested through representatives like Moses M. Strong or James Duane Doty—employed local or itinerant agents to invest their funds. Others came in person, their eyes on the large profits realized already by others, their pockets stuffed with drafts on eastern banks and letters of introduction to influential citizens in the western country.[50]

To meet the tremendous press for lands in Michigan Territory, Congress created two new land districts, with land offices at Ionia (Grand River district) and Genesee (Saginaw district). A flurry of excitement followed in the selected towns, the hum increased with the arrival of the new land officers, and eventually the records appeared from the old districts. Enterprising citizens in Ionia hastily constructed two hotels, "and these and the houses of settlers were filled to overflowing." When the Ionia office opened in September, the register noted that "the crowd of purchasers was immense." In the first eleven days of operation, sales reached $190,000. So great was the rush that the land office closed while the new officers checked their books and accounts against one another. In the final three and one-half months of 1836 the Ionia land office had sales of $461,870.19.[51] The desire for

50. Ann Arbor Michigan Argus, May 12, 1836; Detroit Democratic Free Press, June 1, 8, 1836. A fine example is John Montgomery Gordon of Philadelphia and Baltimore, whose search for Michigan lands is recounted in Douglas H. Gordon and George S. May, eds., "John M. Gordon's 'Michigan Journal, 1836,'" Michigan History, 43 (1959): 1–42, 129–49, 257–93, 433–78. Other accounts of particular interest in describing Michigan in this period are two works by Caroline M. Kirkland, Western Clearings (New York, 1845); and, A New Home—Who'll Follow? or, Glimpses of Western Life (New York, 1840.).
51. "The City of Ionia—Its First Settlement and Early History," Michigan Pioneer and Historical Collections, 3 (1881): 473; Joseph W. Brown to GLO, NA:

lands was not dampened by Andrew Jackson's declaration that after September 1 only specie would be received in payment for public lands. The Bank of Michigan at Detroit quickly ordered specie from the East, acquired $500,000 in hard money from New York in October alone, and supplied land office money to continue the Michigan boom.[52] The land office business of the Michigan Territory careered through the autumn unchecked.

When the Bronson office opened on November 10, 1836, after one of its periodic closures, the register found a mob of five or six hundred in attendance. So quickly did the applications come in that sales soon reached $200,000, and the land officers suspended sales once more. In spite of these periodic interruptions to bring up the books and to seek needed rest, during which times the receiver deposited his funds, the Bronson office sold land to the value of $2,044,167.05 in 1836. It led the nation's land offices in this respect. Michigan's five land offices had sales of $5,241,228.70.[53] Soon after the dawn of the new year Michigan entered the Union, a child of the land office business.

Michigan's experience was the most graphic example of a national impulse. Sales of the public domain in 1836 leaped to nearly $25,000,000, surpassing customs receipts for the first time. The impact of this phenomenon was far broader than simply revenue to the government. Trading city lots, speculation in raw wilderness, gambling in town sites, and investment in timberlands dominated the minds and pocketbooks of citizens everywhere in the Republic. Men at the time were well aware of this fixation. American observers commented upon it, visitors were struck by it, and people returning from abroad were appalled by it. Joseph Baldwin twitted a new generation of cotton kings with their empires of paper rags. Charles Dickens's *Martin Chuzzlewit* satirized the American West, with its speculative enterprise and sharp financial practices, and recounted the adventures and misadventures of two Englishmen wandering about in this new Eden. Perhaps the most seriously disturbed were the American aristocrats of

GLO, Ltrs. Recd., Reg. & Rec., Ionia, Register, Sept. 22, Oct. 3, 1836; *House Executive Documents*, 25 Cong., 2 Sess., #23: 13.
52. Harry N. Scheiber, "The Pet Banks in Jacksonian Politics and Finance, 1833–1841," *Journal of Economic History*, 23 (1963): 206.
53. Edwards to GLO, NA: GLO, Ltrs. Recd., Reg. & Rec., Bronson, Register, Nov. 10, 11, Dec. 19, 1836; *House Executive Documents*, 25 Cong., 2 Sess., #23: 13.

an earlier generation. Returning from Europe after an extensive stay, James Fenimore Cooper shrank from the vulgar marketplace that he found in his homeland. He immediately set down his impressions in *Home as Found,* a novel satirizing the world of commerce and business which he found so dominant in American life. Here the buying, selling, and speculating in lots, farms, and villages took on a ridiculous and sordid air. Later in a shorter piece, *Autobiography of a Pocket-Handkerchief,* he introduced the representative of the new class, a gentlemen by the name of Henry Halfacre, Esq. Halfacre was an enterprising speculator in town lots. His grand paper estate included lots in Manhattan and Brooklyn and large holdings in Milwaukee, Chicago, Rock River, Moonville, and other promising sources of investment. Vulgar, pretentious, and overdrawn as Halfacre may have been, he represented a new class, whose fascination with real estate across the continent dominated the America of the mid-1830's.[54]

54. Baldwin, *The Flush Times of Alabama and Mississippi,* esp. 81–92; Charles Dickens, *Martin Chuzzlewit* (2 vols., Standard Library Edition, Boston and New York, 1894); James Fenimore Cooper, *Home as Found* (New York, 1961, 1st ed., 1838), 110–21; Cooper, *Autobiography of a Pocket-Handkerchief* (Chapel Hill, 1949, 1st ed., 1843).

ADMINISTERING THE
LAND OFFICE BUSINESS,
1830–1837

12

The enormous volume of work generated by the land business between 1830 and 1837 had to be absorbed into the land system. It was a staggering task. In the four years from 1833 through 1836, citizens of the Republic purchased lands to the sum of $52,000,000, a figure that exceeded the sales of all previous years combined. As the land office business grew, so did the land system. The district land offices administered by the Commissioner of the General Land Office numbered thirty-six in 1831, forty-eight by early 1833, fifty-five in November 1834, and finally sixty-two at the climax of the land business in 1837. The number of surveying districts increased in the same period from five to seven with the creation of one each for Arkansas and Louisiana. Unfortunately the staff in the Washington office did not increase as rapidly as the field force.

During this period of expansion the General Land Office was headed by Elijah Hayward. Hayward's career differed markedly from the careers of his predecessors. He was a politician. Born in Bridgewater, Massachusetts, he read some law in his youth, gained admittance to the bar, and moved to Cincinnati in 1819. Like many others who called themselves lawyers, he quickly gravitated to politics. When he became editor of the *National Republican,* the election of 1824 was on the horizon, and he took an active part. Hayward strongly favored DeWitt Clinton, and he attacked the other candidates, including Andrew Jackson. Suddenly, in April 1824, Hayward changed candidates. He became a Jackson man. His conversion can probably be ascribed to a visit from Major William B. Lewis, a close friend of Jackson's. Hayward's zeal and determination—and his influential editorship—carried him to the forefront of the Jackson party in Ohio. His partisan journalism helped to fashion a great victory for the

Jackson cause in 1828. He spent several months in search of a suitable reward, and when Jackson offered him the commissionership of the General Land Office, he eagerly accepted.[1] In this fashion Andrew Jackson deserted the tradition of gentlemen-scholar public servants for a newspaperman-politician. Whether Elijah Hayward could meet the pressing problems of the office remained to be seen.

When Hayward took office, the great Choctaw Treaty was already signed, and it signaled the start of a frantic administrative effort on the part of the government, led by the President, to throw open for public entry enormous quantities of the public domain in Mississippi and Alabama. Instant survey became a necessity, along with an expanding administrative apparatus to meet the needs of incoming settlers; and the attendant rise in bookkeeping and record-keeping assumed pressing proportions. Eventually these same conditions would pervade the remainder of the western country.

By the time Hayward moved to Washington, the seasonal demands of the land system were well established. The spring and autumn were periods of heavy sales, and summer was a time of extensive surveying. The winter months were particularly severe for administrators. In the field the returns of the sales must be finished and sent to the General Land Office, while in the growing number of offices of the surveyors general the field notes of the summer and fall must be translated into plats for the sales of the coming spring. Within the General Land Office itself the winter and spring months were particularly trying. Congress was in session, and its official demands and the unofficial requests of numerous Congressmen must be carefully honored. A recurring battle was fought over additional appropriations—which the General Land Office invariably lost—and the climax of the session was the struggle over the annual appropriations bill. The new legislation must be interpreted, and the proper land officers notified, their questions answered, and legislators conferred with over difficulties with existing legislation and plans for future laws. At the moment when pressure from the Congressional and the Executive branches was heaviest, the great volume of returns from the district land offices (the result of the late autumn sales) poured into the office, demanding the

1. Hayward to Ethan Allen Brown, Dec. 22, 1822, Brown Papers, Ohio State Library, Columbus; Stevens, *The Early Jackson Party in Ohio*, 105; Weisenburger, "The 'Atlas' of the Jacksonian Movement in Ohio," 283–94.

attention of the hard-pressed clerks. Summer brought some relief, even in the stifling heat of Washington. Extensive correspondence had first priority, followed by consultation over the increasing sales, the organization of new land districts established at the recent session of Congress, the transfer of accounts and plats, and the endless inquiries of the new officers.

The paramount concern of Congress was cost. Congress had long been concerned with the expense of administering the public domain—at least since the period of retrenchment following the panic of 1819. It was in this period that Commissioner George Graham had voluntarily reduced the staff of the General Land Office. Graham had estimated that the expense of administering the public lands in the period from 1821 to 1827 amounted to about 6.4 per cent of the gross income. In early February 1829 he confirmed that the future expenses of the land business would not exceed 6 per cent.[2] Many observers chose to read the statistics another way: that 6 per cent of the revenue from the public domain would be channeled into sinecures, into a private trough to which fortunate officials went upon occasion for hearty drafts at public expense. "This is not assertion, but fact: only about 33 millions of dollars have been paid into the Treasury for public lands in 42 years, and of this inconsiderable sum, a great proportion has been swallowed up in expenses," asserted an editorial in the *St. Louis Beacon*. "The expense of keeping up a system so long to sell so little, and the balance not consumed in expenses, has been more than ten times sunk in paying interest on the national debt." So strong was the pressure for retrenchment that, in spite of his voluntary reduction of a sorely pressed staff, Graham found himself constantly importuned in his last months in office to make still further reductions.[3] It was this reduced staff that Elijah Hayward inherited as the land business entered one of its biggest booms.

When the new commissioner took office in October 1830, the next session of Congress was only a few weeks distant, and a report on the condition of the General Land Office would be due. Although Hayward's views were based on only a few weeks of personal observation, he determined to speak forthrightly to Congress. His first report

2. Graham to Rep. Andrew Stevenson (Va.) NA: GLO, Ltrs. Sent, Misc., 23: Feb. 6, 1829.
3. *St. Louis Beacon*, Sept. 9, 1829; Graham to Samuel D. Ingham, Sec. Treas., NA: GLO, Ltrs. Sent, Misc., 25: Jan. 25, 1830.

presented a pessimistic—indeed almost alarmist—view of the land business. Since in the previous session Congress had made no appropriations for surveying, and the Indian cessions of the Southwest had begun and demands for their immediate preparation were already current, the commissioner requested $150,000 for surveys. The new Indian cessions and the movement of population west would also necessitate more land offices. Far more serious was "the present condition of the office, its arrears of business, the embarrassments under which it labors, and the improvements and provisions which are considered necessary to its proper and efficient organization. . . ." The reduction of the clerical staff in 1827 had caused much of the present embarrassment. Continuing Congressional legislation was also a heavy burden, particularly the relief acts whose administration absorbed the attention of the office staff upon several occasions so completely that "a considerable portion of the regular current business" had to be suspended. Hayward's summary suggested the degree to which the General Land Office was unprepared to meet the land office business that lay just ahead. Five hundred private land claims needed decisions, while another fifteen thousand claims awaited patents. All private claims needed to be properly indexed. Twenty-six thousand patents awaited issue, with an annual deficit of five thousand (sales of the level of 1830 required about fifteen thousand patents each year, while facilities existed for writing, recording, issuing, and distributing no more than ten thousand); and work should be resumed on an index of names of patentees of the public lands, a project now suspended since the days of the Relief Act of 1821. The commissioner also noted the demands of the President, the Secretary of the Treasury, Congress, and the several committees of that body, all of whom imposed their desires on the understaffed General Land Office. He closed with a reminder that economy was always "a cardinal virtue," but so were efficiency and promptness in the public service.[4]

When Hayward took office, the most demanding area of the land business was the Southwest, where frantic preparations for a public sale of the Choctaw Cession were under way, hampered by the disorganization of the surveying district South of Tennessee. Gideon Fitz, the incumbent surveyor general, wrote briefly of his predecessors. The first was Isaac Briggs, Fitz began, a man who "had not the advantage

4. *American State Papers, Public Lands*, 6: 191–94.

of a *practical* knowledge of surveying, nor of conducting such business, though he was a fine scholar and a great theorist." Briggs made
large advances to his deputies, and much of the work done under him
went to subcontractors with his tacit approval, as he was concerned
simply with having the work done. Many of the "sub-deputies" were
men with "no practical experience in surveying, and some, it is believed, were unqualified for want of education." This arrangement,
"with the aid of some dishonest surveyors, threw the work into derangement from the very origin of it, and it has never been, nor never
will be, got into the order it should have been." Briggs left the scene
abruptly, and his replacement was Seth Pease. Pease recognized that
much of the surveying was of poor quality, "but the work being cred-
ited on the books, he thought it best for the public good, in many instances, to dispense with scrupulous nicety; the alternative would have
been attended with great expense to the public, and delay of the
sales." The third surveyor general, Thomas Freeman, became intem-
perate, careless, overbearing, partial, and made several alterations for
the worse. Of Freeman's work, Fitz continued, "There are, I believe
about *eighty* township maps of the settled part of the State sent back
for corrections, before patents will be issued, which maps are *now lying in this office for that purpose.*" George Davis occupied his time in
letter writing and did nothing to forward the surveying business.
James P. Turner covered the country with surveyors, many with little
experience, and yet he entrusted them with surveying of the most intricate nature. The result was substantial cost to the government with
little accomplished. Throughout, the records of the office had been
shamefully neglected. "The mice, roaches, and crickets, all have free
access to them; and the mice may and do make beds out of old field
notes." Fitz cautioned the eager administrators in Washington not to
repeat past mistakes in supervision. "If the work is pressed on me, as
has been the case very generally heretofore with my predecessors, too
fast for execution, it must then, from necessity, pass, as they past it,
with slight superficial examination, and the recording must be laid
aside." He concluded, "I dread this state of things in the office." [5]

Hayward achieved tangible results in his first year in office. Acting
on his recommendation, Congress reorganized surveying operations in

5. Fitz to Poindexter, Nov. 9, 1831, *Senate Public Documents,* 22 Cong., 1
Sess., #54.

the Southwest, abolished the cumbersome system of three principal deputies, and created in its place a separate surveying district for the State of Louisiana. In order to assist in the organization and early operation of the new district, Hayward dispatched a clerk from the General Land Office to supervise the transfer of records. The commissioner also directed his agent Samuel Davidson King to examine the office of the surveyor general at Washington (Mississippi) and the district land offices in Mississippi and Louisiana. Hayward outfitted King with letters of credit and introduction and emphasized the importance of the mission by noting that it proceeded directly from the interest of the President.[6]

After a brief stop at Cincinnati, King followed the Ohio to its confluence with the Mississippi, and thence down that great river to the river port of Natchez. By the time he arrived, his spirits had wilted in the debilitating heat of the lower Mississippi Valley, the onset of the fever, and numerous missed transportation connections. The sight of the surveyor general's office in Washington did nothing to restore him. Although he had expected to find "many difficulties, I had not the least idea of the state in which the old papers, more especially, are situated, nor is it in my power at present to give any more particular description of their state than to say that it would be almost impracticable to place them in greater confusion than they are now in," he wrote. King stayed almost three full months, trying to straighten out the affairs of the surveyor general's office, attempting to prevent the same sort of confusion from infecting the new Louisiana office, and examining the surveys returned to the various district land offices. He returned to the General Land Office thoroughly depressed. His final report catalogued the endless difficulties that had dogged the office from the moment of its opening: incompetent and dishonest deputies who subcontracted their districts; the loss of correspondence to George Davis; endless examples of erroneous surveys and resurveys of an even poorer quality; and, finally, a strange catalogue of incumbents, each a talented man in his own way, who failed to perform the duties of the office. King concluded that the work of the office was far in arrears in terms of surveying, platting, correspondence, and administration of private claims, and that little or no reliance could be

6.   4 Stat. 492–94 (March 3, 1831); Hayward to King, NA: GLO, Ltrs. Sent, Misc., 26: June 30, 1831; Hayward to Fitz, *ibid.*, SG, 4: June 30, 1831.

placed on the completed work.[7] A later dispute with Congress over appointments led Andrew Jackson to leave this vital office vacant for a full year. From mid-1835 to mid-1836, with the land office business at its crest, no surveys were contracted, no field notes were accepted, and no progress was made in bringing up the arrears of office. The confusion in the land system in Mississippi and Louisiana can be laid to incompetent, unqualified administrators and ambitious politicians.[8]

Hayward was also determined to create order and uniformity in the various surveying districts. The initial focus was the recalcitrant office South of Tennessee which seemed to defy all attempts to give it order. The commissioner wrote to the surveyor general, Gideon Fitz, for the purpose of showing "what are the requirements of the Department in reference to the township surveys and the mode of making returns thereof in order that you may adopt your contracts with your deputies, and instructions and form of field books precisely to suit these requirements." Hayward described in great detail the duties of each member of the surveying team, the procedures for making surveys in the field, the form of the field book and its contents, and the work to be done in the office of the surveyor general. So pleased was he with this letter that the commissioner sent a copy of it to the other surveyors general.[9] For the first time the surveying business had some order. It was astonishing to think that a system established in 1785 had expanded over half the nation with only slight direction.

Hayward's first year in office was a busy one. The great increase of business evident in 1830 (estimated at twice that of the previous year) continued. New duties fell on the General Land Office, including for the first time the task of adjusting the accounts of the surveyors. Various new laws also had to be administered. Writing to the register at Shawneetown in the middle of the summer, Hayward confessed, "Amidst the multiplicity of the duties of this Office, & the continual pressure of business, the provisions of the 2d Section of the Act for the relief of the citizens of Shawneetown . . . which requires in-

7. King to Hayward, *ibid.*, Ltrs. Recd., Misc., K: July 15, Aug. 8, 1831; King to Hayward, *ibid.*, Oct. 3, 11, 14, 19, 22, Nov. 21, 1831.
8. Cf. Coles, "Applicability of the Public Land System to Louisiana," 39–58, that the land system was at fault.
9. Hayward to Fitz, NA: GLO, Ltrs. Sent, SG, 5: July 28, 1831; Hayward to William McRee, John Coffee, Micah T. Williams, Robert Butler, and Hore B. Trist, *ibid.*, Sept. 23, 1831.

structions from this Office to carry it into effect escaped my observation." [10] Many details of a similar nature went unattended; others were done only tardily.

In Hayward's first year as commissioner, the General Land Office issued more than twenty-five thousand patents. Yet the backlog continued to grow. The problem of patents provided an interesting insight into the mood of Congress and the outmoded procedures of a past era. Under law the President fixed his signature to every patent. During the days of Thomas Jefferson this duty was burdensome but not impossible. John Quincy Adams carried bundles of patents with him to Quincy, where he signed them as part of his regular work schedule. By the 1830's the magnitude of the land business and the forty-acre law made it imperative that Congress change the law requiring the President's signature, and, at the same time, that it provide greater assistance to the General Land Office in the preparation of patents. Congress subjected the commissioner to tremendous pressure over patents, and a flood of letters from constituents complained of the speed at which patents reached the western country. In spite of Hayward's determination that patents should be issued in the order in which the land was sold, elected officials frequently used their privileged position to crowd themselves and their favorites to the head of the patent line. [11]

By 1832 the General Land Office needed to issue forty thousand patents a year simply to meet the annual sales. Even if the office managed to turn out thirty thousand (which was unlikely, since it had produced twenty-five thousand patents in 1831 only with a Herculean effort), the President would need to affix his signature to one hundred land patents every working day. Hayward recommended that Congress dispense with the President's signature and substitute that of the Secretary of the Treasury. Samuel D. Ingham, the present Secretary, demurred on the grounds that his duties were already too heavy. Ingham recommended the Secretary of State, who also declined. While the various land committees and individual Congressmen had much to say about the problems facing the President and expressed sympathy for his plight, no one paid the slightest attention to the problems of the General Land Office in preparing the patents for the President's

10. Hayward to Charles Gordon, *ibid.*, Misc., 26: April 6, 1831; Hayward to James C. Sloo, *ibid.*, Reg. & Rec., 2 (New Series): July 26, 1831.
11. See, e.g., Hayward to Senator David Barton (Mo.), *ibid.*, Misc., 26: Dec. 17, 1830.

signature.[12] Indications of public irritation began to appear in the press, and the Detroit *Democratic Free Press* ran a long editorial on the various inconveniences caused by delayed patents. Congress treated the General Land Office with indifference or felt that the staff was sufficient to its duties. The plight of the President was something else again. Between the opening of Congress in December and the middle of June, Andrew Jackson signed more than 10,000 patents. Yet when he paused for a rest, he was still 10,590 behind and losing ground. The next year Congress passed a law providing for the appointment of a secretary to sign patents in the name of the President.[13] As for the General Land Office, Congress contented itself with small periodic injections of funds and admonitions to greater effort.

Upon occasion various Congressmen roused themselves to criticize. In his annual report for 1832, Elijah Hayward requested fifteen additional clerks, as well as another $5,000 for the writing of patents. With such additional force and annual appropriation, the arrears of the office could probably be brought up within four years, he wrote, but the extra staff would become permanent; so rapidly were the duties of the General Land Office growing that the fifteen clerks could be absorbed into the regular staff at the end of that period.[14] When the commissioner's request came to the floor of the House, Congressman Charles Wickliffe of Kentucky reminded the House that his predecessor had dismissed clerks when requested to do so by the House Committee on Retrenchment; "yet, with this diminished force, Mr. Graham had been able to get along." Wickliffe "had been struck with the increase of arrearages since the time of Mr. Graham," he continued. "They had increased at a rate greatly beyond the increase of the business. Mr. Graham had been able to keep up with the course of business till the time of his lamented death; and yet now, in two years, the House was told that the arrears required fifty-five clerks, and an enlargement of the treasury building. Last year the commissioner had asked for ten clerks, now he asked for fifteen, and next

12.   Hayward to Rep. Jonathan Hunt (Vt.), *ibid.*, 27: Dec. 27, 1831; Hayward to McLane, Sec. Treas., NA: TD, Ltrs. from Comm. GLO to Sec. Treas., 9: Feb. 16, 1832.
13.   Detroit *Democratic Free Press*, Sept. 27, 1832; Hayward to Senator William King (Ala.), NA: GLO, Ltrs. Sent, Misc., 27: June 19, 1832; 4 Stat. 663 (March 2, 1833).
14.   Hayward to Senator William R. King (Ala.), NA: GLO, Ltrs. Sent, Misc., 27: Jan. 23, 1832.

year he supposed he would want twenty." Wickliffe, a Whig, hinted that the General Land Office and its commissioner were deeply involved in politics, which absorbed much of their time and energy. Hayward, too, had his political defenders, notably William Irvin of Ohio. The respected Clement C. Clay of Alabama represented a middle ground. He conjured up frightening visions of stagnated trade and commerce in an economy crippled by lack of land patents; and while he deplored "the effect of this retrenchment mania," he admitted "that great difficulty and delay occurred in getting answers to inquiries from the land commissioner." Hayward settled for a $4,000 increase in his budget and no additional clerks.[15]

Hayward might have added a few comments about these "inquiries" made to the General Land Office. They were numerous and unending. Statistics, maps, reports, investigations—something more could always be discovered about the public lands. Senator George Poindexter's imperious demand for a list of purchasers at the Columbus and Chocchuma sales induced the commissioner to comment, "These two statements embrace . . . in all more than *Fifteen thousand* items of information." In an ordinary session of Congress official requests for information demanded the attention of at least four clerks for two full months; for the shorter session, six weeks. These figures, of course, did not include the unofficial demands of Congressmen, a substantial volume of business in themselves. At the flood tide of the land office business in the months after the autumn of 1834, Hayward often refused requests for information, on the grounds that "the magnitude of the work, and great pressure of business on every branch of the Office, and the very limited means at its disposal to perform the multifarious demands on its attention, which are daily increasing," made such compliance impossible.[16]

Surveys continued to cause trouble. No public sales could take place

15. *Register of Debates*, 22 Cong., 1 Sess., 8: 1847–49. Wickliffe's charge that the General Land Office was deeply involved in politics had a certain justification in the case of the commissioner. Hayward openly continued his interest in Ohio politics. See, e.g., Robert Skinner to Hayward, NA: GLO, Ltrs. Recd., Reg. & Rec., Piqua, 38: March 31, 1831; *Niles' Weekly Register*, 43: 115 (Oct. 20, 1832); Weisenburger, "The 'Atlas' of the Jacksonian Movement in Ohio," 296.
16. Hayward to Vice-President Martin Van Buren, NA: GLO, Ltrs. Sent, Misc., 29: Dec. 15, 1834; Hayward to McLane, Sec. Treas., Jan. 21, 1833; *Senate Public Documents*, 22 Cong., 2 Sess., #50: 10–11; Hayward to Delegate Lucius Lyon (Mich.), NA: GLO, Ltrs. Sent, Misc., 29: Jan. 16, 1835.

until the arrival of the township plats at the office of the district land officer. This was the worst bottleneck in the administrative system, or at least so the experience of the early 1830's suggested. Congressional appropriations for surveys of public lands came through the House with ease. In practical terms, however, these increased appropriations—particularly for rush projects such as the Choctaw Purchase—meant little when they simply resulted in larger stacks of field notes awaiting the attention of a few clerks in the offices of the surveyors general. The end result was the cancellation or postponement of a number of public sales that had been advertised.

Aside from the general aspects of the problem, each district presented its own special difficulties, most often centered in the person of the surveyor general. Robert Butler of Florida was always either ill or on leave to recover from periodic bouts of illness. Absent from his office for nine months from July 1831 to April 1832, he was so weakened on his return that he did nothing for the rest of the year. In his annual report for 1832, Hayward reported that no surveys had been returned from Florida for the past twelve months. The commissioner feared that in the absence of careful supervision "there has been much bad surveying in Florida," and he was alternately apprehensive that Butler would do little or that he would do too much. Fortunately the demand for land in Florida was marginal, and Butler's office was not of central importance.[17]

The same could hardly be said of the district of William McRee, who directed the preparation of lands for sale in Arkansas, Missouri, and Illinois—all at the center of the land business. The successor of William Rector, McRee grew more and more pessimistic over the enormous backlog in his office. Eventually he refused to answer his mail, and from the autumn of 1830 to the autumn of 1831 he did not write a single letter to the General Land Office. In this interval his failure to provide township plats resulted in the cancellation of sales in Franklin and Lexington (Missouri), Little Rock (Arkansas), and Springfield and Palestine (Illinois). Commissioner Hayward finally persuaded the President to order the surveyor general to reply. McRee responded only grudgingly. Congress relieved the pressure somewhat

17. *American State Papers, Public Lands,* 6: 511; Butler to Hayward, NA: GLO, Ltrs. Recd., SG, Fla., 51: April 11, 1832; Hayward to Butler, *ibid.,* Ltrs. Sent, SG, 5: April 15, 1833.

by creating a new surveying district for the Territory of Arkansas—an act that Hayward wholeheartedly supported. McRee's refusal even to describe the condition of his office and his tardy response to proclaimed sales suggested that he was incompetent to deal with the expanding land office business. On March 15, 1832, Andrew Jackson dismissed him. At the time of McRee's removal, more than 5,520 miles of returns were due from him.[18]

Within a year, growing dissatisfaction with Gideon Fitz led to his removal from the office of Surveyor General South of Tennessee.[19] Andrew Jackson then appointed a series of successors that the Senate refused to confirm, and in pique the President left the office vacant for a year. By 1837 surveying affairs in Mississippi were thoroughly disordered.

The propensity of Congressmen to criticize in haphazard fashion increased because of Elijah Hayward's obvious political connections. In early 1833 a series of random comments on inefficiency and high costs led to a House investigation of the "causes of the arrearages of business in the General and other Land Offices," with particular emphasis on the surveying practices in force, on the "fidelity, industry, and punctuality" of the several clerks of the office, and especially on the costs connected with the administration of the public lands. In his reply Hayward pointed out that forty-eight district land offices were now in operation, many of them established very recently. Ill-considered (from an administrator's point of view) legislation added to the administrative burden. A prime example was the forty-acre law, which had greatly increased the paper work of land administrators everywhere. The arrears of the General Land Office were large and growing. "It may be asked, *from what causes have these arrears accumulated?*" asked the commissioner. He immediately replied, "From the physical impossibility of the office to discharge all the duties required of it by law with the force provided for that purpose. . . ." He re-

18.   Hayward to the President, *ibid.*, Misc., 27: Feb. 29, 1832; 4 Stat. 531 (June 15, 1832); McRee to Hayward, NA: GLO, Ltrs. Recd., SG, Mo., 63: March 2, 1832; Hayward to the President, *ibid.*, Ltrs. Sent, Misc., 27: March 20, 1832; Carter, ed., *Territorial Papers*, 21: 511n.
19.   Hayward to Fitz, NA: GLO, Ltrs. Sent, SG, 5: March 30, Dec. 6, 1832; Hayward to the President, *ibid.*, Misc., 27: June 16, 1832; *ibid.*, 29: June 23, 1834; Feb. 9, 1835. Fitz's removal most certainly resulted, at least in part, from political motives. Edwin Arthur Miles, *Jacksonian Democracy in Mississippi* (James Sprunt Studies in history and political science, Vol. 42, Chapel Hill, 1960), 48–54.

vealed that the appropriations of the General Land Office were so inadequate that during the past year it had been forced to borrow
$2,290 from the branch Bank of the United States.[20]

The duties of the office continued to increase, and so did the unfinished business. During 1833 the staff of the General Land Office
wrote more than 6,000 letters. It also completed 40,000 patents. Yet by
January 1, 1834, the number of final certificates awaiting patenting
had reached 70,000. By the spring of 1834 this number was 92,000;
two months later, 110,000. The commissioner estimated that at the
present rate of issue, as many as 5,500 of the patentees would die before receiving their patents—a development that might raise cumbersome legal problems for their heirs.[21] Records of the land districts
filled every corner of the General Land Office; adding to the crush
were the new "Chickasaw business," the unending labor of the draftsmen, and the procession of patent books. Patent records alone increased at the rate of 150 volumes each year. The thirteen rooms on
the lower floor of the State Department Building were no longer adequate to hold the records of the land business, much less provide
working area for the several clerks, and yet these quarters of necessity
continued to provide both. "There are at this time fifty-five land offices
in operation—next year there will be several more," wrote the commissioner in November 1834. "There are only *seven* regular accoun-
tants, receiving occasional aid from three or four Clerks . . . there
should be at least twelve Clerks regularly engaged in registering the
sales. . . ." In February 1835, Hayward wrote that "the pressure of
the business of this office has been so great and the force is so disproportionate to the magnitude of its duties" that the records of the district land offices could not be posted before the next mail brought new
ones.[22]

In early 1833 Hayward suggested that the permanent staff be in-

20. Hayward to Representative Gulian Verplanck (N.Y.), Jan. 7, 1833, *House
Executive Documents*, 22 Cong., 2 Sess., #46: 2–3; Hayward to Louis McLane,
Sec. Treas., Jan. 21, 1833, *Senate Public Documents*, 22 Cong., 2 Sess., #50: 7.
21. *American State Papers, Public Lands*, 6: 623–27; Hayward to Rep. Clement
C. Clay (Ala.), NA: GLO, Ltrs. Sent, Misc., 29: April 9, 1834; Hayward to
Senator George Poindexter (Miss.), *ibid.*, June 5, 1834.
22. John M. Moore, acting, to Levi Woodbury, Sec. Treas., *ibid.*, Sept. 8, 1834;
Hayward to Woodbury, *ibid.*, Nov. 15, 1834; Hayward to Thomas L. Sumrall,
ibid., Reg & Rec., 5 (New Series): Feb. 17, 1835. Cf. Roy M. Robbins, *Our
Landed Heritage* (Princeton, 1942), 55, that the administrative problems of the
land business were well on their way to solution by 1834.

creased from seventeen to thirty. But he was not heeded. In January 1835 the commissioner estimated that the burdens of the General Land Office required at least sixty-nine full-time permanent clerks, but he offered to settle for a permanent staff of forty-five. The number of regular clerks at this time was still seventeen, the figure agreed to by George Graham in 1827.[23] Although much had changed in the intervening eight years, Congress was not moved to add to the permanent force of the General Land Office.

Congress and the Treasury Department rarely responded to the demands of the commissioner. The Secretary of the Treasury occasionally used his authority to divert surveying funds to the various surveyors general for relief of the administrative backlog.[24] Generally, however, the head of the Treasury Department offered the commissioner little support, tangible or moral—an astonishing indifference to the fate of one of the department's responsibilities. Congress, on the other hand, voted money in little driblets: $4,000 in the spring of 1832, and $7,000 a year later. At the same time it turned down an urgent request from the commissioner for $2,500 with which to purchase copies of the statutes and reports of the high courts of the several public-land states. When the commissioner or one of his clerks wished to consult a state law, he sent a messenger to the chambers of the Attorney General. Another $6,000 provided temporary relief in the spring of 1834.

Hayward was in a difficult spot. His many enemies enjoyed themselves immensely at his expense. Charles Hammond of the *Cincinnati Gazette*, a long-time antagonist, led the assault. "The Committee on public lands have had under consideration for some time past, an enquiry into the nature of the expenditures &c by the Commissioner of the General Land Office," he wrote. "I have reason to believe that the developments which have been made, in the progress of that inquiry, must produce the removal of the head of that department." Hayward also suffered attacks from faithful Jacksonians. His role as guardian of the public domain often brought him into conflict with various Con-

23.   Hayward to McLane, Sec. Treas., Jan. 21, 1833, *Senate Public Documents*, 22 Cong., 2 Sess., #50; Hayward to Levi Woodbury, Sec. Treas., NA: GLO, Ltrs. Sent, Misc., 29: Jan. 27, 1835.
24.   E.g. Hayward to Samuel D. Ingham, Sec. Treas., NA: TD, Ltrs. from Comm. GLO to Sec. Treas., 9: Jan. 10, 1831; Ingham to Hayward, *ibid.*, Ltrs. Sent, Misc., 1801–33: April 7, 1831.

gressmen over the issue of patronage, and with the several governors of the states on matters of land grants. These constant conflicts sapped his partisan support.[25]

Hayward's staunch friends also worried about him, but for different reasons. At first his career on the national scene showed every sign of success. Reports affirmed that he was "doing very well at Washington," and that he "is putting the Land Office in much better shape than it has been heretofore." After an auspicious start Hayward began to absent himself from the office for long periods, ostensibly because of illness. Friends and foes alike suspected strong spirits. Micah T. Williams, the Surveyor General Northwest of the Ohio, wrote of Hayward, "You know that charges of habits of *intemperance* have been made against him—I regret to [believe?], not without some cause. His removal, has even been hinted at in the West." The President intervened and ordered Hayward "that he *must* desist entirely from tasting *any spirits*, unless it was a table wine." The whole matter had become dangerous for the Jackson administration. "If he does obey the old man's injunctions all will be well—but if he does not, & shd again fall into the habits of which he has been charged, I am well satisfied from the remarks of the Genl he must go." [26]

Rumors of Hayward's intemperance spread. His supporters in Congress found it necessary to defend his personal habits. The commissioner was frequently incapacitated at times when business required the greatest delicacy and tact. In the summer of 1834, Major William B. Lewis, who had recruited Hayward to the Jackson cause a decade before, wrote Jackson that he intended to cut his contact with Hayward, and that the commissioner might not be able to attend to the office regularly in the future. Hayward's career had come full circle; the end was in sight. In July 1835, Hayward indicated his determination to resign, but he asked to remain in office until August 31. Jackson acquiesced. His days of grace expended, the former commissioner "returns to the west," to search for political influence and power in a world greatly changed and one in which he was to play a minor role. Opposition newspapers rejoiced in his disappearance from the Washington scene (which they termed a "removal") as proof of the

25. *Daily Cincinnati Gazette*, Feb. 22, 1833; Lonnie J. White, *Politics on the Southwestern Frontier: Arkansas Territory, 1819–1836* (Memphis, 1964), 146–51.
26. Micah T. Williams to Ethan Allen Brown, Sept. 25, 1831, Brown Papers, Ohio State Library, Columbus; Williams to Brown, Oct. 13, 1833, *ibid.*

rumors of his intemperance and of the incompetence that stalked Jackson's administration. That "he has been for a long time notoriously incompetent to perform his duties" was now obvious to all.[27]

Hayward's replacement as Commissioner of the General Land Office was Ethan Allen Brown, former Governor of Ohio, member of the diplomatic corps, and a leading Jacksonian politician. Brown had moved to Cincinnati from Connecticut in 1804 and had begun to practice law. He rose quickly in the legal profession, joined the Republican party, and received the post of inspector of the Cincinnati land office in 1807, 1808, and 1809, an honor that showed his growing influence. From 1810 to 1818, Brown served as an associate justice of the Ohio Supreme Court. In 1818 he was elected governor, and from the state house he made an important contribution to the development of Ohio's transportation network. He resigned as governor to serve out the unexpired term of William A. Trimble in the United States Senate, but in 1825 the legislature denied his bid for re-election. In the years that followed, Brown devoted himself to the development of Ohio's canal system. He was an early enthusiast for Andrew Jackson, and the President sent him to Brazil as chargé d'affaires. The Ohioan (for such he was by now) served abroad until April 1834. Upon his return he hastened to Ohio to see old friends and renew political connections. Brown soon received "a very unexpected invitation to the post of Commissioner of the General Land Office." He immediately accepted.[28]

The new commissioner immediately began to publicize the condition of the General Land Office. His first annual report detailed the necessity for reform by contrasting in graphic fashion the vast gap between the obligations of the bureau and the comparatively tiny work force at its disposal.[29] Brown next made use of his years of service to the Jacksonians to gain the ear of the President himself. So persuasive

27. *Register of Debates,* 22 Cong., 1 Sess., 8: 2182–83; Lewis to Jackson, July 25, 1834, Bassett, ed., *Jackson Correspondence,* 5: 276; *Daily National Intelligencer,* July 22, 1835; *Niles' Weekly Register,* 49: 2 (Sept. 5, 1835); Weisenburger, "The 'Atlas' of the Jacksonian Movement in Ohio," 297–99; Little Rock *Arkansas Advocate,* July 10, 1835.

28. Brown to Bento de Silva Lisbon (an official in the Brazilian Foreign Office), Oct. 11, 1836, Brown Papers, Ohio State Library, Columbus. On Brown's public career, see John S. Still, "The Life of Ethan Allen Brown, Governor of Ohio" (Unpublished doctoral dissertation, Ohio State University, 1951).

29. *American State Papers, Public Lands,* 8: 4–7.

were his arguments and so eloquent his presentation that Jackson devoted a part of his annual message to the General Land Office. His recitation of the great increases in sales during the quarter-century since the organization's establishment, the large number of new land districts, the wave of Congressional legislation, and the inadequate work force might have come directly from the mouth of the commissioner. Brown had also made personal appeals to several influential Congressmen, among the most important of whom was C. C. Cambreleng on the House Committee on Ways and Means.[30] Within three months Brown had skillfully laid the groundwork for reform in the land business.

The first result of this careful attention to personal relations was a request by the House Committee on Public Lands, dated January 20, 1836, for the commissioner to draft a bill on the reorganization of the General Land Office. The land business was at "flood-tide," and the returns from the great sales of the previous fourth quarter were pouring into the office. Brown responded with an eloquent description of the needs of the General Land Office and its present condition.

The commissioner's report began by referring to the great rise in sales of recent months. If the district land offices closed their doors on January 1, 1836, he wrote, six or eight years of work would be required for his present staff to bring all the business up to date. But the district land offices would not close. Estimating sales in 1836 at $10,000,000 (they actually reached almost $25,000,000), he found the land business for the three years 1834, 1835, and 1836 would total more than $30,000,000. Based on the rule of experience that "every hundred dollars requiring one patent," the sales of these three years would necessitate the issue of 360,000 patents. In spite of the most determined efforts, the General Land Office had never been able in the past to issue more than 40,000 in any single year. The number of final certificates awaiting patents had now reached 169,107; processing them would require the services of fifty clerks for one year. Each patent required the signature of the Commissioner of the General Land Office; and should Congress make provision to bring up the arrears (admittedly an unlikely contingency), the task of signing patents

30. *Senate Public Documents*, 24 Cong., 1 Sess., #1: 16; Brown to Cambreleng, NA: GLO, Ltrs. Sent, Misc., 6 (New Series): Jan. 5, 1836.

would absorb the commissioner's entire attention for a matter of years.

Auditing and bookkeeping had suffered. The monthly accounts of each land officer had to be audited on receipt of his data, and the entries posted in a ledger. Two hundred and fifty-one monthly accounts from the district land officers remained unadjusted. In light of the defalcations that plagued the land business, such delays in accounting in a period of greatly increased sales carried obvious dangers. In addition to this unfinished business, none of the 123,440 certificates of purchase for 1835 had been entered in the appropriate ledgers. One experienced bookkeeper could make about 150 entries each week (or 8,000 a year); seventeen bookkeepers would be required to bring up these arrears of posting. If these certificates were not entered on time, the certificates for 1836 would soon flood the office and add to the burden. Brown showed that if the same ratio of work force to sales used in 1826 had been maintained, the appropriations for clerk hire in 1835 would have reached $288,318; they were actually $48,950.

Legislation passed during the 1830's had also substantially added to the work of the General Land Office. The forty-acre law of 1832 had greatly increased the burdens of land management. The Pre-emption Law of 1834 had brought fifteen hundred cases to the General Land Office for adjudication. The bureau also had to attend to a large number of Indian titles, claims, and conveyances. The duties connected with the administration of the Virginia military bounty lands, would last another three to five years. Each case involved investigation of the warrant, the survey, the claim of title, and the "singularly tedious task of engrossing the grants upon those surveys," and demanded "attentive and critical investigation, and continual recurrence to indexes and papers. . . ." [31]

The long-standing problem of private claims was also far from solution, the commissioner continued. The Bureau of Private Land Claims had before it work that "can only be estimated by years, in the best possible organization of the General Land Office." For 18,961 confirmed claims in nine states and territories, the General Land Office had issued only 2,473 patents; the figures for Louisiana were 8,857

---

31. Frederick Keller to John M. Moore, chief clerk, Feb. 1, 1836, *Senate Public Documents*, 24 Cong., 1 Sess., #216: 14–19.

and 463. Brown continued by noting that the embarrassments "connected with the *confirmed* claims, form only a small part of the business connected with this branch of the General Land Office." The unconfirmed claims were too many to admit of any estimate of the time needed for their solution.

The surveys of public lands also demanded far more attention than devotees of the rectangular system would admit. "The surveys are at the base of the land system," affirmed Brown. In spite of the wisdom of the men who drew up the system in 1785, and in spite of the compliments paid it by Mansfield, Meigs, and others, the execution of the surveys of the public lands was almost totally uncodified. Each surveyor general—and in some cases, each deputy—attended to matters as he saw fit. "The laws on this subject, having prescribed the mere outline of rectangular surveying, appear to have left the detail to be filled up by the Surveyors General, and to justify the Department in recognizing the certificate of each, however variant their notions of proceeding, as definitively conclusive," the commissioner wrote. Care, attention, and codification of the survey in the period immediately after 1815, "when the immense amount of surveys for military bounty, and sale, in Indiana, Illinois, Missouri, Arkansas, Alabama, &c., were ordered, [might] have prevented much bad surveying. . . ." Elijah Hayward's circular of July 1831 was the first attempt to give order to the surveying business. Much remained to be done. As for immediate problems, the backlog of field notes awaiting transcription and preparation for sale was immense. In the fall of 1833 more than six hundred townships remained to be protracted on the connecting maps of the land districts; in 1836 the number was twice that. The duties of the surveying section of the General Land Office had increased in like proportion in these years.[32]

To meet the needs of a growing land business and to make proper disposition of the extensive arrears of the office, Brown asked for eighty-one permanent clerks plus two principal clerks to direct public lands and private claims respectively, as well as a recorder and a first clerk of surveys. Congress buried his request under a mass of pressing business. While the national legislature debated matters of bank deposits and the rising tide of speculation that was engulfing the entire nation, the land office business reached a peak of activity. By the mid-

32. *Ibid.*, 1–23.

dle of the Congressional session, routine letters to the General Land Office waited thirty days for a response. Requests from individual Congressmen waited three weeks—clear evidence of the press of business. Interest in the public domain also brought urgent demands for information. At times the number of personal inquiries made at the office by Congressmen and private citizens involved one-fifth of the small staff.[33]

In early June the Senate examined the bill for the reorganization of the General Land Office. Senator Thomas Ewing presented the measure and made a few comments. The bill, he said, "looked to an entirely new organization of the General Land Office." It provided a large number of new clerks, and from what Ewing had heard and seen, "every one . . . was absolutely necessary to discharge the duties of this Department." As all members of the Senate knew full well, "an immense mass of business had accumulated upon the hands of its officers, which it would take years of industry and perseverance to bring up to the present time." Not a single voice was raised in opposition. The House was less amenable. Several of its members objected to the permanent aspect of the new organization. Why not limit the tenure of new clerks to two years? they suggested; then Congress could take up the question once more and fix a permanent number. This group was vocal but a minority. Eventually the House agreed to the Senate's version of the bill.[34]

The act of July 4, 1836—"an Act to reorganize the General Land Office"—provided for an extension of the present system and contained, at the same time, elements of a new organization. The clerical staff was enlarged to eighty-eight, and the office was reorganized internally. In addition to the commissioner, the act created three principal clerks: one for public lands, a second for private land claims, and a third for surveys. New officers of importance were also created to handle the many tasks that had devolved on the commissioner since 1812. The President would appoint a recorder to supervise the patent business, a solicitor to give opinions on questions of law, and a secretary to superintend correspondence and sign patents. The act tightened accounting procedures by requiring receivers to make monthly

33.   Brown to Rep. Michael W. Ash (Penn.) NA: GLO, Ltrs. Sent, Misc., 6 (New Series): March 8, 1836; Washington *Globe*, June 22, 1836; Brown to Woodbury, Sec. Treas., NA: GLO, Ltrs. Sent, Misc., 7 (New Series): June 17, 1836.
34.   *Register of Debates*, 24 Cong., 1 Sess., 12: 1676, 4606–09.

returns to the Secretary of the Treasury and the Commissioner of the General Land Office. Hours were fixed at eight in the winter (October 1 to April 1) and a minimum of ten in the summer, with holidays on Christmas and July 4. The act attempted to rectify the tendency of some land officers to use their positions for personal aggrandizement. The register of a district land office was specifically prohibited from giving false information to an applicant for land, particularly from stating that the land had been applied for when it was still vacant. The penalty was five dollars an acre for the land involved. Officers within the General Land Office were forbidden to deal in land, either directly or indirectly. The penalty was immediate dismissal from office.[35]

Thus this act, belatedly recognizing the volume of the land business and its complexity, provided at last the staff and the organization to clear away the bureaucratic debris from the land office business of 1830 to 1837. With the new work force at his disposal, Commissioner Brown—aided by the fall in sales during 1837 and subsequent years— made great strides toward putting the business of the bureau in order.

35.   5 Stat. 107–12 (July 4, 1836).

The Jacksonians and
the Land Business

13

The triumph of Andrew Jackson in the autumn of 1828 brought the spoils system into national politics. That General Jackson's victory would mean wholesale changes in office his supporters did not deny. "The great watchword of our party is '*Jackson and Reform,*'" announced Duff Green, editor of the *United States Telegraph*. "The nation have placed an honest patriot in the executive chair to cleanse the Augean Stable."[1] In consultation with his advisers and those who had directed his campaigns in key states, the new President began a series of removals that included several posts in the administration of the public lands.

Andrew Jackson understood frontier politics, and he and his advisers readily grasped the part that the land business might play in the birth and growth of an aspiring political party. Several clearly defined steps led to preferment: militia officer, justice of the peace, sheriff, commissioner of roads, of prisons, or of canals, and perhaps finally election to the lower house of a state legislature or to a territorial assembly. With such experience and connections behind him, the aspiring frontier politician was ready to strike for the greatest source of patronage in his region, the federal government. The post office, the Indian agency, the land office, the surveyor's district, each was a source of patronage and power with its appointive jobs. Careful dispensation of these gifts created a group of devoted dependents—hardly a well-organized political machine by later standards, but a solid base of support from which to begin or extend a political career. State and territorial politics in the sparsely settled frontier region was a series of

1.   *United States Telegraph*, Nov. 24, 1828.

constantly shifting and fluctuating empires, each with its royal domain
and court, presided over by a regional lord.[2]

The power of the land office patronage was extensive in 1828 and
grew steadily thereafter. By 1833, for example, 53 land districts (each
with a register and a receiver) spanned the western country. The
force needed to prepare and administer the public lands also included
another eight surveyors general, 126 deputy surveyors, and innumerable clerks in the various offices. Four years later the number of land
districts had grown to 62. A Senate committee, reporting on the problems of patronage in the land business in 1840, noted the vast administrative machinery, "with a host of deputies, clerks, draughtsmen,
chain carriers, and axemen, at an aggregate annual expense of upwards of $334,000, on the average of the last two years." Even these
figures gave "a very inadequate conception of the real extent" of the
land business, the report continued. "Few places . . . afford such
ready and certain means of acquiring fortunes, and of extending favors and accommodation to a large and influential portion of the community, as those attached to the land system." In a period of strong
interest in the public lands, "the thorough knowledge which those
who hold them have of all that relates to the public lands, makes their
good will of great importance to the numerous body of individuals
annually emigrating to the west, or engaged in investing or speculating in the public lands." In spite of these insights, the power of this
patronage defied adequate analysis: "The extent of the influence
which the Government might exercise, whenever it thinks proper,
through so many of its dependents, with such ample means of acting upon public opinion, can be more readily conceived than estimated. . . ."[3]

Andrew Jackson was not entirely selfish in his appointment policy,
and he foresaw a number of benefits for the nation. To begin with, rotation in office was important in a democracy. John Quincy Adams
had managed the civil service in such a fashion as to give a life interest in office to a few men. Andrew Jackson and his supporters felt that
the offices of a democracy were open to all. Thus, removals were not
for political reasons, "but upon the principle of rotation in office,

2. A perceptive analysis of politics on the frontier of the Old Northwest is Paul
Wallace Gates, "Introduction," Robertson and Riker, eds., *The John Tipton Papers*,
1: 3–28.
3. *Senate Public Documents*, 26 Cong., 1 Sess., #460: 4–5.

which, we believe, it is Gen. Jackson's intention to establish," ran the argument. "Let him do but this, let this principle once be established, and he will have done more for the perpetuity of the government, than all the acts of the late administration put together." When Gideon Fitz lost his post as Surveyor General South of Tennessee, the local Jackson paper commented, 'Now we do not think that Mr. Fitz has any property in this office of Surveyor General—However satisfactorily he may have discharged its duties; but believe that one citizen who is *qualified* has just as much right to the enjoyment of office as another." The party of Andrew Jackson also brought into office men of the highest talents, "combining at once more of public favor and public security," and invariably "highly respected citizens." The "reformation" sought out defaulters and others who had not served the nation faithfully. An oft-cited example was John Harrison, the former receiver at Vincennes, who supposedly resigned because Jackson removed his father. Harrison turned out to be a defaulter to the sum of $15,000, much to the delight of the Jackson press. "We can now see, that it was not his high sense of honor that induced him to resign, but the fear of the searching operations of *Reform*," cried the *Western Annotator*.[4]

The Jacksonian "reformation" was deep and wide, especially in the Old Northwest. There it swept out of office, among others, the venerable Edward Tiffin, whose career in the administration of the land business spanned almost two decades, as Commissioner of the General Land Office and surveyor general. He had been Surveyor General Northwest of the Ohio for almost fifteen years. His replacement was General William Lytle, a leading Jacksonian in Cincinnati.[5] Jackson failed to reappoint to office Jesse Spencer, register at the Chillicothe office since 1803. Spencer, too, was upset, particularly since he represented himself as a strong supporter of the President and felt that his removal resulted from "misrepresentation" and "intrigue." Pascual Enos' removal as receiver at Springfield (Illinois) distressed him because the office had been so unproductive during his incumbency; he had held office since 1823. To Samuel Gwathmey, who had become

4. Salem Indiana *Western Annotator*, Sept. 5, 1829; Jackson *Mississippian*, Aug. 1, 1834; *St. Louis Beacon*, Feb. 3, 1830; Salem Indiana *Western Annotator*, March 6, 1830.
5. Graham to Tiffin, NA: GLO, Ltrs. Sent, SG, 4: July 7, 1829; Chillicothe *Scioto Gazette*, May 13, 1829.

register at Jeffersonville (Indiana) in 1807, removal was a stain on his character. He immediately requested a copy of the charges. "I wish to transmit to my family a character pure and unsullied," he wrote. "Your answer shall be carefully preserved amongst the records of my family and not otherwise used unless by special permission." Graham replied that his business had been transacted with promptness and ability, to the complete satisfaction of the department. The veteran land officer was mollified. He concluded, "Since my first entry upon the duties of the Office, which is well on to twenty two years, it has been the pride of my heart faithfully to discharge them. . . ." Others displayed bitterness rather than sorrow. Ambrose Whitlock, the receiver at Crawfordsville since 1820, took his removal as a sign of the times. "The change of these offices have been talked of by a rabble rousing set in the country for six months past and it was bruted about previous to the presidential election that every man in office who did not vote for Gen¹ Jackson would be turned out," he wrote. "I merely mention this occurrence to show you what kind of juggling the wiseacres make use of in the country to ride on big men's shoulders, & give them the office, and they will swear allegiance to any man or party of men with whom they can succeed." [6]

Jackson's system of rotation in office drew critical comment from those not sympathetic with the principles of his party. Everywhere they found the new President's appointment policies at variance with the traditions of the nation. Editors of opposition newspapers immediately discovered that the numerous removals inconvenienced prospective purchasers of the public lands. "The public has suffered, and is now suffering great inconvenience from the wanton, and unnecessary change of the Register of the Land Office here," went the protest. Heart-rending tales of pioneers who had trudged scores of miles to a closed land office made their way into print. Also deplored were the reasons for removal: political proscription. "No reasons are given for those changes, none being in fact necessary, 'These offices are natural and lawful spoils of victory,'" commented the *National Intelligencer*. Opponents of the "reformation" charged that the new appointees did not represent talent so much as professional office-seeking. For the

6. Spencer to Graham, NA: GLO, Ltrs. Recd., Reg. & Rec., Chillicothe, 36: March 19, May 19, 20, 1829; Enos to Graham, *ibid.*, Springfield, 15: Aug. 8, 18, 1829; Gwathmey to Graham, *ibid.*, Jeffersonville, 19: Aug. 14, 1829; Whitlock to Graham, *ibid.*, Misc., W: Aug. 17, 1829.

first time the offices of the nation were filled with "candidates," men who actively sought office, rather than waiting for the office to come to them as their just reward for services to country and community.[7]

Opposition to the Jacksonian appointment policy was not confined to the newspapers. It flourished in Congress, where the leading opponents were David Crockett of Tennessee, George Poindexter of Mississippi, and David Barton of Missouri. Barton was especially incensed at the removal of Theodore Hunt, recorder of land titles in Missouri. The Senator from Missouri once made disparaging remarks about "some of the office-hunting loungers around the President. . . ." Of Jackson's appointment program in Missouri, he observed, "It seemed to be a general restoration, as if her Botany Bay and her Siberia were to be emptied in her streets, to mark the epoch of this administration!" A sharp exchange followed, but the opponents of the President held their ground.[8] Jackson suffered defeat in the cases of Moses Dawson, receiver at Cincinnati, and James F. Gardiner, register at Tiffin. Gardiner was the former editor of the *Ohio People's Press*, a staunch Democratic sheet; the opposition strongly criticized his appointment on the grounds of intemperance. Moses Dawson was a pugnacious naturalized Irishman, a rabid Democrat, and editor of the Cincinnati *Advertiser*. From the earliest moment of Jackson's candidacy, Dawson's personality, paper, and organizational ability were a tower of strength. The Senate rejected both nominations by large majorities. The Cincinnati receivership went to Morgan Neville, editor of the *Cincinnati Commercial Register*. Dawson returned to his paper. Gardiner found consolation in an appointment to inspect district land offices. The struggle between Congress and the President continued. Jackson resented Senate opposition as an infringement on the appointment power of the Executive. He fought to preserve that power, and he even refused to give the Senate information about removals.[9]

Changes in land officers were common. When Jackson had been

7. Chillicothe *Scioto Gazette*, April 1, 15, 1829; *Western Herald and Steubenville Gazette*, April 25, 1829; *Daily National Intelligencer*, Sept. 4, 1829; *Daily Cincinnati Gazette*, May 1, 1829.
8. *Register of Debates*, 21 Cong., 1 Sess., 6: 367–68; *United States Telegraph*, April 27, 1830.
9. Chillicothe *Scioto Gazette*, May 13, 1829; Stevens, *The Early Jackson Party in Ohio, passim*; Leonard D. White, *The Jacksonians: A Study in Administrative History* (New York, 1954), 106–11; Richardson, ed., *Messages and Papers of the Presidents*, 3: 132–34 (Feb. 10, 1835).

seven months in office, the *United States Telegraph* reported the removal of sixteen out of forty-two registers, and of a like number of receivers.[10] Since the removals were confined almost entirely to the Old Northwest, and since many officers were Jacksonians to begin with, the sweep was virtually complete. An assessment of the changes in office showed positive and negative results. Certainly the threat of removal prompted much scurrying around and the straightening of records for the first time in several years. It also produced surprises. Debtors came to light. There were cases of men who did not reside in the towns where they held office, as well as of others who rarely attended to official business. One of the more startling examples was Major William Oliver, the receiver at Piqua (Ohio), who resided at Cincinnati for four years, returning to the office only quarterly to draw his salary. At the same time the shuffle in personnel undoubtedly caused inconvenience, much as the opposition press charged.[11]

Far more serious than the inconveniences to individual purchasers (however grave they may have been for those directly involved) was the derangement of the surveying business in Mississippi and Louisiana. At the time that Jackson took office, the surveyor general of this region was James P. Turner, who gave evidence that he was putting the tattered business of the district in some kind of order. At least he had sent deputy surveyors into the field. Turner himself had little interest in politics, but his brother was one of the leading anti-Jacksonians in the State of Mississippi. Rumors immediately circulated that Turner would be removed from office. George Graham, who eschewed politics wherever possible, went so far as to write strongly in favor of Turner's retention in office. Others, who sought office, denounced Turner for his Adams-Clay leanings and demanded his dismissal.[12] Shortly thereafter the President removed Turner. Jackson first offered the post to Thomas Hill Williams, a former Senator from Mississippi, and a man completely innocent of surveying experience,

10. *United States Telegraph*, Sept. 27, 1829; these figures represent about the same proportion as Carl Russell Fish's findings of the removal of 252 of 612 officers holding Presidential appointments. *The Civil Service and the Patronage*, 125.
11. Thomas B. Van Horne to Graham, NA: GLO, Ltrs. Recd., Reg. & Rec., Piqua, 38: May 25, 1829; William P. McKee to Graham, *ibid.*, Edwardsville, 12: Nov. 16, 1829; Gideon Fitz to Graham, *ibid.*, Mount Salus, 29: May 10, 1830.
12. Turner to Graham, *ibid.*, SG, Miss., 58: May 22, 1829; Graham to Turner, *ibid.*, Ltrs. Sent, SG, 4: June 17, 1829; Robert Ward to William T. Barry, Postmaster General, *ibid.*, Ltrs. Recd., Misc., W: Aug. 18, 1829.

techniques, or management. Williams admired the billet in the manner of a man inspecting a prize cow. "It is a very snug office," he wrote; but it did not suit his present needs, and he declined it. Turner was upset at losing the post and at the confusion of the surveying business of the region—and all "for the purpose of gratifying a few Hot-Headed partizan politicians. . . ." [13] In the struggle over the post of surveyor general, concern for efficiency in the land business was no consideration.

The case of James Turner suggested more than that the land business was being prostituted to the demands of partisan politics, however dangerous such prostitution was. It indicated that Andrew Jackson's "reformation" of the administration of the public domain was being used to settle personal grievances against rivals and to promote personal interest. Political proscription opened a golden opportunity for the unscrupulous to undermine official confidence in land officers: it was necessary only to indicate that a land officer had given aid and comfort to the enemy and, finally, expressed imperfect orthodoxy. Neutrality in the administration of the public domain had vanished from the scene. Of the complaints of land officers, Gideon Fitz once remarked, "From my experience of twenty six years in the land department, I am inclined to believe that perhaps nine times out of ten, complaints of public officers are unfounded, and originate with interested persons, or from mistaken prejudice, or vicious motives. . . ." [14] The manner in which Andrew Jackson and his party managed the business of the public domain invited such criticism.

Numerous individuals brought pressure to bear on the President in the matter of appointments, and since Jackson hardly had time to make a thorough examination of every case, some were influential. In appointments to administer the public domain, the Secretary of the Treasury played an important role. This department was a source of patronage, and the Secretary a key figure in its dispensation. [15] The Commissioner of the General Land Office often expressed his opinion on appointments. The partisan orientation of the land business increased under Elijah Hayward, a political figure who took great interest in proper appointments. In all cases, however, Jackson's deci-

13.   Williams to Graham, *ibid.*, Sept. 3, 1829; Turner to Graham, *ibid.*, SG, Miss., 59: Oct. 19, Nov. 12, 1829; Jan. 16, 1830.
14.   Fitz to Graham, *ibid.*, Reg. & Rec., Mount Salus, 29: May 10, 1829.
15.   White, *The Jacksonians*, 163–64.

sion remained final. Within the General Land Office itself the Secretary
of the Treasury exercised final authority. The commissioner always
cleared the appointment of clerks with the head of the department,
although the communication was frequently made in the form of a
message rather than a request for permission. When conflict developed over an appointment, however, the cabinet officer easily prevailed.[16]

Andrew Jackson himself displayed signs of human frailty in a period when men were becoming increasingly flexible in their ethical
standards. Public office meant power, the kind of power useful in retaining that office. The connection was obvious. Political debts must
be paid, and the wherewithal to pay them was readily available. "I request that you and Mr. Woodbury consult together . . . see judge
Hayward and let him give him the office promised worth $1000—or
place him in the office from which Mr. Tyler has been promoted," the
President wrote of one political creditor.[17] The temptation to do
something for his relatives was also strong. Among his favorites was a
nephew of his late wife, Stokley D. Hays. Upon dismissing James
Turner, the President determined to make Hays, a resident of Tennessee, Surveyor General South of Tennessee. The appointment was
doubly vulnerable. Hays had a history of intemperance. "He must get,
and send on here, as early as he can, testimonials of his sobriety and
capacity as a surveyor," wrote Jackson.[18] George Poindexter opposed
the nomination of Hays as surveyor general from the first. The Senator from Mississippi objected to filling this lucrative office with an out-
of-state appointee. His arguments found a warm response among his
colleagues. The Senate rejected Hays and passed a motion affirming
Poindexter's stand. Jackson was furious. He regarded the resolution as
a challenge to the appointment prerogative of the Executive, but in
the end he compromised. Hays was made register of the new land
office in Clinton (Mississippi) and the office of surveyor general went
to Gideon Fitz (whom Jackson later removed), a friend of Poindex-

16.   Woodbury to Hayward, NA: TD, Ltrs. Sent, Misc., 1833–39: June 23, 1835.
17.   Jackson to Livingston, Sec. State, June 28, 1831, Bassett, ed., *Jackson Correspondence*, 4: 306. "Tyler" is probably Charles Tyler, former clerk in the General Land Office, subsequently "promoted" to a land office in Indiana.
18.   Jackson to Robert J. Chester, Nov. 7, 1830, *ibid.*, 199; Jackson to Governor
Thomas Williams, April 30, 1831, Jackson Papers (microfilm), State Historical
Society of Wisconsin, Madison.

ter's.[19] Party unity was preserved, at least for the time being, and the patronage was divided to the satisfaction of the contending parties. Only the land business suffered.

Jackson had not finished filling offices in the Mississippi land business to suit himself and the Democratic party. He also determined to do something for Samuel Gwin, an obscure clerk in the Post Office Department who was the son of an old comrade-in-arms. Because of his wife's failing health—Gwin himself had been crippled since youth—he urgently needed an appointment in the South. Jackson made Gwin register at Mount Salus, a lucrative post. Poindexter secured Gwin's rejection in December 1831, and the battle was joined. Eventually Jackson forced the Senate to accede to his wishes by threatening to leave the offices vacant, but the struggle lasted for two years, and the land business suffered neglect in the interim. His actions had great relevance for the development of his party in Mississippi. Gwin became the acknowledged leader of the Mississippi Democracy and keeper of its patronage. Congressman Franklin E. Plummer complained that Gwin dominated the federal patronage in the state to the exclusion of all other influences, even those of Jacksonian Congressmen. The survey and sale of the great Indian cessions increased the patronage of the land business in the state, and Gwin supervised the staffing of the many new administrative offices with true Jacksonians. He also directed Martin Van Buren's campaign in 1836, carried on an extensive correspondence with the President, and presided over one of the busiest land districts in the nation. Gwin's land office proved an ideal command post from which to direct the political affairs of the Democratic party in Mississippi, provided, of course, that he did not spend too much time attending to the administration of the public lands in his district.[20]

The political situation in Florida changed little as a result of the victory in 1828. At the time Jackson took office, his friends already controlled the land office machinery in Florida Territory. The "land office crowd," "the Tennessee surveyors," or the "nucleus," as they were known to the opposition journals, used the administration of the

19.   Miles, *Jacksonian Democracy in Mississippi*, 44–49.
20.   White, *The Jacksonians*, 107–8; Miles, *Jacksonian Democracy in Mississippi*, 49–54, 164; Edwin A. Miles, "Franklin E. Plummer: Piney Woods Spokesman of the Jackson Era," *Journal of Mississippi History*, 14 (1952): 18.

public domain as a base for their political activities.[21] Surveyor General Robert Butler kept his eye on the various newspapers and indicated those worthy of federal patronage.[22] From the safety of his land office Richard Keith Call, long an intimate of the President, campaigned for the office of territorial delegate. He immediately caught a broadside from those factions that had not enjoyed the patronage of the federal government. "It was not convenient for him to offer until the land office 'tit' was sucked dry," ran the comment, "but now it seems, it no longer gives milk, and he must take to rooting." Opponents attacked Call for seeking public office, while he "continues quietly to wield the patronage of the Land Office, and enjoy its profits. . . ." The question of the "unpopularity of the Land Office and its dependents" became the foremost issue in the campaign. In the midst of this savage struggle Jackson reappointed Call for another four-year term, thus adding fuel to the campaign. Call lost decisively to Colonel Joseph M. White and retired to the land office once more. The remnants of the "land office faction" had to be content with appointive rather than elective office. The patronage power of the "nucleus," at its height in 1830 and 1831, split over the question of allegiance to Andrew Jackson or the nullification doctrines of John C. Calhoun.[23] It had dominated Florida politics for more than a decade.

Many of the important political events in Arkansas Territory also revolved around the administration of the public domain. The dominant political figure was Ambrose H. Sevier, for several years delegate to Congress. Sevier invariably found land office posts for his important supporters. When Benjamin Desha, receiver at the Little Rock land office, had the temerity to challenge Sevier for the seat in Congress, the delegate defeated him handily and then forced his removal. District land officers became known as "pensioners upon Col. Sevier's

21. Herbert J. Doherty, Jr., *Richard Keith Call, Florida Unionist* (Gainesville, 1961), 41–42. The politically powerful and widely despised land office faction included Richard Keith Call and George W. Ward, land officers for the Tallahassee district; Robert Butler, the surveyor general; and Butler's deputy surveyors and clerks. Among the latter were Robert W. Williams, Isham G. Searcy, and later Samuel Overton, nephew of John Overton.
22. Butler to Graham, NA: GLO, Ltrs. Recd., SG, Fla., Nov. 9, 1829; Graham to Samuel D. Ingham, Sec. Treas., *ibid.*, Ltrs. Sent, Misc., 24: Oct. 1, 1829.
23. Tallahassee *Floridian*, April 24, 1833; June 12, 1832; Feb. 9, March 2, 1833; Doherty, *Richard Keith Call,* 70–83.

bounty. . . ." [24] By 1834, with several election victories behind him, an accompanying increase in patronage, and the assistance of the Conway faction (James Conway, surveyor general of the territory, and George Conway, register of the Washington land office) and the Rector brothers (active in Arkansas as well as in Missouri), Sevier had turned the administration of Arkansas public lands into a personal fief. With the approach of statehood, he explained to the President how he wanted things worked out in Arkansas:

Col Rector at this time is agent for the Creek Indians—His brother Elias Rector, is now Marshal and will expect a reappointment under our state, as soon as it is admitted—James Conway, who is now the incumbent, is Rector's cousin, and is the democratic candidate for governor—Conway is my relation also—I am held up for the Senate in Arkansas, and my father in law Judge Johnson, I desire to be appointed federal Judge—I am thus particular, in order to show you that if Rector is appointed in the place of Conway to the exclusion of Cross, who wants it, the people of Arkansas will consider that there is too much monopoly in the offices of Arkansas by my relatives and intimate friends—And this impression may injure the cause in Arkansas, and on that account, I desire the appointment of Cross [as surveyor general].

The only relative I desire office for is for Judge Johnson; Let him be made federal Judge. Elias Rector Marshal—Cross surveyor General, and either Randolph—Childress or Ringo district attorney, and Biscoe register of the land office at Helena, the same I spoke to you about on Friday last, and I pledge myself for a fortunate issue to the administration in the coming contests in Arkansas.

I think I can reconcile all our friends to this arrangement without difficulty.[25]

The election of 1836 was very gratifying to Sevier. Van Buren carried the state. Voters elevated James S. Conway from the office of surveyor general to the governor's mansion. Archibald Yell, former receiver at Little Rock, became Congressman. The first session of the new state legislature chose Sevier and former Governor William S. Fulton to be United States Senators. President Jackson also did his part by appointing Benjamin Johnson a federal judge; Wharton Rector, marshal; Cross, surveyor general; and Biscoe received the register-

24. Little Rock *Arkansas Advocate*, Aug. 14, 1833.
25. Sevier to the President, April 4, 1836, Carter, ed., *Territorial Papers*, 21: 1207–08.

ship at Little Rock. It was a clean sweep for the men who controlled the business of the land office.[26]

Within the Michigan Territory two political factions struggled for control: one was led by John Biddle, register at the Detroit land office and sometime delegate to Congress (1829–1831); the other, by Austin E. Wing, his successor in Congress. Wing's supporters controlled the second Michigan land office at Monroe, and from this vantage point Wing and "his Land-office friends at Monroe" sought to control the boundaries of new districts or of existing ones in order to restrict the profitability of Biddle's district.[27] The emergence of the Democratic party coincided with the rise to political prominence of Lucius Lyon, a man who began service to the government as a deputy surveyor. In the summer of 1833, Lyon defeated Wing and replaced him as territorial delegate. The former deputy surveyor built the patronage strength of the party around new district land offices created at just the right time, New Monroe and Bronson (later Kalamazoo) in 1834, Genesee and Ionia two years later.[28]

In Indiana's factional political scene also, control over the administration of the public domain was a valuable political lever. When he took office, Jackson quickly filled several Indiana land offices with his supporters. James P. Drake became register at Indianapolis, and his office served as party headquarters for the central part of the state. Around the land business swirled the various factions, struggling for the patronage of the Democratic party (each posed under the banner of Andrew Jackson) and discussing the various candidates and their services, their need for reward, and their value to the faction and the Democracy. Of a vacancy in the Fort Wayne land office, one of Senator John Tipton's supporters wrote, "I look upon this appointment as highly important, & I should think it ought to be secured to some friend instead of an enemy. —Old Hickory cannot be too particular in his appointments among us—as they form the surest criterion by which to judge his administration." Tipton captured the ear of the President and steered one of his supporters to the post, but no politi-

26.   White, *Politics on the Southwestern Frontier, Arkansas Territory*, 200; Carter, ed., *Territorial Papers*, 21: 1207n–08n.

27.   *House Committee Reports*, 22 Cong., 1 Sess., #449.

28.   John Shirigian, "Lucius Lyon: His Place in Michigan History" (Unpublished doctoral dissertation, University of Michigan, 1961), Chs. 1 & 2.

cian, however skillful, could find enough land offices to satisfy the mob of applicants. The Senator immediately came under attack from his other backers, who felt their claims equal or superior to that of the fortunate office holder. During a severe fight for re-election, Tipton apparently promised land office appointments to several key figures, and he succeeded in winning a close contest. His friends now demanded their rewards. Tipton succeeded in satisfying James T. Pollock with the receivership at Crawfordsville, but many unfulfilled promises remained. Pollock was virtually illiterate, so Tipton secured the appointment of a second office seeker, A. W. Morris, to act as chief clerk in the office.[29]

Sales of public lands were heavy in the 1830's, receipts were large, and the temptation to use funds for selfish purposes grew with prosperity. In 1831 the Executive surrounded its public officers with a stringent set of regulations to ensure their proper performance of duty. Receivers had to make deposits of public monies within thirty days of a public sale, at least quarterly in case of private sale, and any time the funds on hand reached $10,000. The only notes receivable were those acceptable at par by the banks of deposit. Accounting procedures in the Treasury Department slowed during the decade and leaned toward parsimony, two tendencies that gave much cause for complaint. After 1834, at the height of the land office business, the understaffed General Land Office and the equally overworked Treasury Department were so far in arrears in their accounting that it was impossible to tell whether most of the receivers were meeting their obligations to the government.[30]

In spite of the many rules and regulations surrounding the financial aspects of the land business, Jackson's Secretaries of the Treasury were curiously relaxed in enforcing the rules. In practice all Secretaries demanded the regular forwarding of returns and the punctual deposit of public funds. One Treasury Department circular made

29.   Thomas B. Brown to Tipton, Oct. 5, 1831, Robertson and Riker, eds., *The John Tipton Papers*, 2: 443–44; James T. Pollock to Tipton, Jan. 11, 1832, *ibid.*, 493–94; Dr. J. D. Wolverton to Louis McLane, Sec. Treas., NA: TD, Ltrs. from Land Officers, to 1833, Oct. 18, 1832; Tipton to Calvin Fletcher, Jan. 11, 1833, Robertson and Riker, eds., *The John Tipton Papers*, 2: 772.
30.   Woodbury to Comm. GLO, NA: TD, Ltrs. Sent, Misc., 1833–39: Nov. 12, 1834; Hayward to Woodbury, NA: GLO, Ltrs. Sent, Misc., 29: Nov. 15, 1834; White, *The Jacksonians*, 166.

the twin duties of deposit and transmission of accounts and returns "paramount to all other in your official station." [31] Yet all Secretaries, and particularly Levi Woodbury, whose long career in the Treasury under Jackson (June 27, 1834, to March 3, 1837) coincided with the flood tide of the land office business, were reluctant to take steps against receivers who failed to follow the careful instructions of the department. Men were rarely removed from office. In early 1831, for example, the Commissioner of the General Land Office notified the Secretary of the Treasury that Uriah G. Mitchell, receiver at Cahaba, had a balance due the government in excess of $76,000. No effort was made to call Mitchell to account until 1837, six years later, and only then because he resigned. Mitchell left office in debt for the sum of $54,626.55. In spite of consistent failure to deposit the public monies promptly, William Linn of Vandalia received another four-year appointment from the President. Linn defaulted three years later for $55,962.06. [32]

Several factors combined to produce this relaxed attitude. The slow accounting procedures of the General Land Office, the flood of business, the tardy rendering of accounts by banks of deposit, and the several changes in the Treasury Department all played their part. Most important of all, however, was the emergence of the land office as a political tool. District land officers were increasingly influential political figures. They were also political allies. In a period when the rhetoric of politics divided men into "we" and "they," the tendency to protect one's own can be readily understood. Relations between Wiley P. Harris and the Treasury Department provided an instructive example of this development. Harris was receiver of public monies at Columbus (Mississippi), one of the busiest land offices in the nation. In the spring of 1834, land sales engulfed the office, and Harris's accounts fell five months in arrears. Roger B. Taney, the Secretary of the Treasury, reminded the receiver of his failure to fulfill his obligations to the department. Harris remained silent. A year later the new Secretary, Levi Woodbury, sent a second warning. Harris pleaded "the

31. E.g. Louis McLane, Sec. Treas., to George Dameron, NA: TD, Ltrs. Sent, Misc., 1833–39: April 25, 1833; *House Committee Reports*, 25 Cong., 3 Sess., #313: 151.
32. Hayward to Sec. Treas., NA: GLO, Ltrs. Sent, Misc., 26: Jan 4, 1831; *House Committee Reports*, 25 Cong., 3 Sess., #313: 144, 145; Woodbury to Linn, NA: TD, Ltrs. Sent, Misc., 1833–39: Feb. 12, 1835.

interference of the public land sales at this office" and "such a press of business during the months of November and December that I found it impossible for me to render a correct statement." He promised that "for the future I will give you a correct statement of the different kinds of funds received in each month." Woodbury was not satisfied and wrote that if Harris did not send the missing returns by the next mail, the President would take action against him. No returns appeared. The Secretary next announced that if no returns arrived by October 10—some six weeks hence—the receiver would be "dismissed from office." [33]

Harris immediately sought help from his friends. Representative John F. H. Claiborne led a parade of respectable and influential citizens, all faithful Democrats, who affirmed their faith in Harris. Claiborne wrote the President that "General Harris has never engaged in speculation, either directly or indirectly." To remove Harris would gravely damage the strength of the party in Mississippi and give comfort to its foes, particularly George Poindexter. "Nothing would rejoice him more than the expulsion of General Harris, whom he knows to be one of the main pillars of the democratic cause, and one of the earliest and most distinguished friends of the administration in Mississippi," continued Claiborne. Harris's "family and connexions are extremely influential, and all of them are co-operating with us in the arduous struggle which we are now making. They are true democrats; and the bank, nullifying, and [Hugh Lawson] White parties would shout 'victory' at any blow aimed at them." [34]

As a result of the "assurance" given by "your friends," the President permitted the delinquent receiver another thirty days. At the end of this second period of grace, and in the absence of word from Harris, neither the President nor the Secretary took any action. The receiver's returns were still in arrears, and he had more than $100,000 in his hands at the time. This condition might have continued indefinitely except that the Secretary, under a new policy of increasing the penalty of the bonds posted by land officers, sent Harris a new bond with the penalty set at $200,000. Harris began "a minute examination" of

33. Taney to Harris, March 25, 1834, *House Committee Reports,* 25 Cong., 3 Sess., #313: 169; Woodbury to Harris, March 17, 1835, *ibid.,* 170–71; Harris to Woodbury, April 1, 18, 1835, *ibid.,* 171; Woodbury to Harris, June 25, Aug. 28, 1835, *ibid.,* 171–72.
34. Claiborne to the President, Sept. 15, 1835, *ibid.,* 175.

his accounts, as a result of which he wrote "that there is a deficit against me, which as yet I am unable to account for." The deficit was $109,178.08. Instead of a bond, the receiver sent his resignation in 1836. In his official farewell he recommended as his replacement Colonel Gordon D. Boyd, "throughout an ardent supporter of your administration, and an unyielding advocate of the principles of democracy." Even as the full extent of Harris's debt to the government became known in official Washington, Jackson appointed Colonel Gordon D. Boyd the new receiver of public monies at Columbus. Nine and one-half months later Boyd defaulted for the sum of $50,937.29.[35]

The activities of Israel T. Canby, Crawfordsville (Indiana) receiver, demonstrated different aspects of the same theme. Canby was a former state representative and senator, a staunch Jacksonian, and the party's defeated candidate for governor. Management of one of the busiest land offices in the nation was a consolation reward. Indiana lay in the mainstream of western migration, and the settlers provided a profitable market for eastern goods. Canby used the funds of his office to finance a mercantile enterprise. In order to meet the deposit requirements of the Treasury Department, Canby borrowed money from the Indianapolis receiver and other influential citizens, such as Senator John Tipton (to whom he also lent the public funds upon occasion), and, of course, he filled the mail with letters of excuse.[36] When the department began to press him for funds, Canby sought intercession from men of influence. Hurrying to Cincinnati, he took a leisurely trip down the Ohio with John H. Eaton, a Jackson confidant. Canby was reassured. Eaton had "heard nothing of my business in Washington but assures me there is no danger, that he will see the President in Tennessee and will write me the result."[37] Senators Tipton and Hendricks also wrote letters in support of the receiver. Through his influential friends, including Eaton and two United States Senators, Canby fought off exposure for several months. When accused of laxity in the case, the Secretary of the Treasury could remark with much justification, "The Department has constantly re-

35.   Woodbury to Harris, Oct. 12, 1835, *ibid.*, 177; Harris to Jackson, Aug. 27, 1836, *ibid.*, 181–82.
36.   The full story of Canby's defalcation emerges from his correspondence with John Tipton in Robertson and Riker, eds., *The John Tipton Papers*, 2: *passim.*
37.   Canby to Tipton, Aug. 20, 1832, *ibid.*, 686.

sisted every effort made by Dr. Canby and his friends to excuse a departure from the rules prescribed for the regular and periodical deposit of money coming into his possession. . . ."[38] Unfortunately the Department fell short of success by $39,013.31, the sum Canby owed when he was removed from office in December 1832. Canby was a "defaulter" to the Government of the United States, and at least three important public figures were accessories to his crime.

The Treasury Department did not accept defalcations without resistance. Every land officer posted a bond on taking office, but the task of collecting debts from the principal and his securities was long and rarely successful. In case of default, the traditional procedure began with a letter from the solicitor of the Treasury to the district attorney of the appropriate state (or marshal in case of a territory), instructing him to institute legal proceedings against the debtor. Suits involving the sale of personal property and real estate were long and delicate, for the principals were always among the leading figures in the community and often the state;[39] and they dragged on for several years through state or territorial courts. Property of defaulters could rarely be sold advantageously for the government. At the public sale of Canby's estate in Crawfordsville, "there was a village combination to dissuade from and prevent bidding. The register and his son . . . openly proclaimed in the streets, that 'no *gentleman* would bid on the property.' " Most of the goods, "put up in lots much too large for common purchasers," were bought by Canby's maiden sister and housekeeper, at the minimum price. Canby deeded his goods purchased with government funds to his partners, at least until after the court action, and they could not be seized. He also directed the sale of his lands, to be administered by his friends, in order that the choicest lots be reserved for him. Claims against Canby and his heirs dragged on until 1870, when Congress passed a law absolving the descendants of principal and sureties of further liability.[40]

Another legal check on the conduct of the district land officers was the annual inspection, a system used by the Jacksonians with mixed

38. Louis McLane, Sec. Treas., to the President, NA: TD, Ltrs. Sent, Misc., 1833–39: Aug. 8, 1833.
39. Esarey, *History of Indiana*, 1: 396.
40. James B. Gardiner to Hayward, Aug. 12, 1833, *American State Papers, Public Lands,* 7: 194; Canby to Tiffin, Feb. 3, 1834, Robertson and Riker, eds., *The John Tipton Papers,* 3: 19–20, 20n.

success. Each spring, inspectors visited designated land offices. Upon occasion the commissioner or the Secretary ordered special investigations of a single office where evidence existed of strong "malfeasance or negligence." [41] From the beginning the examiners were faithful and deserving party members, men such as Joseph Watson of the District of Columbia, party organizer and alleged dispenser of patronage in Ohio, who examined the Ohio offices; Elijah Hayward, who examined the Ohio offices before his appointment as Commissioner of the General Land Office; Samuel Milroy, influential party leader in Indiana, where he examined offices; and James B. Gardiner, who received this share of the patronage after his rejection as a land officer by the Senate.[42] Since these inspectors examined the work of other faithful Democrats, their common bond was politics rather than an interest in the careful administration of the public domain. Examinations were supposed to be secret, but this rule was difficult to enforce. Advance notice might be given by one receiver to another. Sometimes the appointed inspectors were extremely lax in this matter. "Sam Judah was here last night on his way to Crawfordsville to examine into the affairs of the Land Office," wrote one of John Tipton's correspondents. "If the expedition was intended as a secret one he conducted very strangely for he arrived here at 3 or 4 o'clock in the evening, told every one where he was going & on what business." [43]

The inspections did prove useful. The threat of observation put several houses in order, and some land officers were removed as a result of adverse reports.[44] Yet the most objective and conscientious inspectors faced a difficult task. They had to make careful judgments, allow for irremediable administrative handicaps (isolation, poor mail service, distant banks of deposit) under which the office operated, make due allowance for the feuds and factions that gave rise to complaints, and perform their labors in three or four days. Deception was widespread. Money might be borrowed to show the inspector. Other devices were also used. When Charles M. Whipple inspected the land

41. Hayward to Woodbury, NA: GLO, Ltrs. Sent, Misc., 30: March 27, 1835.
42. Graham to examiners, *ibid.*, 23: April 1, 1829.
43. Lucius Scott to Tipton, July 17, 22, 1832, Robertson and Riker, eds., *The John Tipton Papers*, 2: 658.
44. Two cases in point were removals at Wapaukonnetta and Helena. See Woodbury to Thomas B. Van Horne, NA: TD, Ltrs. Sent, Misc., 1833–39: June 20, 1835; Woodbury to Littlebury Hawkins, *ibid.*, Dec. 19, 1835.

office at Ionia (Michigan) in May 1837, the receiver's account was $8,000 short; the latter claimed that the funds had been deposited in a Detroit bank, but that unfortunately the bank had not forwarded the promised receipt. The inspector rode in leisurely fashion to Detroit, while the receiver, with $8,000 in hand, rode at breakneck speed by a slightly longer route. Whipple arrived at the main intersection in Detroit just in time to see the receiver emerging from the bank of deposit. With solemn dignity, Whipple counted $8,000 of the same money that he had counted the day before in the receiver's office, mounted his horse, and went to the nearest hotel. The ruse came to light nine months later.[45]

One of the best inspectors was the skilled and perceptive V. M. Garesche of Wilmington, Delaware. Like the others, he was a devout Jacksonian. Unlike them, he placed the administration of the public domain above politics. He also penetrated past the immediate condition of the office to broader matters of administering the public domain. Since the talents of the district land officers did not lie in bookkeeping, he recommended a drastic simplification of the record and bookkeeping system. His recommendations eventually led to a general overhaul of the system. Garesche also asked a modification in the salary scale to provide a living wage to all administrators of the public domain, not simply those in districts with heavy public sales. "As it is now, whilst some enjoy large profits, others are suffered to live in a state of penury," he wrote. This situation was particularly acute in Louisiana, where insignificant public sales limited the stipend of the office to the minimum salary.[46] Garesche also wanted a closer check on surveying, which, in the South at least, "gives general dissatisfaction, either from its members being inefficient or its organization defective." He noted the grave weaknesses of the inspection system as practiced by the Jacksonians. "Although very competent men have been at different times intrusted with that commission, it must be confessed (from different reports I have had) that others, totally inadequate to the task, have been employed, who did not even take the trouble of counting the moneys, but would, in that and everything

45. Whipple to Woodbury, Sec. Treas., Jan. 24, 1838, *House Executive Documents*, 25 Cong., 2 Sess., #297: 376–77.
46. E.g. Joseph Friend to Hayward, NA: GLO, Ltrs. Recd., Reg. & Rec., Ouachita, 24: April 21, 1832; Garesche to Hayward, Jan. 16, 1834, *House Executive Documents*, 25 Cong., 2 Sess., #297: 283.

else, 'take the gentleman's word for it,' and whose examination at any
one office would scarcely last half an hour." Garesche's detailed
reports (his examinations often lasted for weeks and included a complete check of every entry for the past three years) provided ample
evidence that he took no "gentleman's word" for anything. The state
of the land business in Louisiana, Arkansas, Missouri, and Mississippi
was better for it. The inspectors had much to check on. "The constant
conversation everywhere is about the large fortunes that have been
realized by land speculations," wrote Garesche of the situation in
Louisiana.[47]

The politicians who increasingly administered the public domain
did not do so out of a feeling of service but to make a profit. They
had served the party well; the land office was their reward. That a
post in a district land office led "to wealth if not fame" was universally
believed.[48] In a district with heavy public sales, the commissions were
very profitable, and the opportunities for illicit gains were virtually
limitless. An astute observer who watched the operations of the
Cahaba (Alabama) office for eleven years, described the pressure
continually on the land officers: "Without entire disinterestedness in
the transactions of official duties, and without strict justice and honor
or integrity being inherent in their nature, it is difficult to avoid yielding to temptations, continually occurring, of secret acquisitions of un-
just emolument," he concluded.[49] Many succumbed.

Among the most lucrative practices was "shaving," or changing
money for a purchaser at a discount. The receiver had more "land
office money" than anyone in the district, and this practice increased
with the burgeoning sales of the 1830's. In spite of a Treasury Department circular against shaving in 1834, moneychanging in the district
land offices continued unabated. Where exposed, a receiver pleaded
acts of courtesy and convenience. "I consider it very mean and nig-
gardly of him, after the favor which I extended, to present me at the
Treasury Department as a petty *shaver*," protested one land officer.[50]

47.   Garesche to Hayward, March 6, 1834, *ibid.*, 285–90; Garesche to Woodbury,
Sec. Treas., April 21, 1836, *ibid.*, 299.
48.   Vandalia *Advocate and State Register*, March 18, 1835.
49.   Jonathan J. Cracheron to John M. Moore, NA: GLO, Ltrs. Recd., Reg. &
Rec., Cahaba, 3: Oct. 24, 1831.
50.   Roger B. Taney to receivers, Feb. 7, 1834, *House Committee Reports*, 25
Cong., 3 Sess., #313: 168; R. H. Sterling to Woodbury, Sec. Treas., July 30,
1836, *ibid.*, 154; Wiley P. Harris to Taney, Sec. Treas., Feb. 26, 1834, *ibid.*, 168.

The use of district land offices as "shaving shops" reached a peak after Jackson's specie circular, when specie for purchase of the public lands became increasingly scarce.[51] Land officers also profited from dealing in military bounty scrip. Congress authorized the retirement of Virginia military warrants and the issue of assignable scrip acceptable for public lands in Ohio, Illinois, and Indiana. Few of those eligible had any intention of moving to the Old Northwest, and a speculative market quickly developed. Often land officers cooperated. Sometimes they dominated the business themselves. One of the largest scrip dealers was Thomas Flood, the register at Zanesville.[52] Probably no other illicit source of profit was as attractive as the diversion of public funds to private purposes, however, and several land officers fell to the temptation. Israel T. Canby diverted government funds for his own use on a grand scale, but many others simply lent money at interest. Capital was always scarce, the money accumulated, interest rates were high, and the temptations were accordingly great.[53]

Historians have dealt harshly with the land officers of this period.[54] Contemporaries often concurred. Joseph G. Baldwin ridiculed these public officials: "The place men robbed with the gorgeous magnificence of a Governor-General of Bengal." [55] Yet the district officers held the respect of their fellow citizens. The best sources of information on this aspect of the land business were the reports of the inspectors, for one of their assigned tasks was to delve into the reputation of a land officer within his community. Even inspectors whose exposition of malpractice and malfeasance in office was devastating, admitted that the objects of their attacks enjoyed not only the good will but also the confidence of their fellow citizens. Even the notorious

51. *Detroit Post and Tribune,* June 1, 1873, quoted in *Michigan Pioneer and Historical Collections,* 3 (1881): 473–74.
52. Flood to Hayward, NA: GLO, Ltrs. Recd., Reg. & Rec., Zanesville, 43: Nov. 7, 1831; James T. Pollock to the President, NA: TD, Ltrs. from Land Officers, 1833–34: April 27, 1833.
53. Garesche to Brown, April 5, 1836, *Senate Public Documents,* 24 Cong., 2 Sess., #158: 21–22; Garesche to Woodbury, Oct. 12, 1837, *House Executive Documents,* 25 Cong., 2 Sess., #297: 279–80.
54. Aside from those already cited, others to comment are Esarey, *History of Indiana,* 1: 395; Buley, *The Old Northwest,* 2: 154; Reginald C. McGrane, *Panic of 1837; Some Financial Problems of the Jacksonian Era* (Chicago, 1924), 59. All are right to a degree, although Buley accepts without question the findings of a politically motivated investigation, and Esarey frequently quotes James B. Gardiner, whose pronouncements must be used with extreme care.
55. Baldwin, *The Flush Times of Alabama and Mississippi,* 86.

public defaulter, Wiley P. Harris of Columbus (Mississippi), called forth the comment, "He, too, passes for an honest man." [56]

The success of these men in retaining the respect of their fellow citizens provides evidence of the fact that the 1830's was a period of changing ethical standards, which were reflected in the land business.[57] The ambiguous relationships among the government, the land, the citizen, and the administrator increased the uncertainty that characterized the period. Land officers represented an absentee government that owned the most valuable as well as the most essential commodity in the western country. These representatives were placed in positions of grave responsibility, yet they were chosen from among their fellow citizens. To charge them with protecting the interests of the government was far more easily said than done, in spite of solemn oaths and bonds. The land officers and their environment, V. M. Garesche commented, exhibited "a certain looseness in the code of morality, which here does not move in so limited a circle as it does with us at home." The locale of which he spoke was Columbus (Mississippi), in the heart of the new Cotton Kingdom; he could just as well have described the entire western country. Along with this new flexible standard of ethics went a peculiar attitude toward the public domain and the government's ownership of it. Many citizens felt that the government had no right to profit from the public lands: the object of the government should be the swift distribution of the lands, not a careful husbanding of this resource for a profit. Others sought the profit. Of the desire to join schemes of speculation in the public lands, one observer wrote, "Every one is eager to join, honestly *if* they can; but can it be supposed for one moment that they would blow up a scheme by which they hope one day to be benefited themselves?" In a period when the goal of thousands was to accumulate a fortune in land, the claims of the government were the first to be disregarded. To engage in unethical practices with a neighbor in connection with land use was to provoke physical violence; to use unscrupulous devices in acquiring the public domain from the federal government was only to take what rightfully belonged to the citizens of the nation. Of a fraudulent enterprise to cheat the government of tens of thousands

56. Garesche to Woodbury, June 14, 1837, *House Committee Reports*, 25 Cong., 3 Sess., #313: 189.
57. White, *The Jacksonians*, 412.

of dollars' worth of land, Garesche wrote, "Where is the court, where is the jury, that will convict the criminals? I unhesitatingly answer, not one." [58]

The land business also provided some noteworthy examples of character and integrity in public office, the outstanding ones being relics from another age. John Badollet continued to direct affairs at the Vincennes land office very much as he had since 1804; no breath of scandal touched him. Benjamin L. C. Wailes ran the Washington (Mississippi) office with firmness and tact. Alienated from the Jackson administration by political principle and spokesman for the Natchez region which was losing political power to the center of the state, Wailes conducted his office at the highest level of traditional republican standards. So did Valentine King, register at Opelousas. To those who knew or met him, King was always a "very meritorious officer," master of three languages, constant in his untiring effort to cut through the maze of Louisiana's confused public domain which lay wrapped in private land claims. Garesche wrote of King:

The number of persons interested in the Spanish claims who seek information, either personally or by correspondence, is such as to take up his time from daybreak till very late at night. His patience and industry are unbounded, and when it is considered that the duties of his office have made him abandon his profession as a lawyer, and that his salary, not exceeding $650 per annum, is far from affording maintenance to his numerous family, living in this country being very expensive, and that compensation is granted for the sales at auction of public lands, a task far less laborious, one cannot but wish that he should receive some extra compensation commensurate with his daily labors. . . .[59]

King received nothing more. The Treasury Department and Congress rewarded diligence, industry, and integrity as they did dishonesty in office.

Not one of these land officers distinguished by integrity and attention to duty was a Jacksonian appointee. The men put into the land business by Andrew Jackson and his party were politicians, not public servants. They served themselves and the party, not the nation. The

58. Garesche to Woodbury, June 14, 1837, *House Executive Documents*, 25 Cong., 2 Sess., #297: 243; same to same, April 21, 1836, *ibid.*, 299; same to same, June 9, 1836, *ibid.*, 326.
59. Garesche to Hayward, Nov. 1833, *American State Papers, Public Lands*, 7: 218.

district land officers who were appointed after March 3, 1829 and served during Jackson's Presidency, defaulted for more than three-quarters of a million dollars.[60] Perhaps even more serious was the untold and untotaled damage that resulted from their attitude toward the public lands. If the officers of the United States Government looked upon the public domain as another source of their own profit, the public could hardly be expected to do otherwise. The ordinary administration of the public lands was also severely deranged, in part from the great load caused by the land office business of this period, in equal part by the attitude of the public office holders. These men looked upon the proper administration of the public lands as secondary in importance to their own personal gain and to the affairs of the party that had brought them their appointments. V. M. Garesche once commented of the mid-1830's that "Few Curtii are to be found in the present age." [61] There were fewer still in the land business.

60.   The figure to January 26, 1839, was $825,678.28. Thus, $750,000 for the eight years of the Jackson administration is a conservative guess. The figure for the period prior to March 1829 was $248,159.13. *House Committee Reports,* 25 Cong., 3 Sess., #313: 145.
61.   Garesche to Woodbury, April 21, 1836, *House Executive Documents,* 25 Cong., 2 Sess., #297: 298.

The Close of an Era   14

During the half-century from 1789 to 1837, more than four and one-half million people poured into the vast region west of the Appalachians. The public domain was the magnet that attracted one of the greatest mass migrations in the history of the world. The settlement of the land brought ten new states into the Union, with Arkansas in 1836 and Michigan in 1837 rounding out a generation of political revolution. The dominating influence of the nation was land: in its economy of agriculture and speculation, in its political philosophy as enunciated by men like Thomas Jefferson and Andrew Jackson, and in its advance to the West. But almost simultaneously with the end of Jackson's Presidency, the great land era was coming to a close.

Central to the orderly occupation of the land was the administration of the 375 laws dealing with the public domain which the Congress of the United States passed and the President signed in this period. The public sale of land was only one—although admittedly an important one—of the many ways in which land was transferred from the federal government to the citizens of the Republic. The colonial experience had not provided clear precedents; the administrative structure of the Republic was new, and there was much experimentation to determine its dimensions and degrees of power. Gradually administrators came to exercise a decisive influence on the conditions and circumstances under which land passed from the government to the citizen. Their authority developed from their interpretations of the various acts of Congress relative to the public domain. Every administrator from Albert Gallatin on interpreted the law as he saw fit, and sent instructions to the district land officers. After 1812 the Commissioner of the General Land Office assumed this authority. For many years this instruction was done on an informal basis, often only in response to

requests for advice. George Graham made it one of the foremost
duties of the commissioner. It was an extremely significant one, for
here the commissioner's influence was direct and pre-emptive. What
Congress had in mind in passing a piece of legislation was often un-
clear. The loud Congressional objections to a commissioner's interpretation indicated that it did not always meet with complete approval.
Generally speaking, the administrators dealt with the law as written
rather than attempting to interpret Congressional wishes from personal conferences. It was unavoidable that the directives of the Commissioner of the General Land Office and the Secretary of the Treasury were further modified by managers of the land offices. Members
of Congress, the Secretary, the commissioner, and the district land
officers often had separate ideas on the meaning of legislation.

The registers and the receivers of the district land offices were
among the most powerful instruments of the government on the frontier, and their importance grew with the rising value and importance
of the public lands. Their authority came from the opportunity to
make innumerable variations in the interpretation of legislation, in
advising and guiding purchasers, and in setting rules and standards by
which land might be purchased or claimed. Redress from their decisions, large and small, was distant and often impossible to obtain. In
countless indirect and direct ways, the register and the receiver controlled the distribution of the public lands. One inspector of land
offices commented, "These officers have very extraordinary and dangerous powers, both to the community and the Government, and the
Department cannot have too many checks on them." [1] The impact of
a given law on any one citizen in the Republic depended in part on
the land district in which he found himself. Pre-emption laws were interpreted in a variety of ways in different land districts. The mass of
legislation that governed the distribution of the public domain in the
first half-century of the Republic could only be described as forming
a host of land policies.

If the views of the administrators were often decisive in the operation of legislation, their voices were not heeded in the formulation of
legislation. The forty-acre law and the pre-emption acts, both strongly
opposed by administrators, were the outstanding examples. Gideon
Fitz spoke for the bureaucrat when he wrote, "I think it is to be re-

1. Patrick Barry to Sec. Treas., Aug. 14, 1835, *House Executive Documents*, 25
Cong., 2 Sess., #297: 294.

gretted that there is so much feverish activity to make alterations in the land System by members of Congress who have not the practical experience necessary to enable them to avoid confusion and endless difficulties." [2] Administrators from the Treasury building to the Missouri River would have concurred. Perhaps Congress purposely showed little concern about the problems of administration. Upon several occasions Congressmen acted against the advice of the Commissioner of the General Land Office. They appeared to be guided rather by the intangibles found in the elevated phrases echoing through the halls of the Capitol, than by any notion of the practical difficulties involved in putting into operation certain pieces of legislation. At the same time the legislators appeared to understand little of the significance of the public domain and its distribution to the citizens of the Republic. They did not recognize that the relief acts, general pre-emption laws, and the forty-acre law served purposes far removed from order and legal form, and, in the minds of many citizens, far more important.

Thus, the "land system" consisted of Congressional laws that provided guidelines and of an evolving administrative mechanism that issued instructions, answered questions, and kept records. It never worked very well; at least, it never worked as precisely as it had been intended to work. Uniformity was sadly lacking. All observers, even those closely connected with the administration of the public lands, agreed that the components of the "system" were of uneven quality. One of the principal objects of the rectangular survey was a usable system of land description, and here the surveys proved successful. But much of the surveying was bad, and all of it was tardy. The citizens of the western country themselves viewed the surveys of the government as generally inaccurate. In the period after the close of the War of 1812, only in places in the Old Northwest could purchasers and administrators find prompt accurate surveying. Even here conditions varied widely. Elsewhere the results ranged from generally unreliable to terrible.[3]

The record-keeping and bookkeeping functions of the district land

2. Fitz to Hayward, NA: GLO, Ltrs. Recd., Reg. & Rec., Mount Salus, 29: May 16, 1831.
3. E.g. John Pope to Graham, *ibid.*, Cahaba, 3: April 17, 1828; Benjamin L. C. Wailes to Graham, *ibid.*, Washington, 30b: May 29, 1829; V. M. Garesche to Sec. Treas., Nov. 1833, *American State Papers, Public Lands,* 7: 218–19; Garesche to Sec. Treas., July 10, 1833, *ibid.,* 232.

offices were also uncertain. Calculations under the credit system were incredibly complex, and mistakes occurred frequently.[4] Bookkeeping was simpler under the cash entry system, at least until the 1830's when the volume of business outran any system of accounting. Inspectors continually commented on the deranged state of the books and records in the district land offices.[5] If the administrators in Washington indicated displeasure with the condition of the books in the district offices, land officers responded by complaining about the errors in the patents sent them. And everything in the "system" took a long time. Only the public auction was brief, three weeks at most, and an individual tract might be cried off in thirty seconds. Beyond that simple act, the machinery of administration was cumbersome and slow. The patent was often delayed as much as five years.

In spite of the equitable system of selling the public domain and the predominantly democratic philosophy that characterized the Jacksonian period, all men were far from equal in the search for choice tracts of the public domain. The world of enterprise in the public lands was much like the world elsewhere. "One thing is certain, that equal protection and advantages are not afforded to all," wrote one official.[6] Some aspiring purchasers were wealthy, others poor; some were influential, others unknown; some acquired special privileges commensurate with their importance, others had none. The advantage always accrued to the wealthy man of influence, regardless of what the law said. While the mass of citizens formed outside the office door, a man of influence went in the back door with letters of introduction. While he was there, the register gave him much sound advice about lands and might outfit him with letters of introduction to other land officers. When an influential citizen or a Congressman went west, the Commissioner of the General Land Office himself often wrote a letter of introduction. Members of Congress always had special advantages. In securing patents, work on private land claims, and information

4.   Valentine King once wrote Commissioner Graham to report the discovery of thirty-four cases of deficient payments arising from miscalculations of interest, amounting in all to $67.23. Graham told King to forget the whole thing. Graham to King, NA: GLO, Ltrs. Sent, Misc., 18: Sept. 9, 1826.
5.   Numerous examples may be found in the reports of the inspectors printed in *House Executive Documents*, 25 Cong., 2 Sess., #297; and *American State Papers, Public Lands*, 7: 174–271.
6.   Benjamin F. Linton to Andrew Jackson, Aug. 25, 1835, *Senate Public Documents*, 24 Cong., 2 Sess., #168: 5.

about the marketing of tracts, theirs was a special world, very much as it is today. The man of money bought for cash in large quantities. The squatter or the small settler often bought only after paying a premium to a "shaver" or on credit from a moneylender. In either case, his cost was greater, a difference that he could ill afford to pay. The man of means also acquired other advantages, such as "office privileges." These were

the privilege of obtaining township plats; lists of donation claims, with the lands located by each; lists of seminary lands; surveys under contract; surveys received and approved; and the plats of which are not yet received at the land offices; copies or a list of bounty and military lands, with the names of the patentees: all these, with many other items of information, are essential to citizens as well as traders in lands, and can only be obtained from our Surveyor General's office and our several land offices.[7]

Many others engaged in the land business bought these same privileges. Clerks, surveyors, and the land officers themselves sold this information openly and considered it a part of the prerequisites of office.

The settlers of the West took the view that the land was there to be taken, and that the rules and regulations of the government did not change their natural rights as citizens. This attitude had its simplest manifestation in squatting. Surely the government had no right to deny a man sustenance from the land.[8] This spirit was reflected also in acts of fraud, violence, intimidation, combinations in restraint of competition, all directed against the government and its unenforceable regulations. "Governments, like corporations, are considered without souls, and, according to the code of some people's morality, should be swindled and cheated on every occasion," wrote Benjamin F. Linton to Andrew Jackson of the "float" frauds in Louisiana.[9]

If the citizens of the West obtained land by every known device

7. William B. Duncan to Lewis Randolph, Dec. 1, 1835, *House Executive Documents*, 25 Cong., 2 Sess., #297: 399. Duncan described himself as a man "engaged in land operations."
8. Robert Mitchell of Pensacola once wrote George Graham that the man without means to purchase land "avails himself of the remote tie existing between him and his Government, to take forcible possession. . . ." NA: GLO, Ltrs. Recd., Misc., M: Aug. 21, 1828.
9. Linton to Jackson, Aug. 25, 1835, *Senate Public Documents*, 24 Cong., 2 Sess., #168: 5.

and stratagem, legal and illegal, they were substantially aided by the federal government itself. Their duly elected representatives legalized pre-emption on a national scale and successfully blocked every effort by Presidents to move against trespassers on the public lands. Laws emerged from Congress that were difficult if not impossible to administer; others were worded so vaguely that to control the distribution of the public domain in the face of such legislation was impossible. It was impossible to say whether laws such as the one donating land to victims of the New Madrid earthquakes were written with deliberate ambiguity. What was certain was that a large number of these land laws opened the way to fraud. Among others must be numbered the pre-emption acts, whose "float" provisions provided an opportunity to engross choice tracts at the minimum price. Of the Pre-emption Act of 1830, Gideon Fitz wrote, "It is believed by many that the law itself was intended for fraud, because if it had been the object of him who drew it, to give the Settler his improvement only, it was wholly unnecessary to give him floating rights. . . ." [10] One of the most fertile sources of illicit engrossment of the public domain was the so-called Lovely Donations: tracts of land given to settlers who resided west of an Indian treaty line drawn in 1828 between the Territory of Arkansas and the Cherokee nation. In spite of instructions from the General Land Office (interpreted in two different ways at two different Arkansas land offices), Lovely Donations were granted freely and soon circulated at a high price. "There are two claims that have cost the Government much more land than was ever settled by the claimants: I allude to the New Madrid and Lovely claims," wrote V. M. Garesche. "The latter, above all, has been a fruitful source of villany; for, in addition to the numerous grants made as a compensation, there are still in the hands of speculators claims to a large amount." [11] These were only several of many such cases of legislative carelessness.

Of more far-reaching importance than the matter of profit and loss to the government was the impact of the land and the land system on the nation. The land system itself had a great influence on the West, not in its many forms and details, but simply through its presence. Through control of the public domain, the federal government

10.   Fitz to Hayward, NA: GLO, Ltrs. Recd., Reg. & Rec., Mount Salus, 29: May 8, 1831.
11.   Garesche to Hayward, March 6, 1834, *House Executive Documents,* 25 Cong., 2 Sess., #297: 289.

touched the lives of thousands of remote citizens, who had previously neither known nor acknowledged its existence. The management of the public domain lay at the center of life on the frontier. Nothing was of more importance to the citizens of the far-flung western country, be they planters, lawyers, yeomen, or squatters. The government's control of this commodity was an extension of federal power into the western country. It may even be that the confused and cumbersome administration prevented the imposition of property requirements for suffrage, as the long delay before the receipt of title made such restrictions unfeasible.[12]

The distribution of the public domain had a profound effect on the economic life of the nation. It was the source of a great agricultural empire which developed during this half-century.

These were direct profits from the land; there were also indirect ones. In the first fifty years of the Republic's history, men spent much time devising ways to get something for nothing from the public domain. An early Indiana settler summarized the temper of the times when he wrote, "The love of speculation seems inherent in the minds of men, and there has been no greater field for its operation than land sales in new districts and in and about towns and cities."[13] Speculation was everywhere. Everyone engaged in it to a greater or a lesser degree. Large entrepreneurs bought great tracts and parceled them out. Squatters sold their improvements. Both expected to profit.[14]

The specie circular of Andrew Jackson and the panic of 1837 marked the decline of the land office business as a dominant force in American life. Sales increased for the first two quarters of 1837, but by the summer the effects of the economic crisis were felt in the West, and sales dropped sharply. The total for the year still reached almost $7,000,000. Demand for the public lands continued steady in the next two years, and as late as 1839 sales reached almost $6,500,000. The depression that struck the nation that year made deep inroads in the

12. William T. Hutchinson, "Unite to Divide; Divide to Unite: The Shaping of American Federalism," *Journal of American History*, 46 (1959): 15.

13. Logan Esarey, ed., *The Pioneers of Morgan County, Memoirs of Noah J. Major* (Publications of the Indiana Historical Society, Vol. 5, no. 5, Indianapolis, 1915), 233.

14. R. Carlyle Buley has written, "The speculations and peculations of a few dozen large-scale operators are easily spotted; the same activities on the part of the ten thousand and one pass unnoticed. The difference was mainly in size, not in the nature of the operations." *The Old Northwest*, 2: 151.

land business; and by 1841 sales had sunk to $1,500,000, or about half the level of demand for public lands in the middle of the 1820's.

The depression marked the passing of a period in which the land business dominated the thoughts and dreams of the nation. A new world was emerging. It was a world in which people would be drawn to cities rather than the land, in which the rise of the factory system would sharply distinguish a laboring class, in which great industrial complexes would attract the investment capital of the nation, and in which an expanding railroad network would forge a national economy. Congress would enact fewer laws concerned with the public domain, and the colorful defenses of the squatters in the halls of Congress would fade before the increasingly strident threats of the sections over slavery. As the great land office business of the years from 1830 to 1837 faded, an era was closing.

ACKNOWLEDGMENTS

Over a period of years I have accumulated a variety of debts for services rendered in the completion of this project. My work has taken me to several libraries, and I should like to express my appreciation to the librarians and the staffs of the following institutions: Cincinnati Historical Society; Library of Congress; William L. Clements Library, Ann Arbor; Harvard University Library; Library of the University of Iowa; Library of the State Historical Society of Iowa; Michigan Historical Collections, University of Michigan; Library of the University of Michigan; Library of the Ohio Historical Society, Columbus; Ohio State Library, Columbus; Princeton University Library; Library of the University of Wisconsin; and the Library of the State Historical Society of Wisconsin, Madison.

Miss Jane F. Smith and Mr. Richard Maxwell of the Social and Economic Records Division, National Archives, offered every assistance in making available the correspondence of the land business. I am also indebted to Mr. Buford Rowland of the Legislative Division for guiding me through the labyrinth of the Washington bureaucracy. Miss Ruth Davis of the State Historical Society of Wisconsin has performed innumerable favors for me over the last decade. Hamilton Osborne III, of Princeton University, John N. Schacht, Thomas K. Moore, and particularly Alan F. January, all of the University of Iowa, also assisted in the preparation of this work. Financial aid for a summer of research was provided by the Princeton University Research Council, and the Graduate College of the University of Iowa helped to defray the expense of typing the manuscript.

I have three debts of greater magnitude. Professor Vernon Carstensen of the University of Washington generously took of his time to read and criticize the entire manuscript, and to share with the writer his extensive knowledge of the distribution of the public domain and his insight into that curious and uncertain spectacle of a people moving west. My father, George Irwin Rohrbough, offered strength, encouragement, and support in numerous tangible and intangible ways. My wife, Barbara Gustine Rohrbough, contributed extensively to the preparation of the manuscript while at the same time discharging her domestic duties to a growing family. No acknowledgment, however fluent, can discharge the debts I owe to these three people.

BIBLIOGRAPHY

The numerous works used in the preparation of this volume are cited throughout in the notes. The following listings are concerned only with sources of great value and interest or those secondary works central to the study.

The heart of this study is the voluminous correspondence of the General Land Office and the Treasury Department relative to the administration of the public lands. The countless letters found here show the slow creation of an administrative system, its operations, periodic collapses, and endless variations. The letters received in Washington from the field are far more than a recitation of minutiae relative to the land business. They demonstrate graphically the vitality of the public domain in the life of the West. They are also a valuable source for the political struggles, economic development, and social life of the frontier in the first half-century of the Republic. As such they deserve careful study for far more than simply as a prime source for information on the administration of the public domain. No one was better stationed to observe the formation and transformation of the western country than the district land officers and the surveyors general.

Correspondence of the General Land Office. National Archives, Washington, D.C.

LETTERS SENT:

> Miscellaneous, 30 vols., 1796–1830.
> Miscellaneous, 7 vols. (New Series), 1830–37.
> Surveyors General, 6 vols., 1796–1837.
> Registers and Receivers, 6 vols. (New Series), 1831–37.
> Private Land Claims, 2 vols., 1833–37.
> Circulars, four folders, 1818–37.

LETTERS RECEIVED:

> Miscellaneous, 40 vols., 1803–33.
> Miscellaneous, 2 vols. (Registers), 1821–37.

Registers and Receivers, 43 vols., 1803–32.
Registers and Receivers, miscellaneous volumes (Registers), 1832–37.
Registers and Receivers, miscellaneous boxes by land office, 1832–37.
Surveyors General, 22 vols., 1803–30.
Surveyors General, miscellaneous volumes (Registers), 1830–37.

Correspondence of the Treasury Department. National Archives, Washington, D.C.

LETTERS SENT:

Secretary of the Treasury to the Commissioner of the General Land Office, 3 vols., 1814–33.
Private Land Claims, 2 vols.
Miscellaneous, 2 vols., 1801–39.

LETTERS RECEIVED:

From Land Officers, 2 vols., to 1834.
Commissioner of the General Land Office to the Secretary of the Treasury, 12 vols., 1815–37.
At the Office of the 1st Comptroller relative to public lands, 3 vols.

Reports of the House Committee on Public Lands. Legislative Division, National Archives, Washington, D.C.

Private Land Claims: 1 vol., 14 Cong., 2 Sess. to Cong., 2 Sess. (1816–33).
Public Lands: 2 vols., 9 Cong., 1 Sess. to 22 Cong., 2 Sess. (1805–33).

Manuscript Letter Collections

Several manuscript letter collections provide useful supplementary material. Of particular importance are the Papers of Albert Gallatin and Andrew Jackson, both available on microfilm. Both these men presided over the administration of the public domain at critical periods, separated by the better part of a generation. In a sense, their respective periods of administration mark the limits of this study. The Papers of James Madison, James Monroe, and John Quincy Adams, also on microfilm, offer a contrast by their paucity of material on the administration of the public lands.

Other collections of less eminent figures are also of some assistance. The Papers of Thomas Worthington and Ethan Allen Brown (Ohio State Library, Columbus) examine the land business sporadically at the period of its inception and floodtide. The Papers of Jared Mansfield, Thomas Worthington, and Ethan Allen Brown (Ohio Historical Society Library, Columbus) do the same in a more extensive fashion. The Papers of General William Lytle and Robert Todd Lytle, both surveyors general (Cincinnati Historical Society), have few references to the management of the public lands.

Newspapers and Periodicals
(*On file in the Library of Congress unless noted otherwise*)

ALABAMA

    Cahawba Press and Alabama State Intelligencer, 1820–26.
    Huntsville *Alabama Republican,* 1819–25.
    Huntsville *Southern Advocate,* 1825–28, 1834–37.
    Mobile Commercial Register, 1825–30, 1833–36.
    St. Stephens *Halcyon and Tombeckbe Public Advertiser,* 1819–22.
    Tuscaloosa *American Mirror,* 1824–25.

ARKANSAS

    Little Rock *Arkansas Gazette,* 1819–37.
    Little Rock *Arkansas Advocate,* 1830–37.

DISTRICT OF COLUMBIA

    The Globe, 1830–37.
    Daily National Intelligencer, 1812–37.
    United States Telegraph, 1826–37.

FLORIDA

    Pensacola Gazette, 1824–27, 1836–37.
    Pensacola *Floridian,* 1823.
    St. Augustine *Florida Herald,* 1829–30, 1835–37.
    Tallahassee *Floridian,* 1829–32, 1834–36.

ILLINOIS

    Edwardsville Spectator, 1819–26.
    Galena *Galenian,* 1833–34.
    Galena *North Western Gazette and Galena Advertiser,* 1834–37.
    Jacksonville *Illinois State Gazette & Jacksonville News,* 1835–36.
    Kaskaskia *Illinois Intelligencer,* 1818–20.
    Kaskaskia *Western Intelligencer,* 1816–18.
    Shawneetown *Illinois Gazette,* 1821–26, 1828–30.
    Vandalia *Illinois Advocate,* 1833–36.
    Vandalia *Illinois Intelligencer,* 1821–32.
    Vandalia Whig and Illinois Intelligencer, 1832–34.

INDIANA

Brookville Enquirer, 1821–25.
Brookville *Franklin Repository,* 1825–26, 1828.
Evansville Gazette, 1822–25.
Indianapolis *Indiana Democrat,* 1833–34.
Indianapolis *Indiana Journal,* 1825–29.
Lawrenceburgh *Indiana Palladium,* 1835–36.
Richmond *Public Ledger,* 1824–25.
Salem *Western Annotator,* 1829–31.
Vincennes *Indiana Gazette,* 1804–05.
Vincennes *Western Sun,* 1807–13, 1819–24, 1826.

LOUISIANA

Alexandria *Louisiana Herald,* 1820–25.
Baton-Rouge Gazette, 1826–27.
Natchitoches Courier, 1825–27.
New Orleans *Louisiana Advertiser,* 1820–21, 1823–24, 1826–28.
New Orleans *Louisiana Courier,* 1831–36.
New Orleans *Louisiana Courier for the Country,* 1821–31.
New Orleans *Louisiana Gazette,* 1804–12.
St. Francisville *Louisianian,* 1819–20.

MARYLAND

Niles' Weekly Register, 1811–40.

MICHIGAN

Ann Arbor *Emigrant,* 1829–33 (Michigan Historical Collections, Ann Arbor).
Ann Arbor *Michigan Argus,* 1835–37 (Michigan Historical Collections, Ann Arbor).
Detroit Gazette, 1817–30.
Detroit *Democratic Free Press,* 1831–36.
Detroit *Michigan Herald,* 1826, 1828–29.
Monroe *Michigan Sentinel,* 1825–30, 1834–36.
Niles Gazette and Advertiser, 1835–36.
White Pigeon *Michigan Statesman,* 1835.

MISSISSIPPI

Jackson *Weekly Mississippian,* 1834–36.
Natchez *Ariel,* 1827–29.
Natchez Gazette, 1825–26, 1830–33.
Natchez *Mississippi Messenger,* 1805–08.

Natchez *Mississippi Republican,* 1813–23.
Natchez *Mississippi State Gazette,* 1818–25.
Port-Gibson Correspondent, 1819–28.

MISSOURI

Franklin *Missouri Intelligencer,* 1821–26.
Jackson *Independent Patriot,* 1822–26.
Jefferson City *Jeffersonian Republican,* 1833–36.
St. Charles *Missourian,* 1820–22.
St. Louis Beacon, 1829–32.
St. Louis *Daily Commercial Bulletin and Missouri Literary Register,* 1836.
St. Louis Enquirer, 1819–24.
St. Louis *Missouri Argus,* 1835–37.
St. Louis *Missouri Gazette,* 1809–18 (William L. Clements Library, Ann Arbor).
St. Louis *Missouri Gazette and Public Advertiser,* 1819–22.
St. Louis *Missouri Republican,* 1822–28.

OHIO

Cincinnati *Centinel of the North-Western Territory,* 1793–96.
Cincinnati Daily Gazette, 1828–29, 1833–37.
Cincinnati *Liberty Hall,* 1808–12, 1814–15, 1820–27, 1828–29.
Cincinnati *National Republican,* 1829–30.
Cincinnati *Western Spy,* 1815–20.
Cleveland Herald, 1820–25, 1827–30.
Columbus *Ohio State Journal,* 1811–37.
Painesville Telegraph, 1822–25.
Steubenville *Western Herald,* 1819–26, 1829, 1834–36.

WISCONSIN

Du Buque Visitor, 1836–37 (State Historical Society of Wisconsin, Madison).
Green-Bay Intelligencer, 1833–36 (State Historical Society of Wisconsin, Madison).
Milwaukee Advertiser, 1836–37 (State Historical Society of Wisconsin, Madison).

Secondary Studies Emphasizing Topics of Special Interest

LAND

Abbey, Kathryn T. "The Land Ventures of General Lafayette in the Territory of Orleans and State of Louisiana," *Louisiana Historical Quarterly,* 16 (1933): 359–73.

Abramoske, Donald J. "The Federal Land Leasing System in Missouri," *Missouri Historical Review*, 54 (1959): 27–38.

———. "The Public Lands in Early Missouri Politics," *Missouri Historical Review*, 53 (1959): 295–305.

Adams, Herbert Baxter. *Maryland's Influence Upon Land Cessions to the United States.* Johns Hopkins University Studies in Historical and Political Sciences, Series 3, vol. 1. Baltimore, 1885.

Bailey, Hugh C. "John W. Walker and the Land Laws of the 1820's," *Agricultural History*, 32 (1958): 120–26.

Belote, Theodore Thomas. *The Scioto Speculation and the French Settlement at Gallipolis.* University of Cincinnati Studies, Series 2, vol. 3, no. 3. Cincinnati, 1907.

Benton, Elbert Jay, ed. "Side Lights on the Ohio Company of Associates from the John May Papers," *Western Reserve Historical Society, Tracts,* vol. 7, no. 97 (1917): 63–231.

Billington, Ray Allen. "The Origin of the Land Speculator as a Frontier Type," *Agricultural History*, 19 (1945): 204–12.

Bogue, Allan G. *From Prairie to Corn Belt, Farming on the Illinois and Iowa Prairies in the Nineteenth Century.* Chicago, 1963.

———. "The Iowa Claim Clubs: Symbol and Substance," *Journal of American History*, 45 (1958): 231–53.

Bogue, Allan G. and Margaret B. " 'Profits' and the Frontier Land Speculator," *Journal of Economic History*, 17 (1957): 1–24.

Brooks, Philip C. "Spain's Farewell to Louisiana, 1803–1821," *Journal of American History*, 27 (1940): 29–42.

Burns, Francis P. "The Spanish Land Laws of Louisiana," *Louisiana Historical Quarterly*, 11 (1928): 557–81.

Carlson, Theodore L. *The Illinois Military Tract: A Study of Land Occupation, Utilization and Tenure.* University of Illinois Studies in the Social Sciences, vol. 32, no. 2. Urbana, 1951.

Carstensen, Vernon, ed. *The Public Lands: Studies in the History of the Public Domain.* Madison, 1963.

Chappell, Gordon T. "Some Patterns of Land Speculation in the Old Southwest," *Journal of Southern History*, 15 (1949): 463–77.

Craven, Wesley Frank. "Diversity and Unity—Two Themes in American History." The Inaugural Lecture of Wesley Frank Craven, George Henry Davis '86 Professor of American History in Princeton University. Princeton, 1965.

Cole, Arthur H. "Cyclical and Sectional Variations in the Sale of Public Lands, 1816–60," *Review of Economic Statistics*, 9 (1927): 41–53.

Coles, Harry L. "Applicability of the Public Land System to Louisiana," *Journal of American History*, 43 (1956): 39–58.

———. "The Confirmation of Foreign Land Titles in Louisiana," *Louisiana Historical Quarterly*, 38 (1955): 1–22.

Cotterill, Ralph H. "The National Land System in the South: 1803–1812," *Journal of American History*, 16 (1930): 495–506.

Davis, T. Frederick. "The Alagon, Punon Rostro, and Vargas Land Grants," *Florida Historical Quarterly*, 25 (1946): 175–90.

Doster, James F. "Land Titles and Public Land Sales in Early Alabama," *Alabama Review*, 16 (1963): 108–24.

Duckett, Kenneth W. *Frontiersman of Fortune: Moses M. Strong of Mineral Point*. Madison, 1955.

Egleston, Melville. *The Land System of the New England Colonies*. Johns Hopkins Studies in Historical and Political Science, Series 4, Parts 11–12. Baltimore, 1886.

Emerick, C. F. *The Credit System and the Public Domain*. Publications of the Vanderbilt Historical Society, no. 3. Nashville, 1899.

Ford, Amelia Clewley. *Colonial Precedents of Our Land System as it Existed in 1800*. Bulletin of the University of Wisconsin, no. 352, History Series, vol. 2, no. 2. Madison, 1910.

Freund, Rudolf. "Military Bounty Lands and the Origins of the Public Domain," *Agricultural History*, 20 (1946): 8–18.

Gabler, Ina. "Lovely's Purchase and Lovely County," *Arkansas Historical Quarterly*, 19 (1960): 31–39.

Gara, Larry. *Westernized Yankee: The Story of Cyrus Woodman*. Madison, 1956.

———. "Yankee Land Agent in Illinois," *Journal of the Illinois State Historical Society*, 44 (1951): 120–41.

Gates, Paul Wallace. "Cattle Kings in the Prairies," *Journal of American History*, 35 (1948): 379–412.

———. "Charts of Public Land Sales and Entries," *Journal of Economic History*, 24 (1964): 22–28.

———. The Disposal of the Public Domain in Illinois, 1848–1856," *Journal of Economic and Business History*, 3 (1931): 216–40.

———. "From Individualism to Collectivism in American Land Policy," Chester McArthur Destler, ed., *Liberalism as a Force in History: Lectures on Aspects of the Liberal Tradition*, pp. 14–35. New London, 1953.

———. *Frontier Landlords and Pioneer Tenants*. Ithaca, 1945.

———. "Frontier Landlords and Pioneer Tenants," *Journal of the Illinois State Historical Society*, 38 (1945): 143–206.

———. "Hoosier Cattle Kings," *Indiana Magazine of History*, 44 (1948): 1–24.

———. "Land Policy and Tenancy in the Prairie Counties of Indiana," *Indiana Magazine of History*, 35 (1939): 1–26.

———. "Land Policy and Tenancy in the Prairie States," *Journal of Economic History*, 1 (1941): 60–82.

———. "Private Land Claims in the South," *Journal of Southern History*, 22 (1956): 183–204.

Gates, Paul Wallace. "Research in the History of American Land Tenure: A Review Article," *Agricultural History,* 28 (1954): 121–26.

————. "The Role of the Land Speculator in Western Development," *Pennsylvania Magazine of History and Biography,* 66 (1942): 314–33.

————. "Southern Investments in Northern Lands before the Civil War," *Journal of Southern History,* 5 (1939): 155–85.

Haggard, J. Villasana. "The Neutral Ground Between Louisiana and Texas, 1806–1821," *Louisiana Historical Quarterly,* 28 (1945): 1001–28.

Harris, Marshall Dees. *Origin of the Land Tenure System in the United States.* Ames, 1953.

Haskins, Charles H. "The Yazoo Land Companies," American Historical Association, *Papers,* vol. 5, pt. 4, no. 5 (1891): 61–103. New York, 1891.

Havighurst, Walter E. *Wilderness for Sale; The Story of the First Western Land Rush.* New York, 1956.

Haynes, Robert V. "The Disposal of Lands in the Mississippi Territory," *Journal of Mississippi History,* 24 (1962): 226–52.

Hibbard, Benjamin Horace. *A History of the Public Land Policies.* New York, 1924.

Higgins, Jerome S. *Subdivisions of the Public Lands, described and illustrated with diagrams and maps.* St. Louis, 1894.

Hulbert, Archer B. "The Methods and Operations of the Scioto Group of Speculators," *Journal of American History,* 1 (1915): 502–515; 2 (1915): 56–73.

Jensen, Merrill. "The Creation of the National Domain, 1781–1784," *Journal of American History,* 26 (1939): 232–42.

————. "The Cession of the Old Northwest," *Journal of American History,* 23 (1936): 27–48.

Johnson, Jack T. "Pioneers and Preemption," *Palimpsest,* 22 (1941): 257–77.

Keppel, Ann M. "Civil Disobedience on the Mining Frontier," *Wisconsin Magazine of History,* 41 (1958): 185–95.

Klein, Ada Paris, ed. "Ownership of the Land under France, Spain, and United States," *Missouri Historical Review,* 44 (1950): 274–94.

Knight, George W. "History and Management of Federal Land Grants for Education in the Northwest Territory," American Historical Association, *Papers,* vol. 1, no. 3. New York, 1886.

Livermore, Shaw. *Early American Land Companies; Their Influence on Corporate Development.* New York, 1939.

Lokken, Roscoe L. *Iowa Public Land Disposal.* Iowa City, 1942.

Lux, Leonard. *The Vincennes Donation Lands.* Indiana Historical Society Publications, vol. 15, no. 4, pp. 419–89. Indianapolis, 1949.

McCloskey, John C. "Land Speculation in Michigan in 1835–36 as Described in Mrs. Kirkland's *A New Home—Who'll Follow?*" *Michigan History,* 42 (1958): 26–34.

McCorvey, Thomas C. "The Vine and Olive," *Alabama Historical Sketches*, 77–89. Charlottesville, 1960.

McNall, Neil A. "John Grieg: Land Agent and Speculator," *Business History Review*, 33 (1959): 524–34.

Markle, A. R. "The Terre Haute Company," *Indiana Magazine of History*, 12 (1916): 158–60.

Martin, Sidney Walter. "The Public Domain in Territorial Florida," *Journal of Southern History*, 10 (1944): 174–87.

Mitchell, Jennie O'Kelly, and Calhoun, Robert D. "The Marquis De Maison Rouge, the Baron De Bastrop, and Colonel Abraham Morhouse—Three Ouachita Valley Soldiers of Fortune. The Maison Rouge and Bastrop Spanish Land 'Grants,'" *Louisiana Historical Quarterly*, 20 (1937): 289–462.

Mowat, Charles L. "The Land Policy in British East Florida," *Agricultural History*, 14 (1940): 75–77.

Neu, Irene D. *Erastus Corning: Merchant and Financier, 1794–1872*. Ithaca, 1960.

O'Callaghan, Jerry A. "The War Veteran and the Public Lands," *Agricultural History*, 28 (1954): 163–68.

Pelzer, Louis. "The Public Domain as a Field for Historical Study," *Iowa Journal of History and Politics*, 12 (1914): 568–78.

———. "The Private Land Claims of the Old Northwest Territory," *Iowa Journal of History and Politics*, 12 (1914): 373–93.

———. "The Spanish Land Grants of Upper Louisiana," *Iowa Journal of History and Politics*, 11 (1913): 3–37.

Philbrick, Francis S. "Introduction," *Laws of the Indiana Territory, 1801–1809*. Collections of the Illinois State Historical Library, vol. 21, pp. ix–cclxxxii. Springfield, 1930.

Reves, Haviland F. "The Reves Farm—Private Claim 49," *Michigan History*, 45 (1961): 237–58.

Richardson, Lemont K. "Private Land Claims in Missouri," *Missouri Historical Review*, 50 (1955–56): 132–44, 271–86, 387–99.

Robbins, Roy Marvin. *Our Landed Heritage; The Public Domain, 1776–1936*. Princeton, 1942.

———. "Preemption—A Frontier Triumph," *Journal of American History*, 18 (1931): 331–49.

Sakolski, Aaron Morton. *The Great American Land Bubble*. New York, 1932.

Sampson, F. A. "Cities That Were Promised," *Missouri Historical Review*, 6 (1911): 11–13.

Sato, Shosuke. *History of the Land Question in the United States*. Johns Hopkins University Studies in Historical and Political Science, Series 4, nos. 7–9. Baltimore, 1886.

Schafer, Joseph. "A Yankee Land Speculator in Wisconsin," *Wisconsin Magazine of History*, 8 (1925): 377–92.

Shambaugh, Benjamin F. "Frontier Land Clubs or Claim Associations," *American Historical Association, Annual Report for 1900*, pp. 67–84. Washington, 1901.

Silver, James W. "Land Speculation Profits in the Chickasaw Cession," *Journal of Southern History*, 10 (1944): 84–92.

Smith, Alice E. *George Smith's Money; A Scottish Investor in America.* Madison, 1966.

———. *James Duane Doty, Frontier Promoter.* Madison, 1954.

Smith, Dwight L. "Indian Land Cessions in Northern Ohio and Southeastern Michigan," *Northwest Ohio Quarterly*, 29 (1956–57): 27–55.

Swartzlow, Ruby J. "The Early History of Lead Mining in Missouri," *Missouri Historical Review*, 28 (1933–34): 184–94, 287–95; 29 (1934–35): 27–34, 109–14, 195–205.

Tatter, Henry. "State and Federal Land Policy during the Confederation Period," *Agricultural History*, 9 (1935): 176–86.

Treat, Payson Jackson. *The National Land System, 1785–1820.* New York, 1910.

Trowbridge, Frederick N. "Confirming Land Titles in Early Wisconsin," *Wisconsin Magazine of History*, 26 (1943): 314–22.

Violette, Eugene Morrow, "Spanish Land Claims in Missouri," *Washington University Studies*, vol. 8, Humanistic Series, no. 2, pp. 167–200. St. Louis, 1921.

Wellington, Raynor Greenleaf. *The Political and Sectional Influence of the Public Lands, 1828–1842.* Cambridge, 1914.

———. "The Tariff and the Public Lands from 1828 to 1833," *American Historical Association, Annual Report for 1911*, pp. 177–85. Washington, 1913.

Whitfield, Gaius, Jr. "The French Grant in Alabama: A History of the Founding of Demopolis," *Transactions of the Alabama Historical Society*, 4 (1904): 321–55.

Williams, Clanton W. "Conservatism in Old Montgomery, 1817–1861," *Alabama Review*, 10 (1957): 96–110.

Young, Mary E. "The Creek Frauds: A Study in Conscience and Corruption," *Journal of American History*, 42 (1955): 411–37.

———. "Indian Removal and Land Allotment: The Civilized Tribes and Jacksonian Justice," *American Historical Review*, 64 (1958): 31–45.

———. *Redskins, Ruffleshirts and Rednecks; Indian Allotments in Alabama and Mississippi, 1830–1860.* Norman, 1961.

SETTLEMENT

Allen, J. C. "Palestine, Its Early History," *Transactions of the Illinois State Historical Society*, 10 (1905): 122–27.

Anderson, Hattie M. "Missouri, 1804–1828: Peopling a Frontier State," *Missouri Historical Review*, 31 (1937): 150–80.

Barnett, Mrs. I. N. "Early Days of Batesville," *Arkansas Historical Quarterly,* 11 (1952): 15–23.

Billington, Ray Allen. "The Frontier in Illinois History," *Journal of the Illinois State Historical Society,* 43 (1950): 28–45.

Boewe, Charles E. *Prairie Albion: An English Settlement in Pioneer Illinois.* Carbondale, 1962.

Boggess, Arthur Clinton. *The Settlement of Illinois, 1778–1830.* Chicago Historical Society's Collection, vol. 5. Chicago, 1908.

Bryan, Charles W., Jr. "Flanders Callaway, A Frontier Type," *Missouri Historical Society Collections,* 6 (1928): 1–18.

Buck, Solon J. "The New England Element in Illinois Politics Before 1833," Organization of American Historians, *Proceedings,* 6 (1912–13): 49–61.

Buley, R. Carlyle. "The Political Balance in the Old Northwest, 1820–1860," *Indiana University Studies,* 12 (1925): 405–55.

Burnet, Jacob. *Notes on the Early Settlement of the North-western Territory.* New York, 1847.

Burton, C. M. "Detroit in the Year 1832," *Michigan Pioneer and Historical Collections,* 28 (1897–98): 163–71.

Calkins, Earnest Elmo. *They Broke the Prairie.* New York, 1937.

Colgrove, Kenneth W. "The Attitude of Congress Toward the Pioneers of the West from 1789 to 1820," *Iowa Journal of History and Politics,* 8 (1910): 3–129.

Doster, James F. "Early Settlements on the Tombigbee and Tensaw Rivers," *Alabama Review,* 12 (1959): 83–94.

Downes, Randolph Chandler. *Frontier Ohio, 1788–1803.* Ohio Historical Collections, vol. 3. Columbus, 1935.

Ellis, James Fernando. *The Influence of Environment on the Settlement of Missouri.* St. Louis, 1929.

Fuller, George Newman. *Economic and Social Beginnings of Michigan: A Study of the Settlements of the Lower Peninsula during the Territorial Period, 1805–1837.* Michigan Historical Publications: University Series I. Lansing, 1916.

———. "An Introduction to the Settlement of Southern Michigan from 1815 to 1835," *Michigan Pioneer and Historical Collections,* 38 (1912): 539–79.

———. "Settlement of Michigan Territory," *Journal of American History,* 2 (1915): 25–55.

Gordon, Leon M., II. "Effects of the Michigan Road on Northern Indiana, 1830–60," *Indiana Magazine of History,* 46 (1950): 377–402.

———. "Settlements in Northwestern Indiana, 1830–1860," *Indiana Magazine of History,* 47 (1951): 37–52.

Hamilton, Peter J. "Early Roads of Alabama," *Transactions of the Alabama Historical Society,* 2 (1897–98): 39–56.

———. "St. Stephens; Spanish Fort and American Town," *Transactions of the Alabama Historical Society,* 3 (1898–99): 227–33.

Hamilton, William B. "The Southwestern Frontier, 1795–1817: An Essay in Social History," *Journal of Southern History*, 10 (1944): 389–403.

Howe, Daniel Wait. "Making a Capital in the Wilderness," *Indiana Historical Society Publications*, 4 (1908): 301–38.

Kaatz, Martin R. "The Settlement of the Black Swamp of Northwestern Ohio: Early Days," *Northwest Ohio Quarterly*, 25 (1952–53): 23–36, 134–56, 201–17.

Kelton, Dwight H. "County of Mackinac—From the Annals of Fort Mackinac," *Michigan Pioneer and Historical Collections*, 6 (1883): 343–49.

Lawlis, Chelsea L. "Settlement of the Whitewater Valley, 1790–1810," *Indiana Magazine of History*, 43 (1947): 23–40.

———. "The Great Migration and the Whitewater Valley," *Indiana Magazine of History*, 43 (1947): 125–39.

Lynch, William O. "The Westward Flow of Southern Colonists before 1861," *Journal of Southern History*, 9 (1943): 303–27.

Mitchell, Waldo F. "Indiana's Growth, 1812–1820," *Indiana Magazine of History*, 10 (1914): 369–95.

Moores, Charles. "Old Corydon," *Indiana Magazine of History*, 13 (1917): 20–41.

Owsley, Frank L. "The Pattern of Migration and Settlement on the Southern Frontier," *Journal of Southern History*, 11 (1945): 147–76.

Pelzer, Louis. "Squatter Settlements," *Palimpsest*, 14 (1933): 77–84.

Perejda, Andrew D. "Sources and Dispersal of Michigan's Population," *Michigan History*, 32 (1948): 355–66.

Petersen, William J. "Population Advance to the Upper Mississippi Valley, 1830–1860," *Iowa Journal of History and Politics*, 32 (1934): 312–53.

Pooley, William V. *The Settlement of Illinois from 1830 to 1850*. Bulletin of the University of Wisconsin, no. 220, History Series, vol. 1, no. 4, pp. 287–595. Madison, 1908.

Power, Richard L. "Wet Lands and the Hoosier Stereotype," *Journal of American History*, 22 (1935): 33–48.

Schafer, Joseph. "The Epic of a Plain Yankee Family," *Wisconsin Magazine of History*, 9 (1925–26): 140–56, 285–309.

———. *The Wisconsin Lead Region*. Wisconsin Domesday Book. General Studies, vol. 3. Madison, 1932.

Schockel, B. H. "Settlement and Development of the Lead and Zinc Mining Region of the Driftless Area with Special Emphasis upon Jo Daviess County, Illinois," *Journal of American History*, 4 (1917): 169–92.

Silver, James W. "General Edmund P. Gaines and the Protection of the Southwestern Frontier," *Louisiana Historical Quarterly*, 20 (1937): 183–91.

Stilwell, Lewis Dayton. *Migration from Vermont. The Growth of Vermont*, vol. 5. Montpelier, 1948.

Taylor, Thomas Jones. "Early History of Madison County," *Alabama Historical Quarterly*, 1 (1930): 101–11, 149–68, 308–17, 489–505; (1940): 86–91, 239–47, 342–64, 493–536.

Thwaites, Reuben G. "Notes on Early Lead Mining in the Fecer (or Galena) River Region," *Wisconsin Historical Collections*, 13 (1895): 271–92.

————. "Early Lead-Mining in Illinois and Wisconsin," American Historical Association, *Annual Report for 1893*, pp. 189–96. Washington, 1894.

Tower, J. Allen. "The Shaping of Alabama," *Alabama Review*, 12 (1959): 132–39.

Turner, Frederick Jackson. "The Colonization of the West, 1820–1830," *American Historical Review*, 11 (1906): 303–27.

Viles, Jonas. "Old Franklin: A Frontier Town of the Twenties," *Journal of American History*, 9 (1923): 269–82.

————. "Missouri in 1820," *Missouri Historical Review*, 15 (1920): 36–52.

Walz, Robert B. "Migration into Arkansas, 1820–1880: Incentives and Means of Travel," *Arkansas Historical Quarterly*, 17 (1958): 309–24.

Wilgus, James A. "The Century Old Lead Region in Early Wisconsin History," *Wisconsin Magazine of History*, 10 (1927): 401–10.

Worley, Ted R. "Glimpses of an Old Southwestern Town," *Arkansas Historical Quarterly*, 8 (1949): 133–59.

————. "Helena on the Mississippi," *Arkansas Historical Quarterly*, 13 (1954): 1–15.

ADMINISTRATION AND PATRONAGE

Aaronson, Sidney H. *Status and Kinship in the Higher Civil Service; Standards of Selection in the Administration of John Adams, Thomas Jefferson, and Andrew Jackson.* Cambridge, 1964.

Agnew, Dwight L. "The Government Land Surveyor as a Pioneer," *Journal of American History*, 28 (1941): 369–82.

Balinky, Alexander. *Albert Gallatin: Fiscal Theories and Policies.* New Brunswick, 1958.

Bassett, John Spencer. "James K. Polk and his Constituents, 1831–1832," *American Historical Review*, 28 (1922): 68–77.

Bush, Evelyn. "United States Land Offices in Alabama, 1803–1879," *Alabama Historical Quarterly*, 17 (1955): 146–53.

Caldwell, Lyton Keith. *The Administrative Theories of Hamilton and Jefferson; their contribution to thought on public administration.* Chicago, 1944.

Chatelain, Verne E. "The Public Land Officer on the Northwestern Frontier," *Minnesota History*, 12 (1931): 379–89.

Conover, Milton. *The General Land Office; Its History, Activities and Organization. Institute of Government Research Publications*, Brookings Institute, vol. 13. Baltimore, 1923.

Eriksson, Erik McKinley. "The Federal Civil Service under President Jackson," *Journal of American History*, 13 (1927): 517–40.

Fish, Carl Russell. *The Civil Service and the Patronage.* New York, 1905.

————. "The Crime of W. H. Crawford," *American Historical Review*, 21 (1916): 545–546.

————. "Removal of Officials by the Presidents of the United States,"

American Historical Association, *Annual Report for 1899,* pp. 67–86. Washington, 1900.

Harrington, Earl G. "Cadastral Surveys for the Public Lands of the United States," *Surveying and Mapping,* 9 (1949): 82–86.

Harrison, Robert W. "Public Land Records of the Federal Government," *Journal of American History,* 41 (1954): 277–88.

Henlein, Jay C. "Albert Gallatin: A Pioneer in Public Administration," *William and Mary Quarterly,* Series 3, 7 (1950): 64–94.

Hotchkiss, Willard Eugene. *The Judicial Work of the Comptroller of the Treasury, as compared with Similar Functions in the Governments of France and Germany; A Study in Administrative Law.* Cornell Studies in History and Political Science, vol. 3. Ithaca, 1911.

Hunt, Gaillard. "Office-Seeking during Washington's Administration," *American Historical Review,* 1 (1896): 270–83.

————. "Office-Seeking during the Administration of John Adams," *American Historical Review,* 2 (1897): 241–61.

————. "Office-Seeking during Jefferson's Administration," *American Historical Review,* 3 (1898): 270–91.

Hutchinson, William T. "Unite to Divide; Divide to Unite: The Shaping of American Federalism," *Journal of American History,* 46 (1949): 3–18.

Jamison, Knox. "The Survey of the Public Lands in Michigan," *Michigan History,* 42 (1958): 197–214.

Logan, Robert R., "Notes on the First Land Surveys in Arkansas," *Arkansas Historical Quarterly,* 19 (1960): 260–70.

Mansfield, Harvey Claflin. *The Comptroller General: A Study in the Law and Practice of Financial Administration.* New Haven, 1939.

Mendenhall, Herbert D. "The History of Land Surveying in Florida," *Surveying and Mapping,* 10 (1950): 278–83.

Merriam, J. M. "Jefferson's Use of the Executive Patronage," American Historical Association, *Papers,* vol. 2, no. 1, pp. 47–52. New York, 1887.

Pattison, William D. *Beginnings of the American Rectangular Land Survey System, 1784–1800.* Chicago, 1957.

————. "The Survey of the Seven Ranges," *Ohio Historical Quarterly,* 68 (1959): 115–40.

Powell, Fred Wilbur, comp. *Control of Federal Expenditures; a Documentary History, 1775–1894.* Washington, 1939.

Smith, Darrell H. *The General Accounting Office, its History, Activities and Organization.* Baltimore, 1927.

Stewart, Lowell. *Public Land Surveys: History, Instructions, Methods.* Ames, 1935.

Thrower, Norman J. W. *Original Survey and Land Subdivision: A Comparative Study of the Form and Effect of Contrasting Cadestral Surveys.* Chicago, 1966.

Treat, Payson Jackson. "Origin of the National Land System Under the Confederation," American Historical Association, *Annual Report for 1905,* pp. 231–39. Washington, 1906.

White, Leonard D. *The Federalists: A Study in Administrative History.* New York, 1948.
―――. *The Jacksonians: A Study in Administrative History, 1829–1861.* New York, 1954.
―――. *The Jeffersonians: A Study in Administrative History, 1801–1829.* New York, 1951.
Whittlesey, Charles. "Surveys of the Public Lands in Ohio," Western Reserve Historical Society, *Tracts*, vol. 2, no. 61, pp. 279–86.
―――. "Ohio Surveys," Western Reserve Historical Society, *Tracts*, vol. 2, no. 59, pp. 187–91.
Wilmerding, Lucius, Jr. *The Spending Power: A History of the Efforts of Congress to Control Expenditures.* New Haven and London, 1943.
Wilson, Alma Winston. "An Early Indiana Surveyor—Lazarua B. Wilson." *Indiana Magazine of History*, 10 (1914): 47–52.
Wilson, George R. "Early Indiana Trails and Surveys," Indiana Historical Society Publications, vol. 6, no. 3, pp. 347–457. Indianapolis, 1919.
Woodard, C. S. "The Public Domain, Its Surveys and Surveyors," *Michigan Pioneer and Historical Collections*, 27 (1896): 306–23.
―――. "The First Public Land Surveys in Indiana: Freeman's Lines," *Indiana Magazine of History*, 12 (1916): 1–33.

Theses

Abbott, Phyllis Ruth. "The Development and Operation of an American Land System to 1800," Ph.D., University of Wisconsin, 1959.
Barber, William DeA. "The West in National Politics, 1784–1804," Ph.D., University of Wisconsin, 1961.
Bayard, Charles Judah. "The Development of the Public Land Policy, 1783–1820, with Special Reference to Indiana," Ph.D., Indiana University, 1956.
Cain, Marvin R. "Edward Bates, The Rise of a Western Politician, 1814–1842," M.A., University of Missouri, 1957.
Coffee, Thomas P. "The Territory of Orleans, 1803–1812," Ph.D., St. Louis University, 1956.
Coles, Harry L., Jr. "A History of the Administration of Federal Land Policies and Land Tenure in Louisiana, 1803–1860," Ph.D., Vanderbilt, 1949.
Conoley, Rudolph Evander. "History of Public Land Policies in Florida, 1819–1900," Ph.D., Duke University, 1941.
Ernst, Joseph W. "With Compass and Chain: Federal Land Surveyors in the Old Northwest, 1785–1816," Ph.D., Columbia University, 1958.
Ferguson, John Lewis. "William E. Woodruff and the Territory of Arkansas, 1819–1836," Ph.D., Tulane University, 1960.
Folz, William E. "The Financial Crisis of 1819—A Study in Post War Economic Readjustment," Ph.D., University of Illinois, 1955.

Hamilton, William B. "American Beginnings in the Old Southwest: The Mississippi Phase," Ph.D., Duke University, 1937.

Hatfield, Joseph T. "The Public Career of William C. C. Claiborne," Ph.D., Emory University, 1962.

Haynes, Robert Vaughn. "A Political History of the Mississippi Territory," Ph.D., Rice University, 1958.

Helms, James M., Jr. "Land Tenure in Territorial Mississippi, 1798–1809," M.A., University of Virginia, 1954.

Hutchinson, William Thomas. "The Bounty Lands of the American Revolution in Ohio," Ph.D., University of Chicago, 1927.

Jones, Dallas Lee. "The Survey and Sale of the Public Lands in Michigan, 1815–1862," M.A., Cornell University, 1952.

Lichtenberg, Caroline. "Beginnings of the United States Military Land Bounty Policy, 1637–1812," M.A., University of Wisconsin, 1945.

Lindegren, Alina Marie. "The History of the Land Bonus of the War of 1812," M.A., University of Wisconsin, 1922.

McCandless, Perry G. "Thomas H. Benton: His Source of Political Strength in Missouri from 1815 to 1838," Ph.D., University of Missouri, 1952–53.

Page, Joseph F., III. "The Private Land Claims in Florida," B.A., Princeton University, 1964.

Roberts Frances C. "Background and Formative Period in the Great Bend and Madison County," Ph.D., University of Alabama, 1956.

Rohrbough, Malcolm Justin. "The General Land Office, 1812–1826: An Administrative Study," Ph.D., University of Wisconsin, 1963.

Rose, Allen Henry. "The Extension of the United States Land System to Missouri, 1804–1817," M.A., Washington University, St. Louis, 1940–41.

Shirigian, John. "Lucius Lyon: His Place in Michigan History," Ph.D., University of Michigan, 1961.

Still, John S. "The Life of Ethan Allen Brown, Governor of Ohio," Ph.D., Ohio State University, 1951.

Tatter, Henry. "The Preferential Treatment of the Actual Settler in the Primary Disposition of the Vacant Lands in the United States to 1841: Pre-Emption, Prelude to Homesteadism," Ph.D., Northwestern University, 1933.

Taylor, J. W. "The Leasing of the Mineral Lands of the United States up to 1850," Ph.D., University of Wisconsin, 1915.

Westfall, Frank W. "Politics in Territorial Missouri, 1804–1821," M.A., State University of Iowa, 1938.

Wheaton, Philip Damon. "Levi Woodbury, Jacksonian Financier," Ph.D., University of Maryland, 1955.

White, Francis Harding. "The Administration of the General Land Office, 1812–1911," Ph.D., Harvard University, 1912.